original story by HIDEYUKI KURATA
art & comic by TOMOMASA TAKUMA

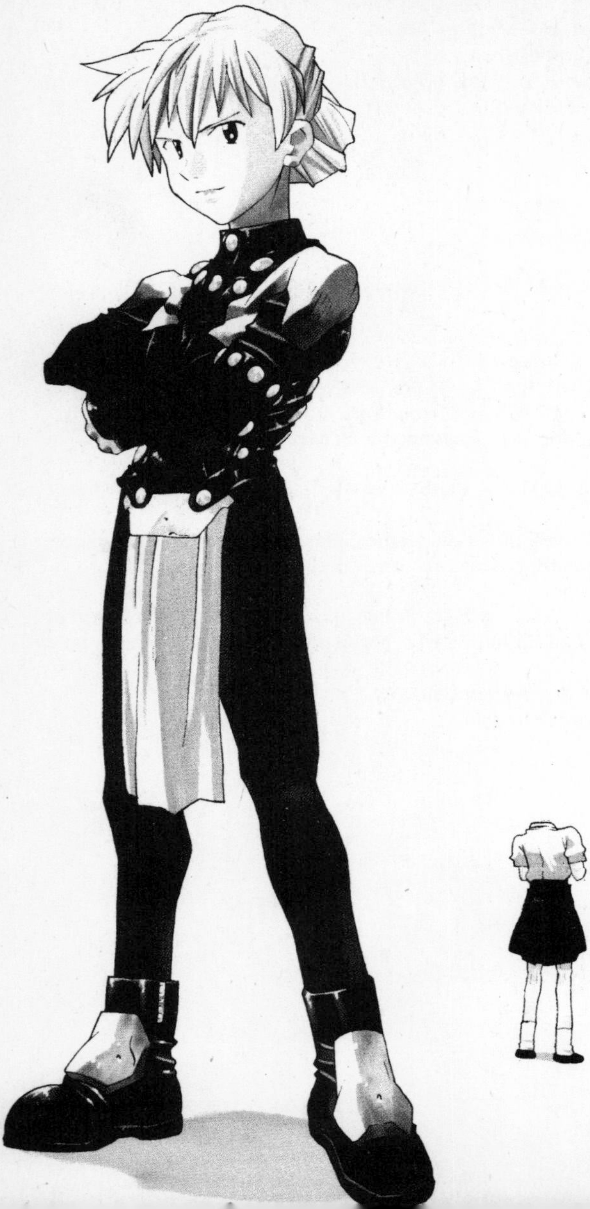

Translation and Adaptation – Christine Schilling
Editorial Assistant – Mallory Reaves
Lettering – TeamPokopen
Production Manager – James Dashiell
Editor – Brynne Chandler

A Go! Comi manga

Published by Go! Media Entertainment, LLC

Train + Train Volume 4
© HIDEYUKI KURATA - TOMOMASA TAKUMA 2002
First published in 2002 by Media Works Inc., Tokyo, Japan.
English translation rights arranged with Media Works Inc.

Visit us online at www.gocomi.com
e-mail: info@gocomi.com

ISBN 978-1-933617-38-1

First printed in October 2007

1   2   3   4   5   6   7   8   9

Manufactured in the United States of America

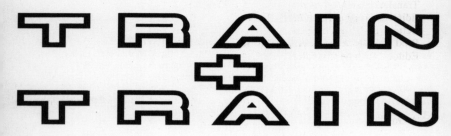

# TRAIN + TRAIN

## Volume 4

Original Story by

## HIDEYUKI KURATA

Art by

## TOMOMASA TAKUMA

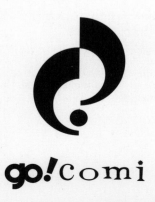

go!comi

# Concerning Honorifics

At Go! Comi, we do our best to ensure that our translations read seamlessly in English while respecting the original Japanese language and culture. To this end, the original honorifics (the suffixes found at the end of characters' names) remain intact. In Japan, where politeness and formality are more integrated into every aspect of the language, honorifics give a better understanding of character relationships. They can be used to indicate both respect and affection. Whether a person addresses someone by first name or last name also indicates how close their relationship is.

Here are some of the honorifics you might encounter in reading this book:

-san: This is the most common and neutral of honorifics. The polite way to address someone you're not on close terms with is to use "-san." It's kind of like Mr. or Ms., except you can use "-san" with first names as easily as family names.

-chan: Used for friendly familiarity, mostly applied towards young girls. "-chan" also carries a connotation of cuteness with it, so it is frequently used with nick-names towards both boys and girls (such as "Na-chan" for "Natsu").

-kun: Like "-chan," it's an informal suffix for friends and classmates, only "-kun" is usually associated with boys. It can also be used in a professional environment by someone addressing a subordinate.

-sama: Indicates a great deal of respect or admiration.

Sempai: In school, "sempai" is used to refer to an upperclassman or club leader. It can also be used in the workplace by a new employee to address a mentor or staff member with seniority.

Sensei: Teachers, doctors, writers or any master of a trade are referred to as "sensei." When addressing a manga creator, the polite thing to do is attach "-sensei" to the manga-ka's name (as in Takuma-sensei).

Onii: This is the more casual term for an older brother. Usually you'll see it with an honorific attached, such as "onii-chan."

Onee: The casual term for older sister, it's used like "onii" with honorifics.

[blank]: Not using an honorific when addressing someone indicates that the speaker has permission to speak intimately with the other person. This relationship is usually reserved for close friends and family.

# TRAIN + TRAIN
## VOLUME 4

Episode. 20 ——————————— 7

Episode. 21 ——————————— 35

Episode. 22 ——————————— 65

Episode. 23 ——————————— 97

Episode. 24 ——————————— 127

Episode. 25 ——————————— 163

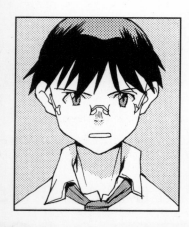
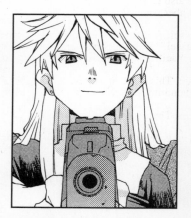

TRAIN
+
TRAIN

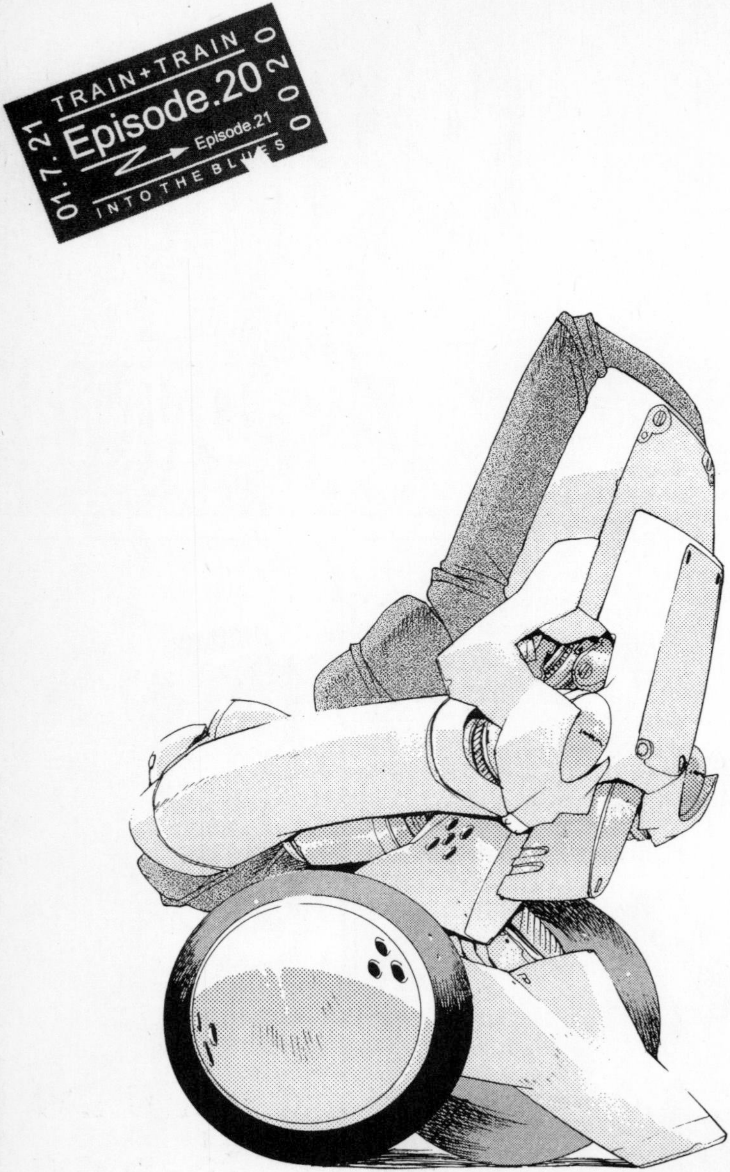
01.7.21
TRAIN+TRAIN
Episode.20
Episode.21
INTO THE BLUES
0020

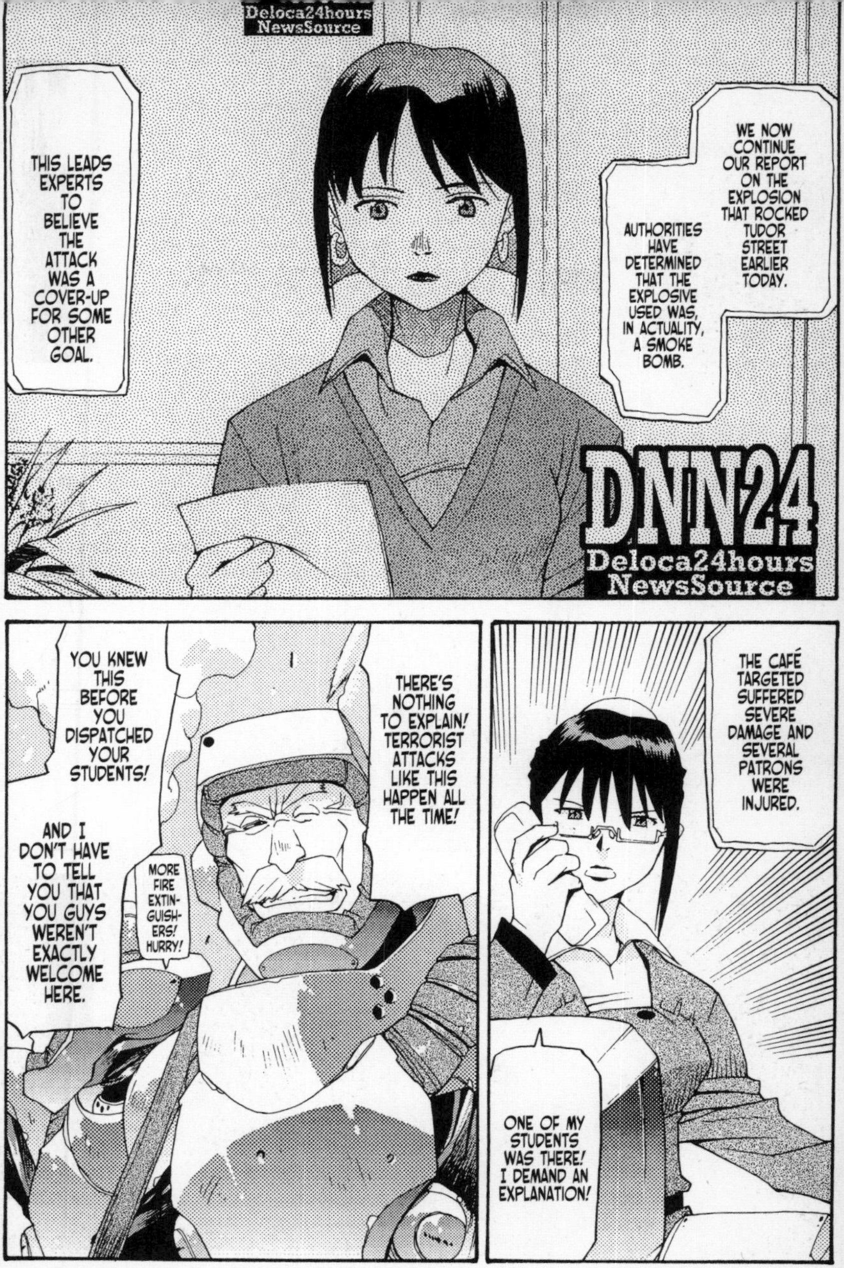
Deloca24hours NewsSource
WE NOW CONTINUE OUR REPORT ON THE EXPLOSION THAT ROCKED TUDOR STREET EARLIER TODAY.
AUTHORITIES HAVE DETERMINED THAT THE EXPLOSIVE USED WAS, IN ACTUALITY, A SMOKE BOMB.
THIS LEADS EXPERTS TO BELIEVE THE ATTACK WAS A COVER-UP FOR SOME OTHER GOAL.
DNN24
Deloca24hours NewsSource
THE CAFÉ TARGETED SUFFERED SEVERE DAMAGE AND SEVERAL PATRONS WERE INJURED.
ONE OF MY STUDENTS WAS THERE! I DEMAND AN EXPLANATION!
THERE'S NOTHING TO EXPLAIN! TERRORIST ATTACKS LIKE THIS HAPPEN ALL THE TIME!
YOU KNEW THIS BEFORE YOU DISPATCHED YOUR STUDENTS!
MORE FIRE EXTIN-GUISH-ERS! HURRY!
AND I DON'T HAVE TO TELL YOU THAT YOU GUYS WEREN'T EXACTLY WELCOME HERE.

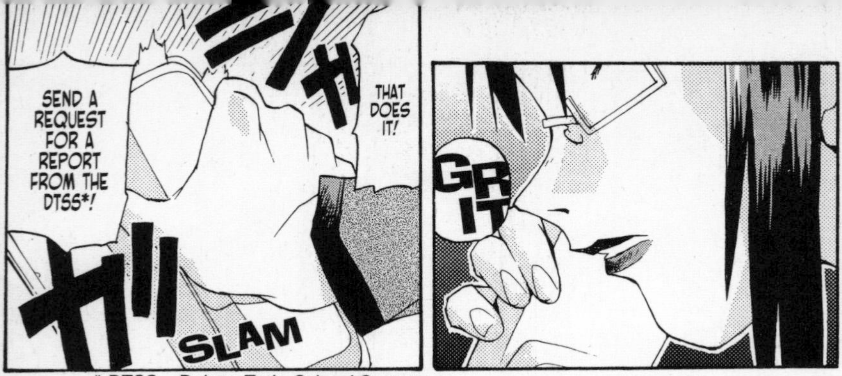
GRIT
THAT DOES IT!
SEND A REQUEST FOR A REPORT FROM THE DTSS*!
SLAM

* DTSS = Deloca Train School System

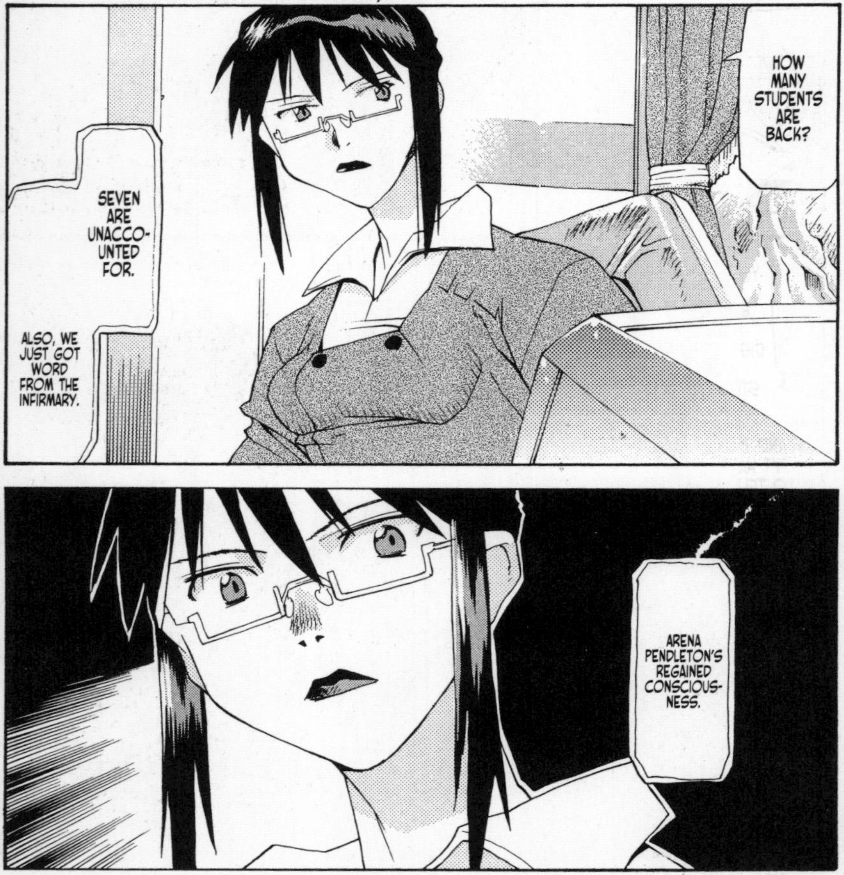
HOW MANY STUDENTS ARE BACK?
SEVEN ARE UNACCOUNTED FOR.
ALSO, WE JUST GOT WORD FROM THE INFIRMARY.
ARENA PENDLETON'S REGAINED CONSCIOUSNESS.

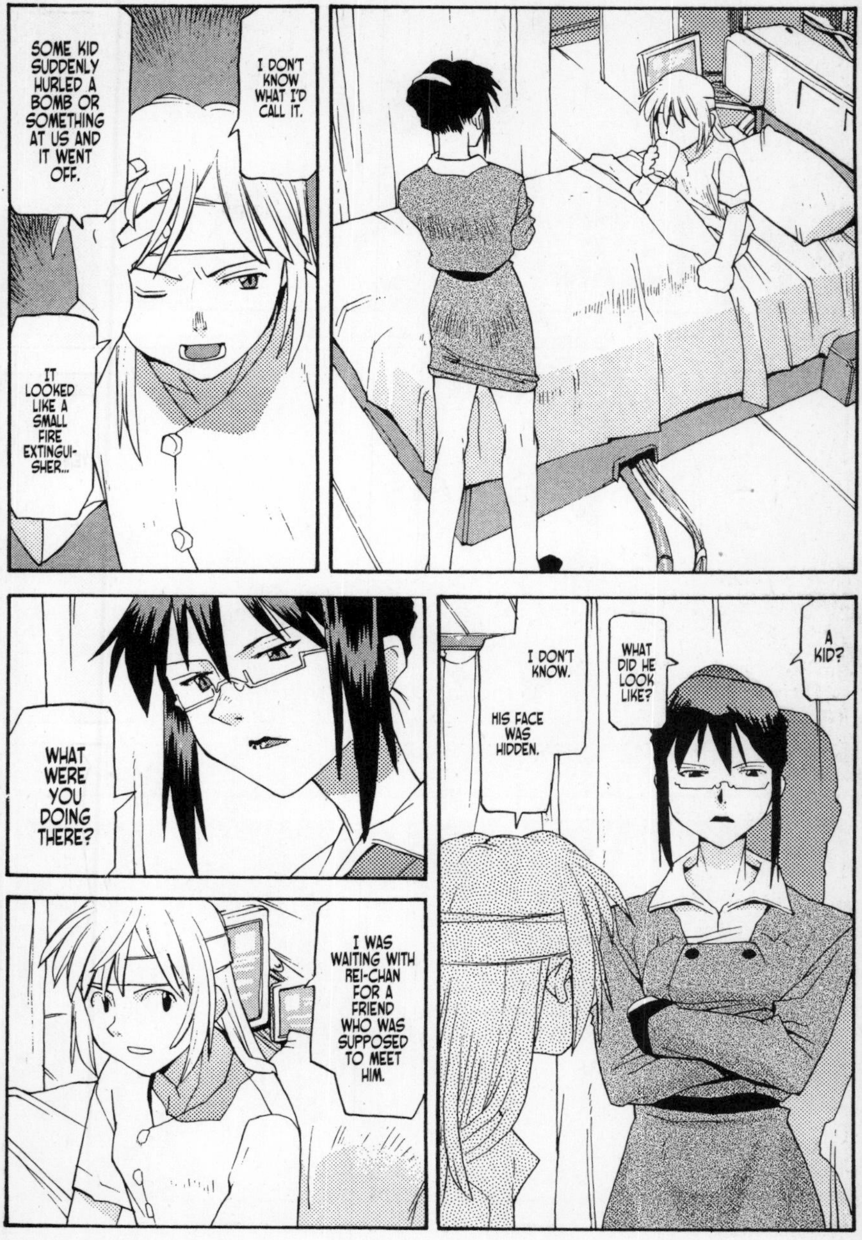
I DON'T KNOW WHAT I'D CALL IT.
SOME KID SUDDENLY HURLED A BOMB OR SOMETHING AT US AND IT WENT OFF.
IT LOOKED LIKE A SMALL FIRE EXTINGUISHER...
A KID?
WHAT DID HE LOOK LIKE?
I DON'T KNOW.
HIS FACE WAS HIDDEN.
WHAT WERE YOU DOING THERE?
I WAS WAITING WITH REI-CHAN FOR A FRIEND WHO WAS SUPPOSED TO MEET HIM.

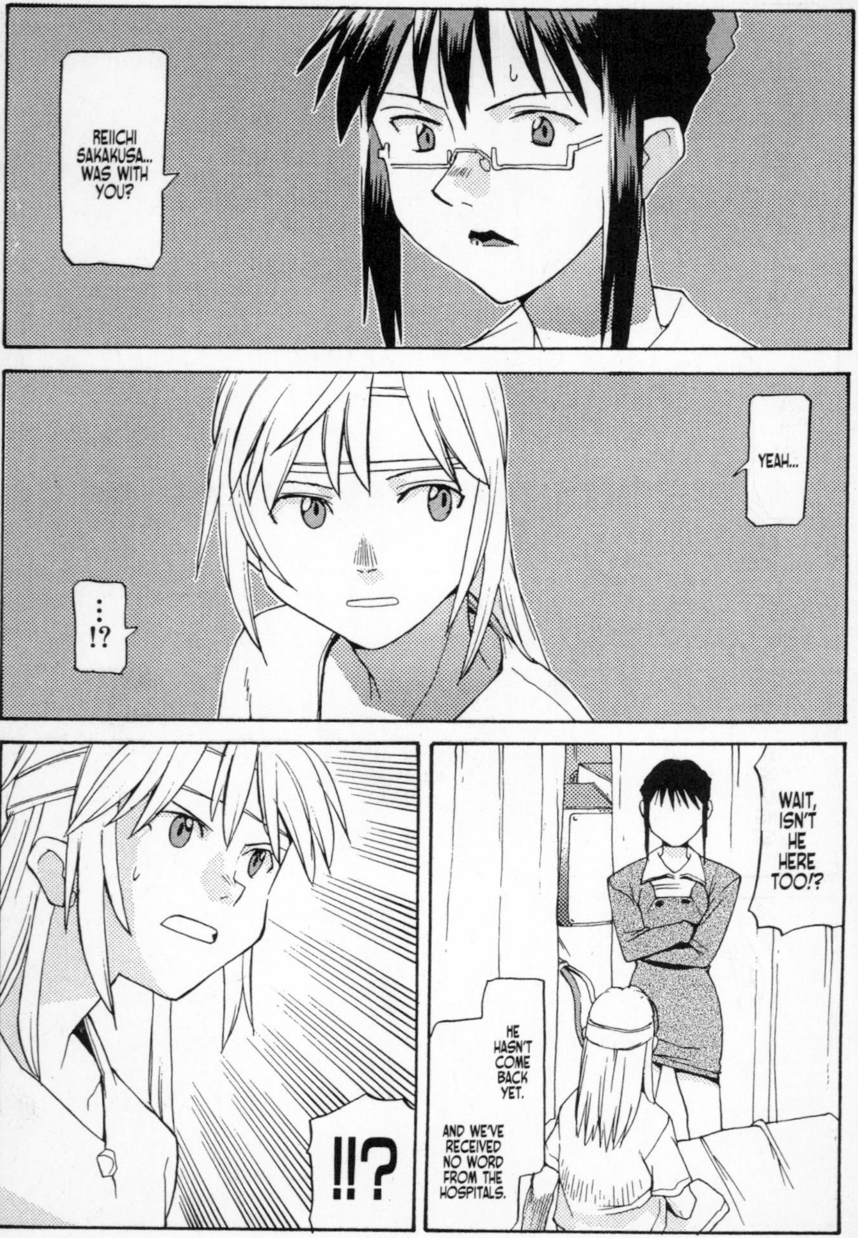
REIICHI SAKAKUSA... WAS WITH YOU?
YEAH...
...!?
WAIT, ISN'T HE HERE TOO!?
HE HASN'T COME BACK YET.
AND WE'VE RECEIVED NO WORD FROM THE HOSPITALS.
!!?

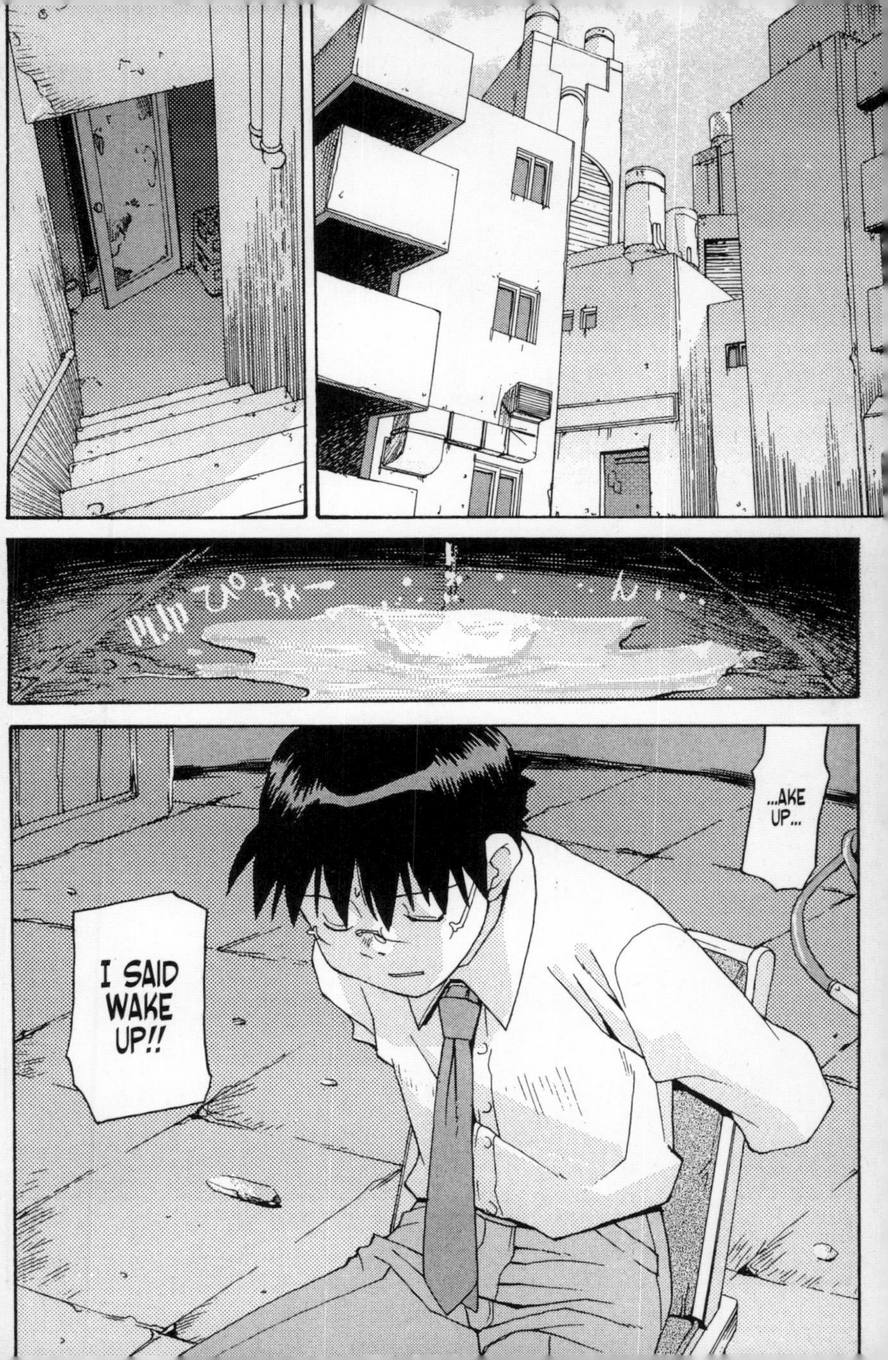
PLIP
ぴちゃー…ん…
...AKE UP...
I SAID WAKE UP!!

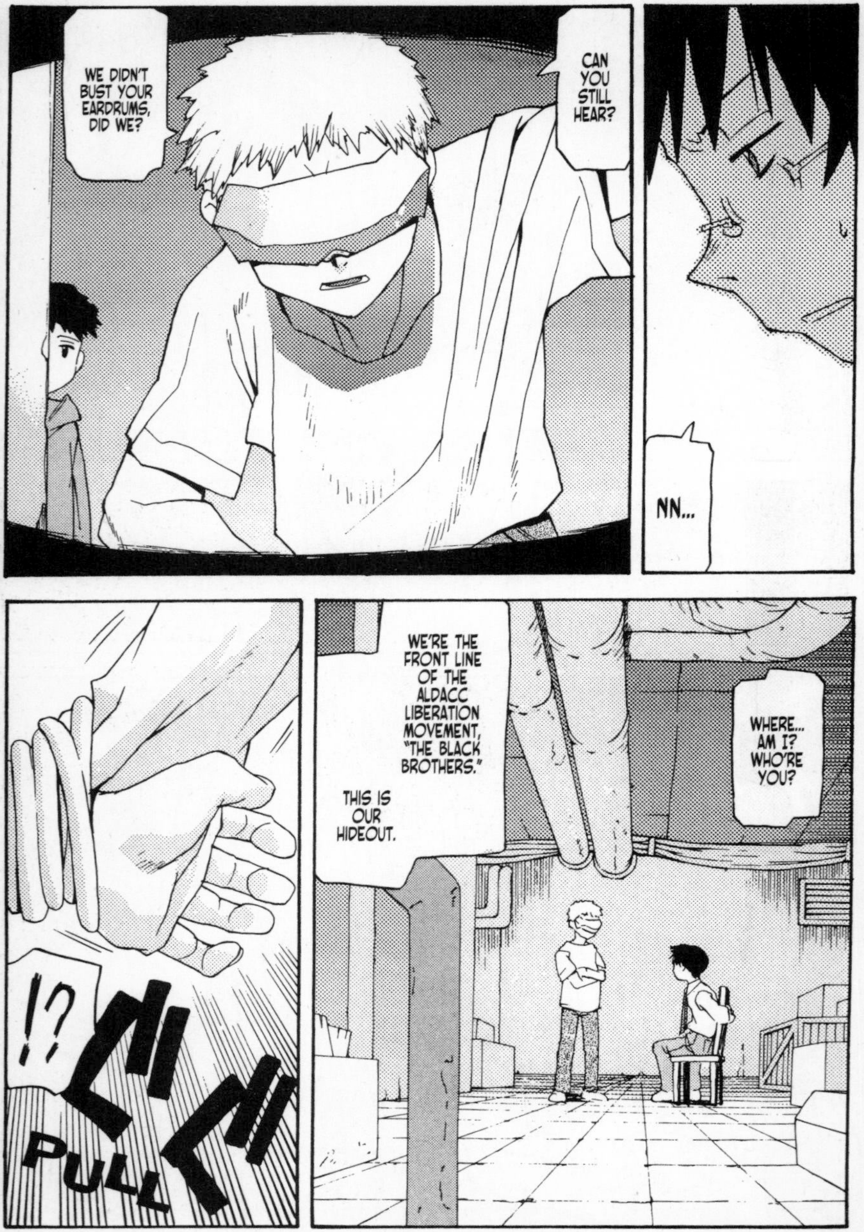
NN...
CAN YOU STILL HEAR?
WE DIDN'T BUST YOUR EARDRUMS, DID WE?
WHERE... AM I? WHO'RE YOU?
WE'RE THE FRONT LINE OF THE ALDACC LIBERATION MOVEMENT, "THE BLACK BROTHERS."
THIS IS OUR HIDEOUT.
!?
PULL

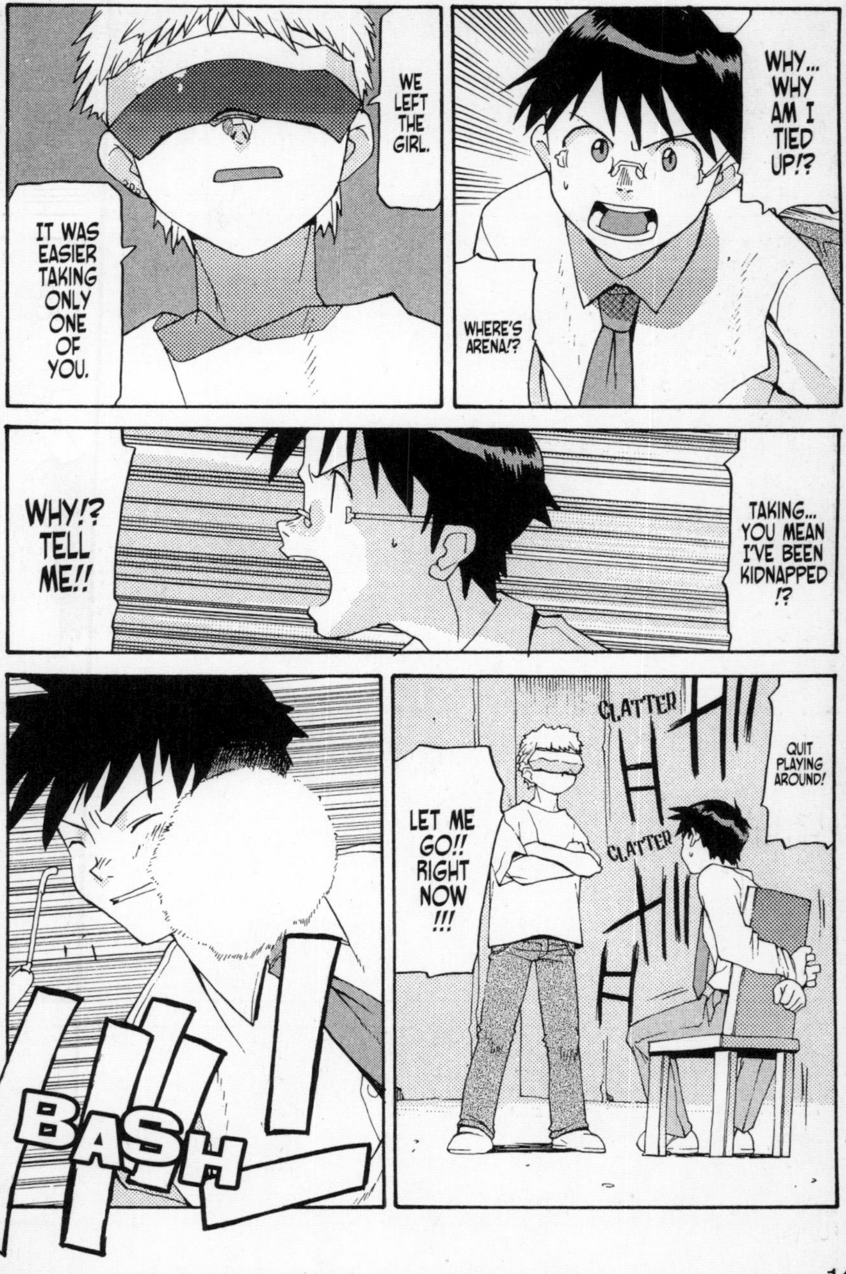
WHY... WHY AM I TIED UP!?
WHERE'S ARENA!?
WE LEFT THE GIRL.
IT WAS EASIER TAKING ONLY ONE OF YOU.
TAKING... YOU MEAN I'VE BEEN KIDNAPPED!?
WHY!? TELL ME!!
QUIT PLAYING AROUND!
CLATTER
CLATTER
LET ME GO!! RIGHT NOW!!!
BASH

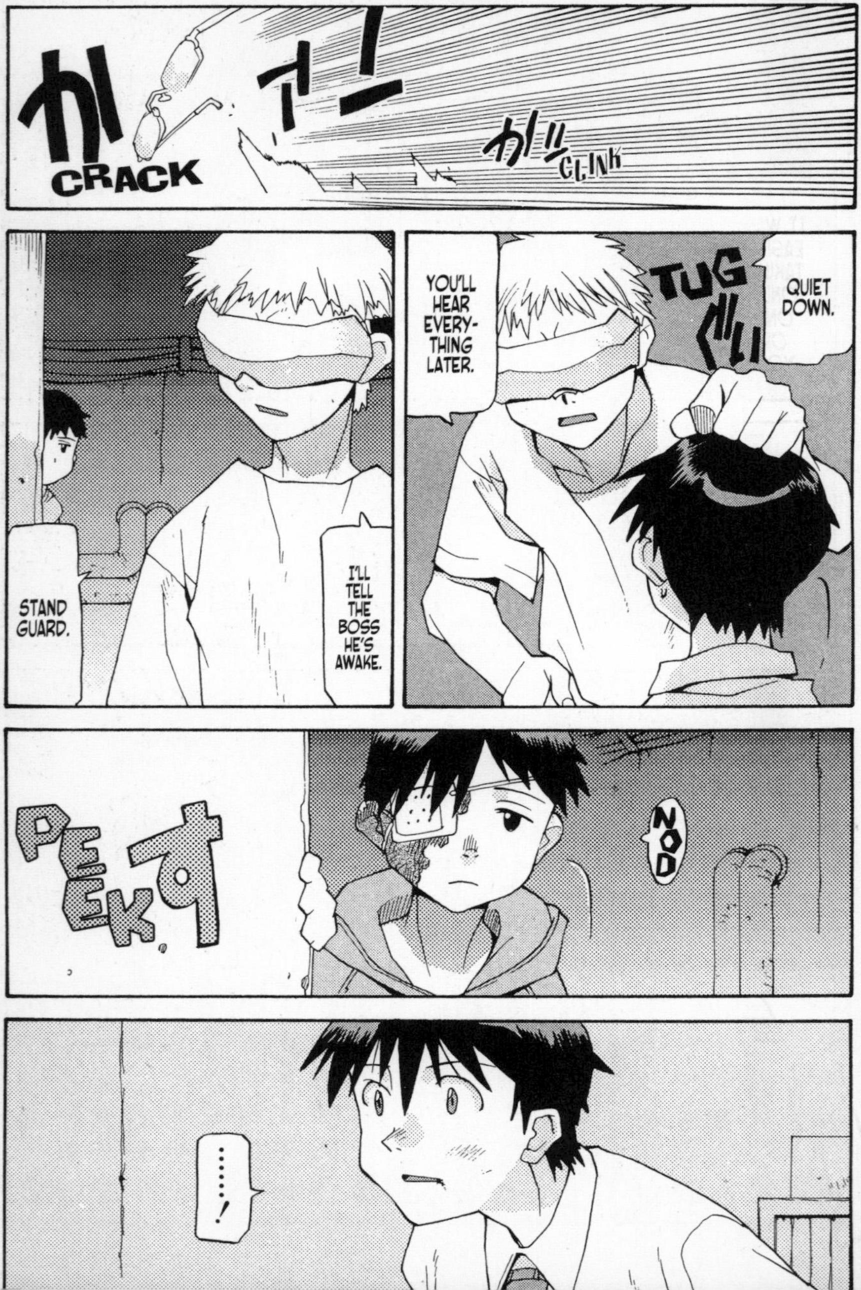
CRACK
CLINK
TUG
QUIET DOWN.
YOU'LL HEAR EVERY-THING LATER.
I'LL TELL THE BOSS HE'S AWAKE.
STAND GUARD.
NOD
PEEK
……!

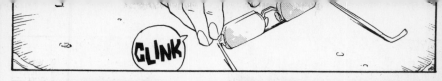

CLINK

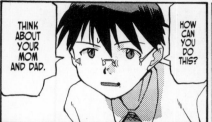

THINK ABOUT YOUR MOM AND DAD.

HOW CAN YOU DO THIS?

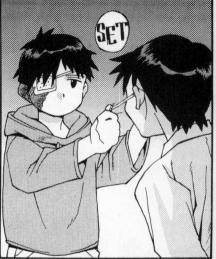

SET

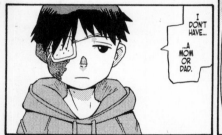

I DON'T HAVE...

...A MOM OR DAD.

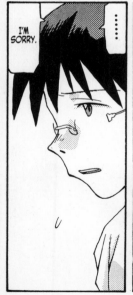

I'M SORRY.

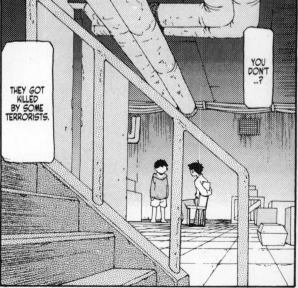

THEY GOT KILLED BY SOME TERRORISTS.

YOU DON'T ...?

16

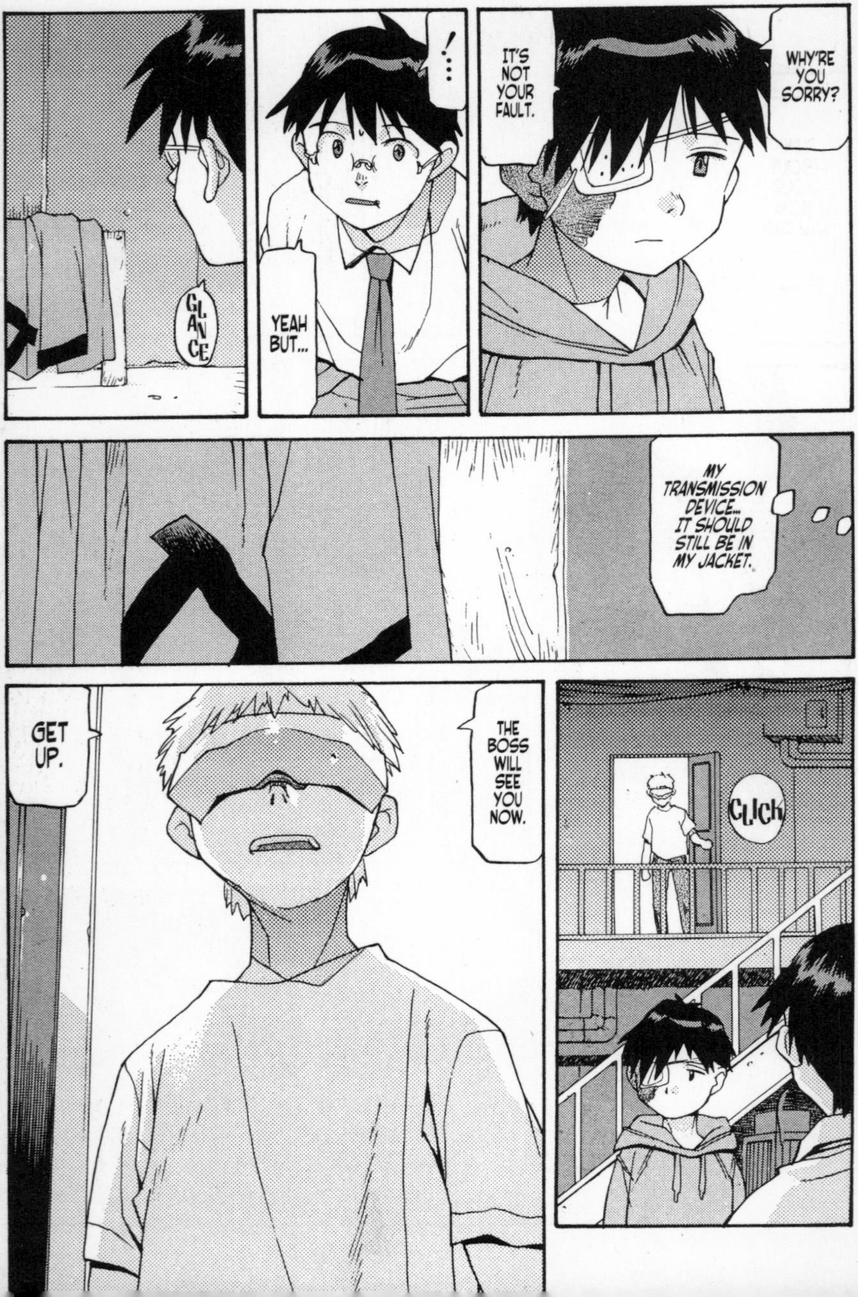
WHY'RE YOU SORRY?
IT'S NOT YOUR FAULT.
!...
YEAH BUT...
GLANCE
MY TRANSMISSION DEVICE... IT SHOULD STILL BE IN MY JACKET.
CLICK
THE BOSS WILL SEE YOU NOW.
GET UP.

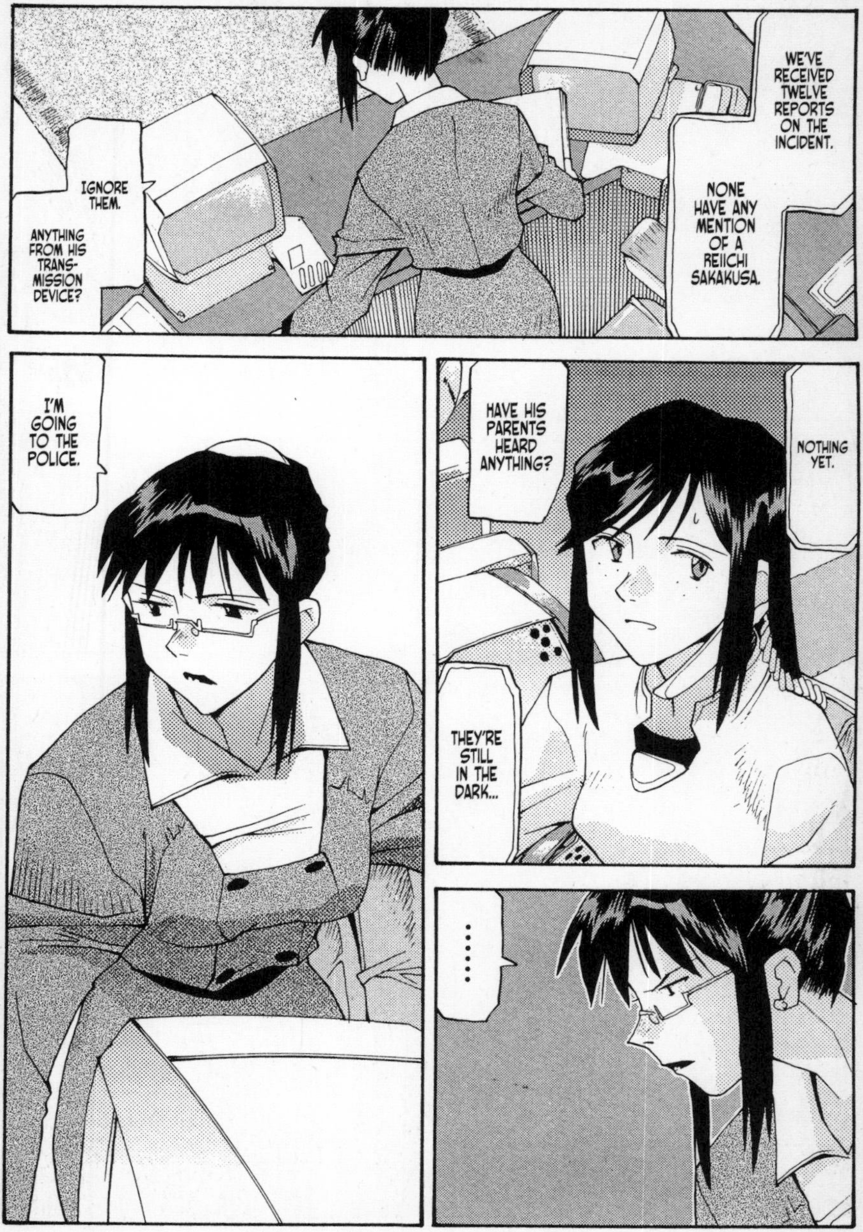

WE'VE RECEIVED TWELVE REPORTS ON THE INCIDENT.
NONE HAVE ANY MENTION OF A REIICHI SAKAKUSA.
IGNORE THEM.
ANYTHING FROM HIS TRANS-MISSION DEVICE?
NOTHING YET.
HAVE HIS PARENTS HEARD ANYTHING?
THEY'RE STILL IN THE DARK...
......
I'M GOING TO THE POLICE.

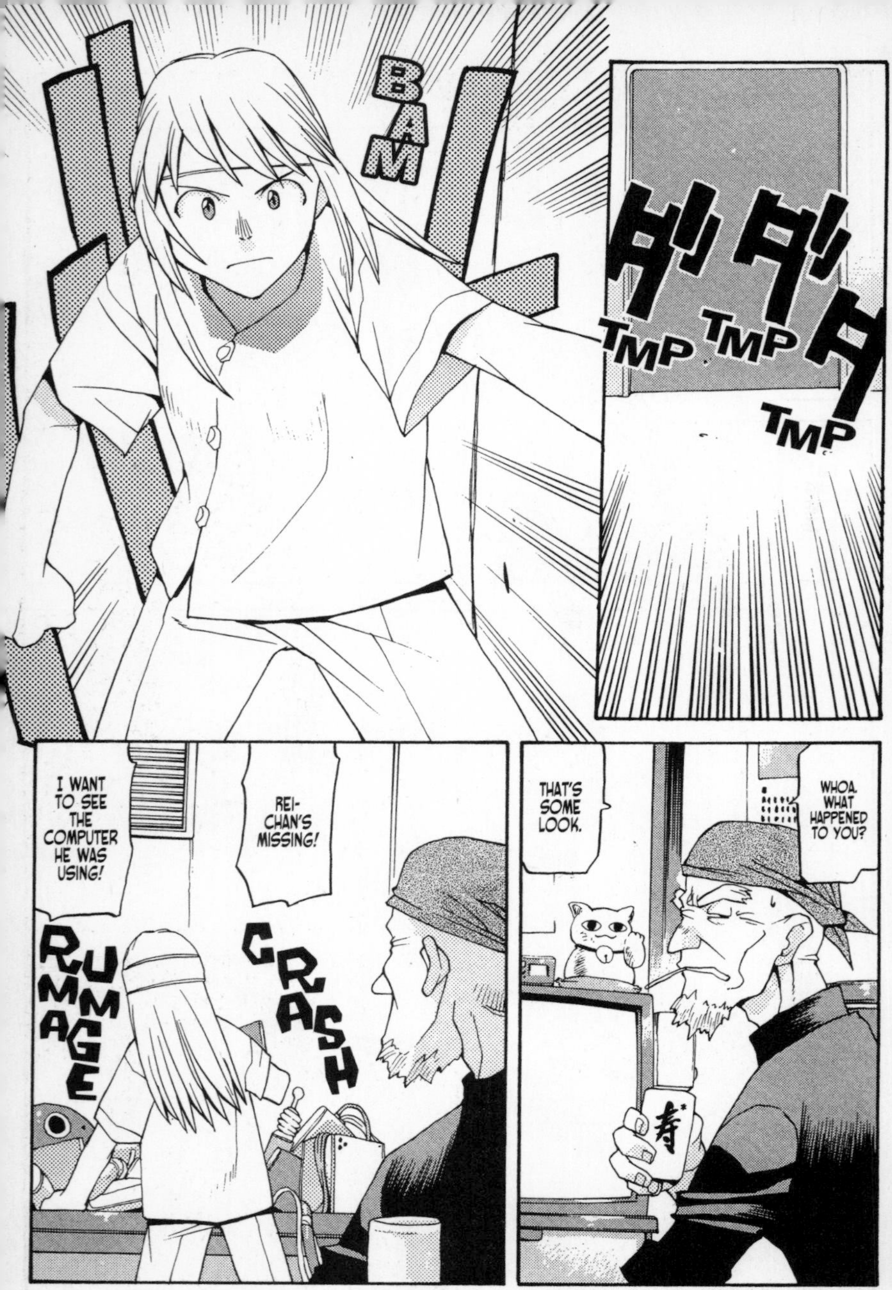
ダダダ
TMP TMP TMP
BAM
WHOA. WHAT HAPPENED TO YOU?
THAT'S SOME LOOK.
寿*
REI-CHAN'S MISSING!
I WANT TO SEE THE COMPUTER HE WAS USING!
CRASH
RUMMAGE

* "Kotobuki" – means congratulations or long life.

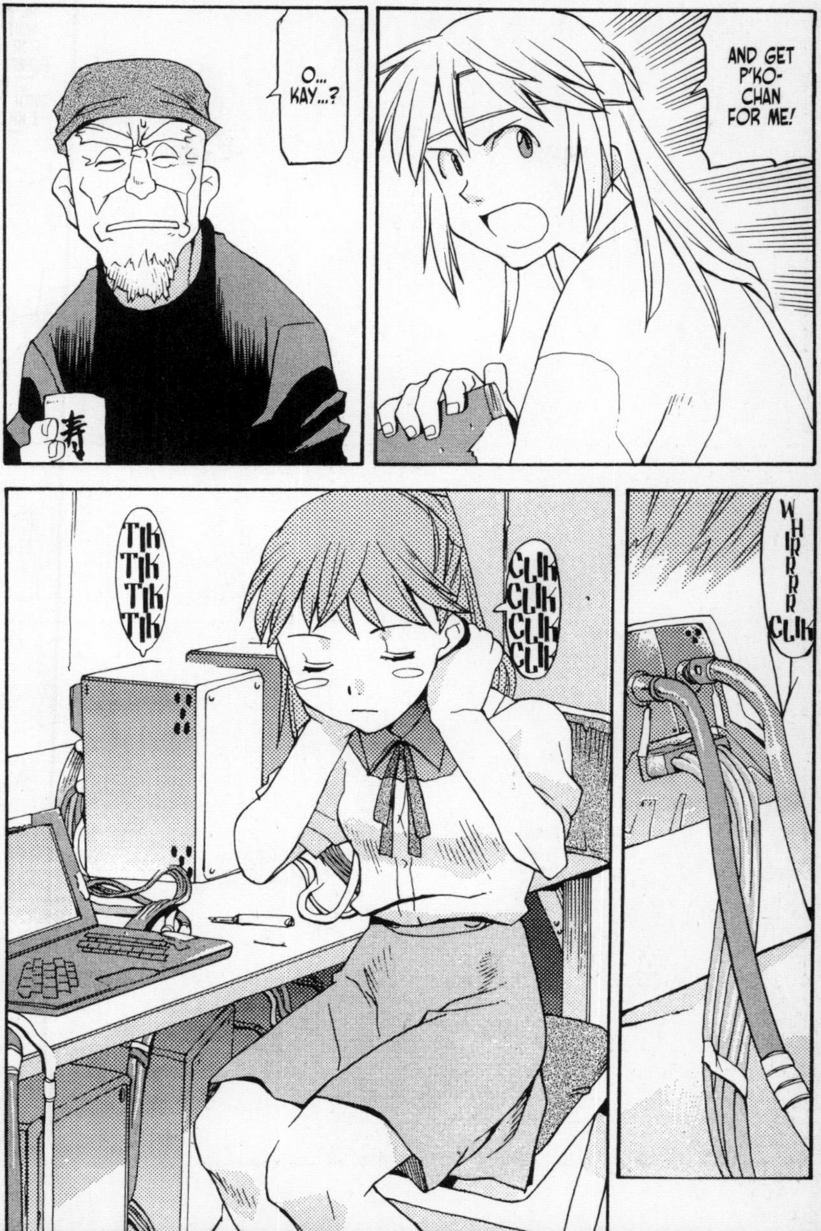
AND GET P'KO-CHAN FOR ME!
O... KAY...?
寿
WHIRRRR CLIK
CLIK CLIK CLIK CLIK
TIK TIK TIK TIK

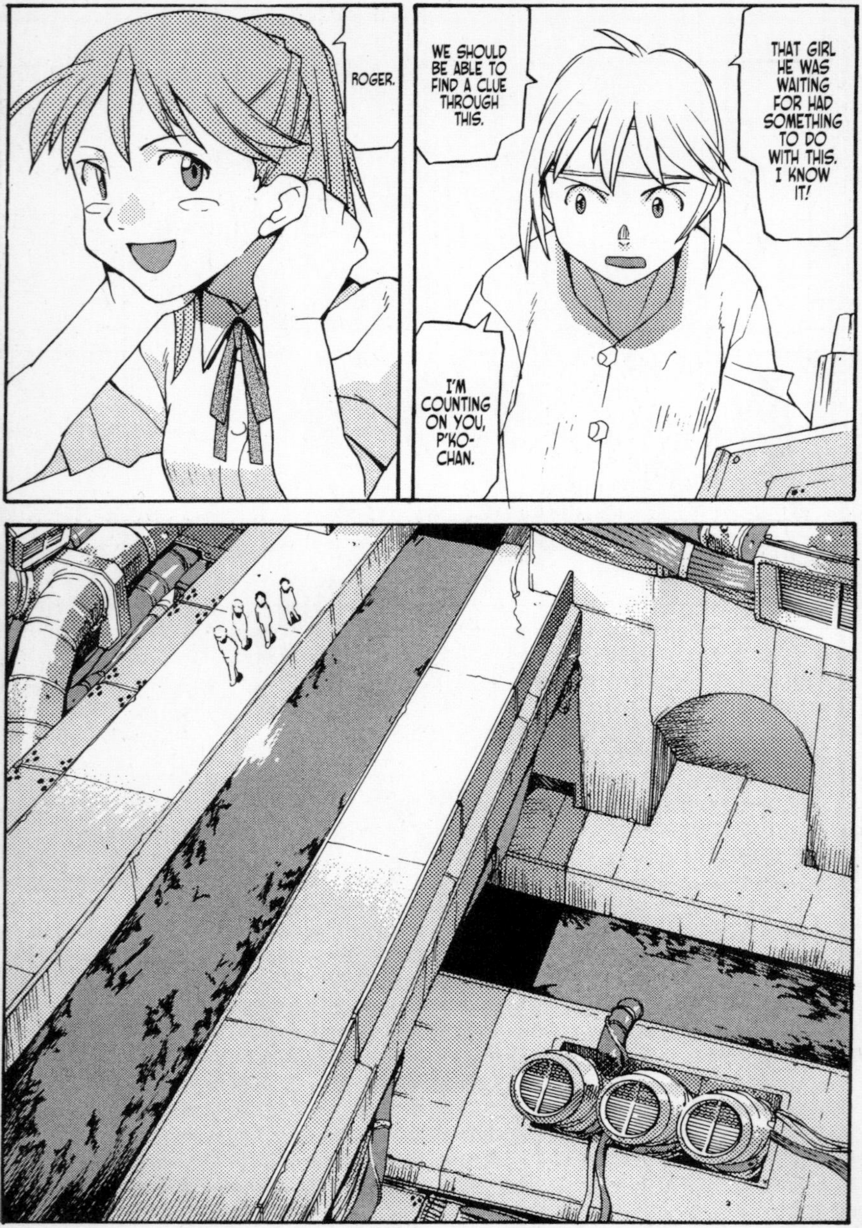
THAT GIRL HE WAS WAITING FOR HAD SOMETHING TO DO WITH THIS. I KNOW IT!
WE SHOULD BE ABLE TO FIND A CLUE THROUGH THIS.
I'M COUNTING ON YOU, P'KO-CHAN.
ROGER.

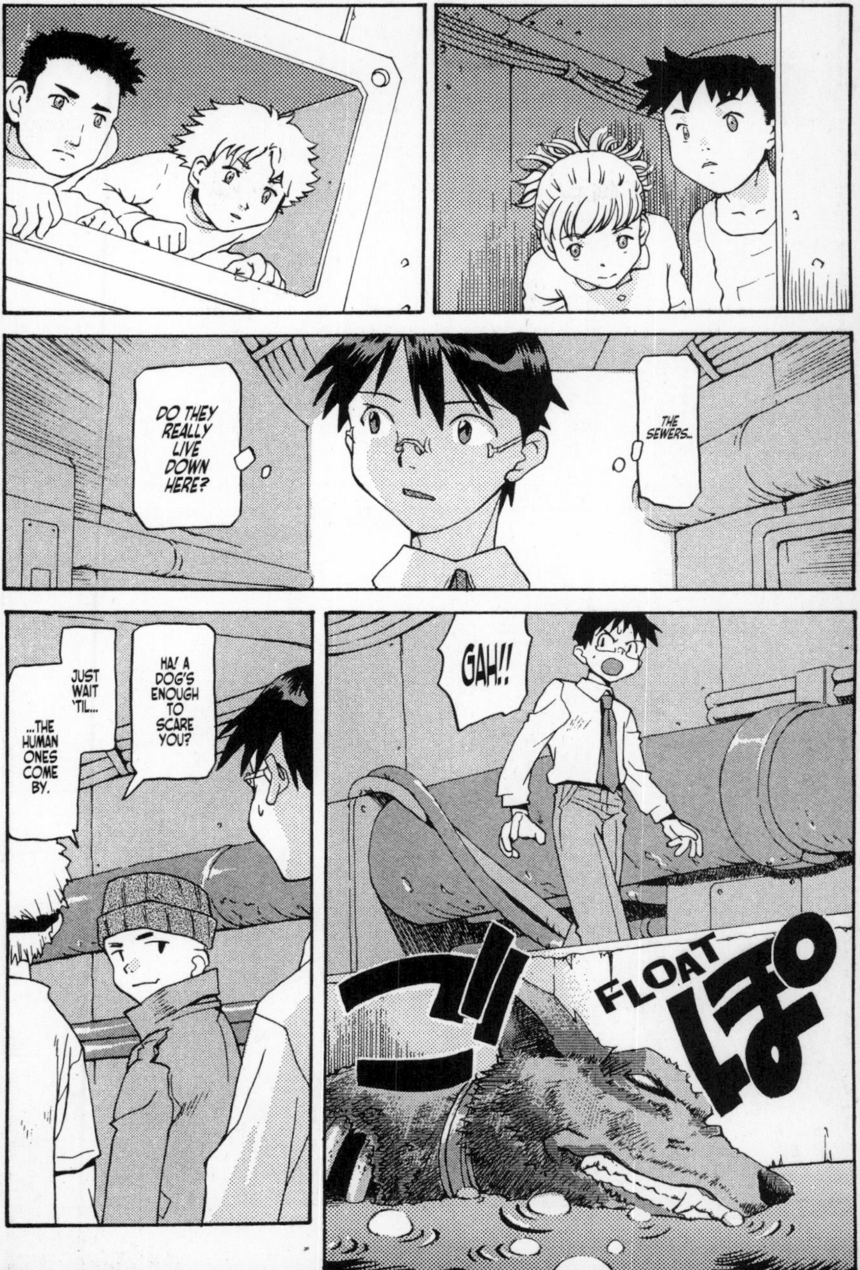
THE SEWERS...
DO THEY REALLY LIVE DOWN HERE?
GAH!!
FLOAT
HA! A DOG'S ENOUGH TO SCARE YOU?
JUST WAIT 'TIL...
...THE HUMAN ONES COME BY.

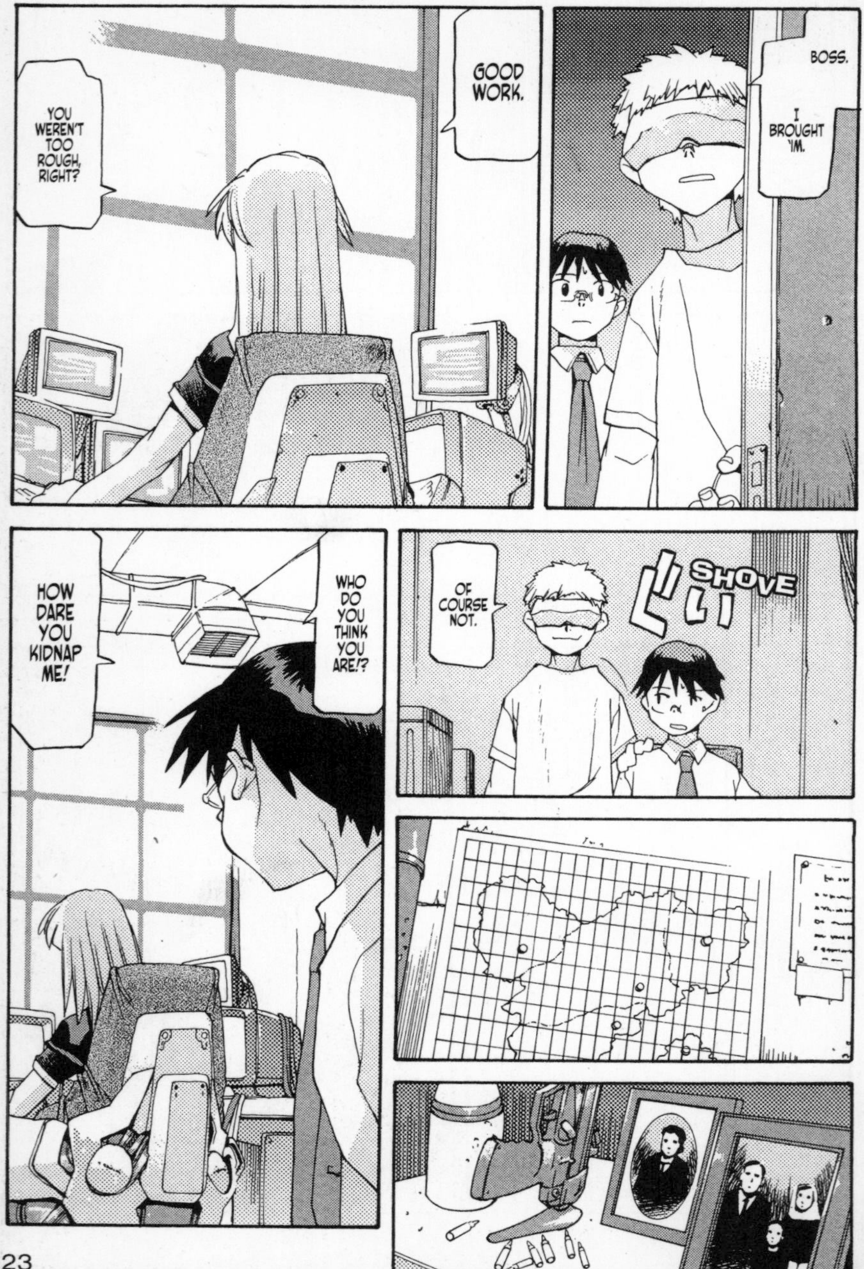
BOSS.
I BROUGHT 'IM.
GOOD WORK.
YOU WEREN'T TOO ROUGH, RIGHT?
SHOVE
OF COURSE NOT.
WHO DO YOU THINK YOU ARE!?
HOW DARE YOU KIDNAP ME!

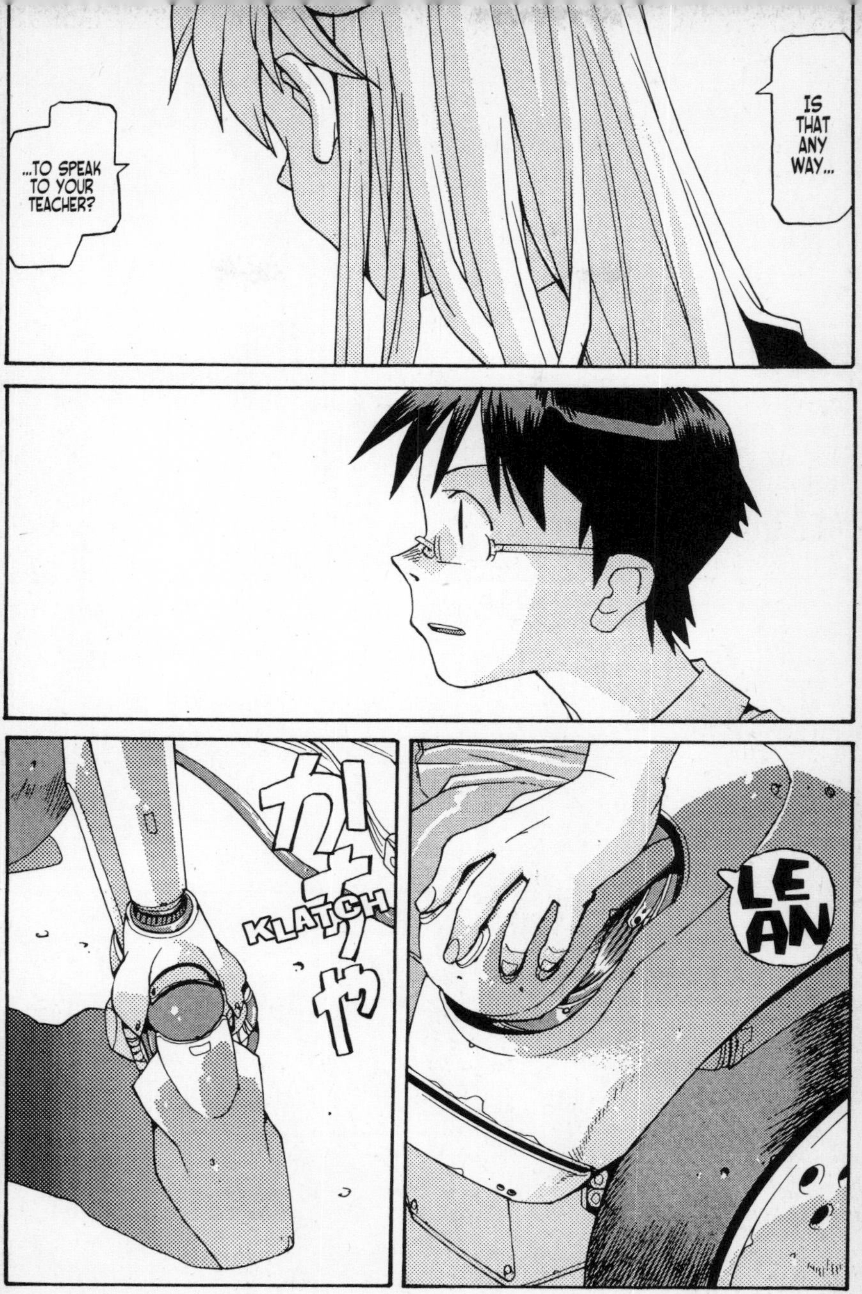
IS THAT ANY WAY...
...TO SPEAK TO YOUR TEACHER?
LEAN
かちゃ
KLATCH

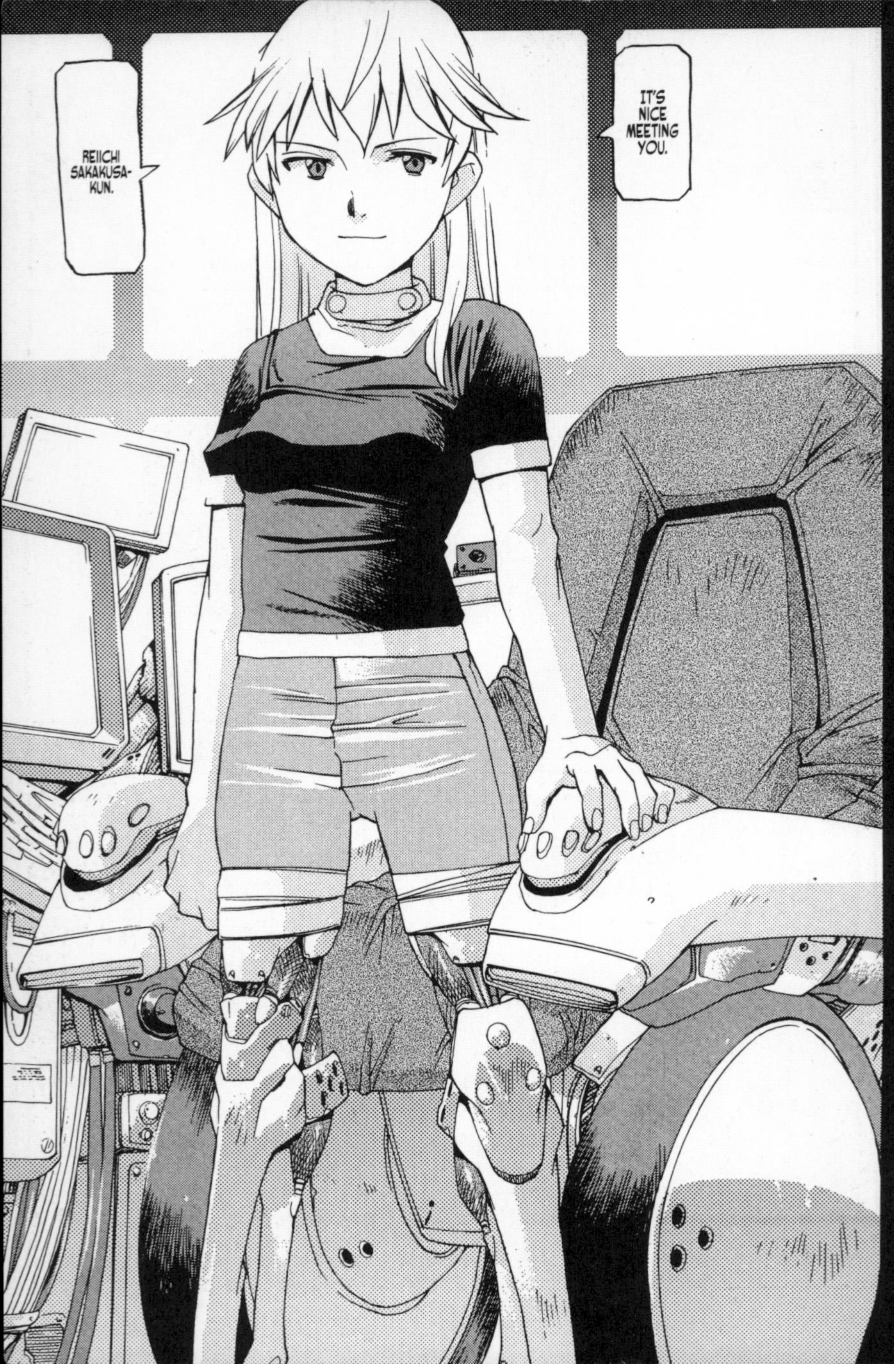
IT'S NICE MEETING YOU.
REIICHI SAKAKUSA-KUN.

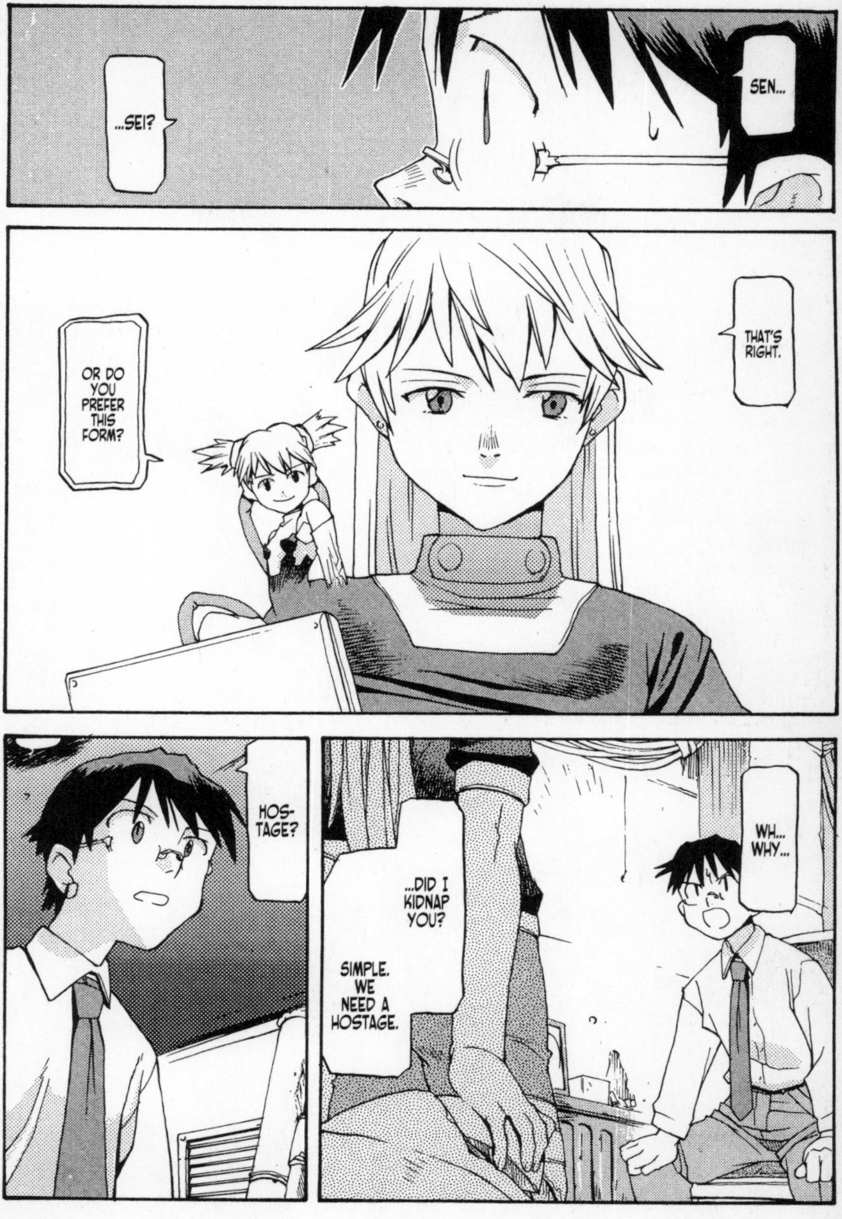
SEN...
...SEI?
THAT'S RIGHT.
OR DO YOU PREFER THIS FORM?
WH... WHY...
...DID I KIDNAP YOU?
SIMPLE. WE NEED A HOSTAGE.
HOS-TAGE?

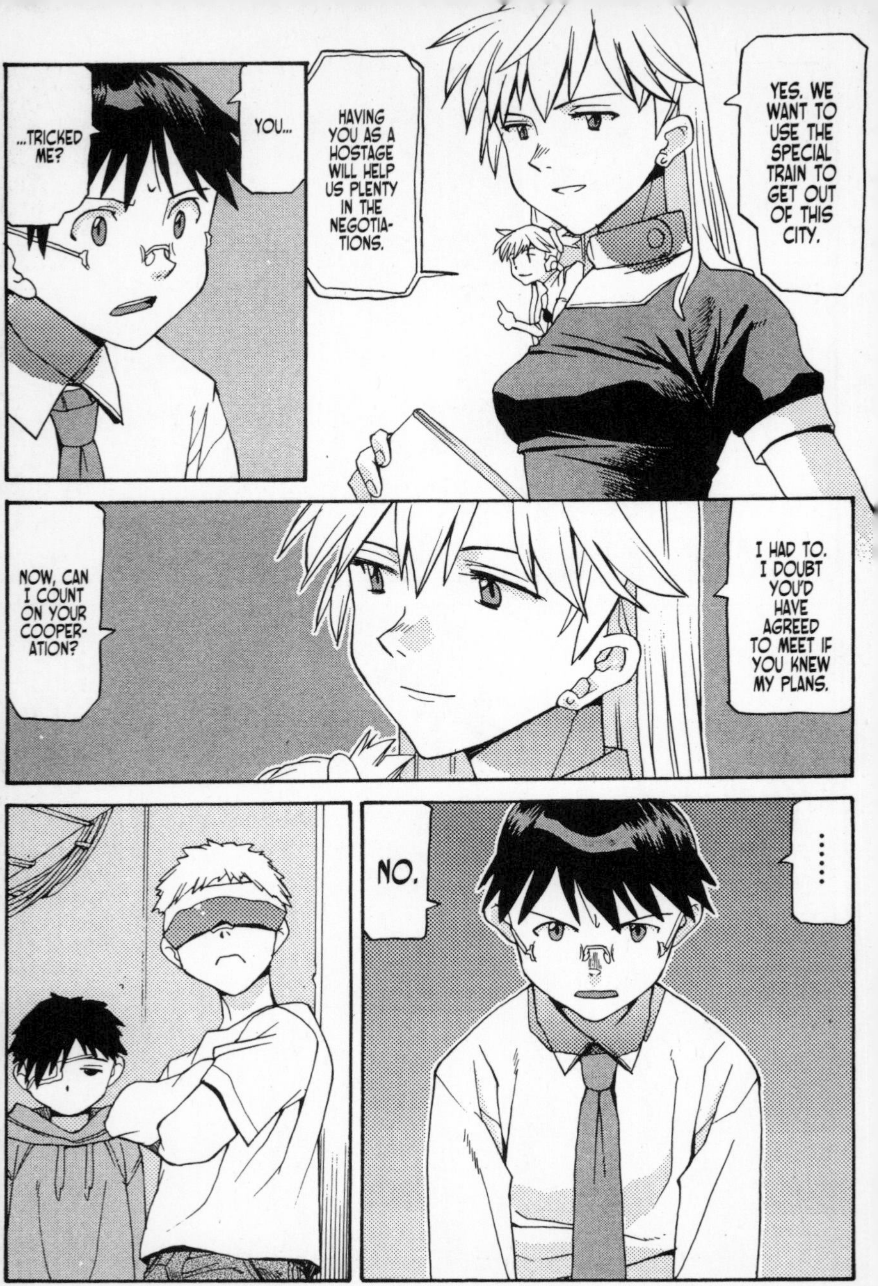
YES. WE WANT TO USE THE SPECIAL TRAIN TO GET OUT OF THIS CITY.
HAVING YOU AS A HOSTAGE WILL HELP US PLENTY IN THE NEGOTIATIONS.
YOU...
...TRICKED ME?
I HAD TO. I DOUBT YOU'D HAVE AGREED TO MEET IF YOU KNEW MY PLANS.
NOW, CAN I COUNT ON YOUR COOPERATION?
......
NO.

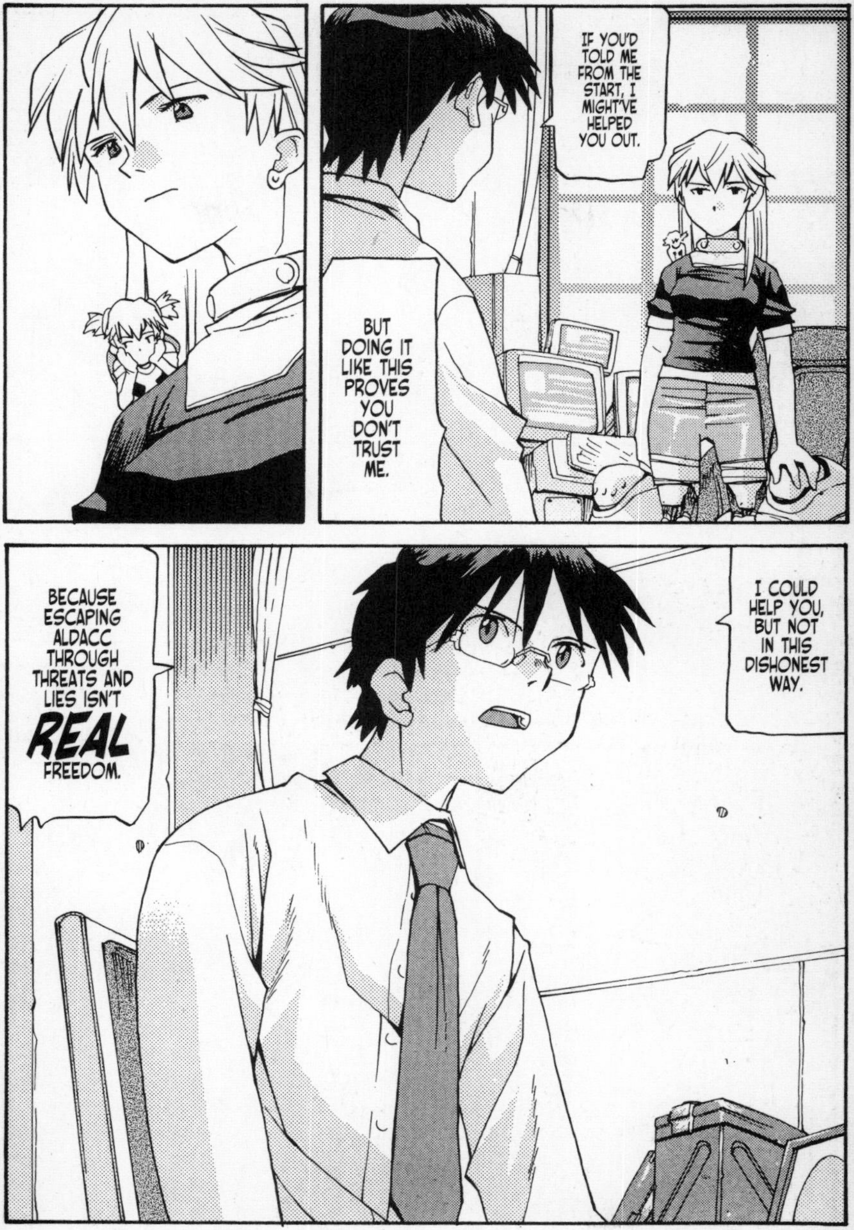
IF YOU'D TOLD ME FROM THE START, I MIGHT'VE HELPED YOU OUT.
BUT DOING IT LIKE THIS PROVES YOU DON'T TRUST ME.
I COULD HELP YOU, BUT NOT IN THIS DISHONEST WAY.
BECAUSE ESCAPING ALDACC THROUGH THREATS AND LIES ISN'T REAL FREEDOM.

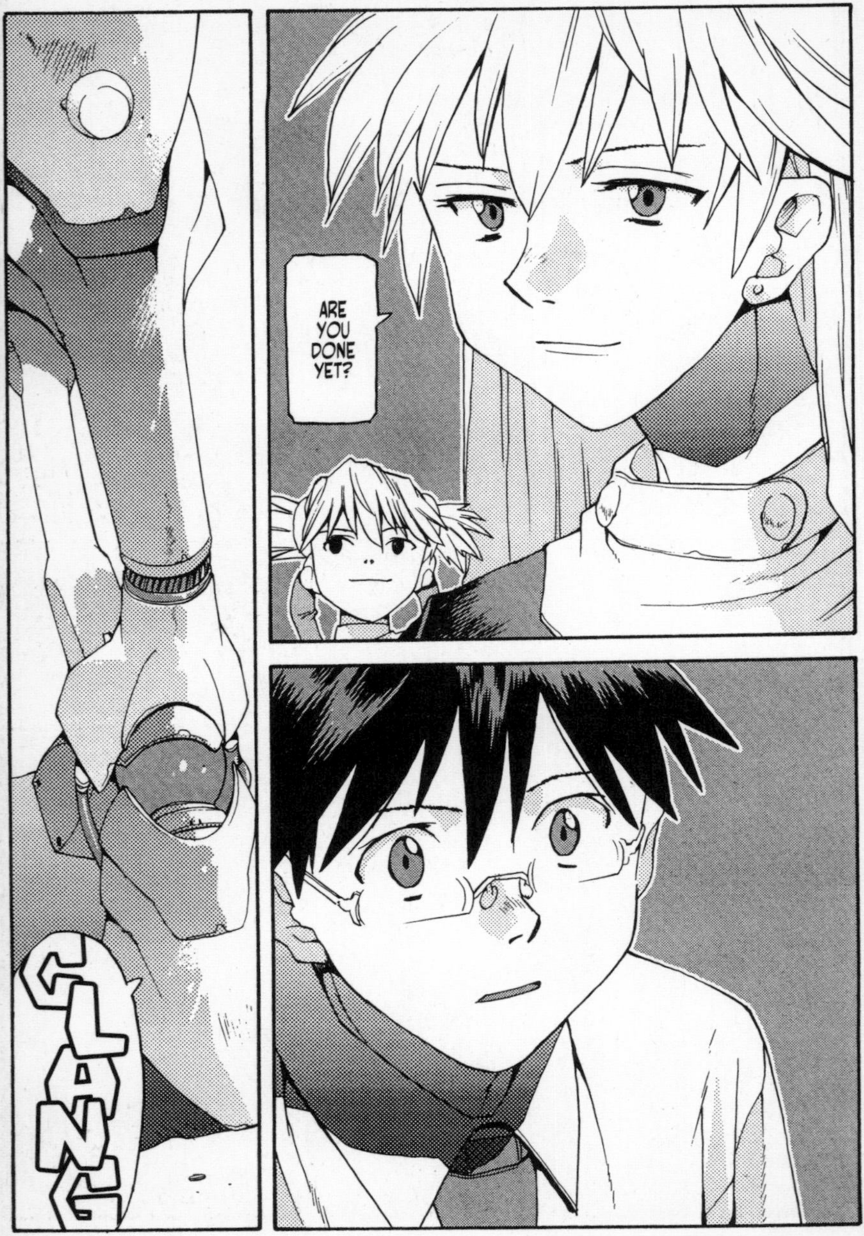
ARE YOU DONE YET?
CLANG

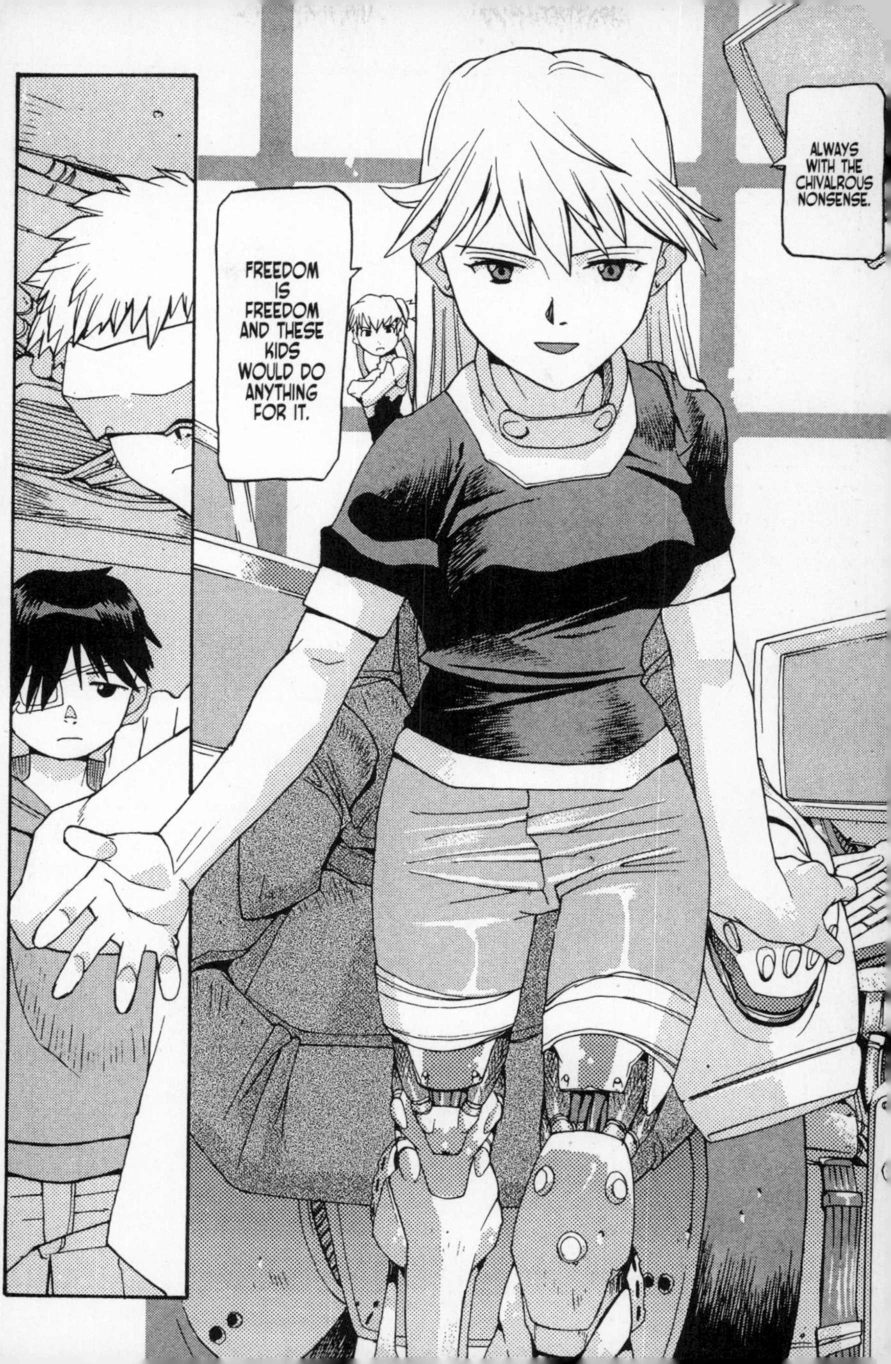
ALWAYS WITH THE CHIVALROUS NONSENSE.
FREEDOM IS FREEDOM AND THESE KIDS WOULD DO ANYTHING FOR IT.

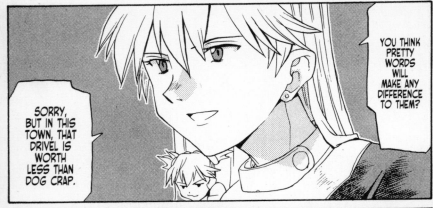

YOU THINK PRETTY WORDS WILL MAKE ANY DIFFERENCE TO THEM?

SORRY, BUT IN THIS TOWN, THAT DRIVEL IS WORTH LESS THAN DOG CRAP.

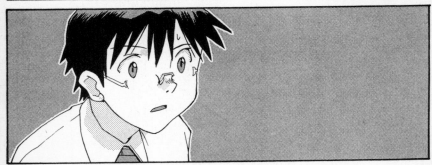

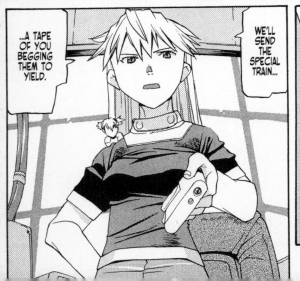

...A TAPE OF YOU BEGGING THEM TO YIELD.

WE'LL SEND THE SPECIAL TRAIN...

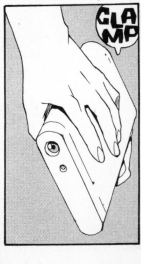

CLA MP

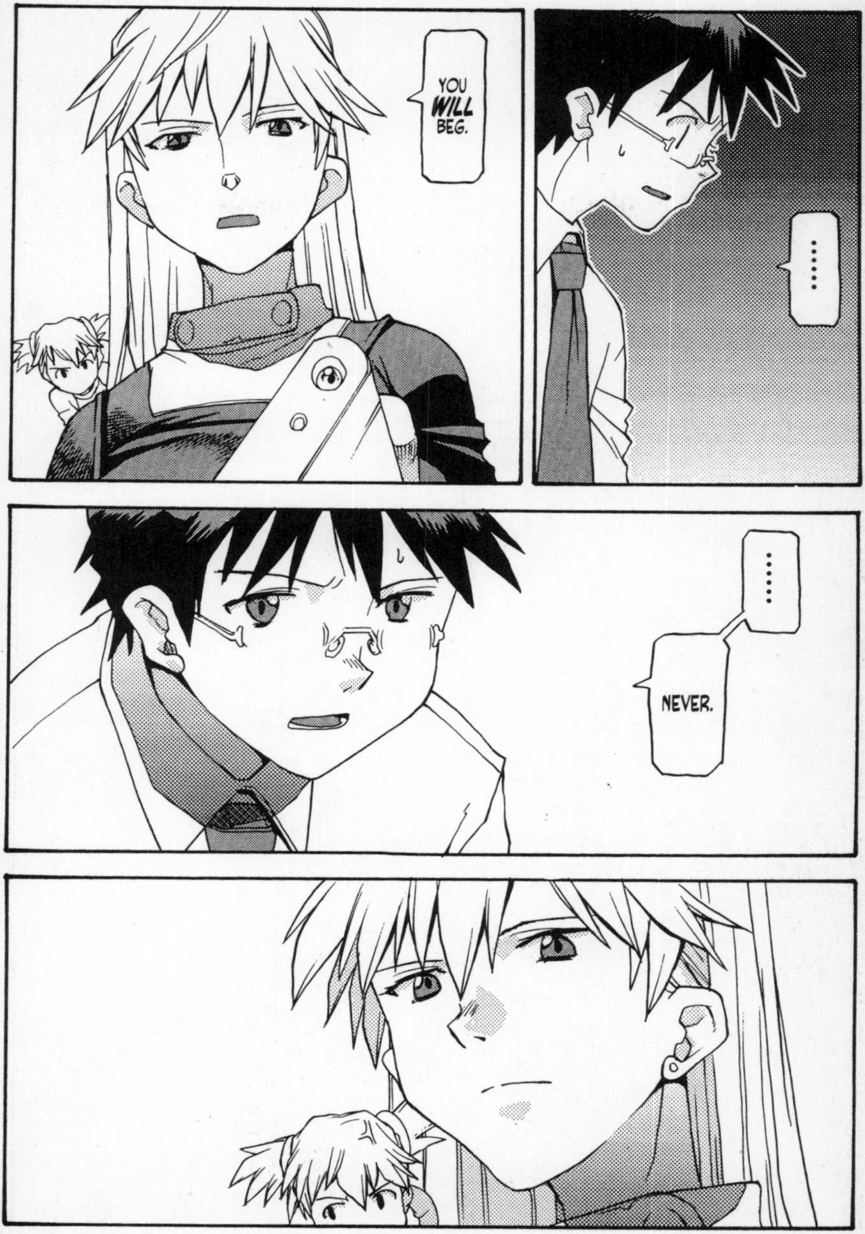
......
YOU **WILL** BEG.
......
NEVER.

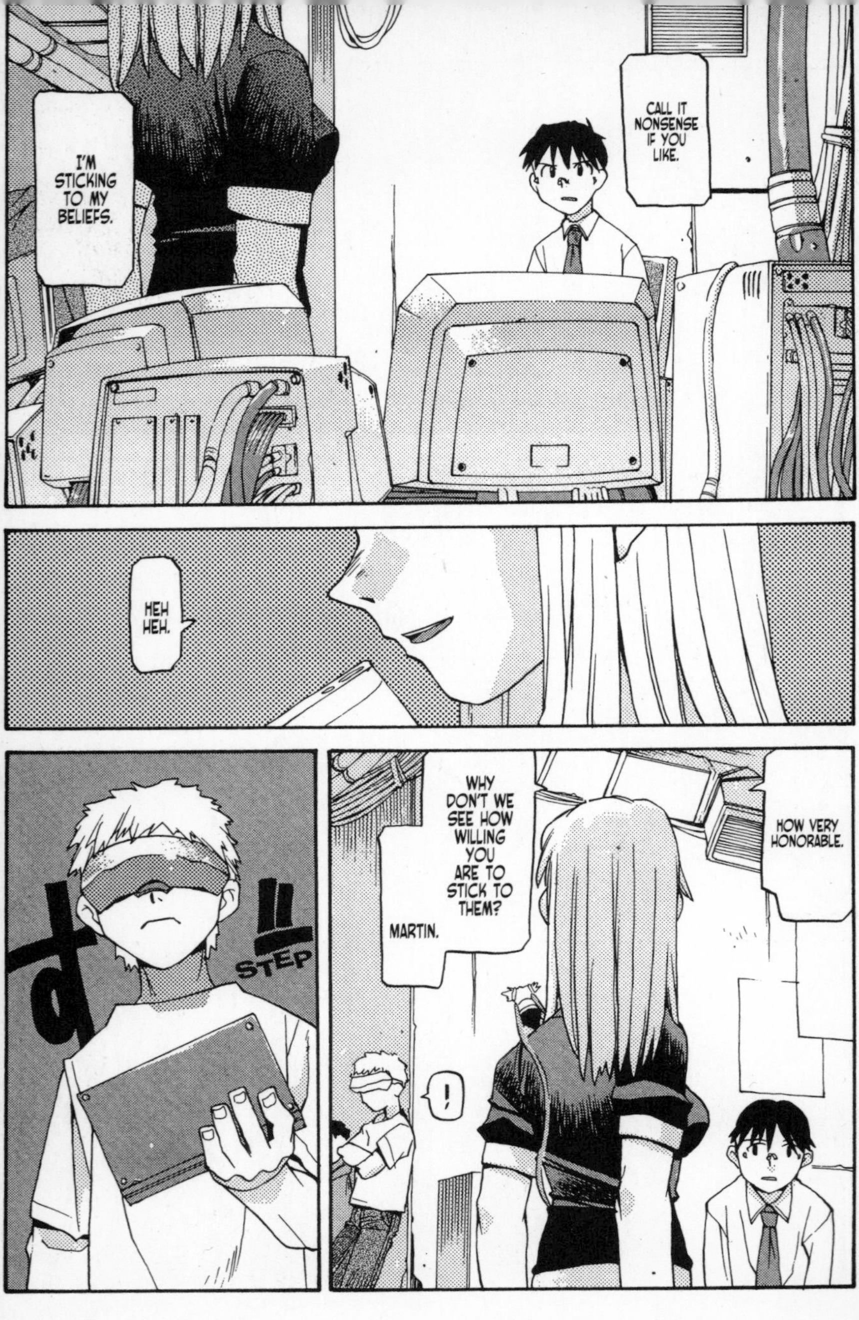
CALL IT NONSENSE IF YOU LIKE.
I'M STICKING TO MY BELIEFS.
HEH HEH.
HOW VERY HONORABLE.
WHY DON'T WE SEE HOW WILLING YOU ARE TO STICK TO THEM?
MARTIN.
!
STEP

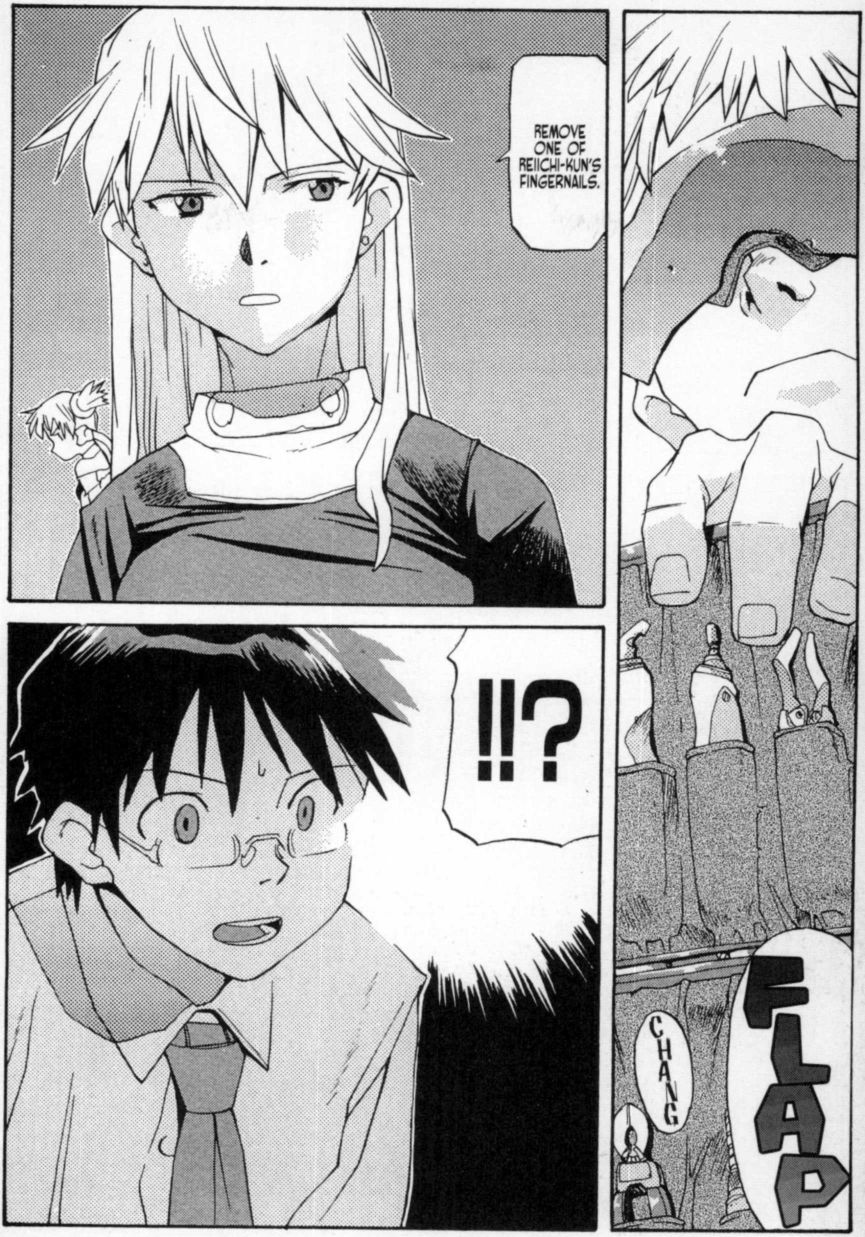
CHANG
FLAP
REMOVE ONE OF REIICHI-KUN'S FINGERNAILS.
!!?

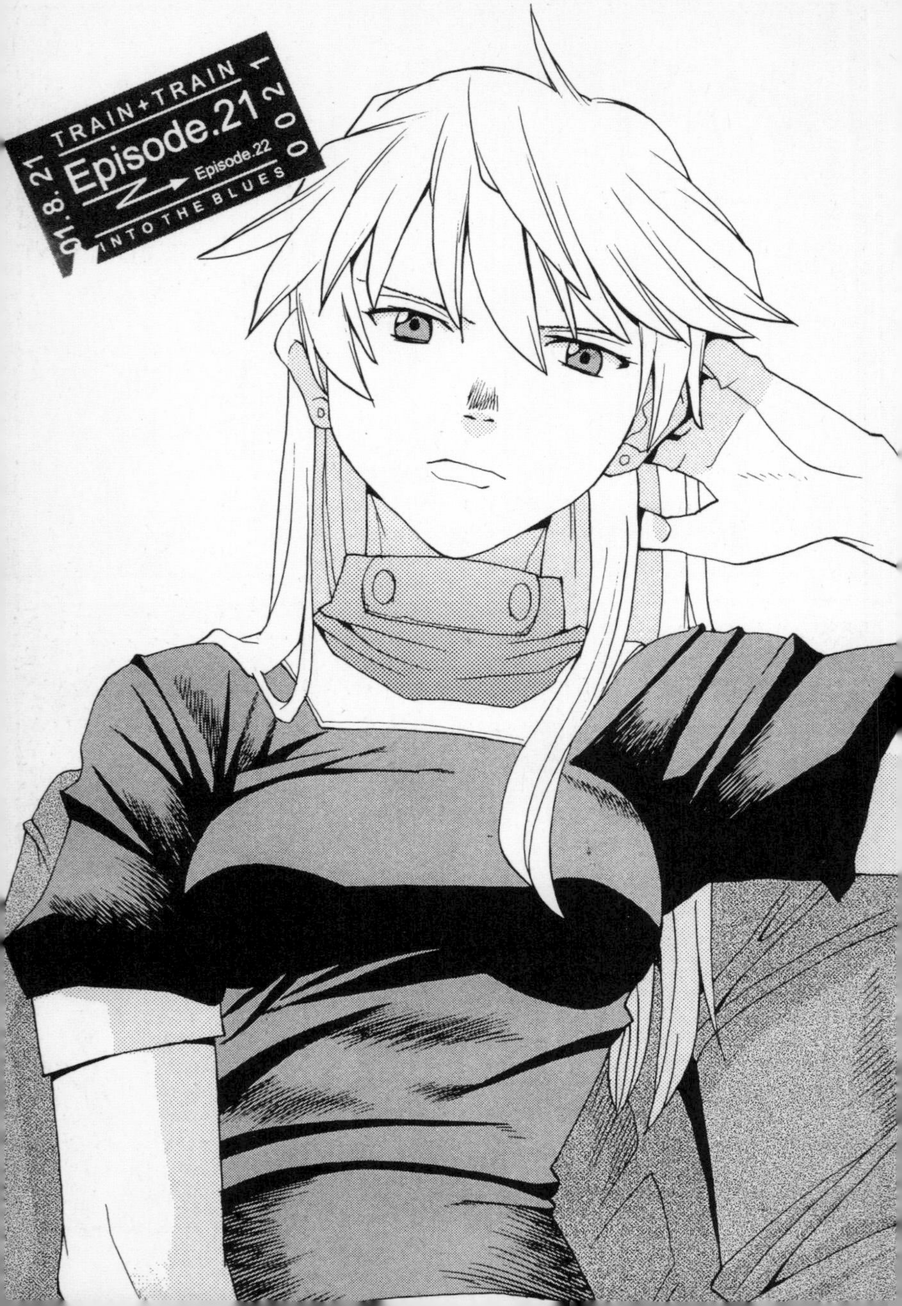
TRAIN+TRAIN
Episode.21
Episode.22
INTO THE BLUES
01.8.21

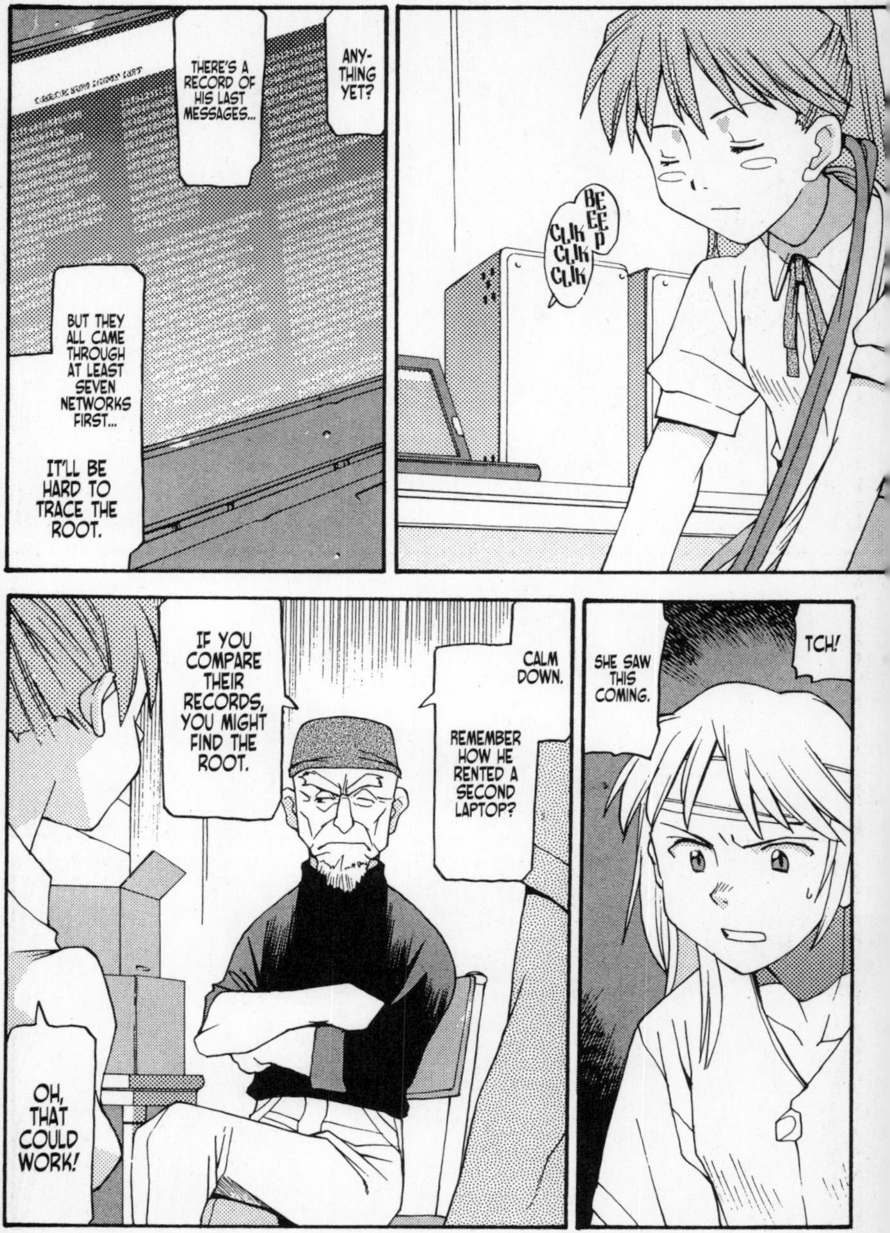
BEEEP
CLIK CLIK CLIK
ANY-THING YET?
THERE'S A RECORD OF HIS LAST MESSAGES...
BUT THEY ALL CAME THROUGH AT LEAST SEVEN NETWORKS FIRST...
IT'LL BE HARD TO TRACE THE ROOT.
TCH!
SHE SAW THIS COMING.
CALM DOWN.
REMEMBER HOW HE RENTED A SECOND LAPTOP?
IF YOU COMPARE THEIR RECORDS, YOU MIGHT FIND THE ROOT.
OH, THAT COULD WORK!

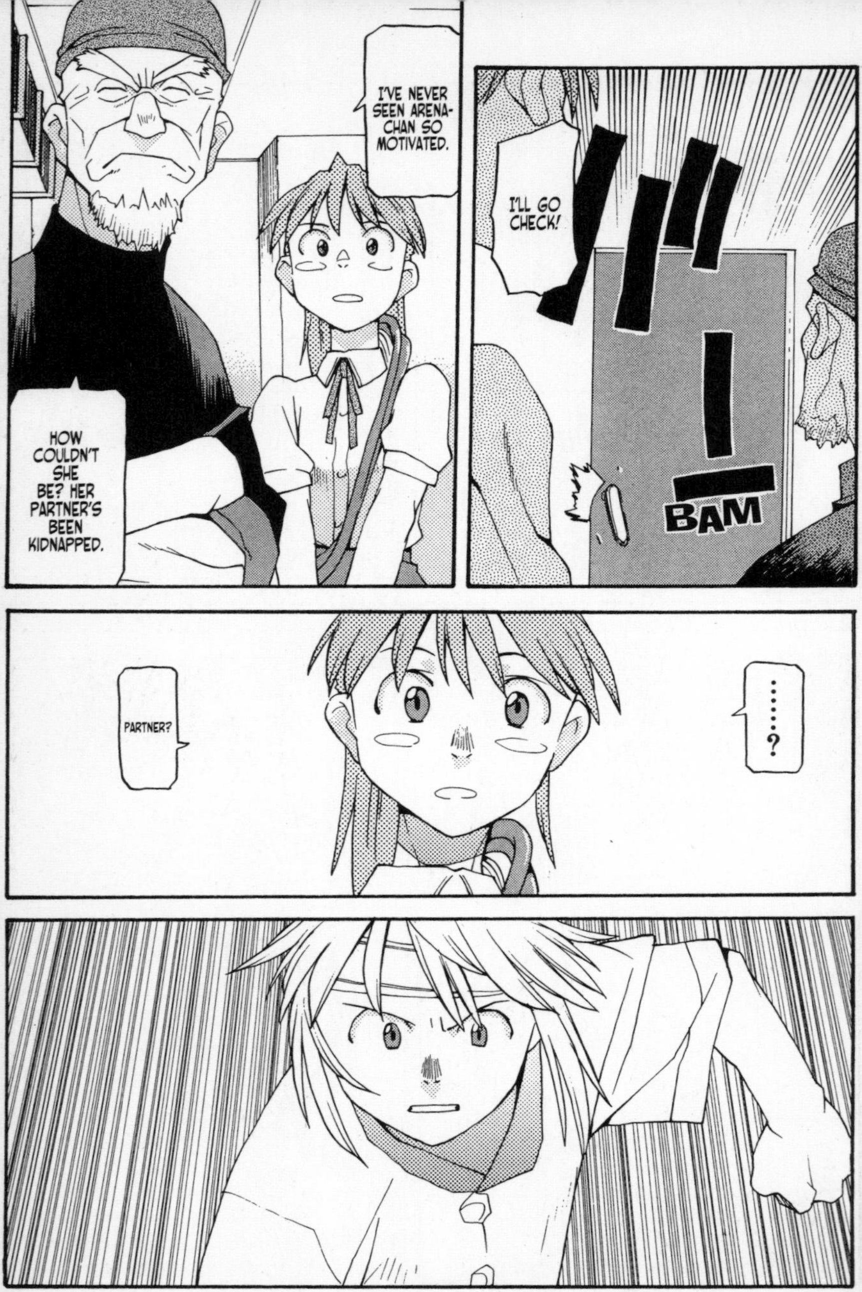
I'LL GO CHECK!
BAM
I'VE NEVER SEEN ARENA-CHAN SO MOTIVATED.
HOW COULDN'T SHE BE? HER PARTNER'S BEEN KIDNAPPED.
......?
PARTNER?

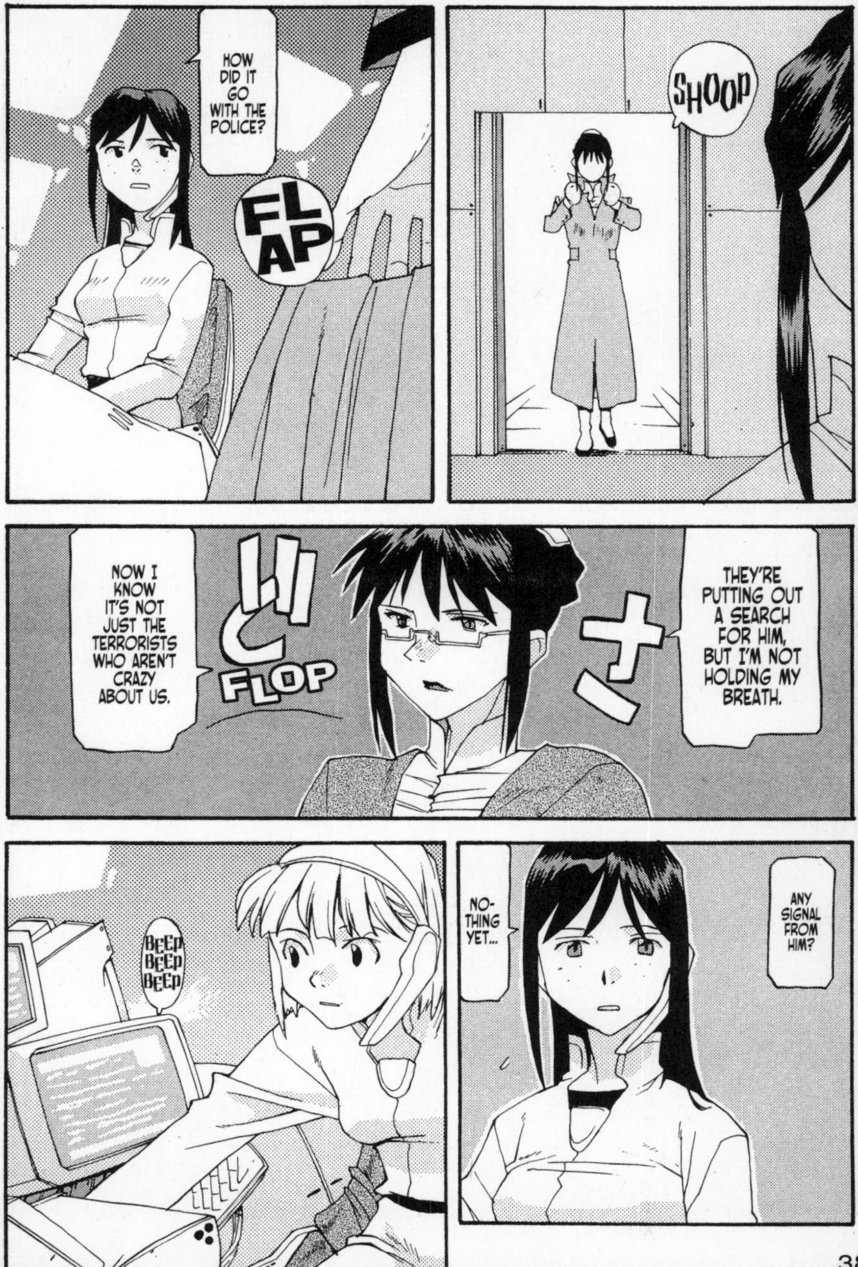
SHOOP
HOW DID IT GO WITH THE POLICE?
FLAP
THEY'RE PUTTING OUT A SEARCH FOR HIM, BUT I'M NOT HOLDING MY BREATH.
FLOP
NOW I KNOW IT'S NOT JUST THE TERRORISTS WHO AREN'T CRAZY ABOUT US.
ANY SIGNAL FROM HIM?
NO-THING YET...
BEEP BEEP BEEP

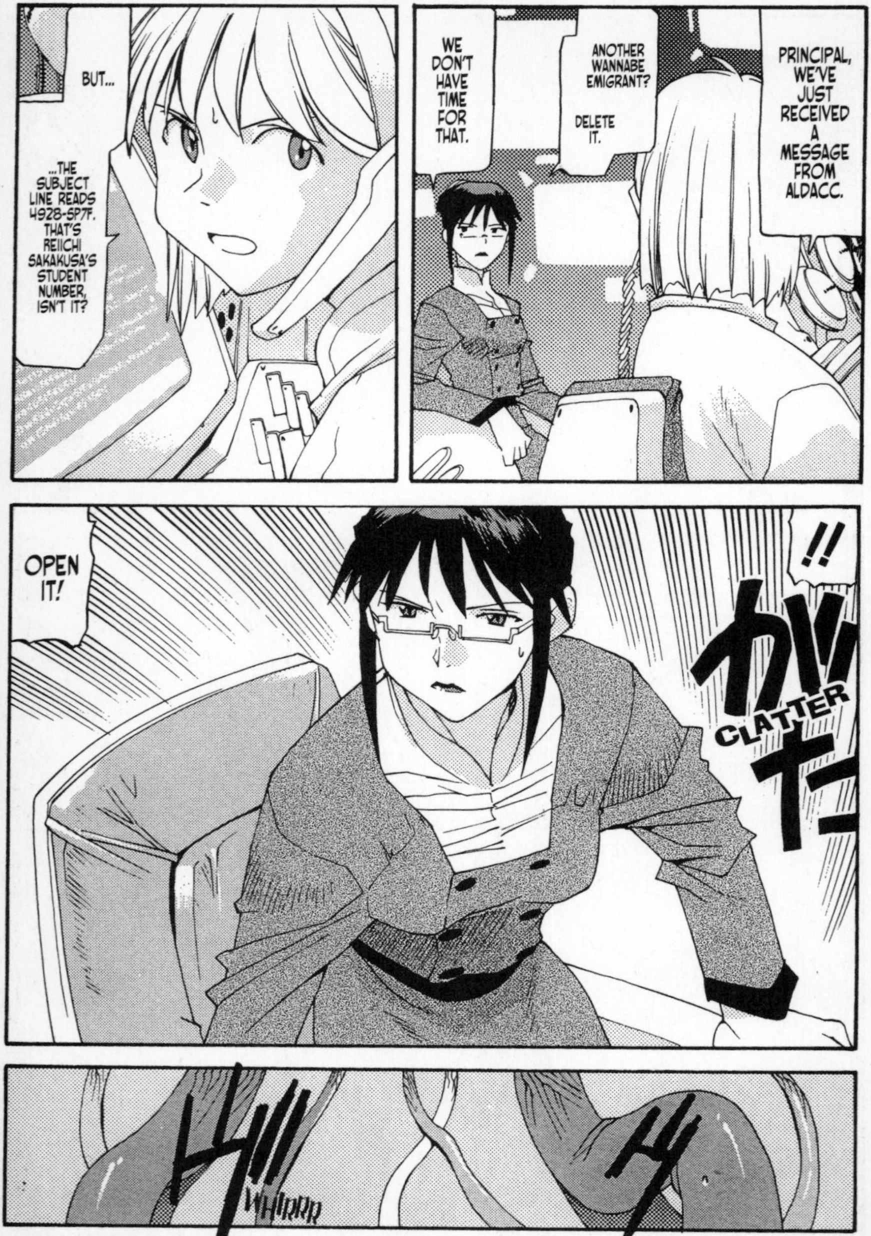

PRINCIPAL, WE'VE JUST RECEIVED A MESSAGE FROM ALDACC.
ANOTHER WANNABE EMIGRANT?
DELETE IT.
WE DON'T HAVE TIME FOR THAT.
BUT...
...THE SUBJECT LINE READS 4928-SP7F. THAT'S REIICHI SAKAKUSA'S STUDENT NUMBER, ISN'T IT?
!!
CLATTER
OPEN IT!
WHIRRR

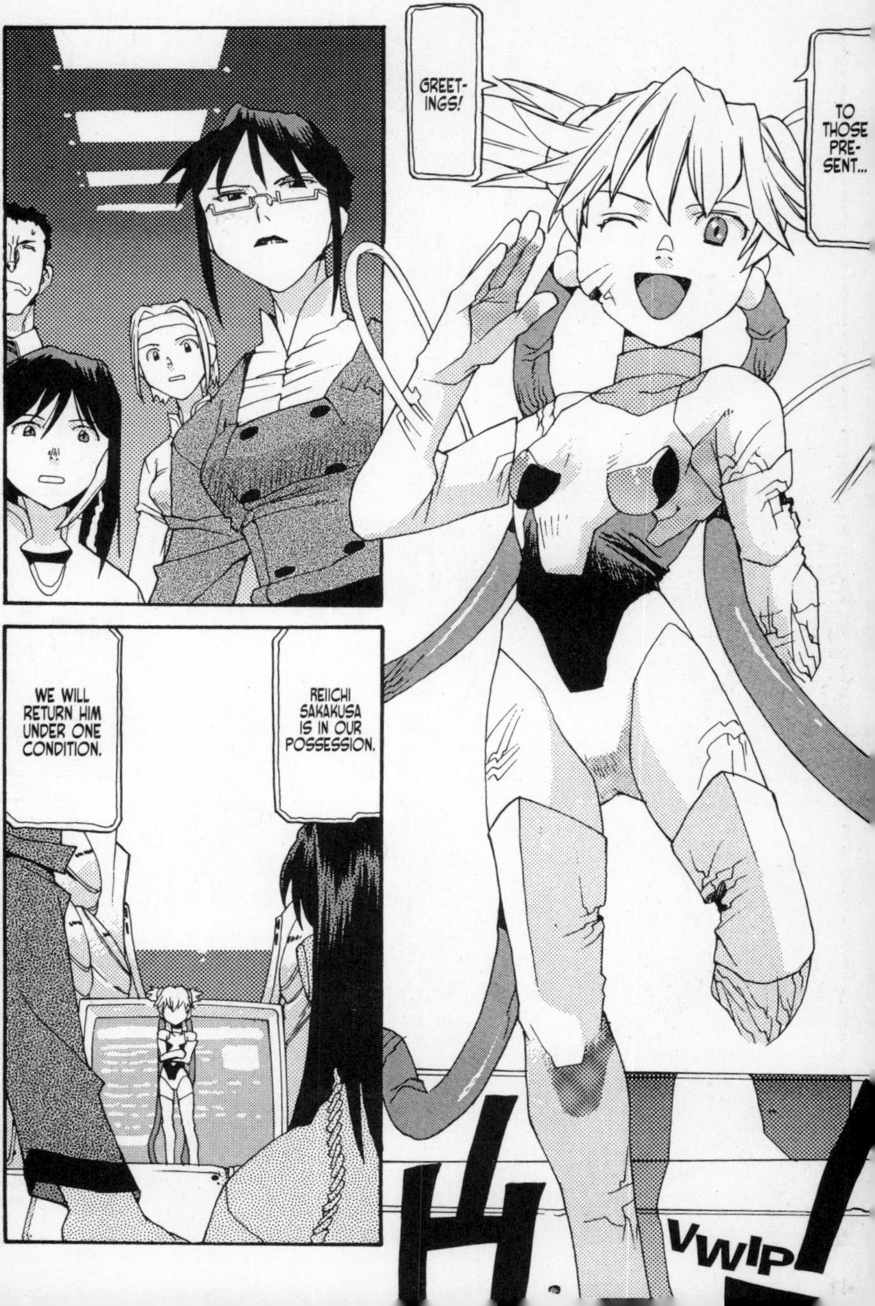
TO THOSE PRESENT...
GREETINGS!
HH
VWIP
REIICHI SAKAKUSA IS IN OUR POSSESSION.
WE WILL RETURN HIM UNDER ONE CONDITION.

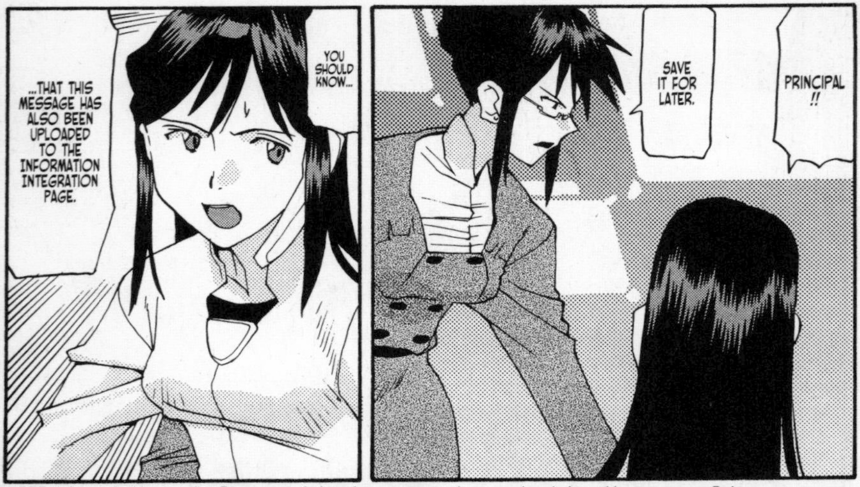
PRINCIPAL!!
SAVE IT FOR LATER.
YOU SHOULD KNOW...
...THAT THIS MESSAGE HAS ALSO BEEN UPLOADED TO THE INFORMATION INTEGRATION PAGE.

NOTE: Information Integration Page = a website where news can be posted and viewed by anyone on Deloca.

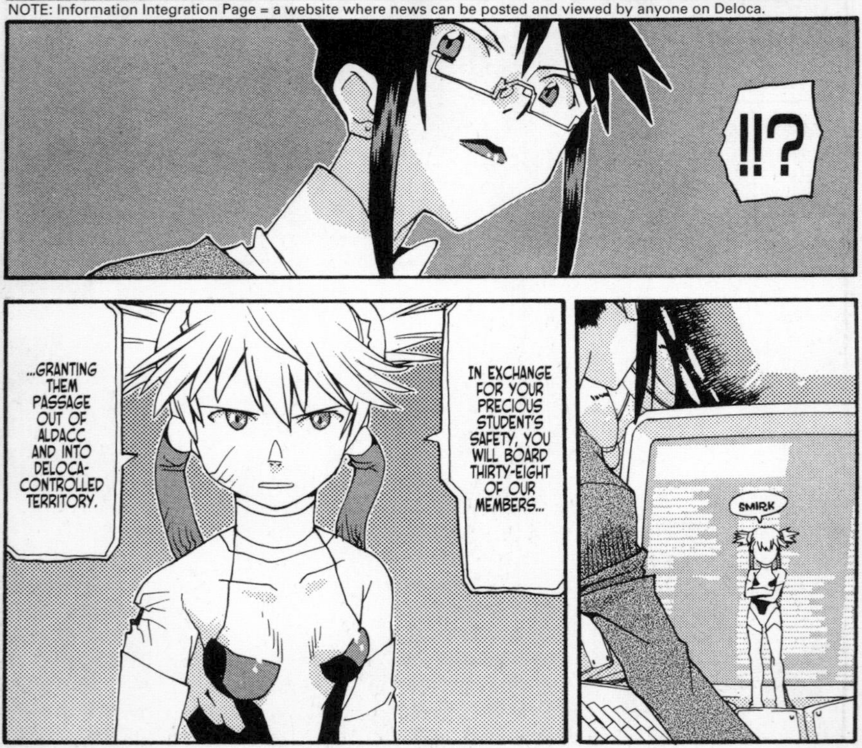
!!?
SMIRK
IN EXCHANGE FOR YOUR PRECIOUS STUDENT'S SAFETY, YOU WILL BOARD THIRTY-EIGHT OF OUR MEMBERS...
...GRANTING THEM PASSAGE OUT OF ALDACC AND INTO DELOCA-CONTROLLED TERRITORY.

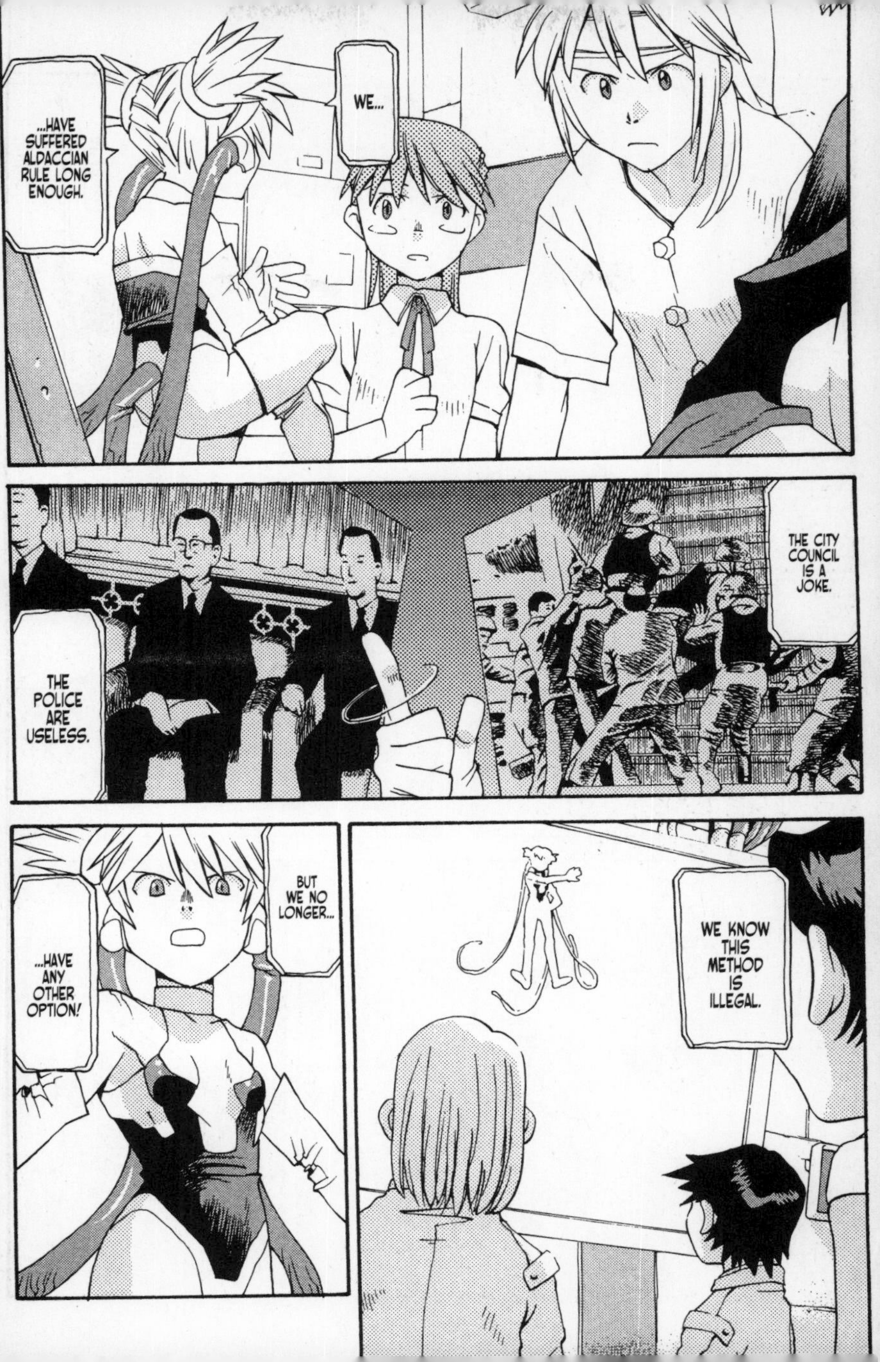
WE...
...HAVE SUFFERED ALDACCIAN RULE LONG ENOUGH.
THE CITY COUNCIL IS A JOKE.
THE POLICE ARE USELESS.
WE KNOW THIS METHOD IS ILLEGAL.
BUT WE NO LONGER...
...HAVE ANY OTHER OPTION!

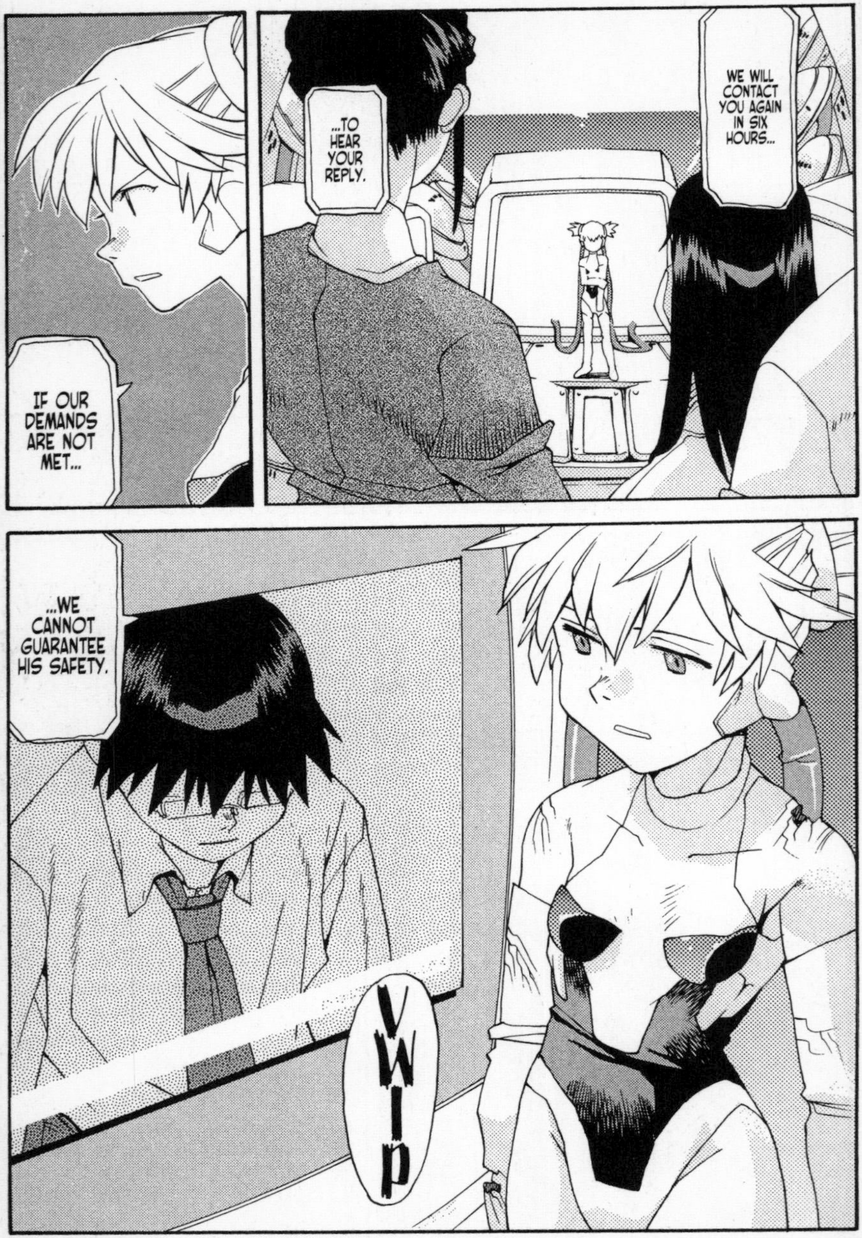
WE WILL CONTACT YOU AGAIN IN SIX HOURS...
...TO HEAR YOUR REPLY.
IF OUR DEMANDS ARE NOT MET...
...WE CANNOT GUARANTEE HIS SAFETY.
VWIp

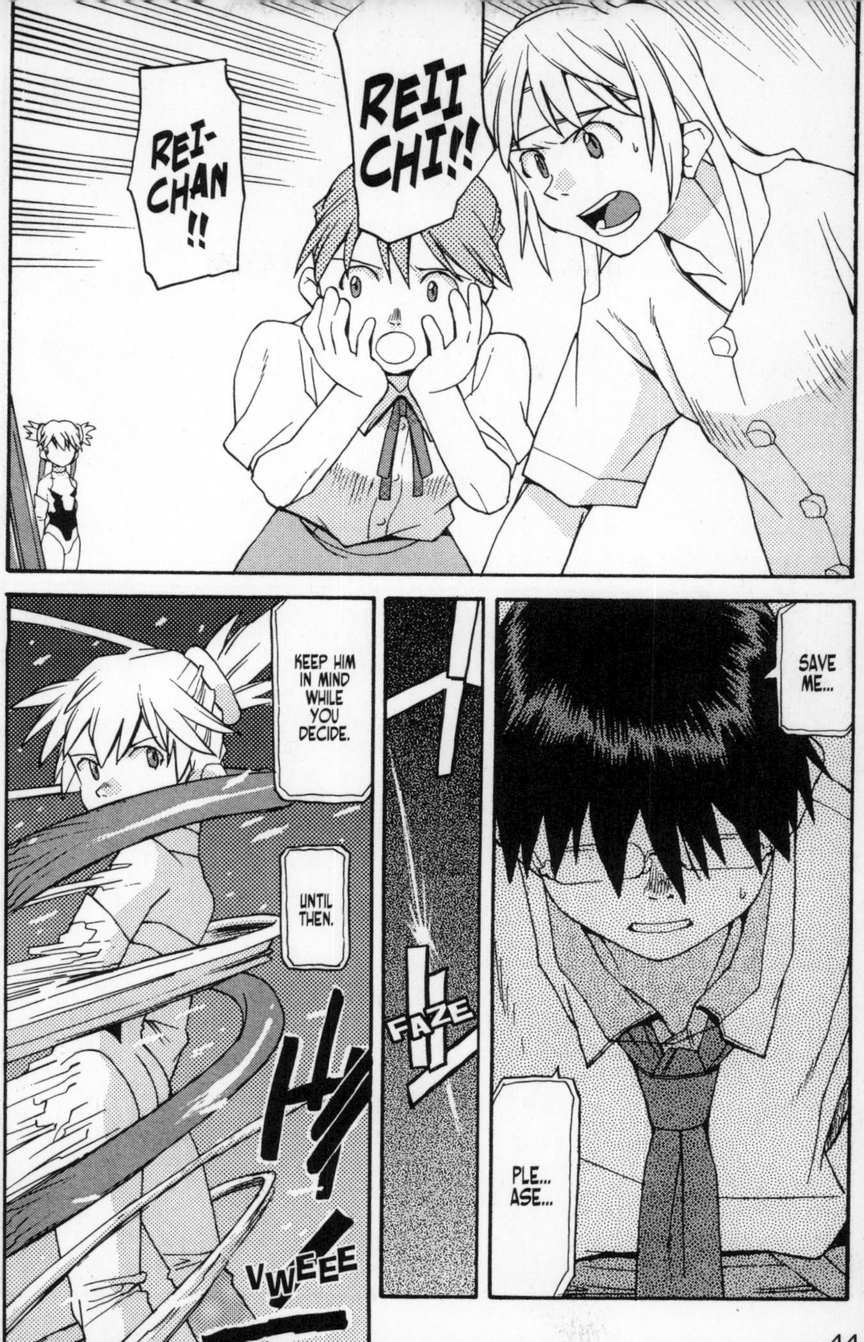
REII CHI!!
REI-CHAN!!
SAVE ME...
PLE... ASE...
FAZE
KEEP HIM IN MIND WHILE YOU DECIDE.
UNTIL THEN.
VWEEE

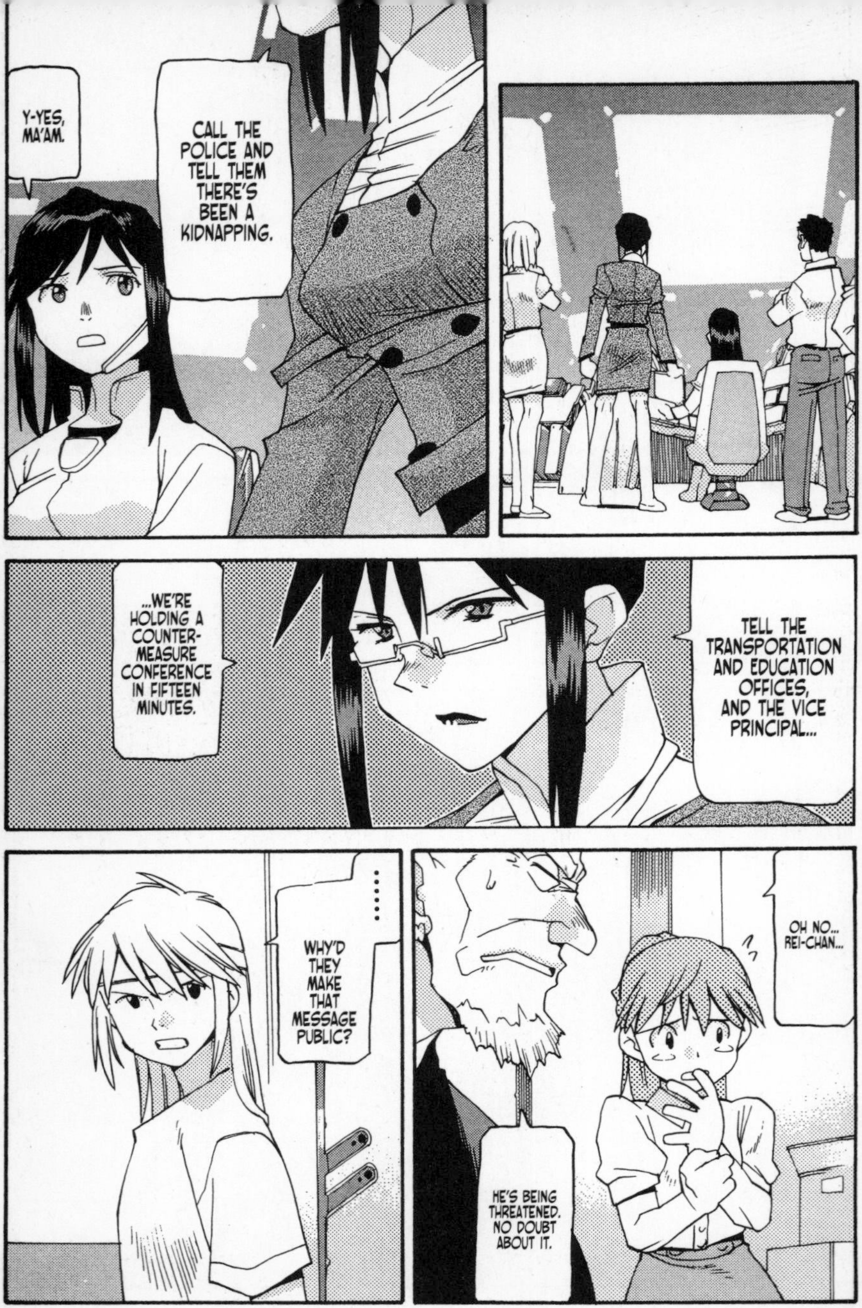
CALL THE POLICE AND TELL THEM THERE'S BEEN A KIDNAPPING.
Y-YES, MA'AM.
TELL THE TRANSPORTATION AND EDUCATION OFFICES, AND THE VICE PRINCIPAL...
...WE'RE HOLDING A COUNTER-MEASURE CONFERENCE IN FIFTEEN MINUTES.
OH NO... REI-CHAN...
HE'S BEING THREATENED. NO DOUBT ABOUT IT.
......
WHY'D THEY MAKE THAT MESSAGE PUBLIC?

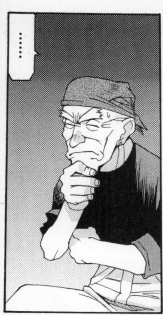

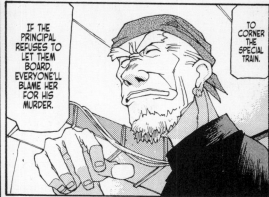

TO CORNER THE SPECIAL TRAIN.

IF THE PRINCIPAL REFUSES TO LET THEM BOARD, EVERYONE'LL BLAME HER FOR HIS MURDER.

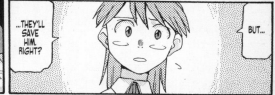

...THEY'LL SAVE HIM, RIGHT?

BUT...

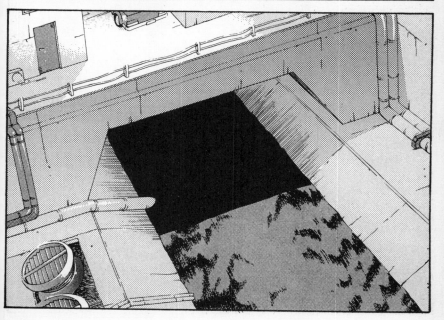

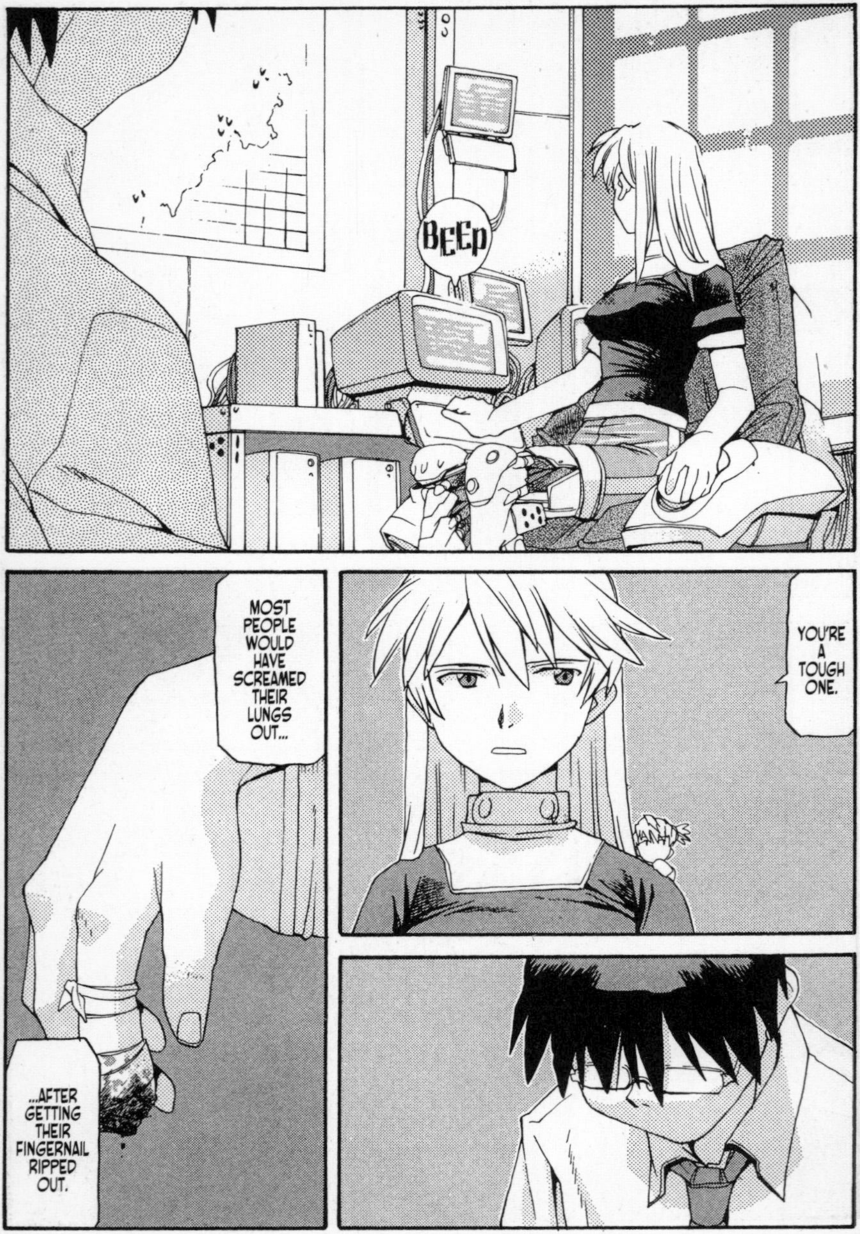
BEEp
YOU'RE A TOUGH ONE.
MOST PEOPLE WOULD HAVE SCREAMED THEIR LUNGS OUT...
...AFTER GETTING THEIR FINGERNAIL RIPPED OUT.

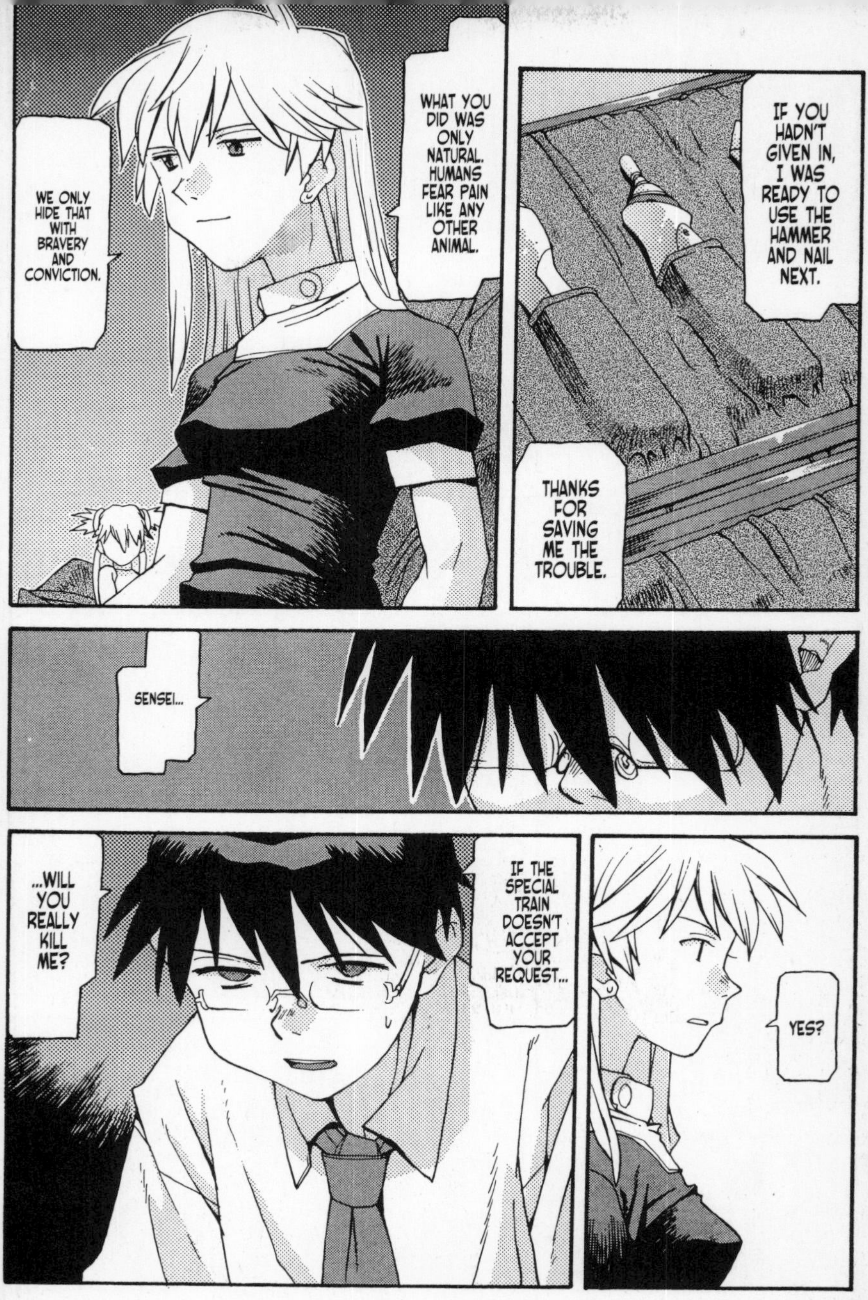
IF YOU HADN'T GIVEN IN, I WAS READY TO USE THE HAMMER AND NAIL NEXT.
THANKS FOR SAVING ME THE TROUBLE.
WHAT YOU DID WAS ONLY NATURAL. HUMANS FEAR PAIN LIKE ANY OTHER ANIMAL.
WE ONLY HIDE THAT WITH BRAVERY AND CONVICTION.
SENSEI...
YES?
IF THE SPECIAL TRAIN DOESN'T ACCEPT YOUR REQUEST...
...WILL YOU REALLY KILL ME?

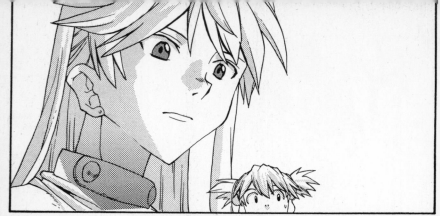

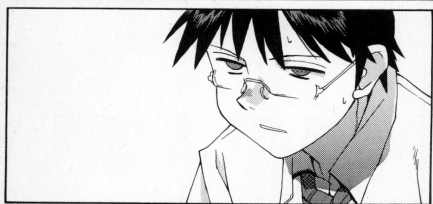

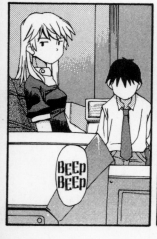

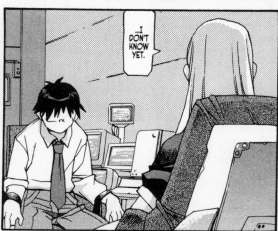

...I DON'T KNOW YET.

BEEP BEEP

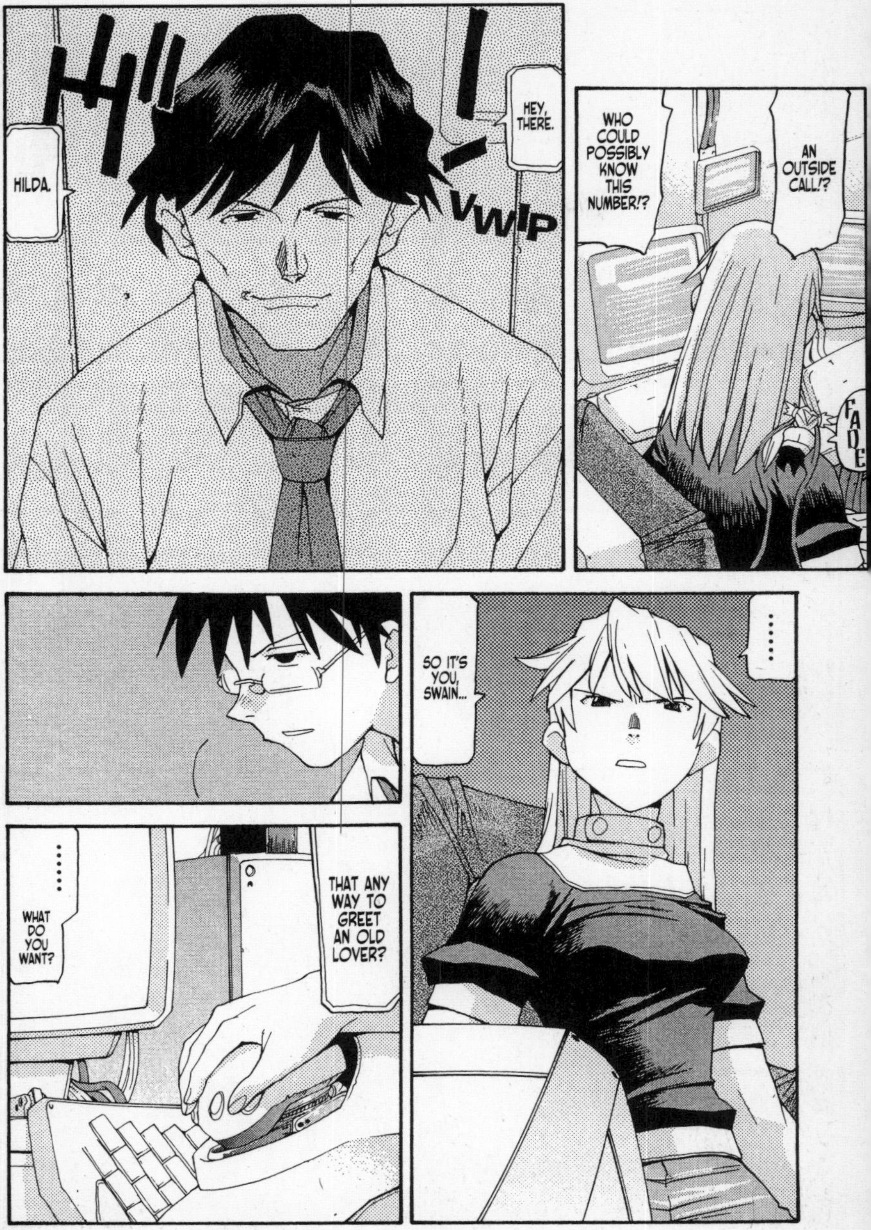
AN OUTSIDE CALL!?
WHO COULD POSSIBLY KNOW THIS NUMBER!?
FADE
HEY, THERE.
VWIP
HILDA.
......
SO IT'S YOU, SWAIN...
THAT ANY WAY TO GREET AN OLD LOVER?
......
WHAT DO YOU WANT?

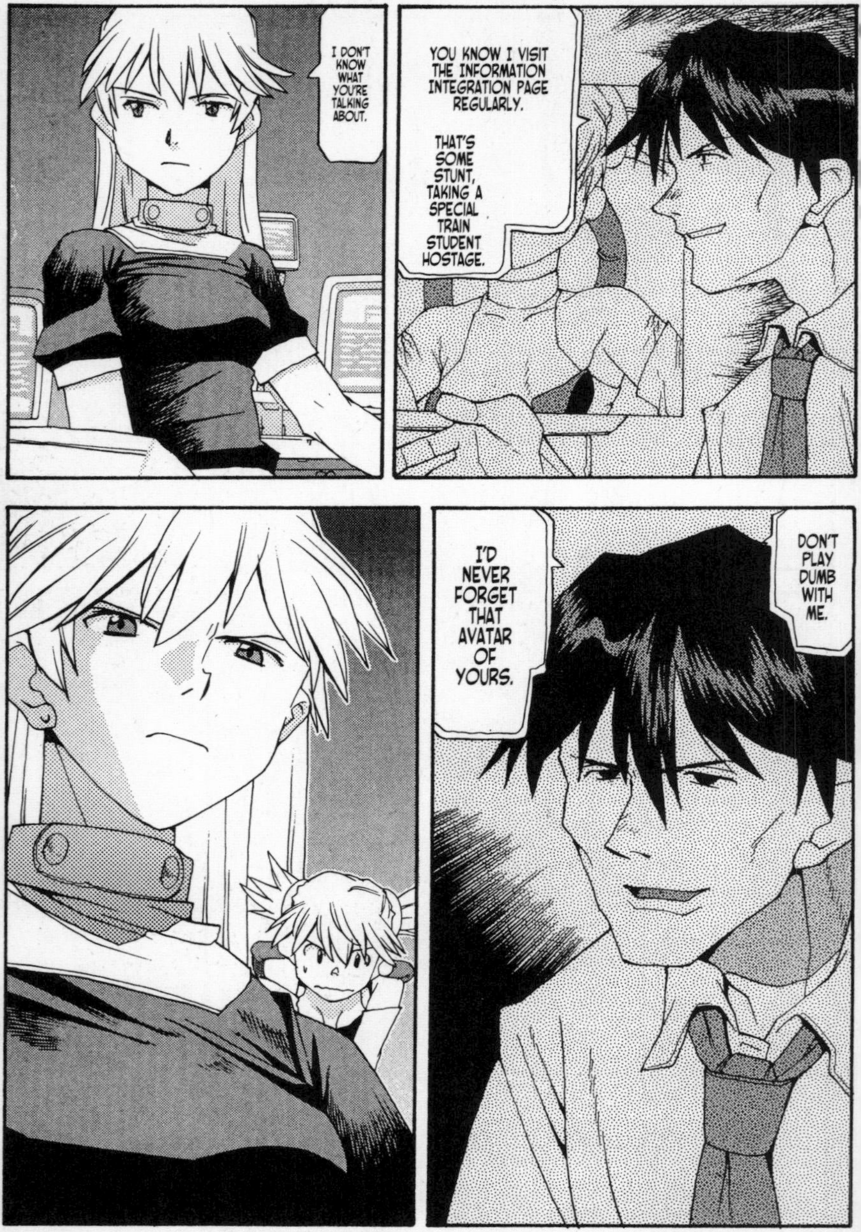
YOU KNOW I VISIT THE INFORMATION INTEGRATION PAGE REGULARLY.
THAT'S SOME STUNT, TAKING A SPECIAL TRAIN STUDENT HOSTAGE.
I DON'T KNOW WHAT YOU'RE TALKING ABOUT.
DON'T PLAY DUMB WITH ME.
I'D NEVER FORGET THAT AVATAR OF YOURS.

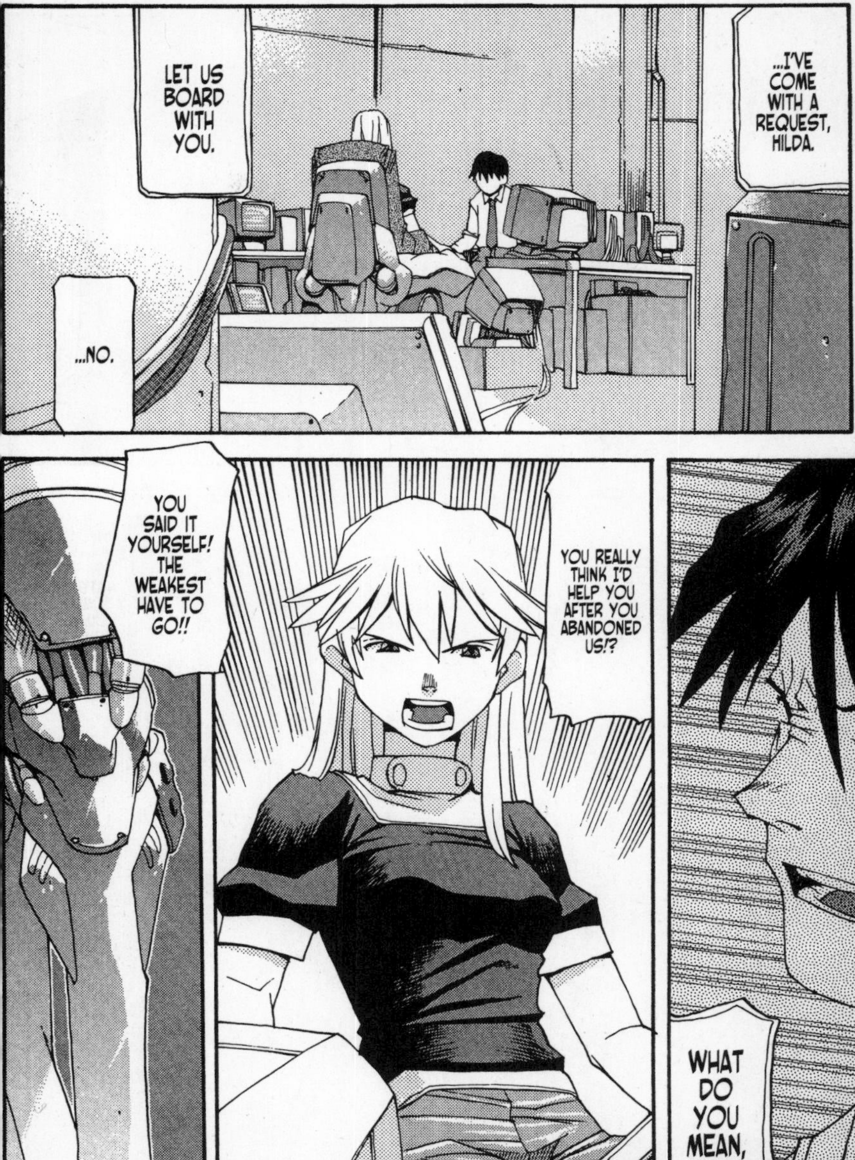
...I'VE COME WITH A REQUEST, HILDA.
LET US BOARD WITH YOU.
...NO.
WHAT DO YOU MEAN, NO!?
YOU REALLY THINK I'D HELP YOU AFTER YOU ABANDONED US!?
YOU SAID IT YOURSELF! THE WEAKEST HAVE TO GO!!

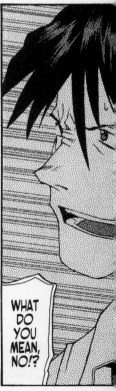

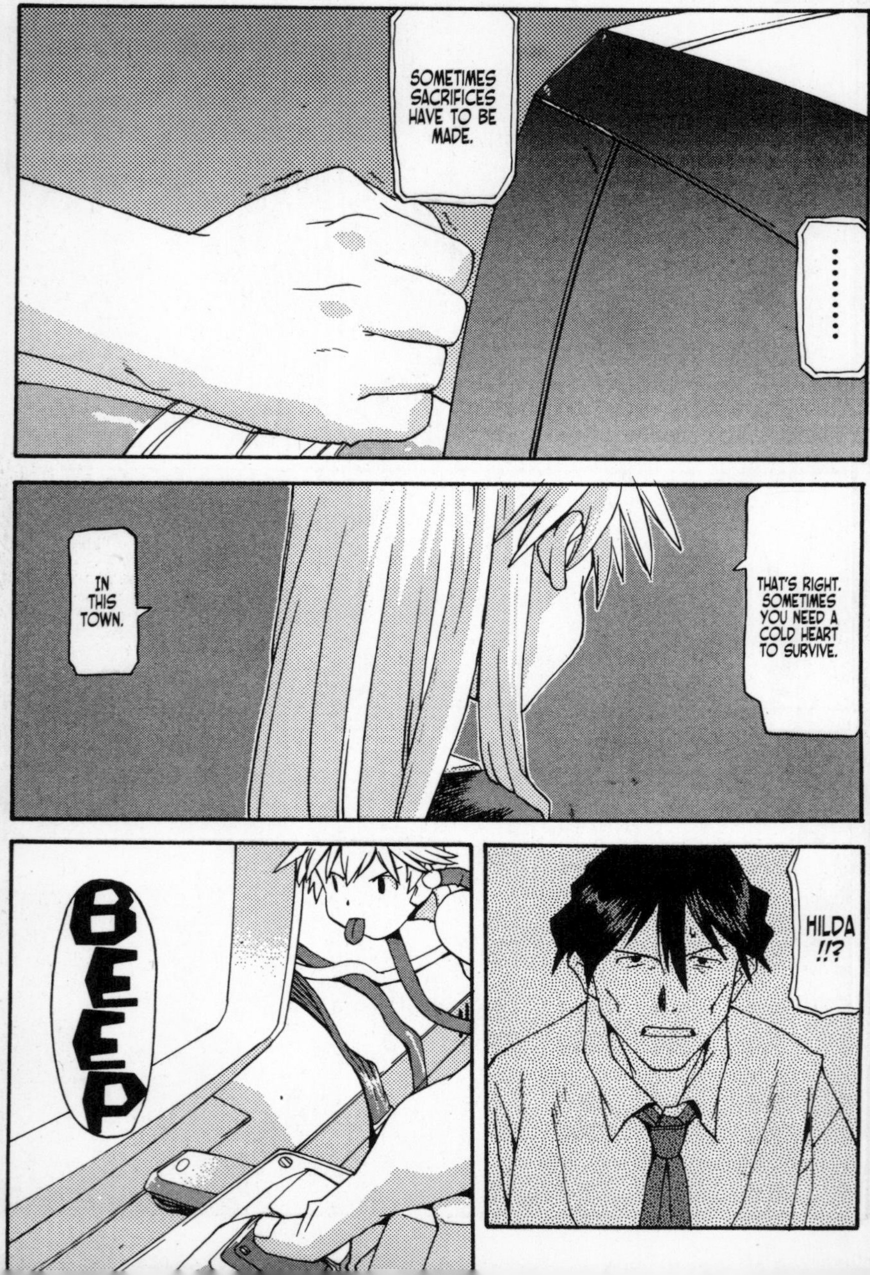
SOMETIMES SACRIFICES HAVE TO BE MADE.
........
THAT'S RIGHT. SOMETIMES YOU NEED A COLD HEART TO SURVIVE.
IN THIS TOWN.
HILDA !!?
BEEP

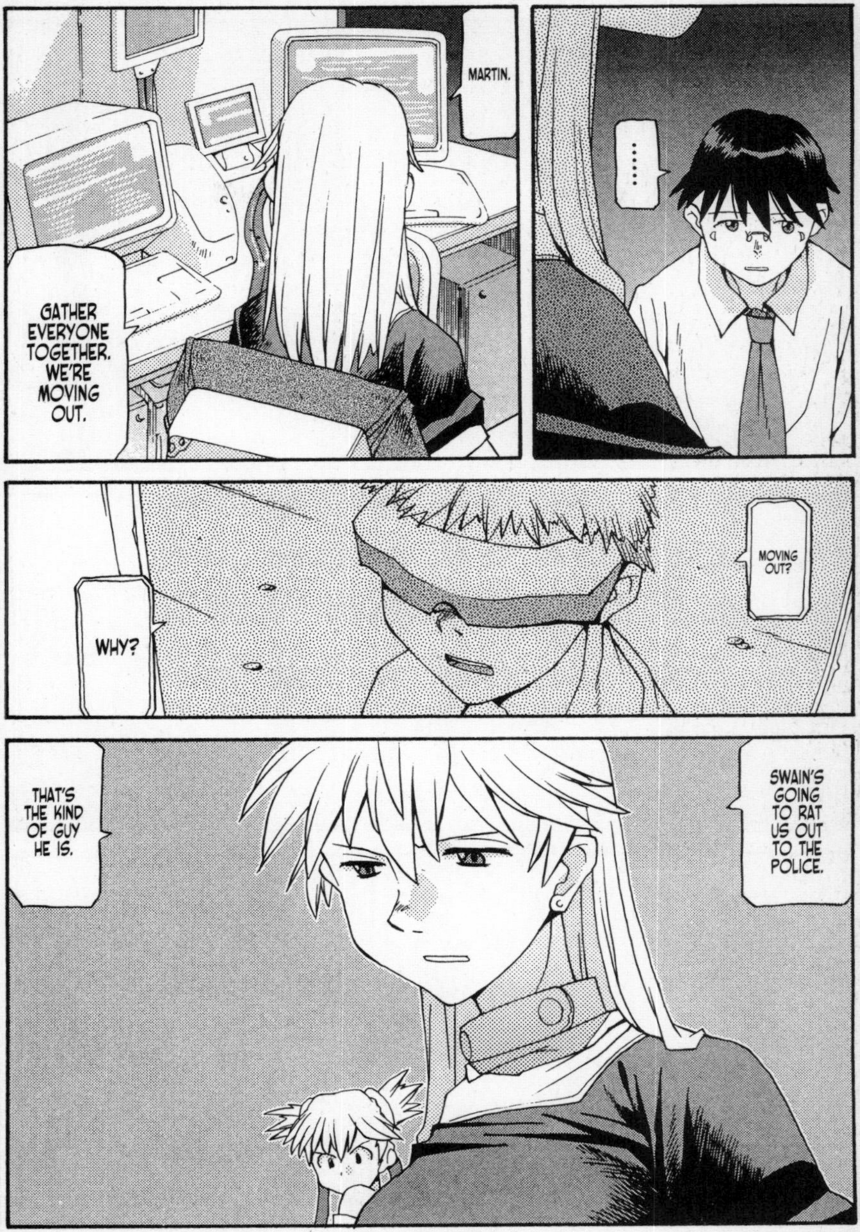
......
MARTIN.
GATHER EVERYONE TOGETHER. WE'RE MOVING OUT.
MOVING OUT?
WHY?
SWAIN'S GOING TO RAT US OUT TO THE POLICE.
THAT'S THE KIND OF GUY HE IS.

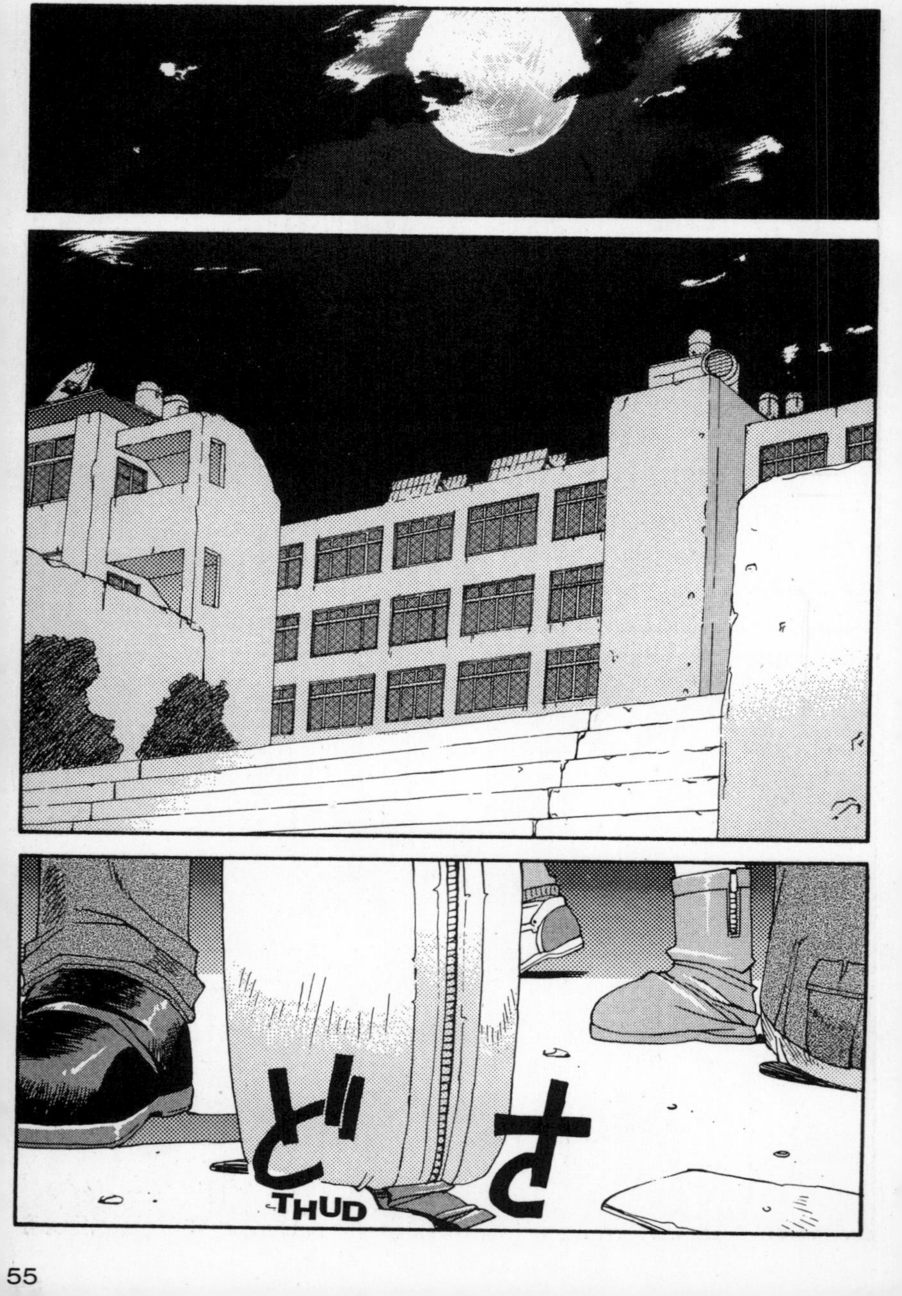
どさ
THUD

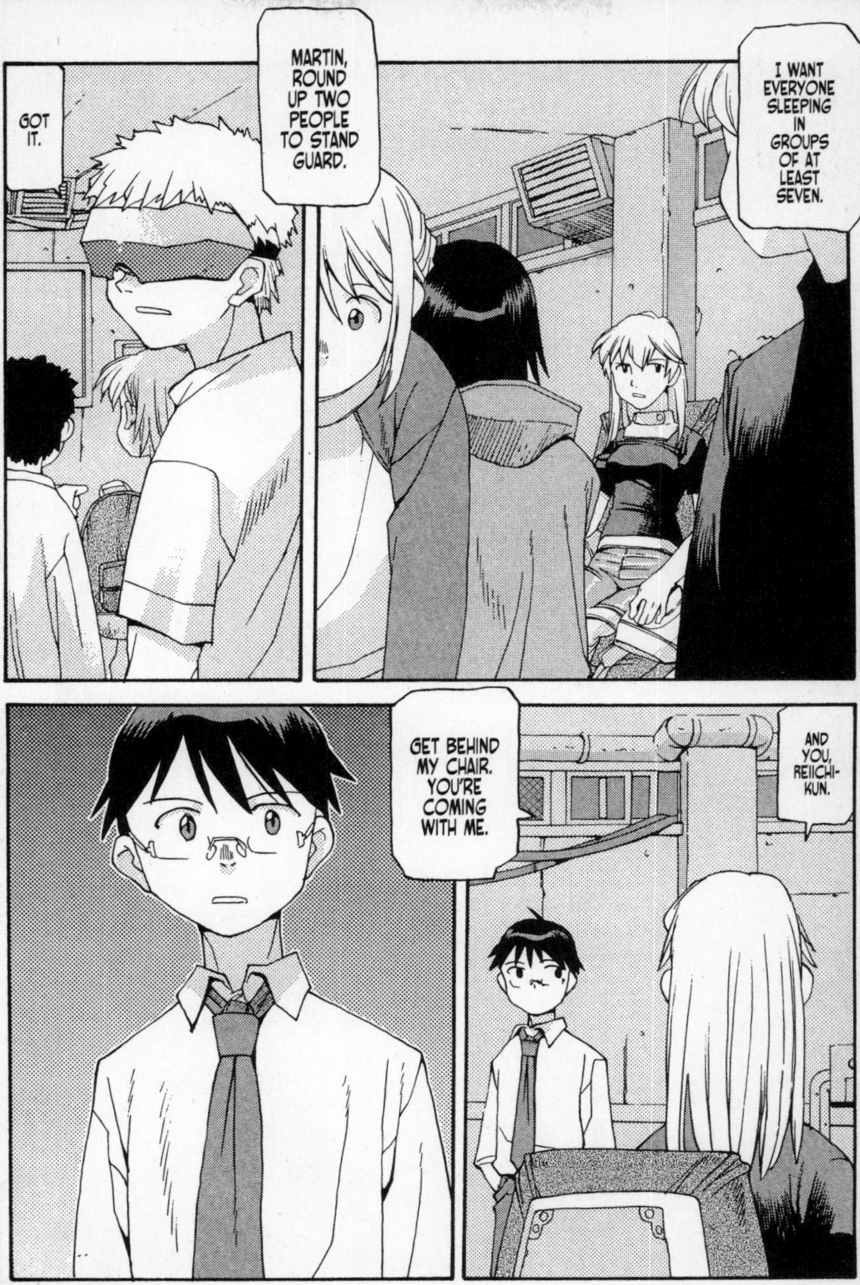

I WANT EVERYONE SLEEPING IN GROUPS OF AT LEAST SEVEN.
MARTIN, ROUND UP TWO PEOPLE TO STAND GUARD.
GOT IT.
AND YOU, REIICHI-KUN.
GET BEHIND MY CHAIR. YOU'RE COMING WITH ME.

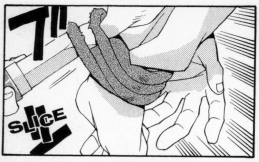

SLICE

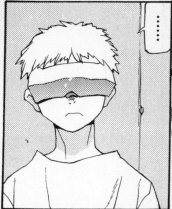

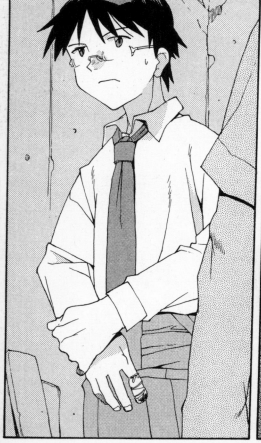

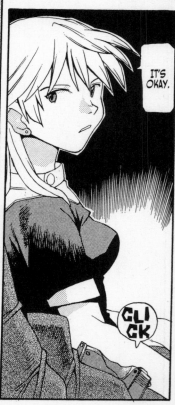

IT'S OKAY.

GLICK

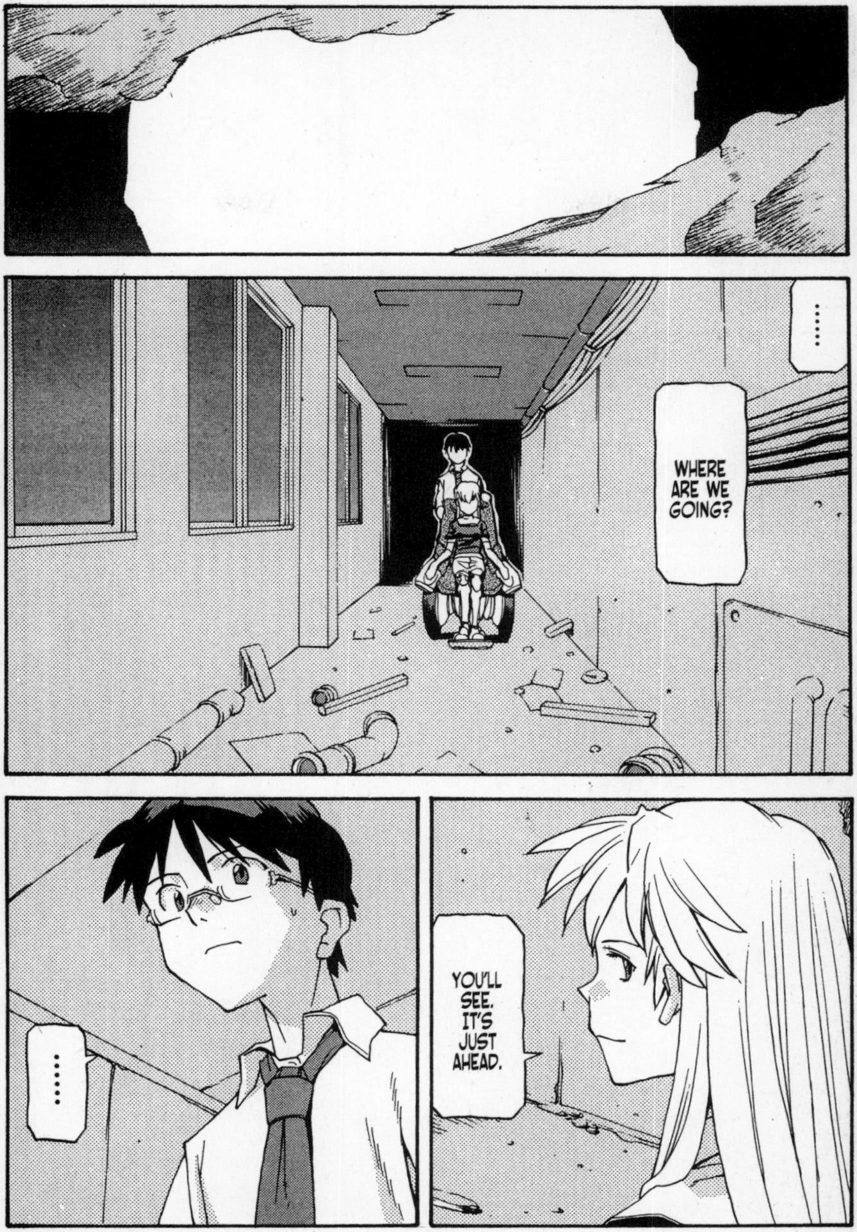
.....
WHERE ARE WE GOING?
YOU'LL SEE. IT'S JUST AHEAD.
......

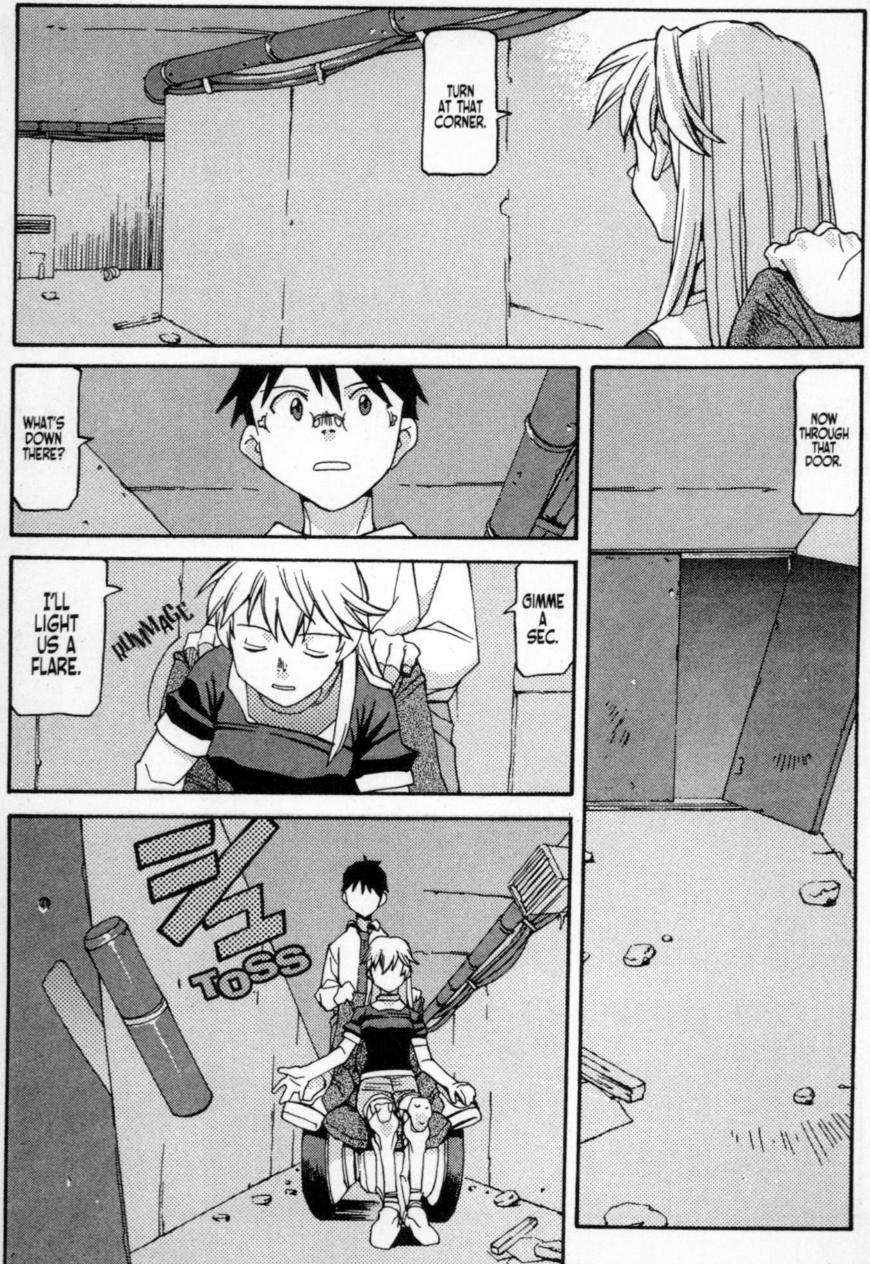
TURN AT THAT CORNER.
NOW THROUGH THAT DOOR.
WHAT'S DOWN THERE?
GIMME A SEC.
RUMMAGE
I'LL LIGHT US A FLARE.
TOSS

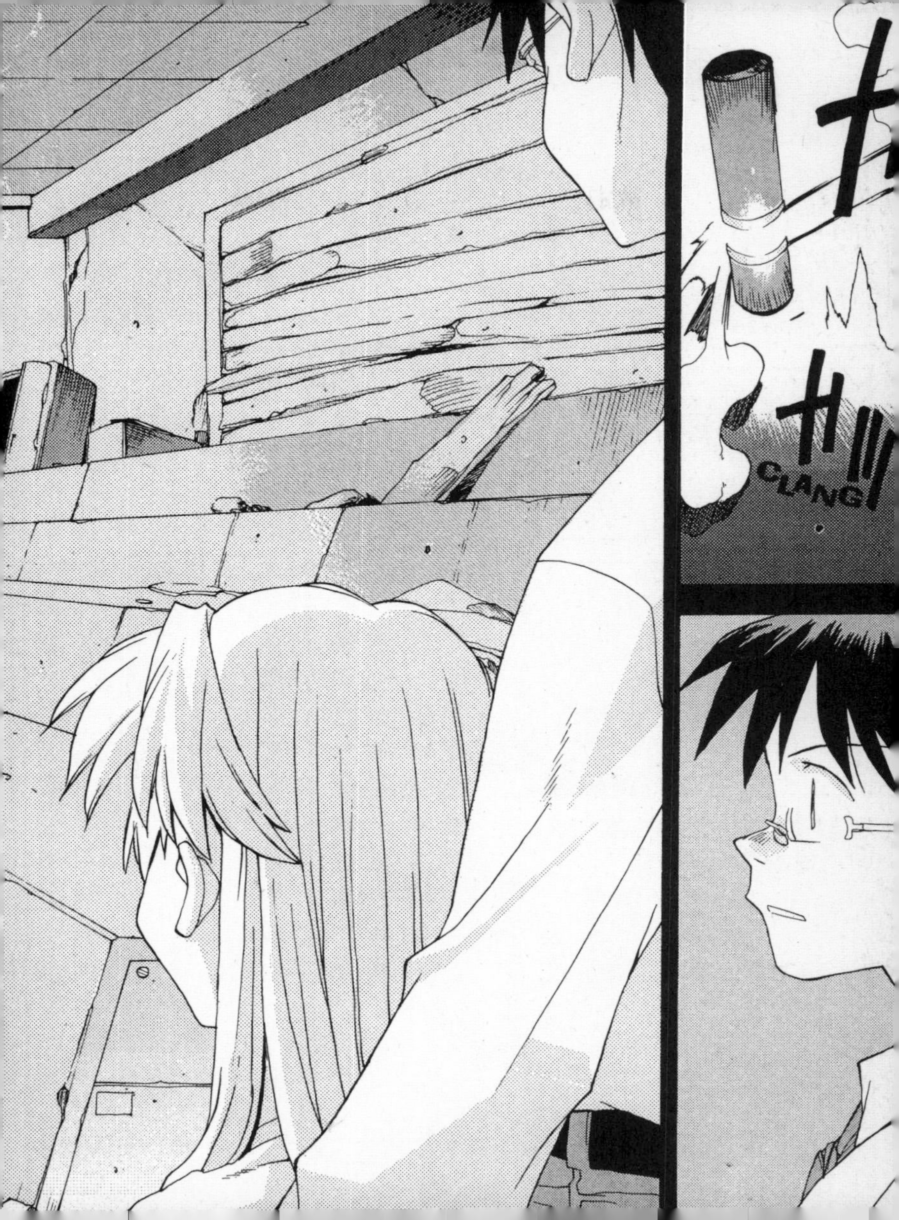
CLANG!

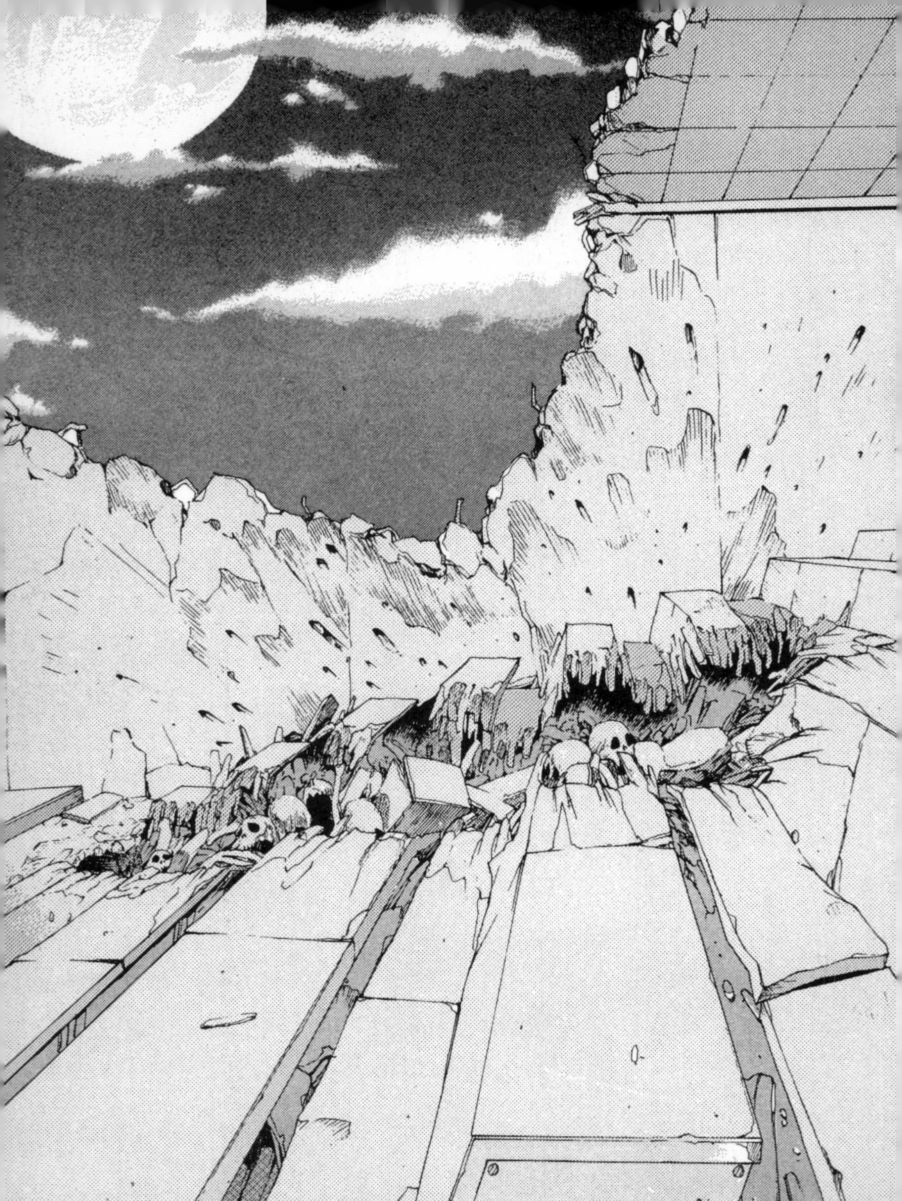

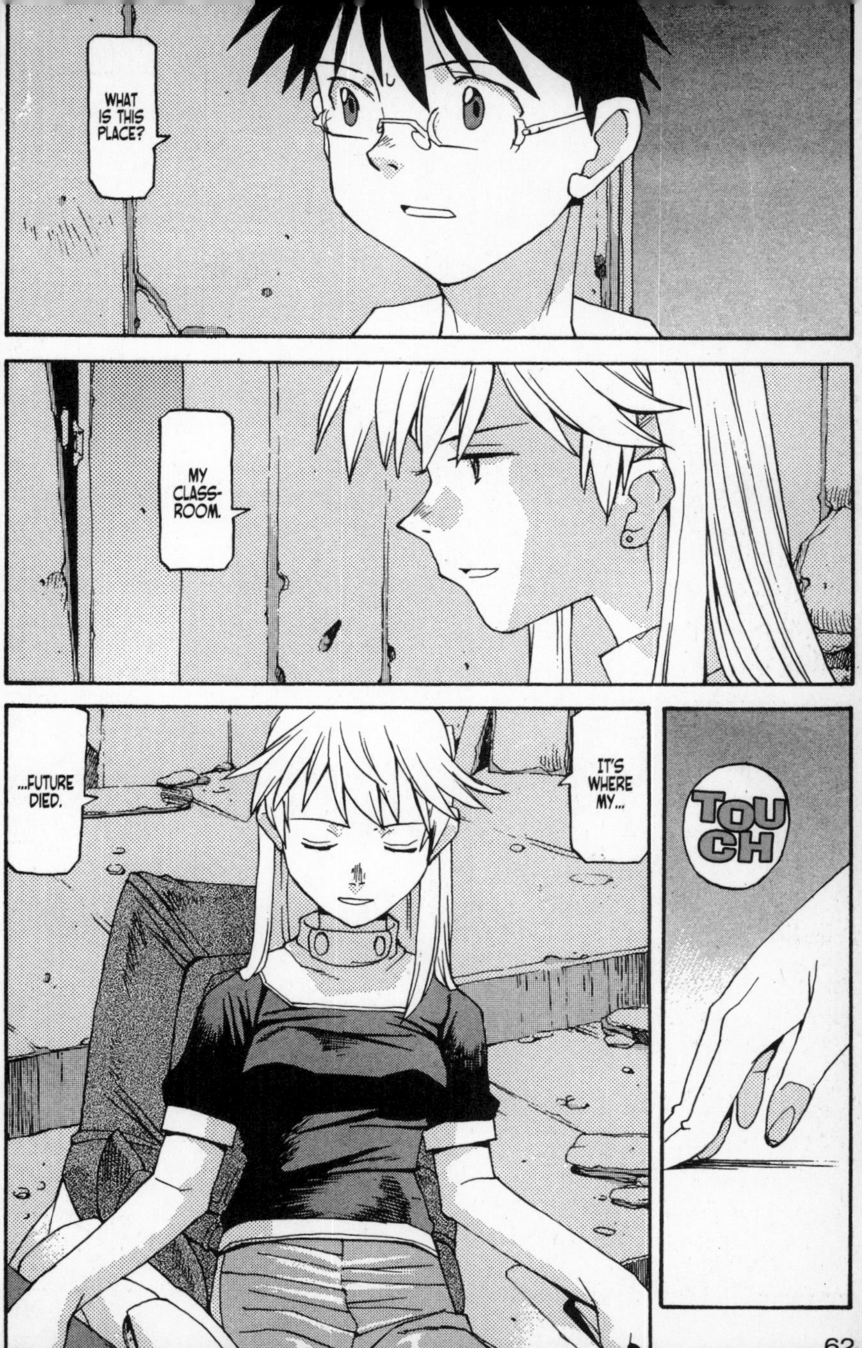
WHAT IS THIS PLACE?
MY CLASS-ROOM.
TOUCH
IT'S WHERE MY...
...FUTURE DIED.

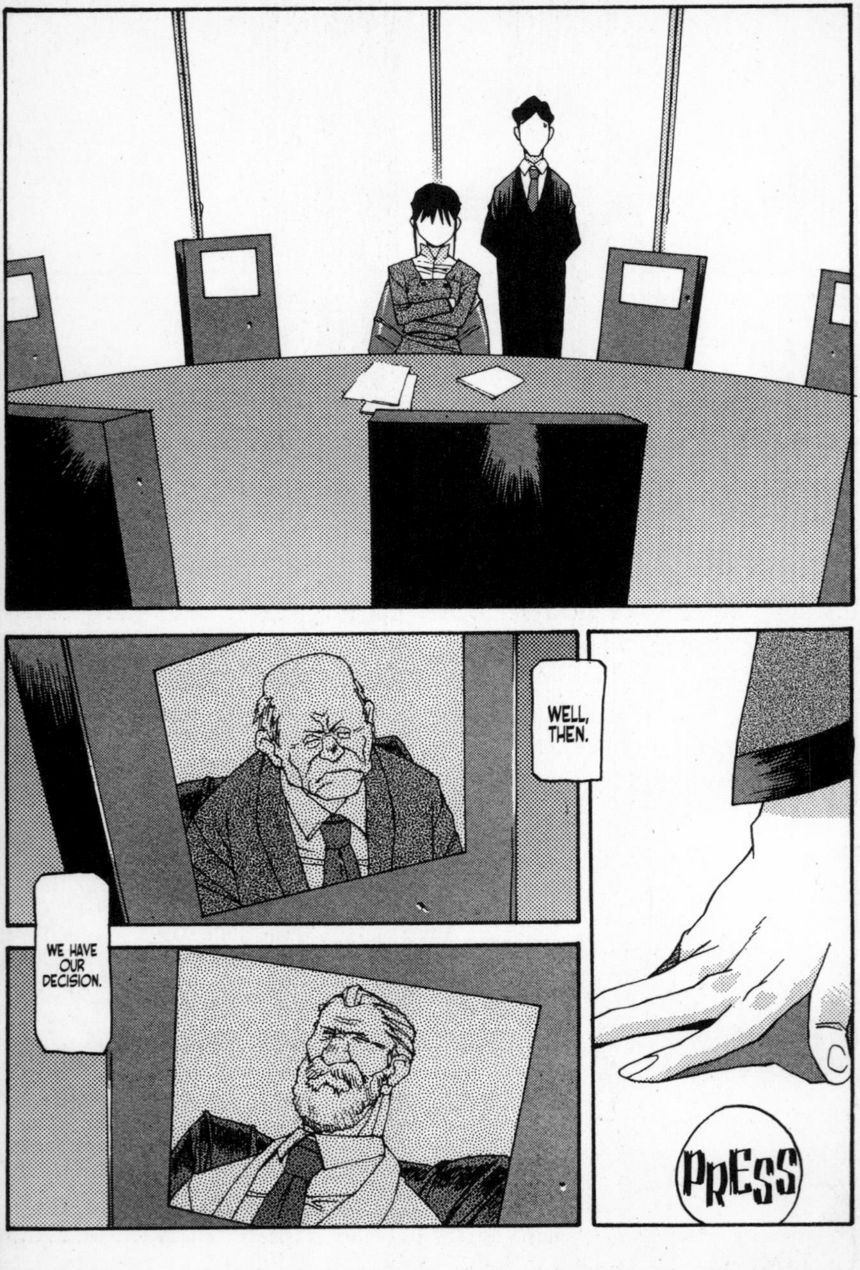
PRESS
WELL, THEN.
WE HAVE OUR DECISION.

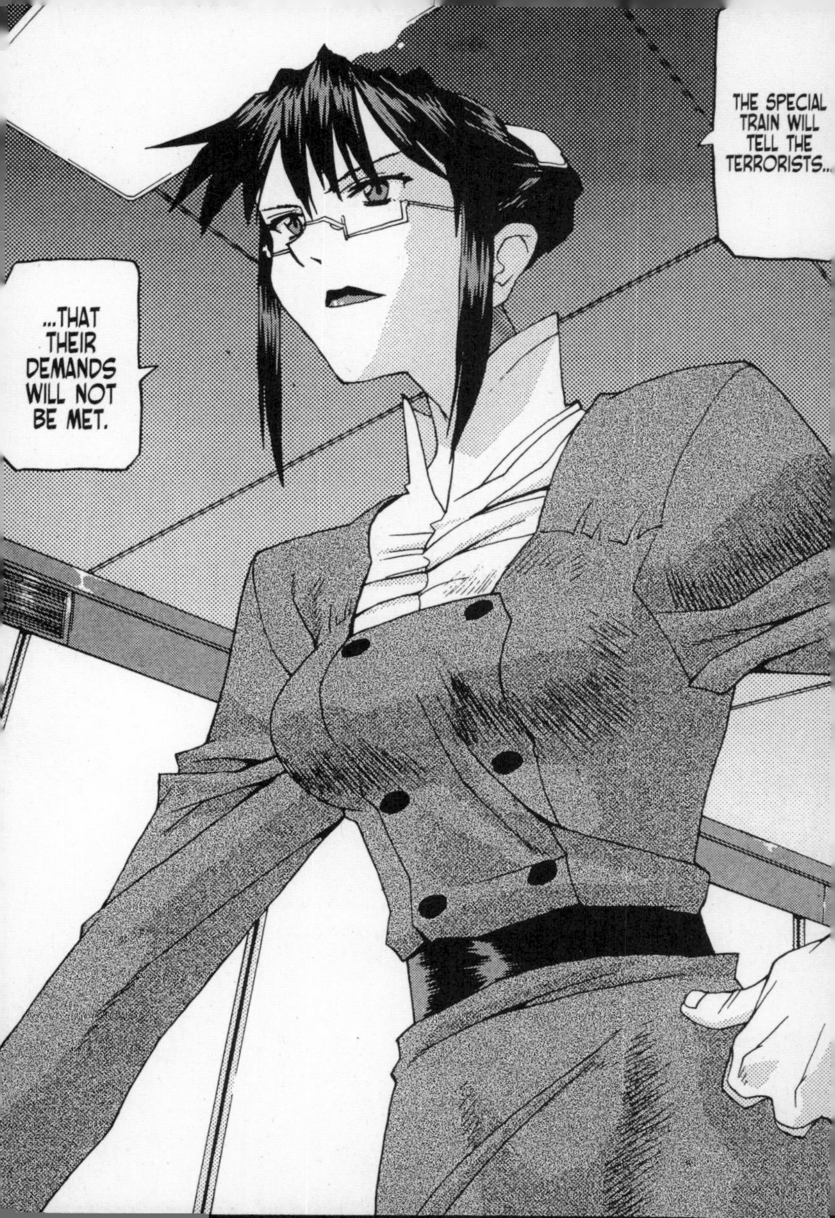
THE SPECIAL TRAIN WILL TELL THE TERRORISTS...
...THAT THEIR DEMANDS WILL NOT BE MET.

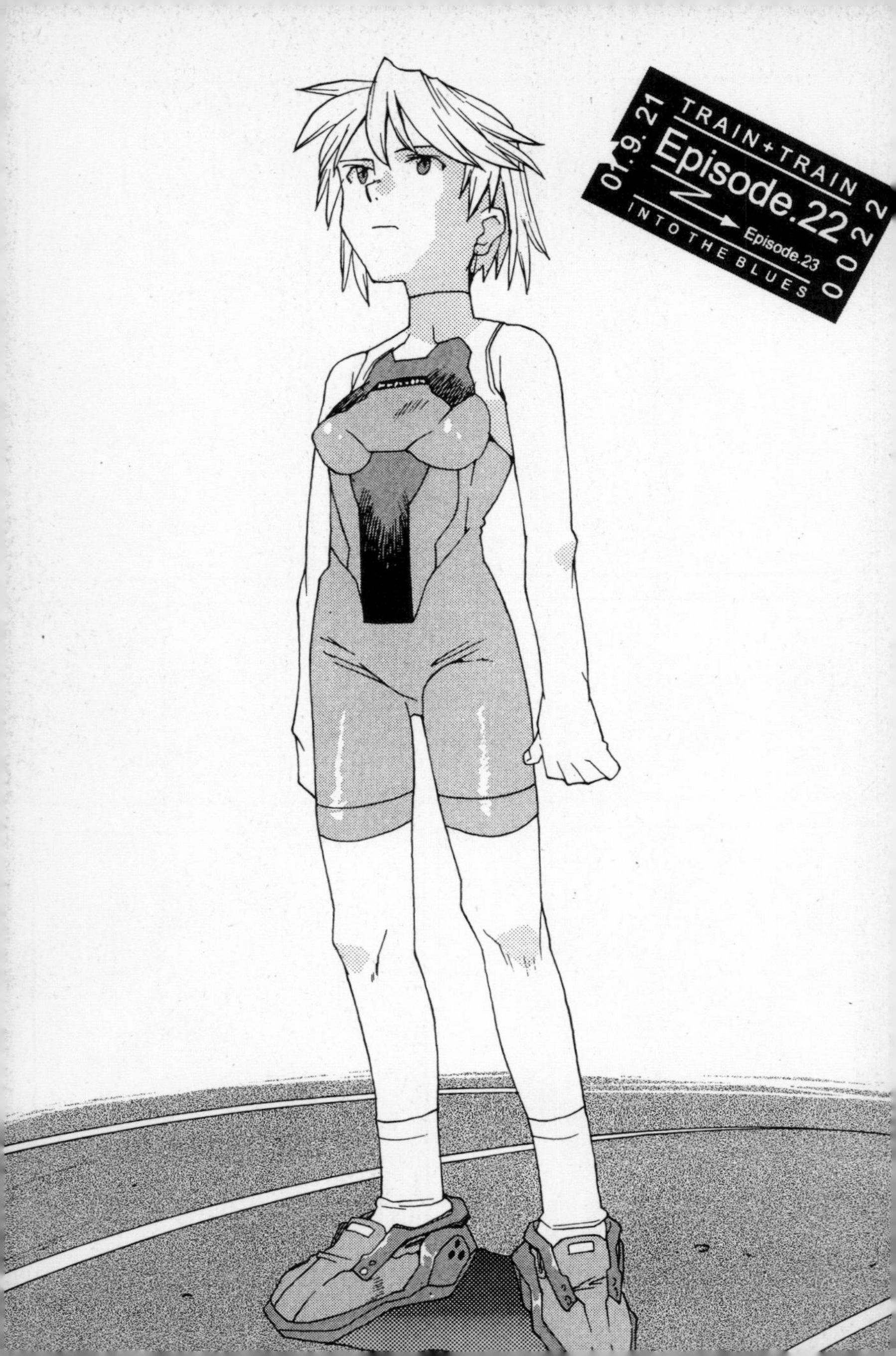

TRAIN+TRAIN
Episode.22
Episode.23
INTO THE BLUES
01.9.21
0022

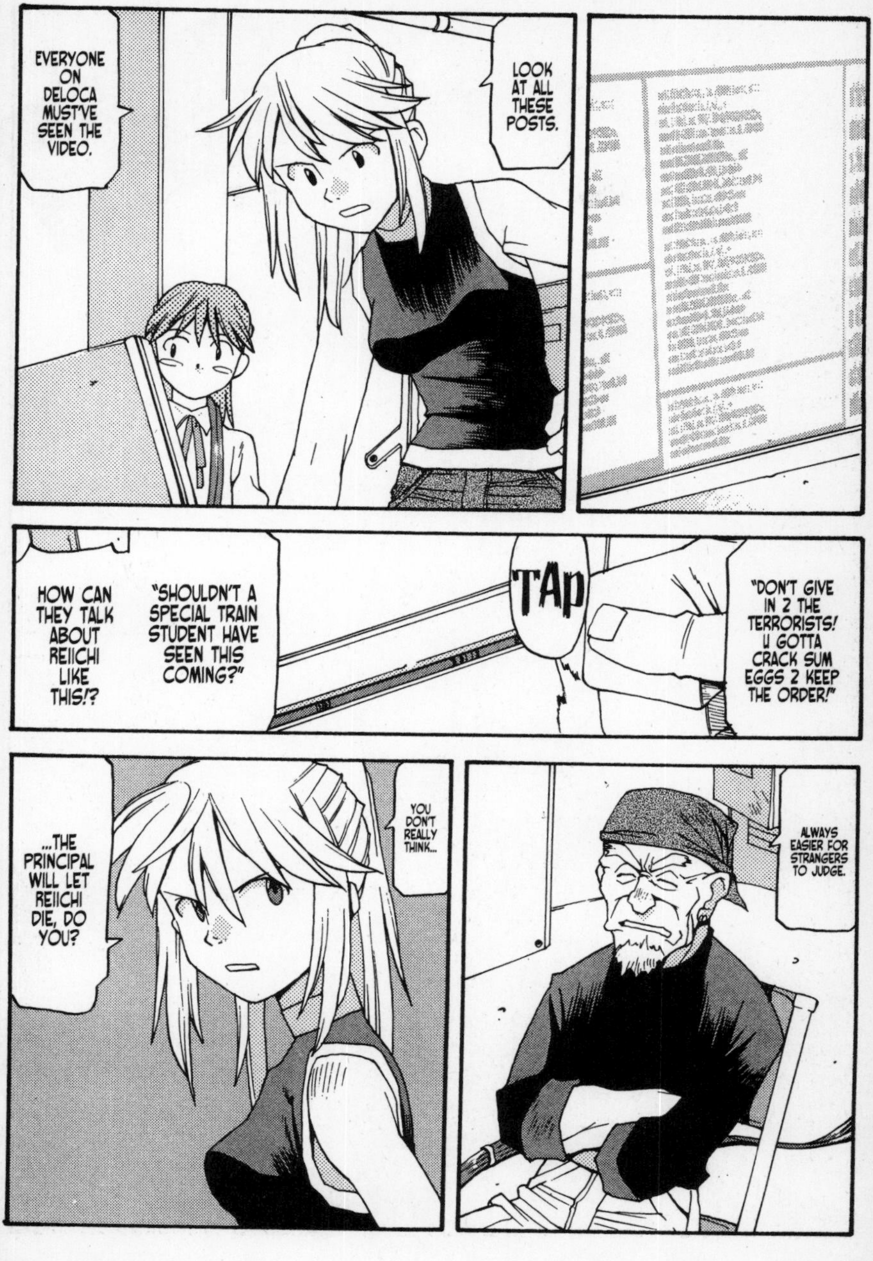
LOOK AT ALL THESE POSTS.
EVERYONE ON DELOCA MUST'VE SEEN THE VIDEO.
"DON'T GIVE IN 2 THE TERRORISTS! U GOTTA CRACK SUM EGGS 2 KEEP THE ORDER!"
TAp
"SHOULDN'T A SPECIAL TRAIN STUDENT HAVE SEEN THIS COMING?"
HOW CAN THEY TALK ABOUT REIICHI LIKE THIS!?
ALWAYS EASIER FOR STRANGERS TO JUDGE.
YOU DON'T REALLY THINK...
...THE PRINCIPAL WILL LET REIICHI DIE, DO YOU?

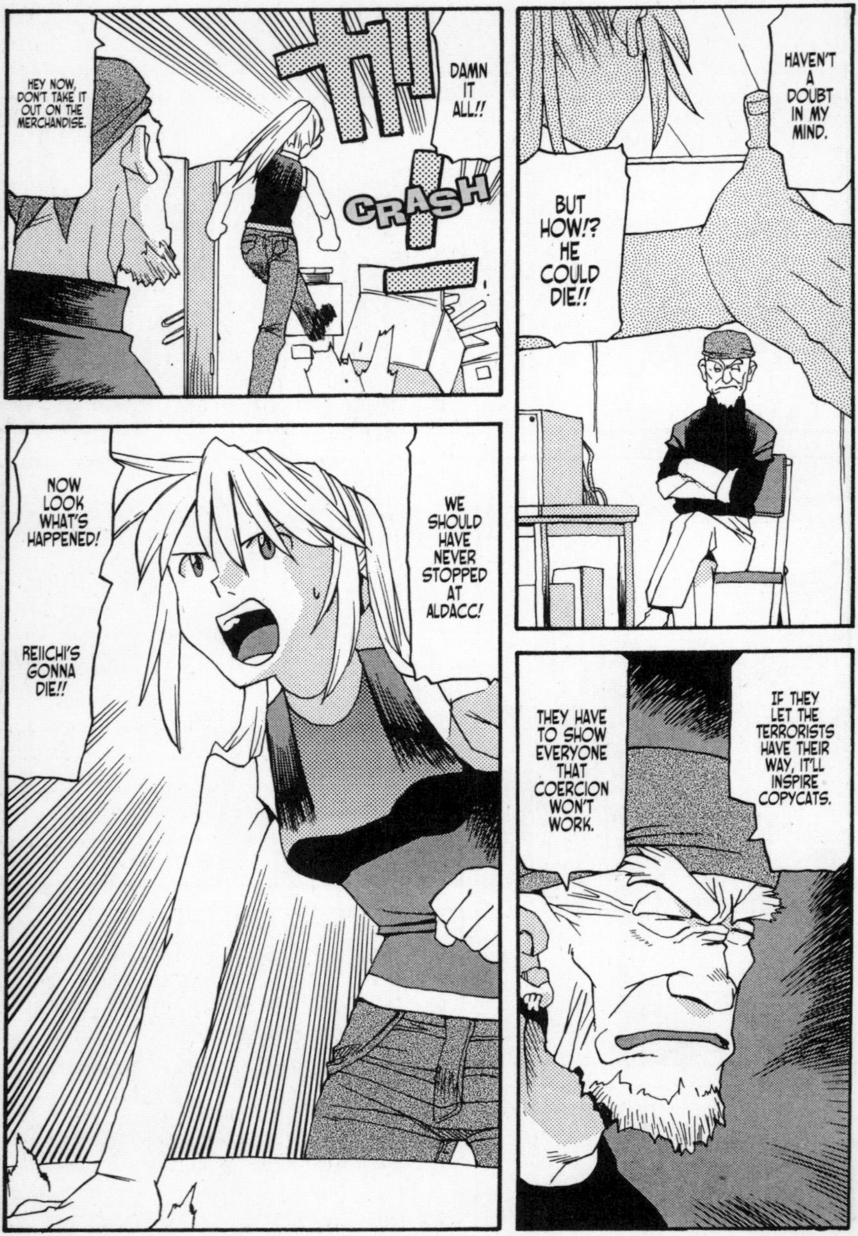

HAVEN'T A DOUBT IN MY MIND.
BUT HOW!? HE COULD DIE!!
DAMN IT ALL!!
CRASH
HEY NOW, DON'T TAKE IT OUT ON THE MERCHANDISE.
IF THEY LET THE TERRORISTS HAVE THEIR WAY, IT'LL INSPIRE COPYCATS.
THEY HAVE TO SHOW EVERYONE THAT COERCION WON'T WORK.
WE SHOULD HAVE NEVER STOPPED AT ALDACC!
NOW LOOK WHAT'S HAPPENED!
REIICHI'S GONNA DIE!!

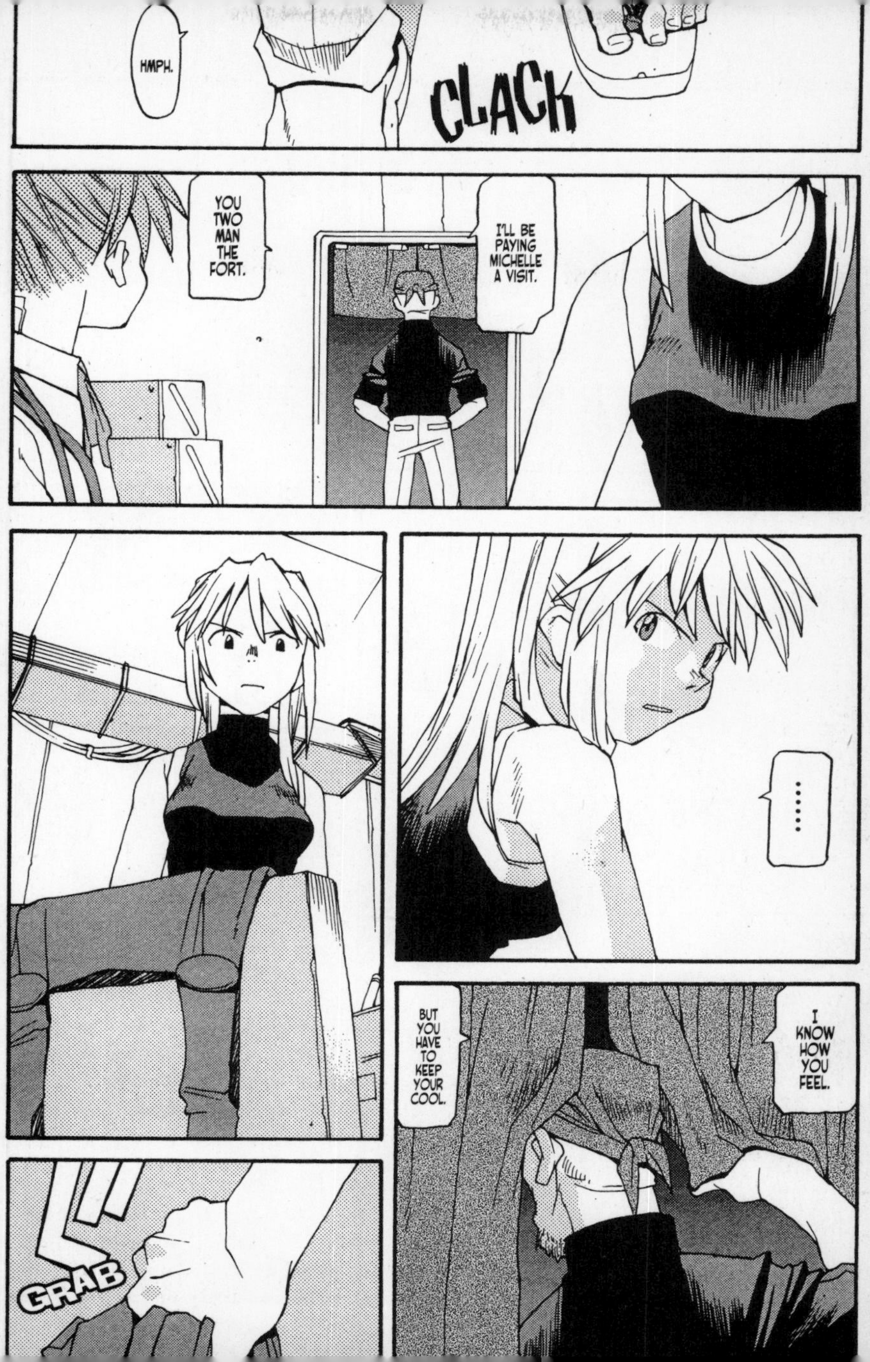
HMPH.
CLACK
I'LL BE PAYING MICHELLE A VISIT.
YOU TWO MAN THE FORT.
......
I KNOW HOW YOU FEEL.
BUT YOU HAVE TO KEEP YOUR COOL.
GRAB

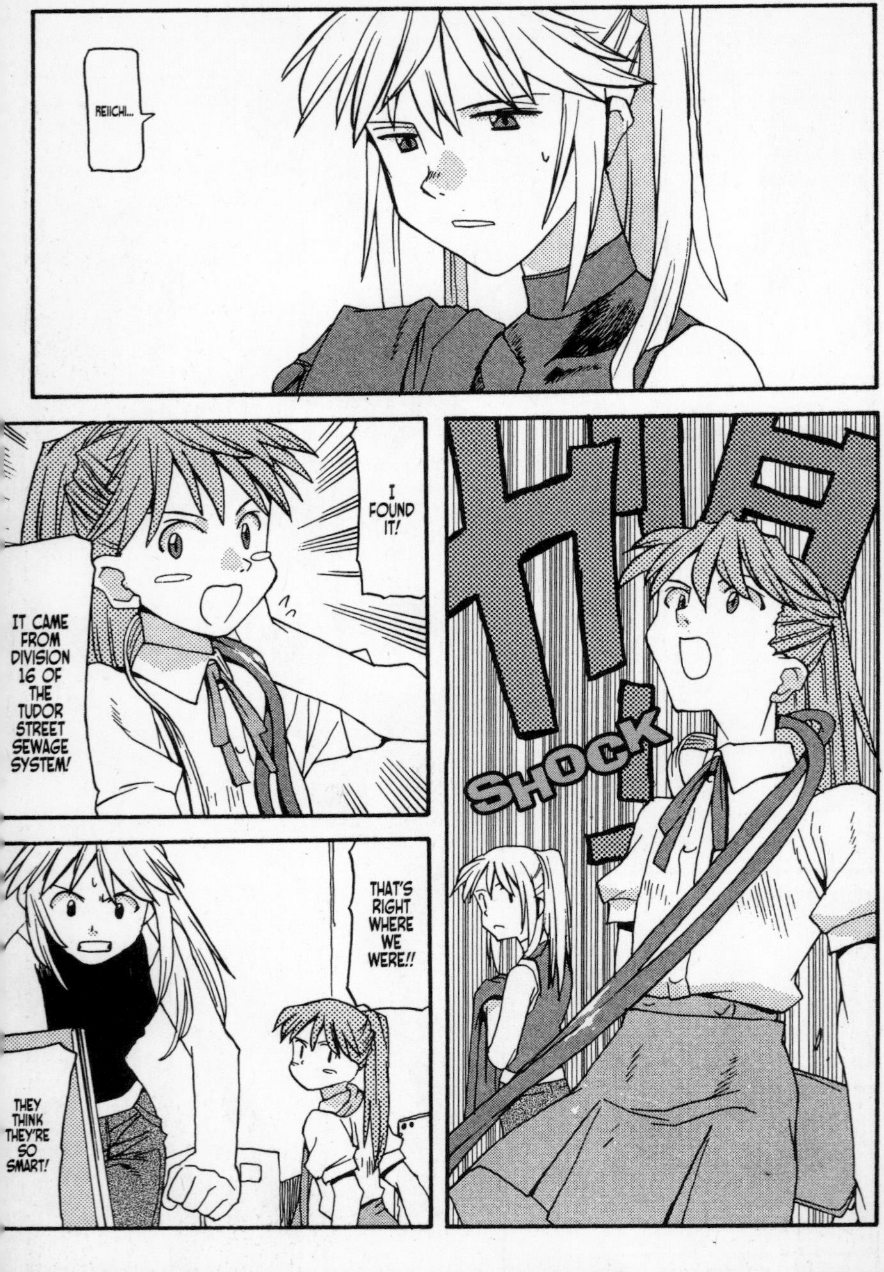
REIICHI...
SHOCK
I FOUND IT!
IT CAME FROM DIVISION 16 OF THE TUDOR STREET SEWAGE SYSTEM!
THAT'S RIGHT WHERE WE WERE!!
THEY THINK THEY'RE SO SMART!

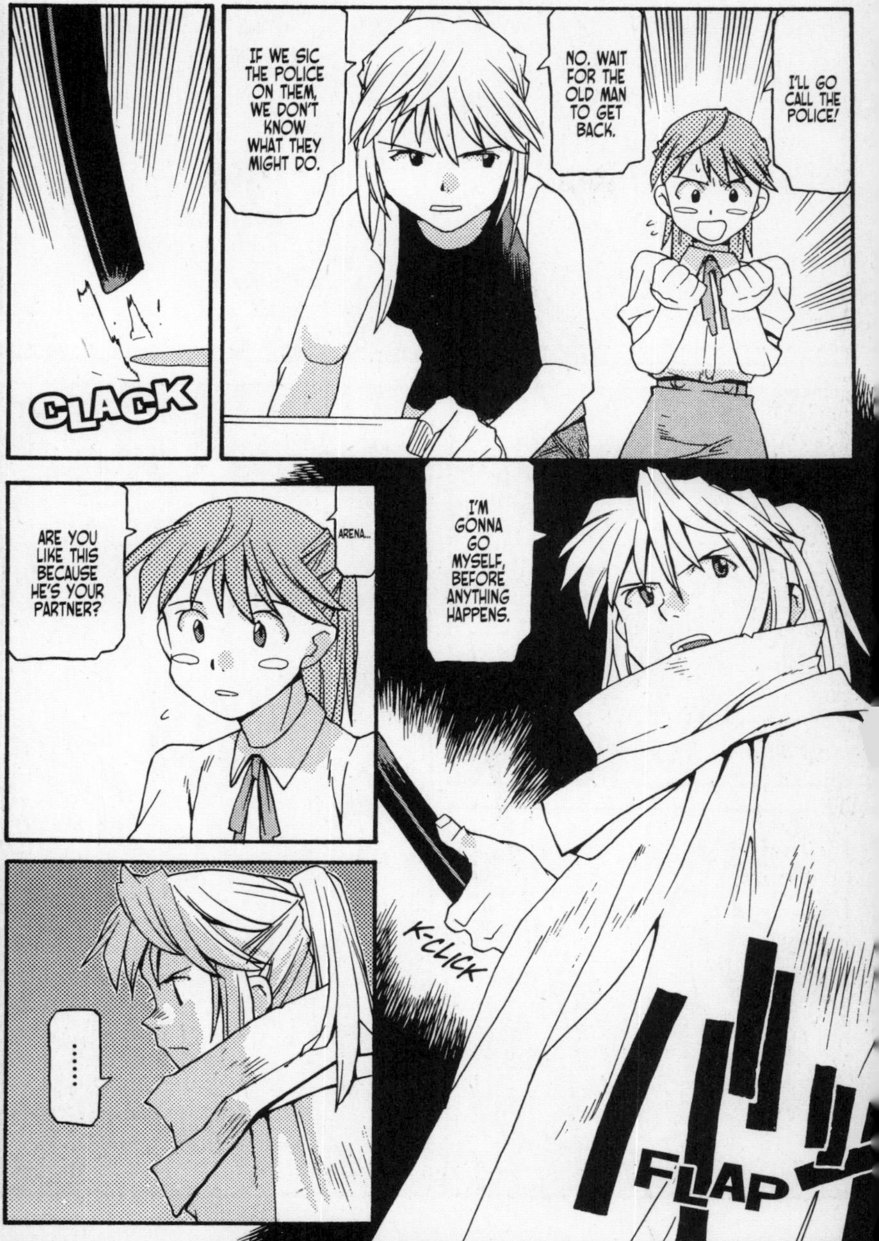
I'LL GO CALL THE POLICE!
NO. WAIT FOR THE OLD MAN TO GET BACK.
IF WE SIC THE POLICE ON THEM, WE DON'T KNOW WHAT THEY MIGHT DO.
CLACK
I'M GONNA GO MYSELF, BEFORE ANYTHING HAPPENS.
K-CLICK
FLAP
ARENA...
ARE YOU LIKE THIS BECAUSE HE'S YOUR PARTNER?
......

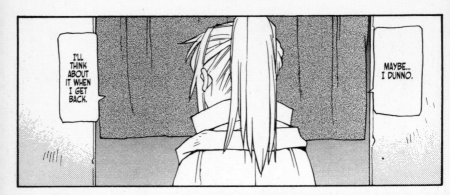

I'LL THINK ABOUT IT WHEN I GET BACK.

MAYBE... I DUNNO.

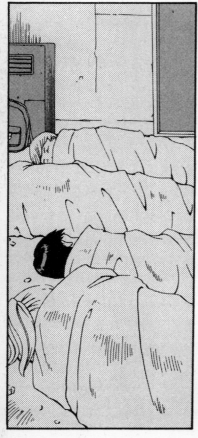

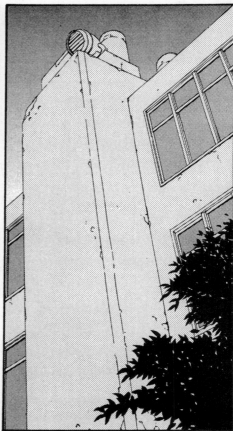

71

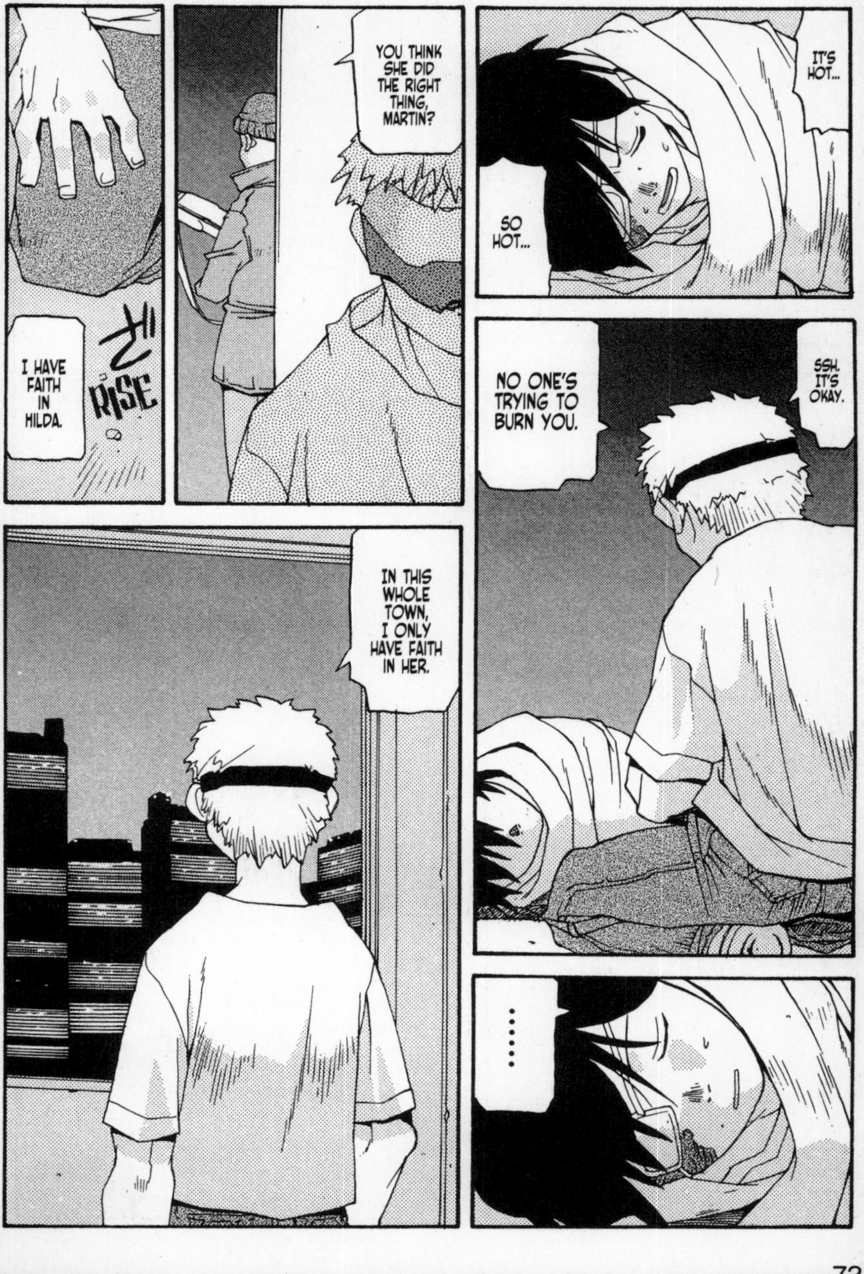
IT'S HOT...
SO HOT...
YOU THINK SHE DID THE RIGHT THING, MARTIN?
RISE
I HAVE FAITH IN HILDA.
SSH. IT'S OKAY.
NO ONE'S TRYING TO BURN YOU.
IN THIS WHOLE TOWN, I ONLY HAVE FAITH IN HER.
......

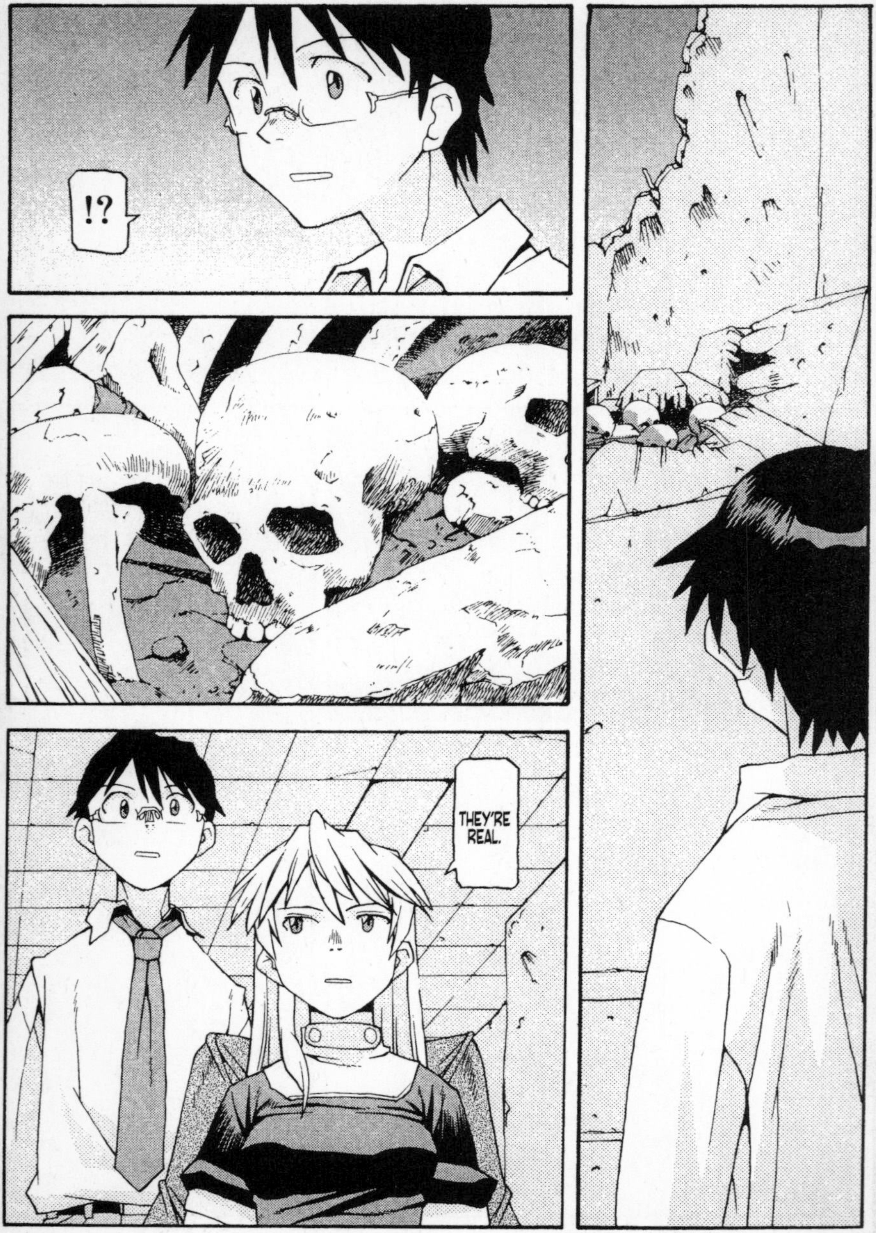
!?
THEY'RE REAL.

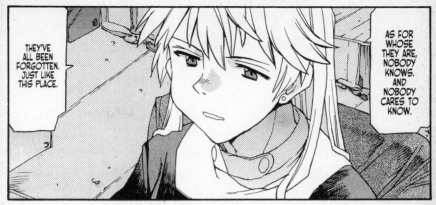

AS FOR WHOSE THEY ARE, NOBODY KNOWS. AND NOBODY CARES TO KNOW.
THEY'VE ALL BEEN FORGOTTEN. JUST LIKE THIS PLACE.
BUT THIS CLASSROOM BRINGS BACK MEMORIES.
LEAN
YES...
THIS IS WHERE I WAS TAUGHT.
R. O'BRIEN

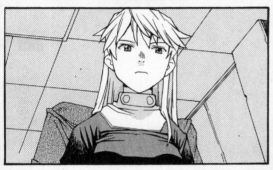

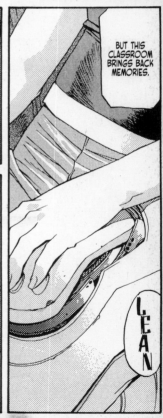

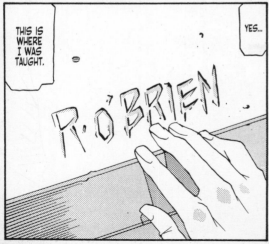

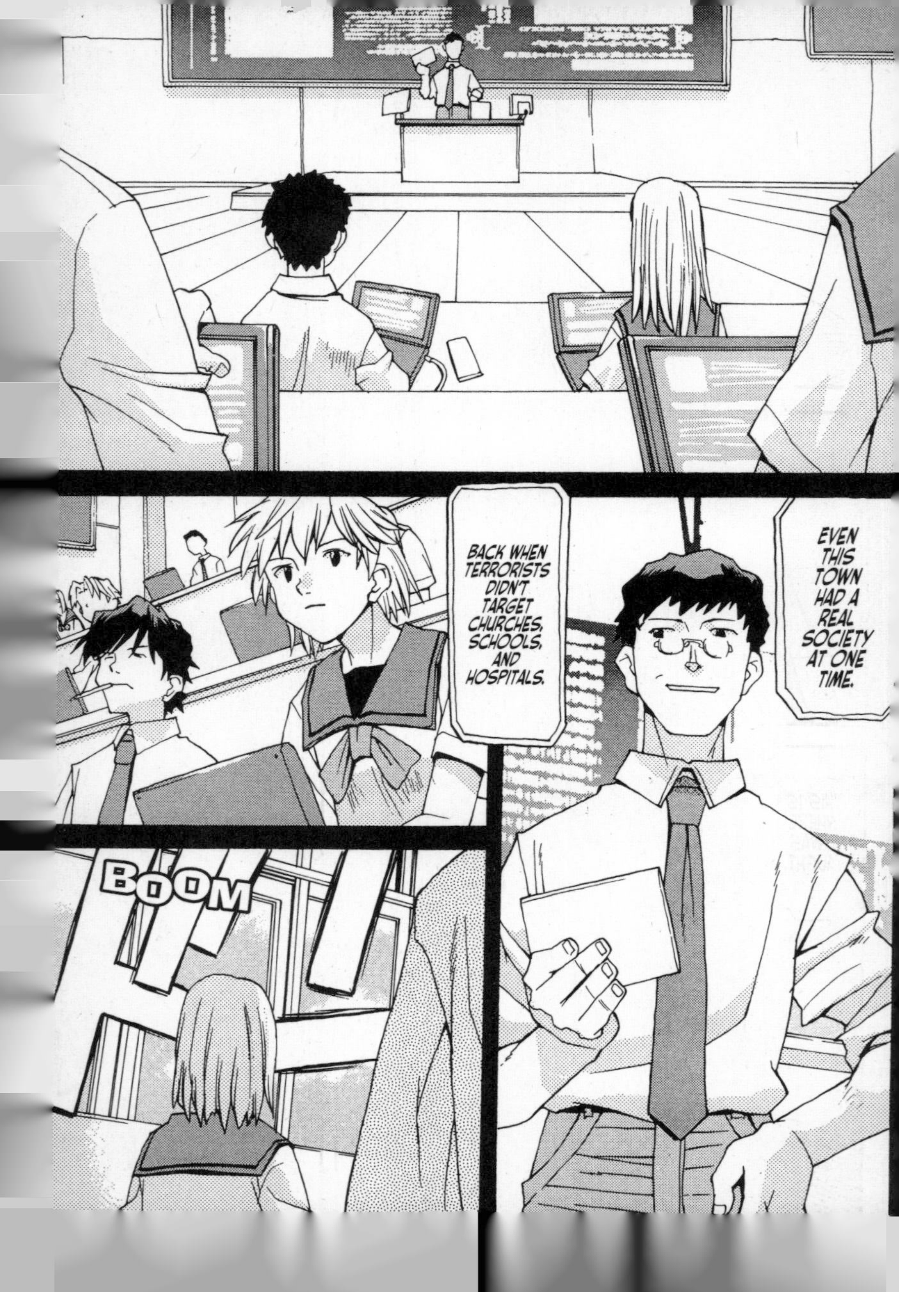
EVEN THIS TOWN HAD A REAL SOCIETY AT ONE TIME.
BACK WHEN TERRORISTS DIDN'T TARGET CHURCHES, SCHOOLS, AND HOSPITALS.
BOOM

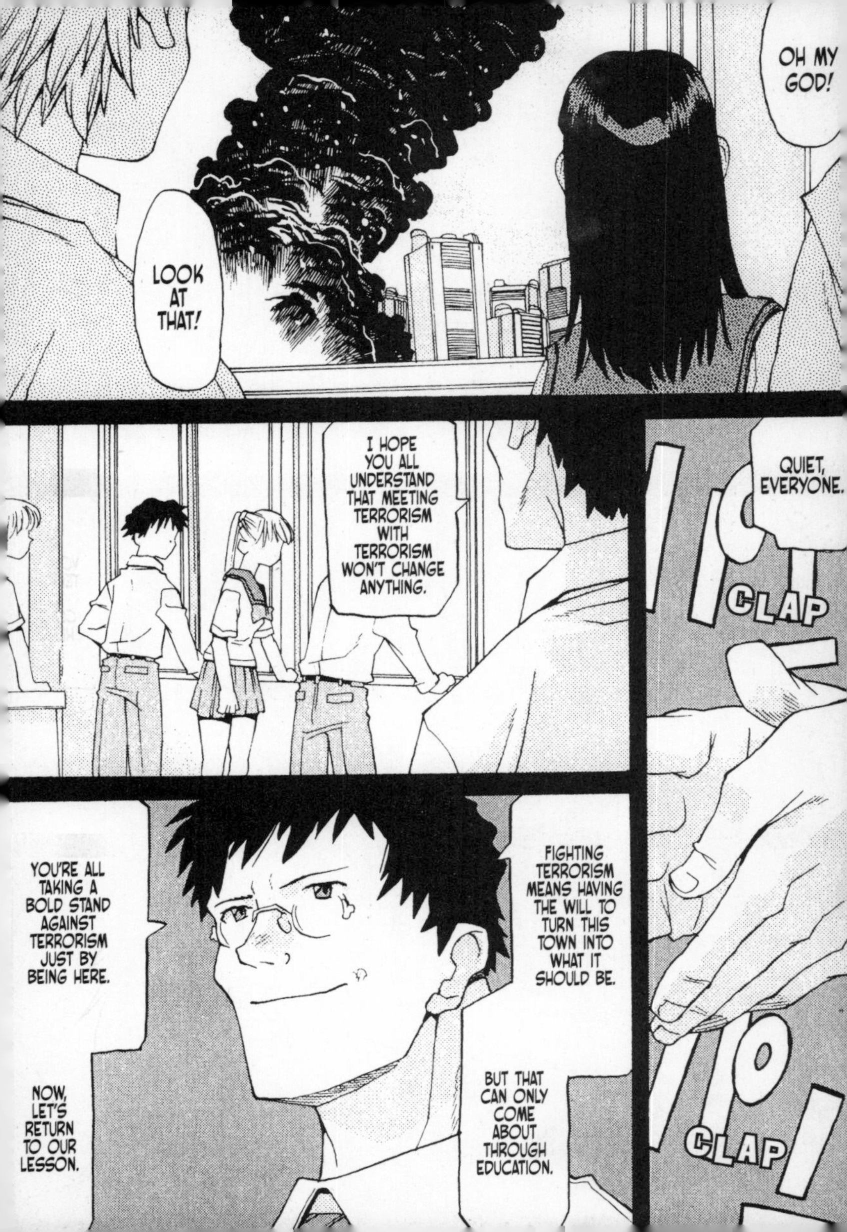
OH MY GOD!
LOOK AT THAT!
QUIET, EVERYONE.
CLAP
CLAP
I HOPE YOU ALL UNDERSTAND THAT MEETING TERRORISM WITH TERRORISM WON'T CHANGE ANYTHING.
FIGHTING TERRORISM MEANS HAVING THE WILL TO TURN THIS TOWN INTO WHAT IT SHOULD BE.
BUT THAT CAN ONLY COME ABOUT THROUGH EDUCATION.
YOU'RE ALL TAKING A BOLD STAND AGAINST TERRORISM JUST BY BEING HERE.
NOW, LET'S RETURN TO OUR LESSON.

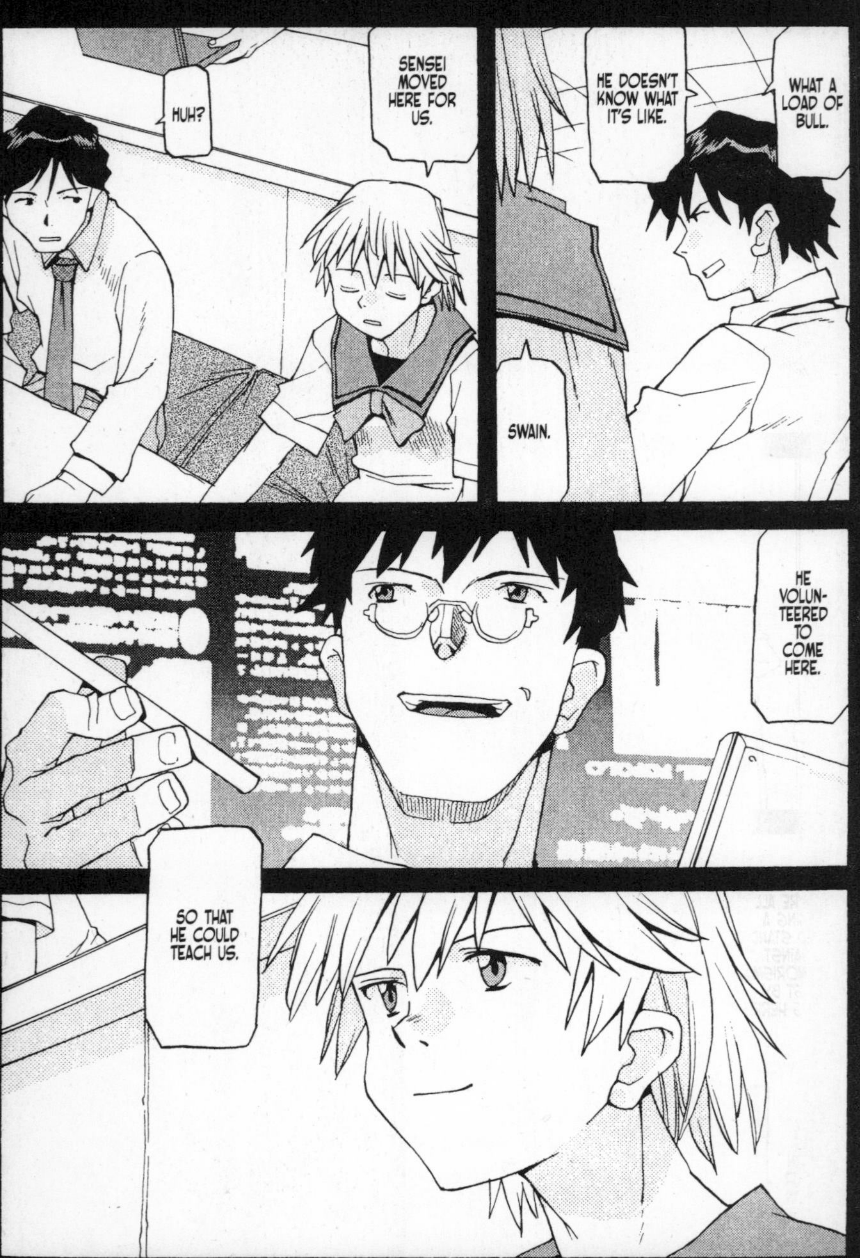
WHAT A LOAD OF BULL.
HE DOESN'T KNOW WHAT IT'S LIKE.
SWAIN.
SENSEI MOVED HERE FOR US.
HUH?
HE VOLUN-TEERED TO COME HERE.
SO THAT HE COULD TEACH US.

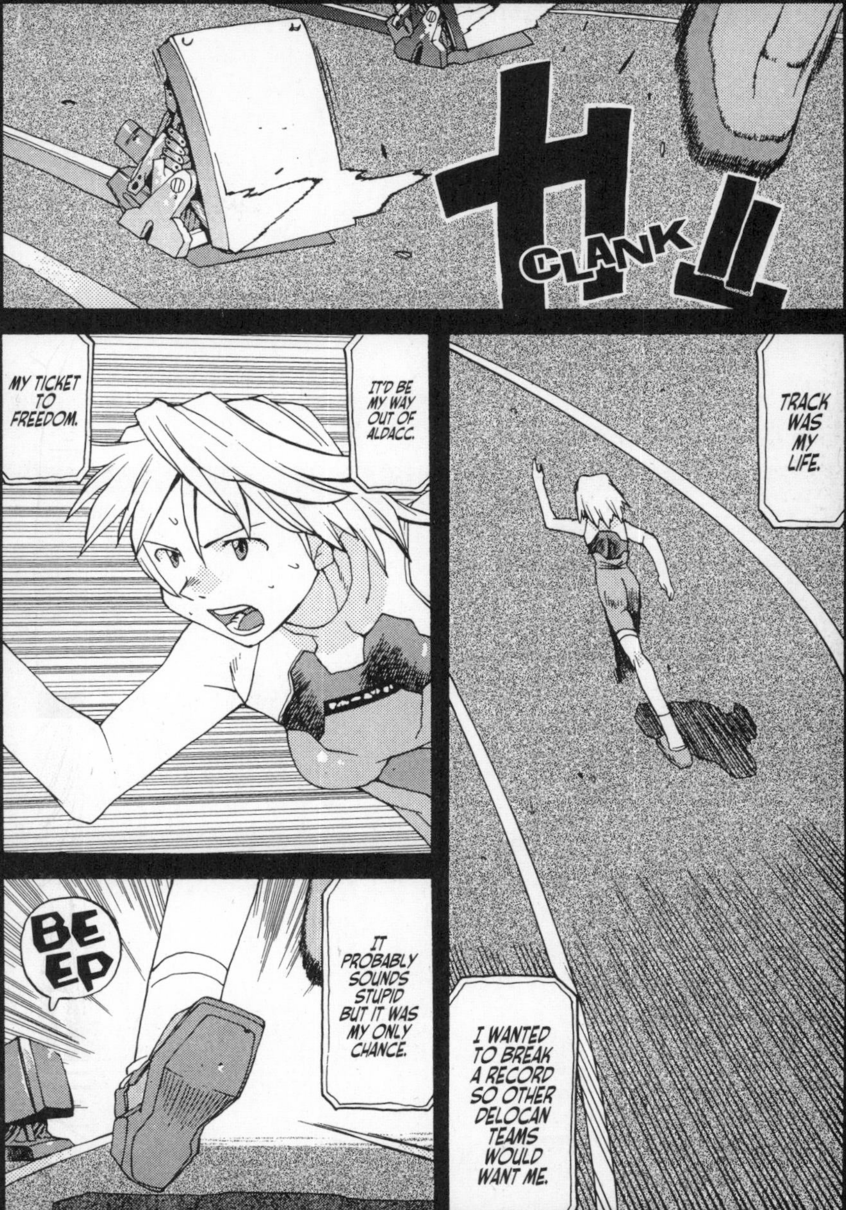
CLANK
TRACK WAS MY LIFE.
I WANTED TO BREAK A RECORD SO OTHER DELOCAN TEAMS WOULD WANT ME.
IT'D BE MY WAY OUT OF ALDACC.
MY TICKET TO FREEDOM.
IT PROBABLY SOUNDS STUPID BUT IT WAS MY ONLY CHANCE.
BEEP

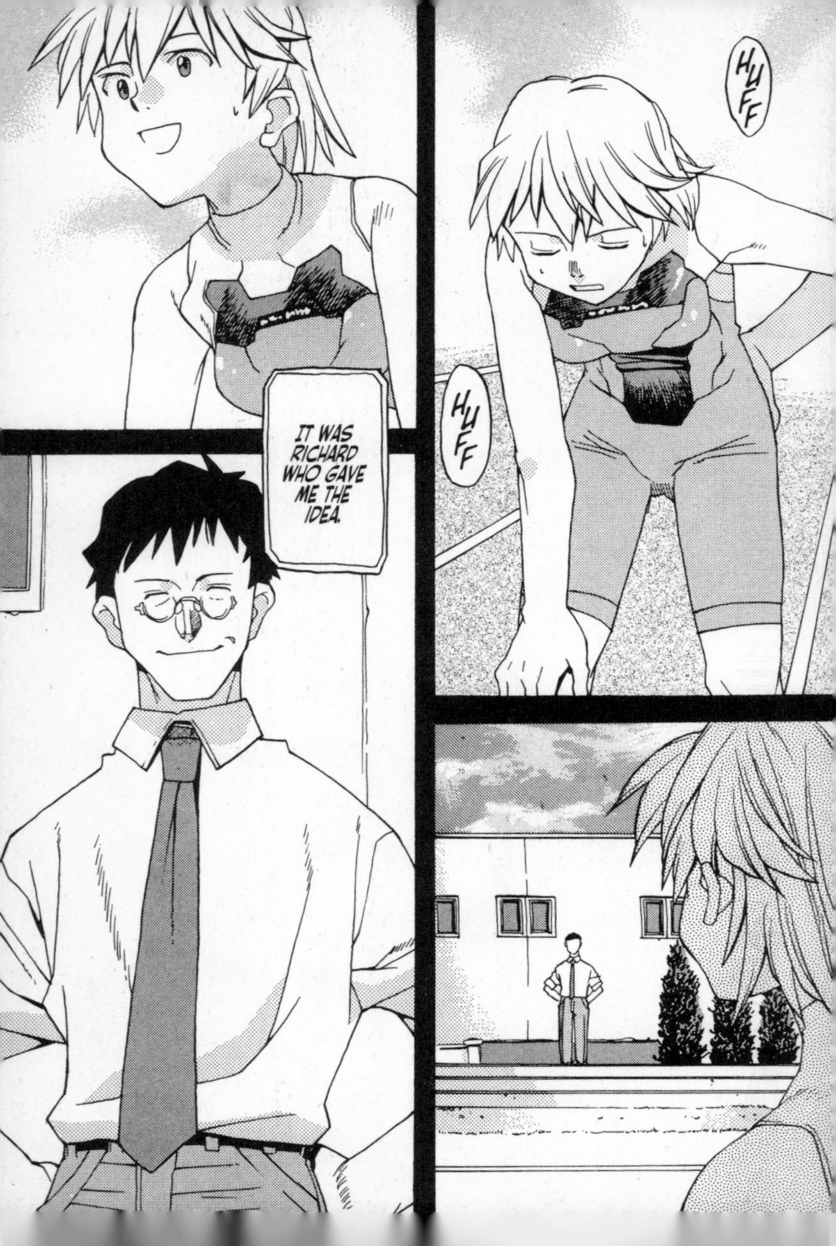
HUFF
HUFF
IT WAS RICHARD WHO GAVE ME THE IDEA.

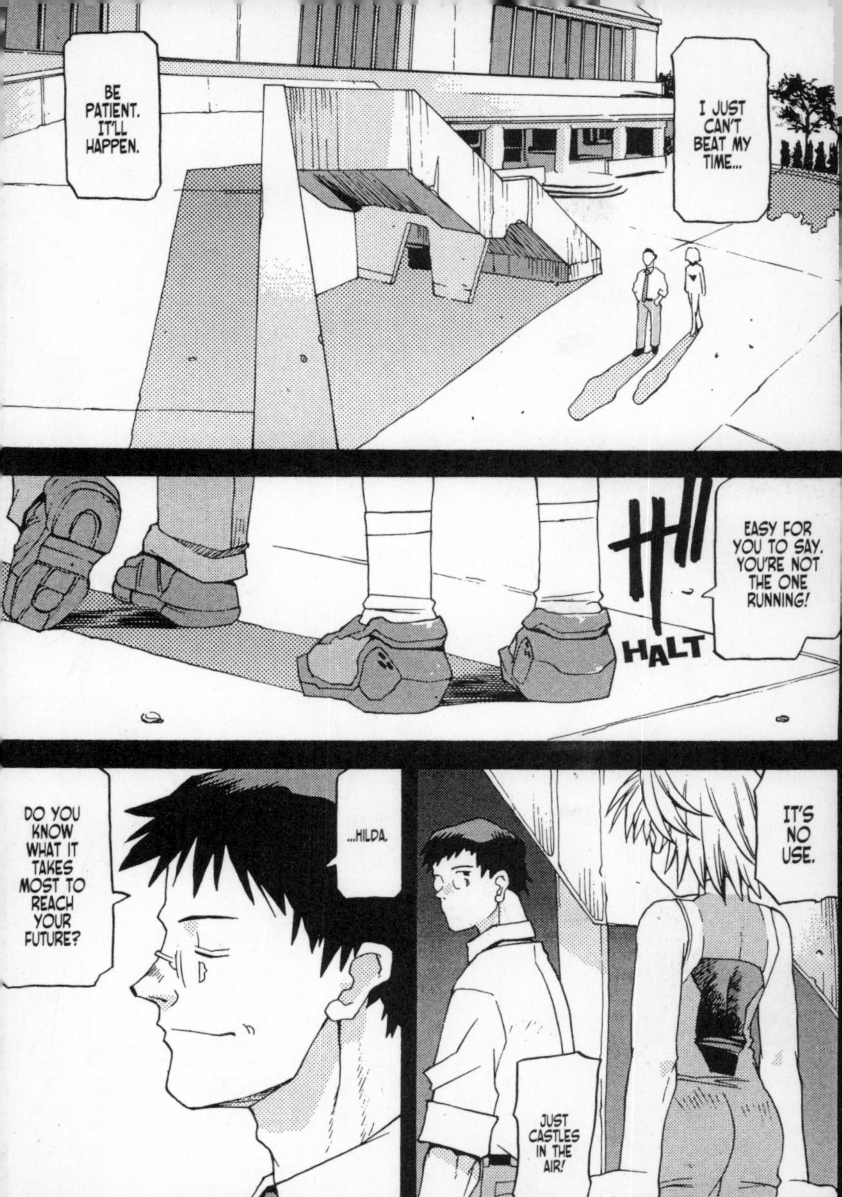
I JUST CAN'T BEAT MY TIME...
BE PATIENT. IT'LL HAPPEN.
EASY FOR YOU TO SAY. YOU'RE NOT THE ONE RUNNING!
HALT
IT'S NO USE.
JUST CASTLES IN THE AIR!
...HILDA.
DO YOU KNOW WHAT IT TAKES MOST TO REACH YOUR FUTURE?

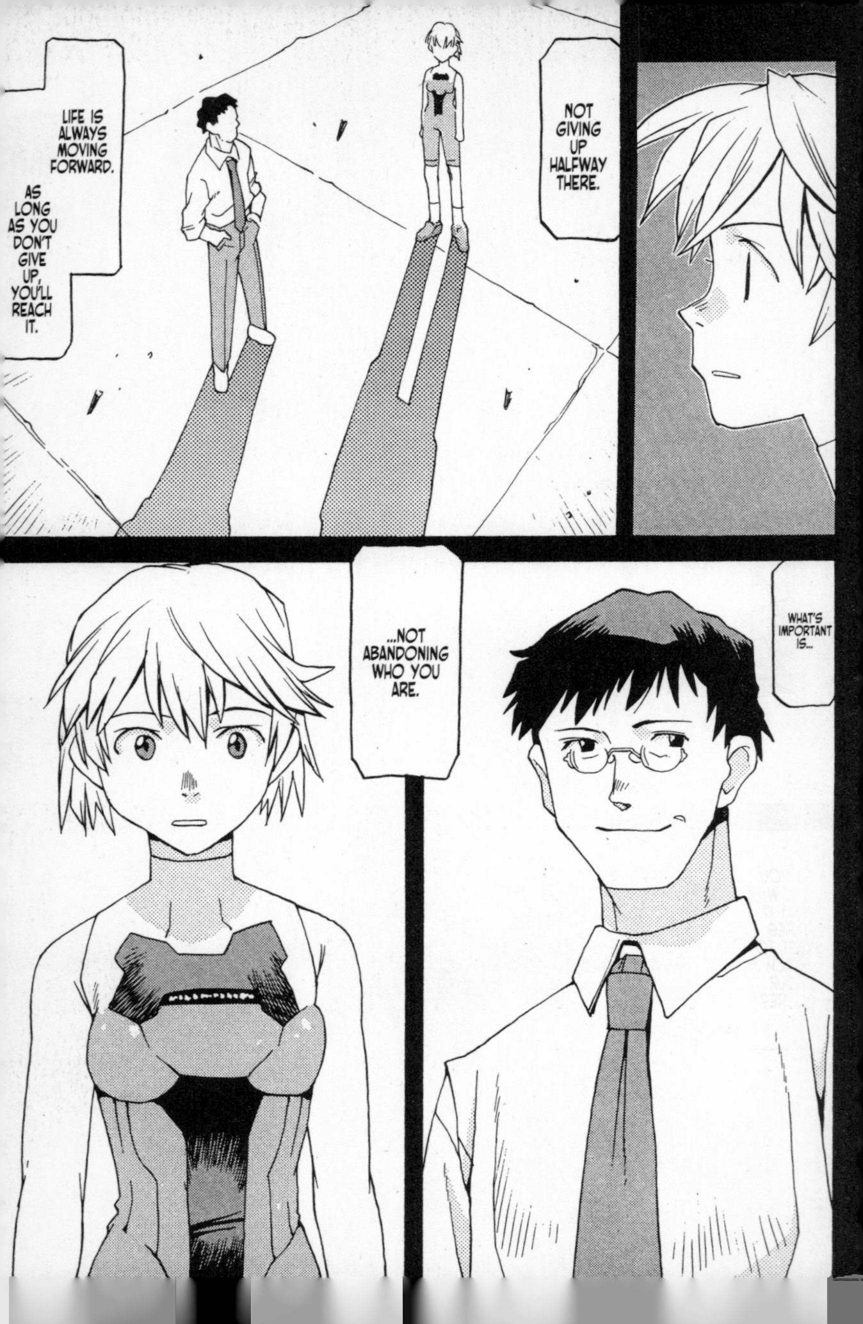
NOT GIVING UP HALFWAY THERE.
LIFE IS ALWAYS MOVING FORWARD.
AS LONG AS YOU DON'T GIVE UP, YOU'LL REACH IT.
WHAT'S IMPORTANT IS...
...NOT ABANDONING WHO YOU ARE.

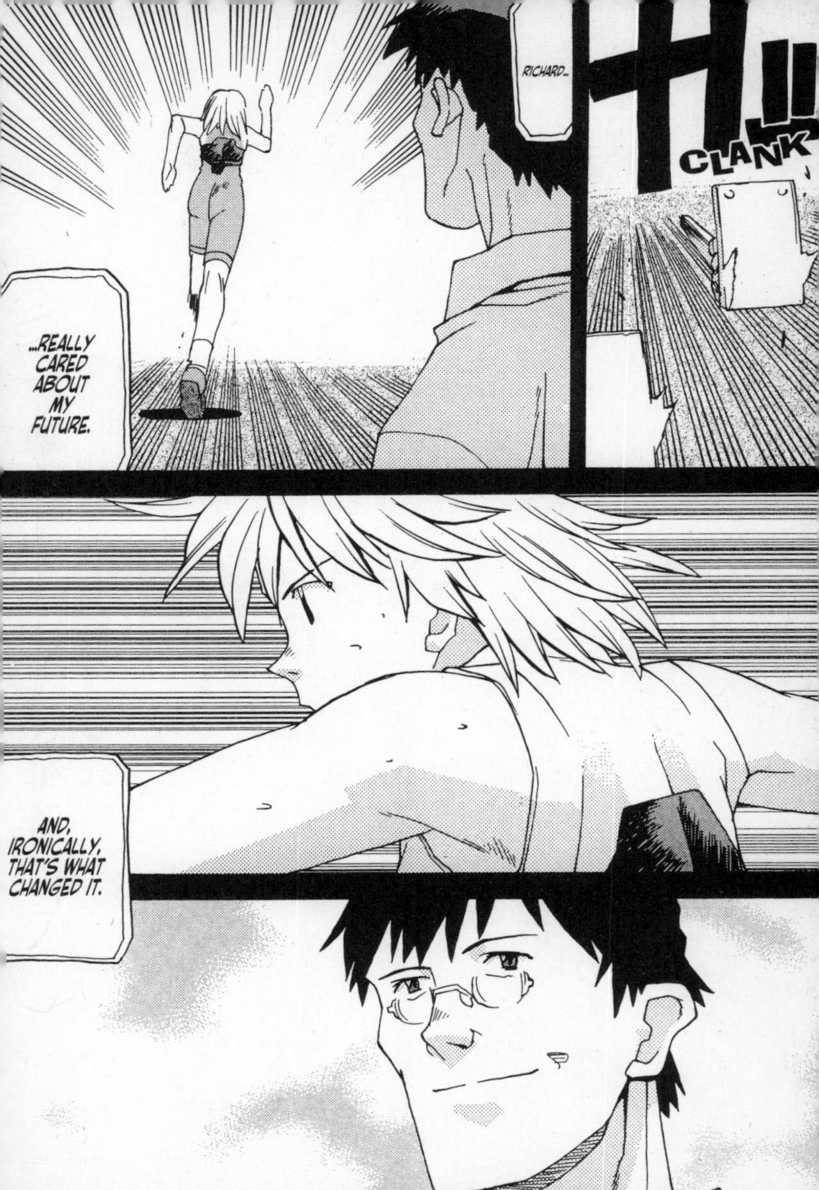
CLANK
RICHARD...
...REALLY CARED ABOUT MY FUTURE.
AND, IRONICALLY, THAT'S WHAT CHANGED IT.

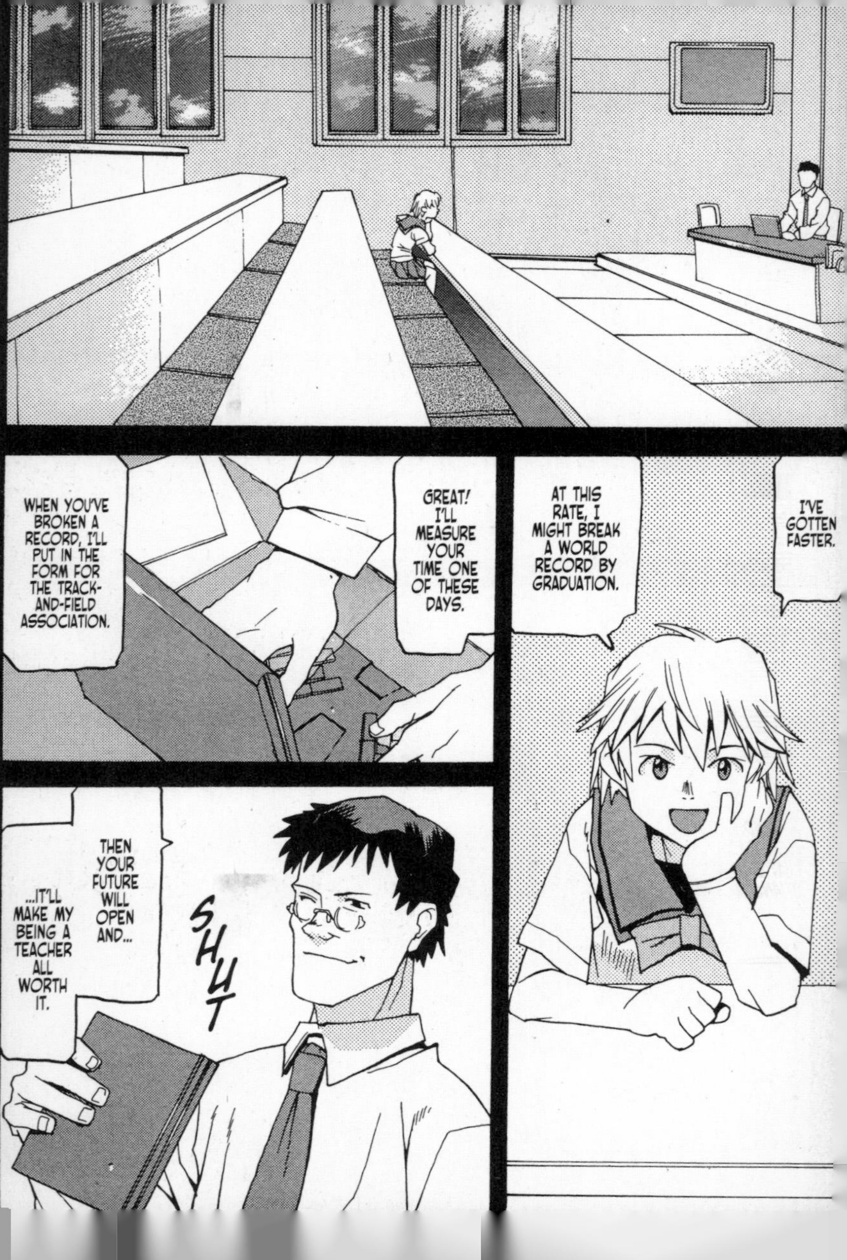
I'VE GOTTEN FASTER.
AT THIS RATE, I MIGHT BREAK A WORLD RECORD BY GRADUATION.
GREAT! I'LL MEASURE YOUR TIME ONE OF THESE DAYS.
WHEN YOU'VE BROKEN A RECORD, I'LL PUT IN THE FORM FOR THE TRACK-AND-FIELD ASSOCIATION.
THEN YOUR FUTURE WILL OPEN AND...
SHUT
...IT'LL MAKE MY BEING A TEACHER ALL WORTH IT.

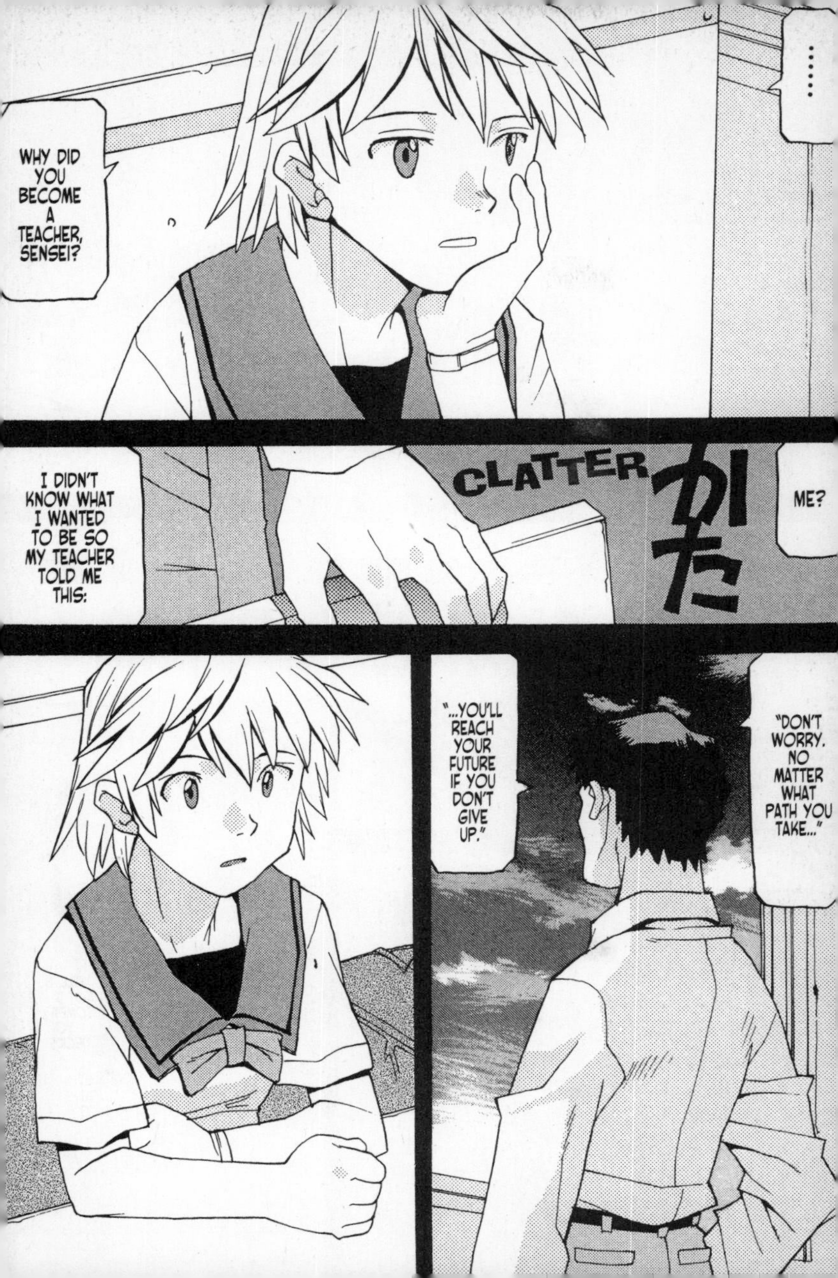
......
WHY DID YOU BECOME A TEACHER, SENSEI?
ME?
CLATTER
かた
I DIDN'T KNOW WHAT I WANTED TO BE SO MY TEACHER TOLD ME THIS:
"DON'T WORRY. NO MATTER WHAT PATH YOU TAKE..."
"...YOU'LL REACH YOUR FUTURE IF YOU DON'T GIVE UP."

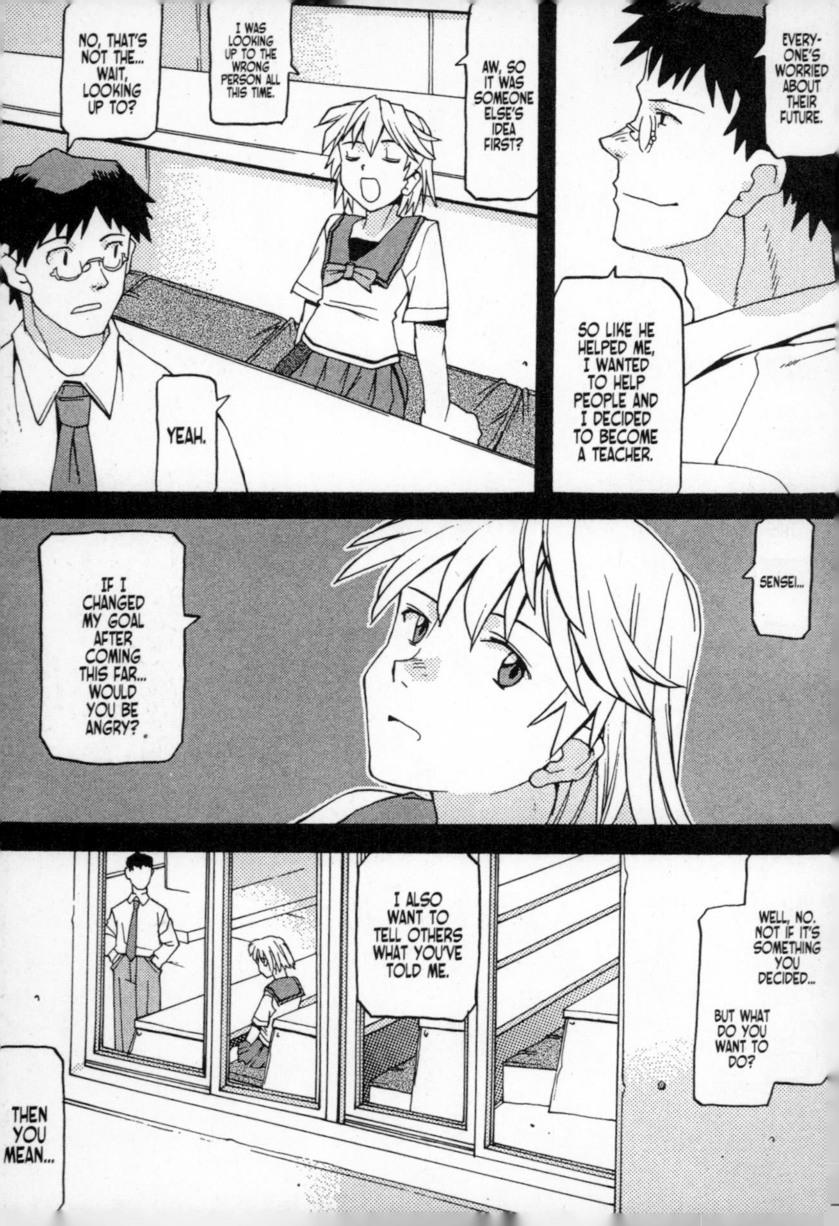
EVERY-ONE'S WORRIED ABOUT THEIR FUTURE.
SO LIKE HE HELPED ME, I WANTED TO HELP PEOPLE AND I DECIDED TO BECOME A TEACHER.
AW, SO IT WAS SOMEONE ELSE'S IDEA FIRST?
I WAS LOOKING UP TO THE WRONG PERSON ALL THIS TIME.
NO, THAT'S NOT THE... WAIT, LOOKING UP TO?
YEAH.
SENSEI...
IF I CHANGED MY GOAL AFTER COMING THIS FAR... WOULD YOU BE ANGRY?
WELL, NO. NOT IF IT'S SOMETHING YOU DECIDED...
BUT WHAT DO YOU WANT TO DO?
I ALSO WANT TO TELL OTHERS WHAT YOU'VE TOLD ME.
THEN YOU MEAN...

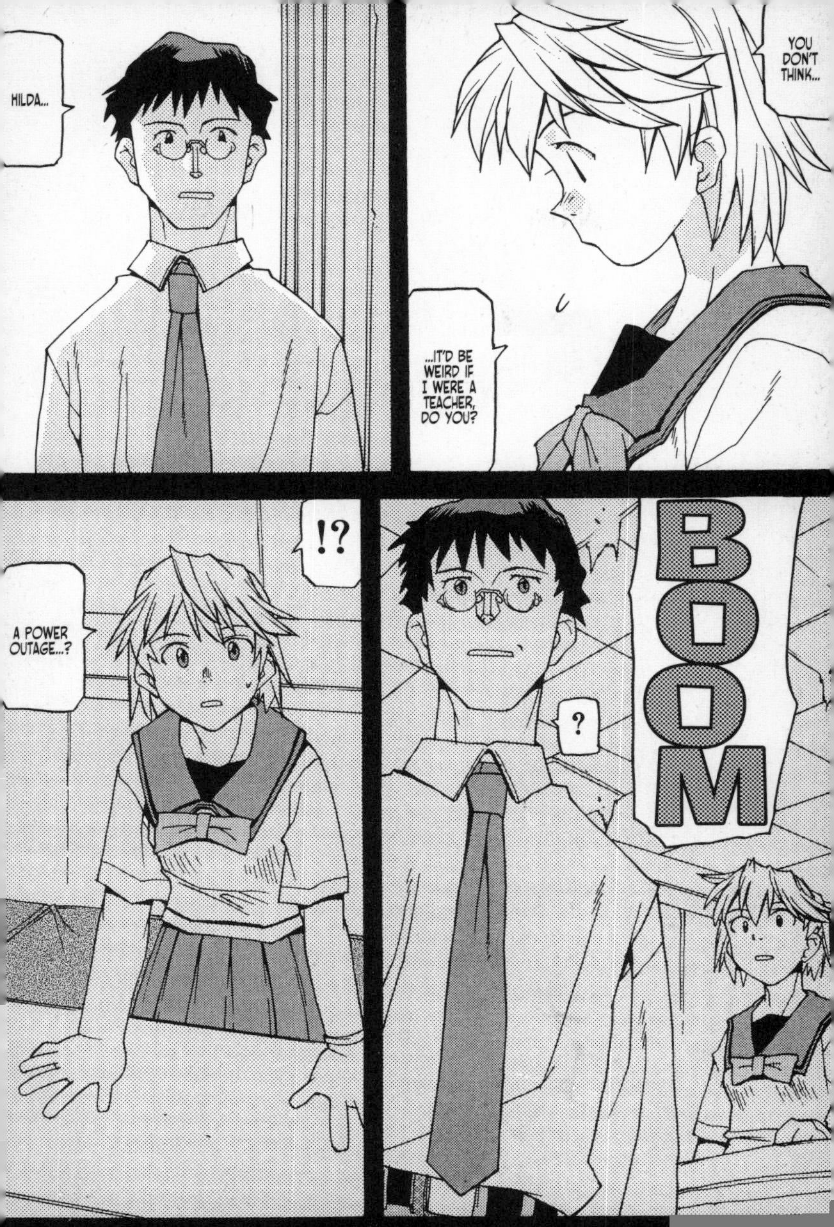
YOU DON'T THINK...
...IT'D BE WEIRD IF I WERE A TEACHER, DO YOU?
HILDA...
BOOM
?
!?
A POWER OUTAGE...?

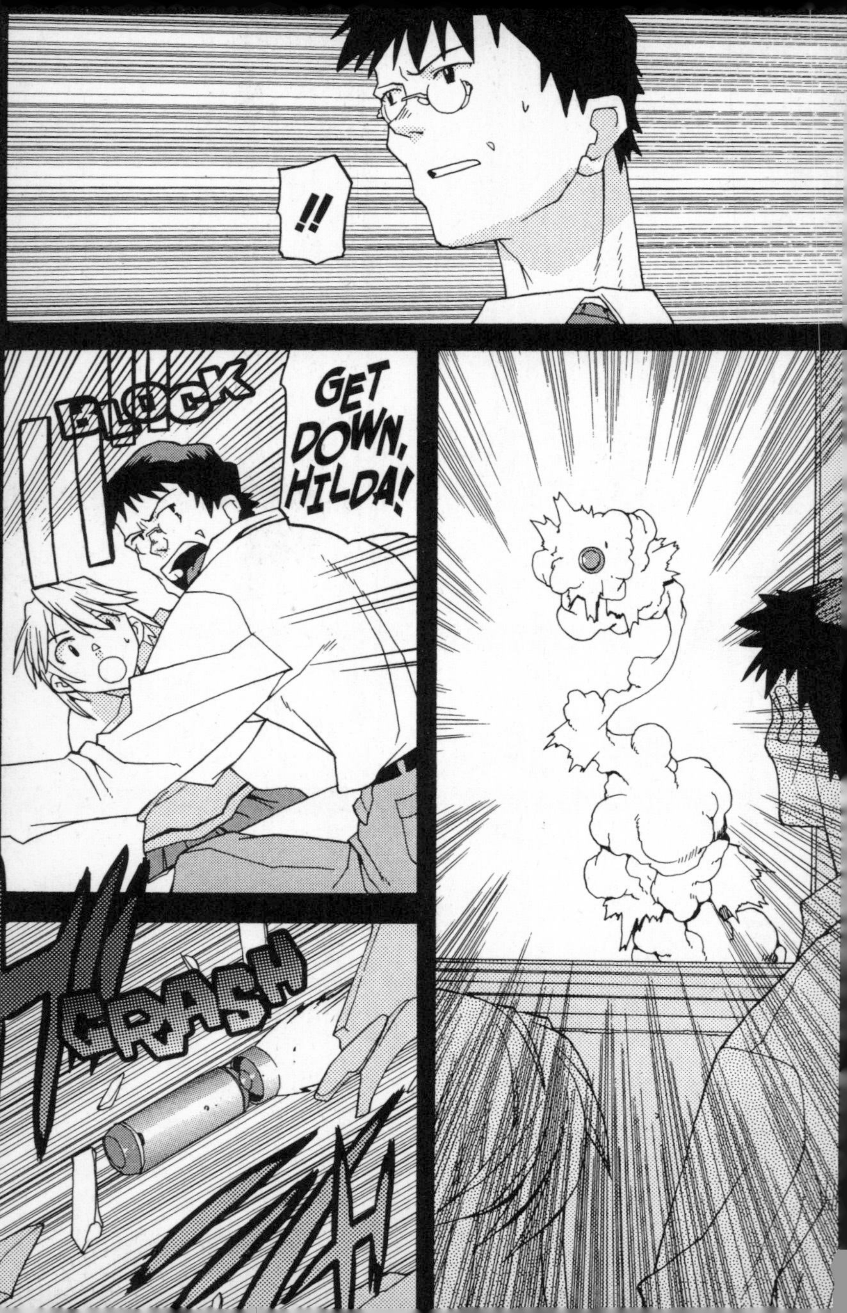
!!
GET DOWN, HILDA!
BLOCK
CRASH

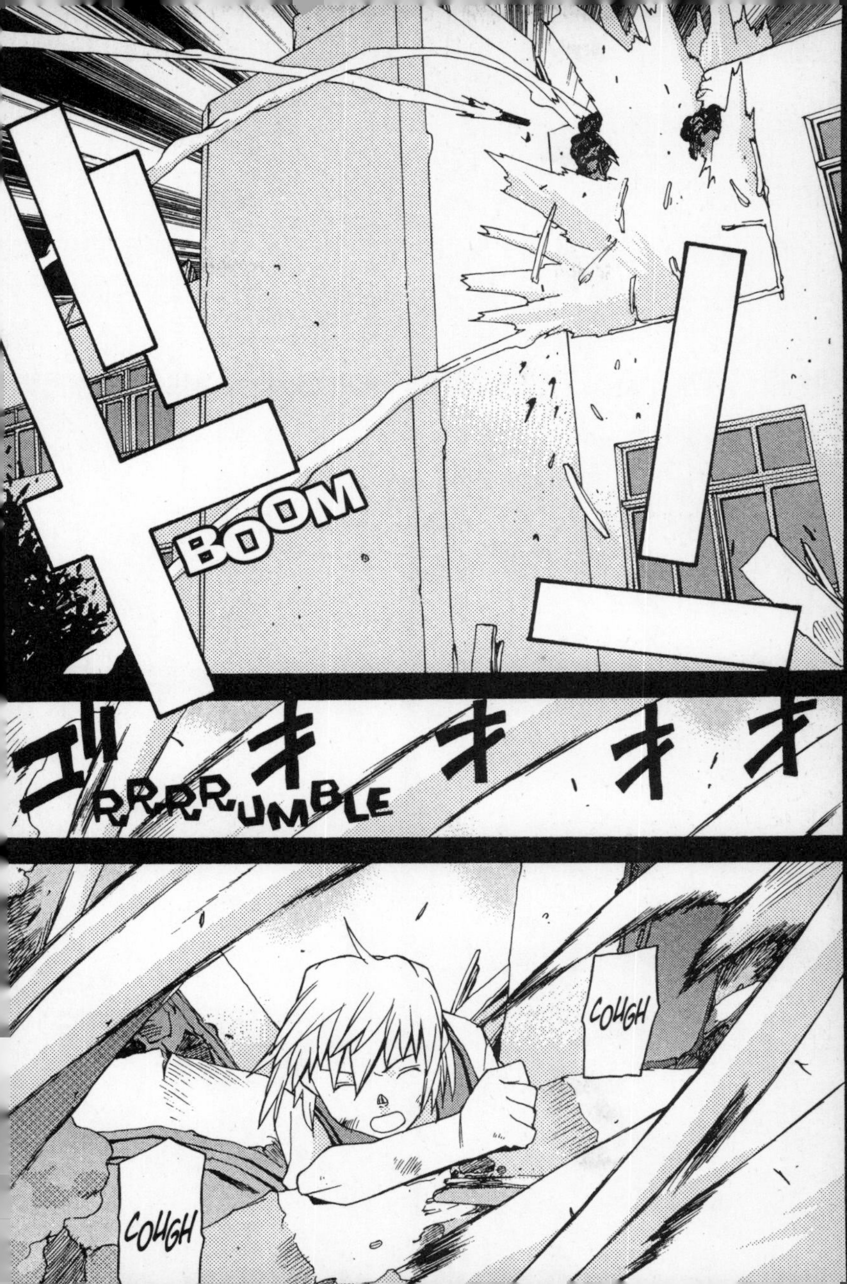
BOOM
RRRRRUMBLE
COUGH
COUGH

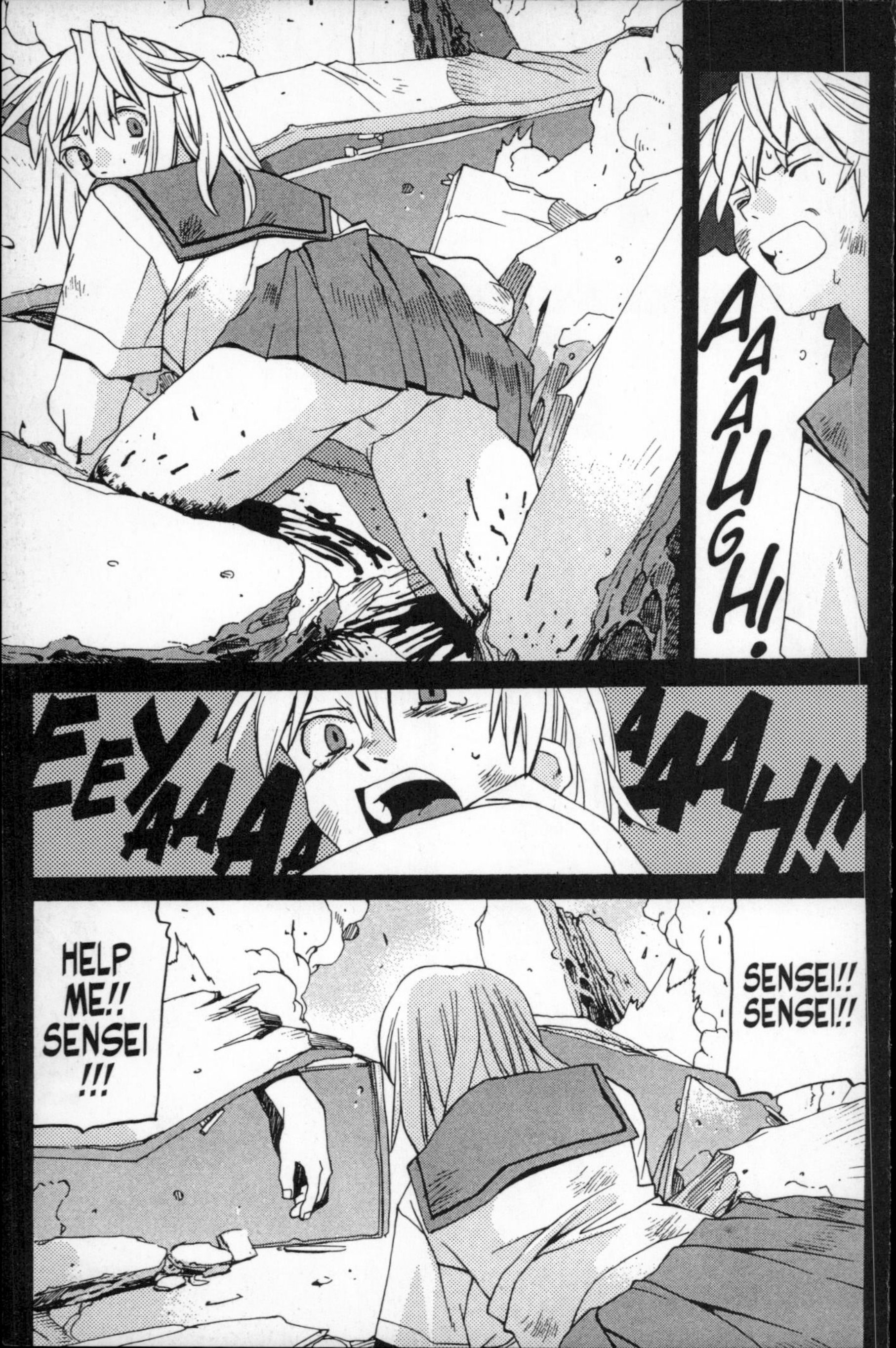
AAAUGH!!
EEYAAAAAAAAH!!
SENSEI!! SENSEI!!
HELP ME!! SENSEI!!!

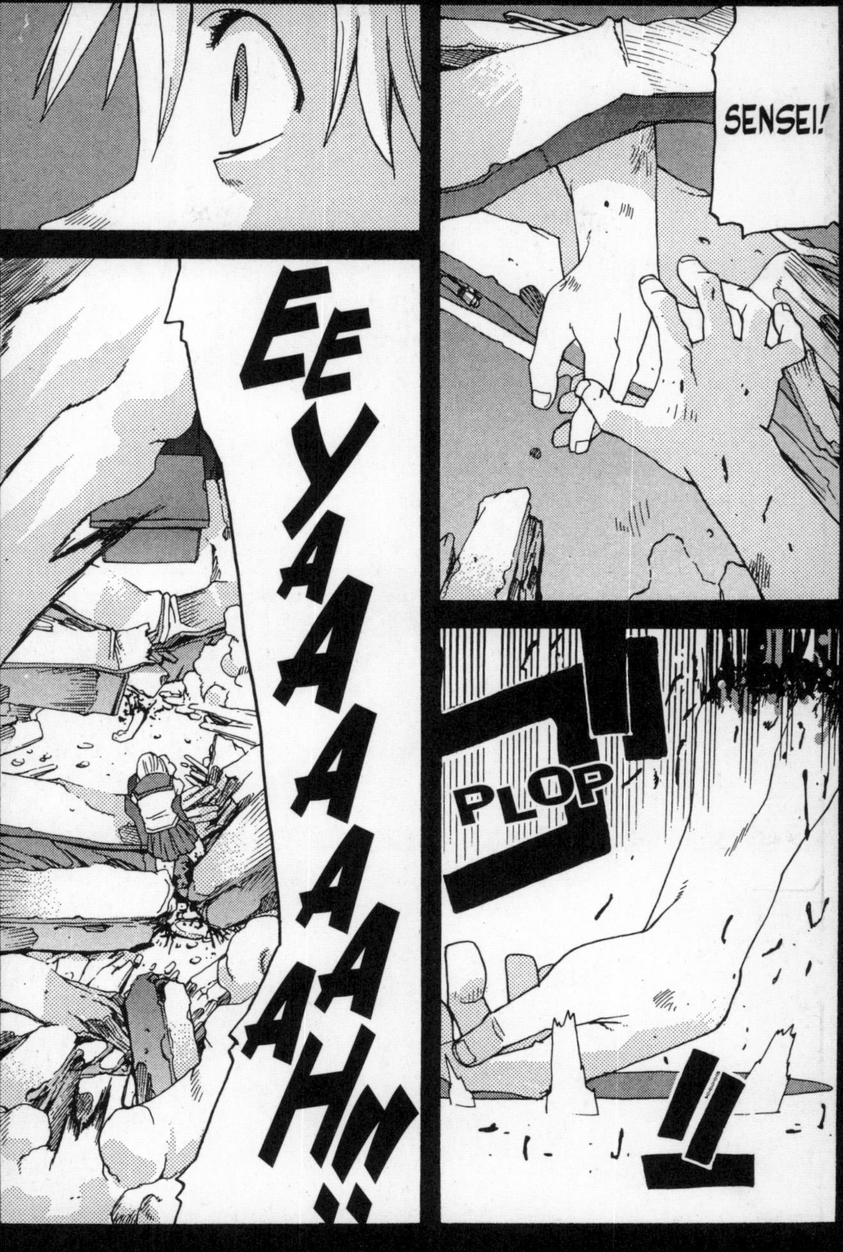
SENSEI!
PLOP
EEYAAAAAAH!!

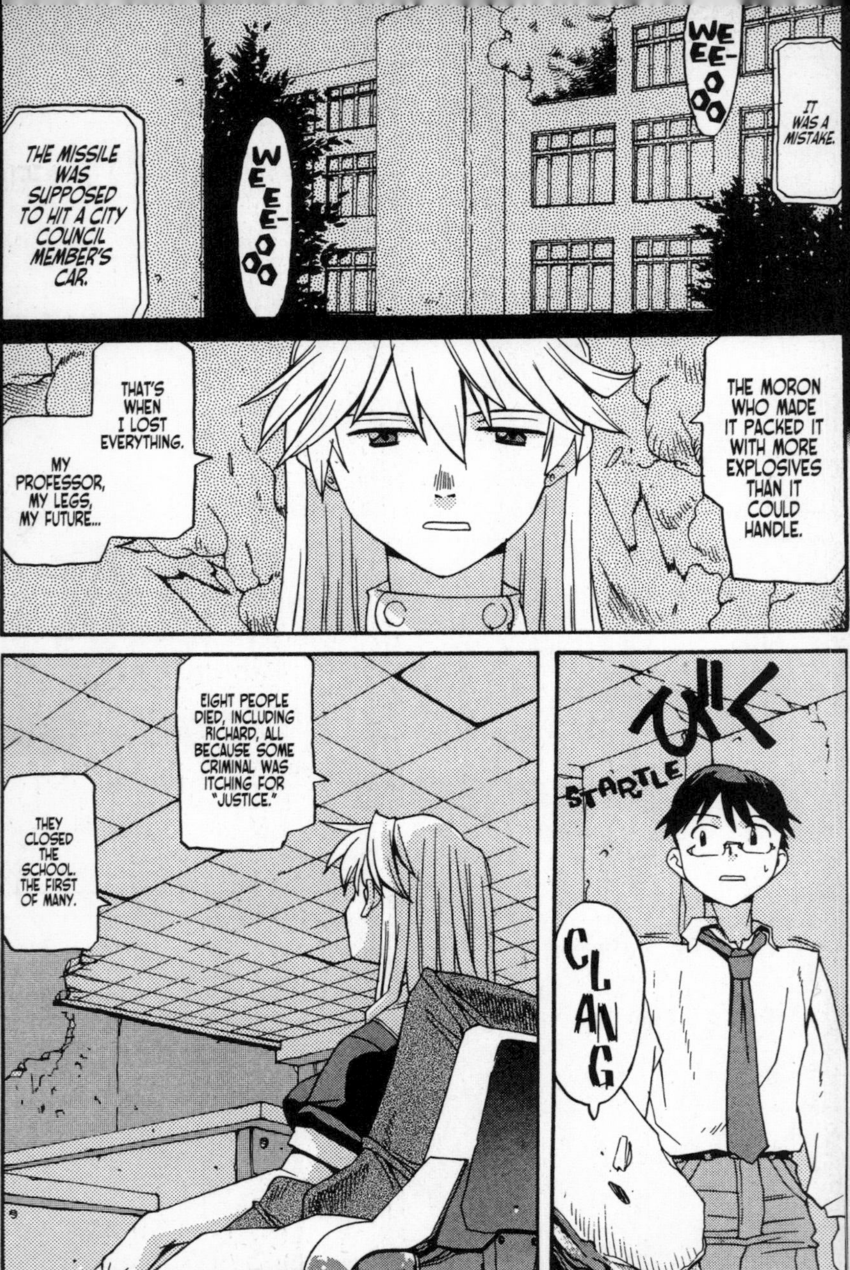
IT WAS A MISTAKE.
WEEE-OOO
WEEE-OOO
THE MISSILE WAS SUPPOSED TO HIT A CITY COUNCIL MEMBER'S CAR.
THE MORON WHO MADE IT PACKED IT WITH MORE EXPLOSIVES THAN IT COULD HANDLE.
THAT'S WHEN I LOST EVERYTHING.
MY PROFESSOR, MY LEGS, MY FUTURE...
びく
STARTLE
CLANG
EIGHT PEOPLE DIED, INCLUDING RICHARD, ALL BECAUSE SOME CRIMINAL WAS ITCHING FOR "JUSTICE."
THEY CLOSED THE SCHOOL. THE FIRST OF MANY.

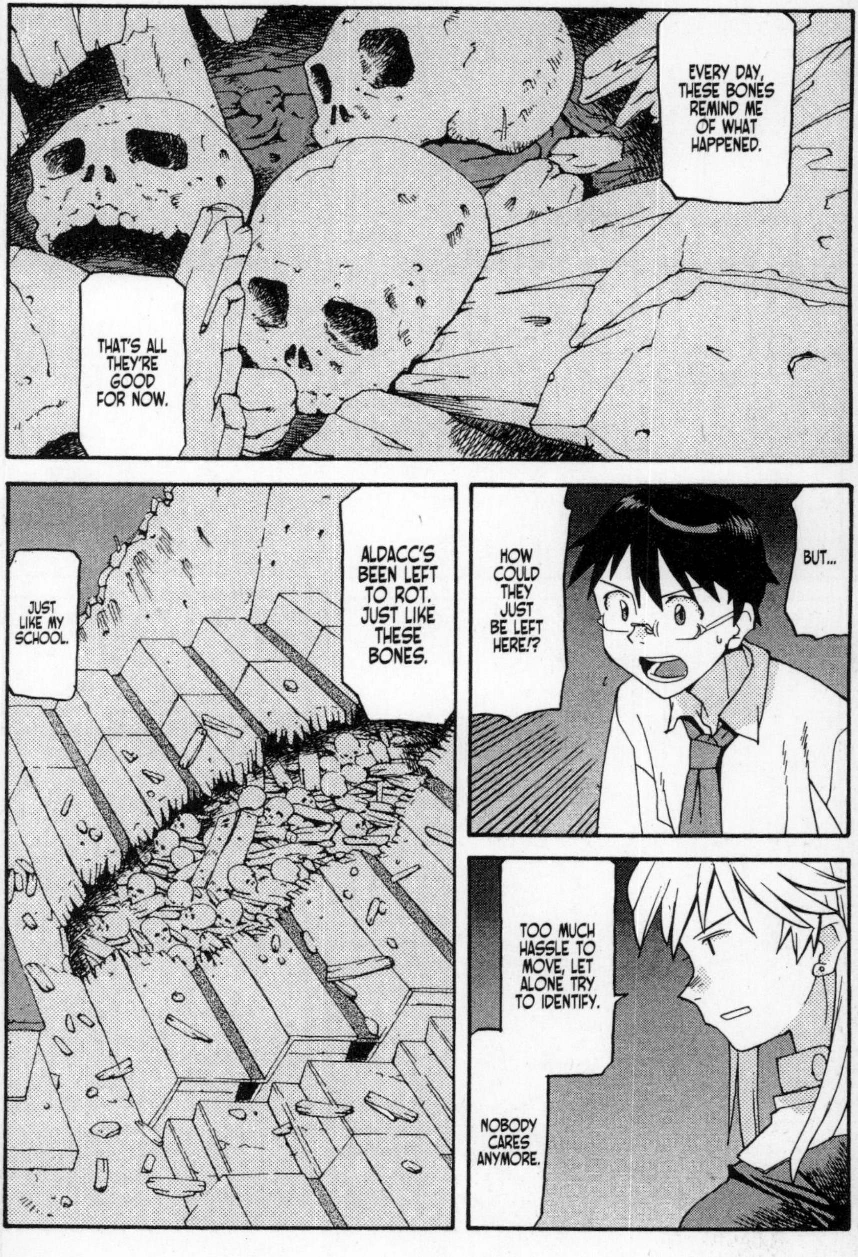
EVERY DAY, THESE BONES REMIND ME OF WHAT HAPPENED.
THAT'S ALL THEY'RE GOOD FOR NOW.
BUT...
HOW COULD THEY JUST BE LEFT HERE!?
TOO MUCH HASSLE TO MOVE, LET ALONE TRY TO IDENTIFY.
NOBODY CARES ANYMORE.
ALDACC'S BEEN LEFT TO ROT. JUST LIKE THESE BONES.
JUST LIKE MY SCHOOL.

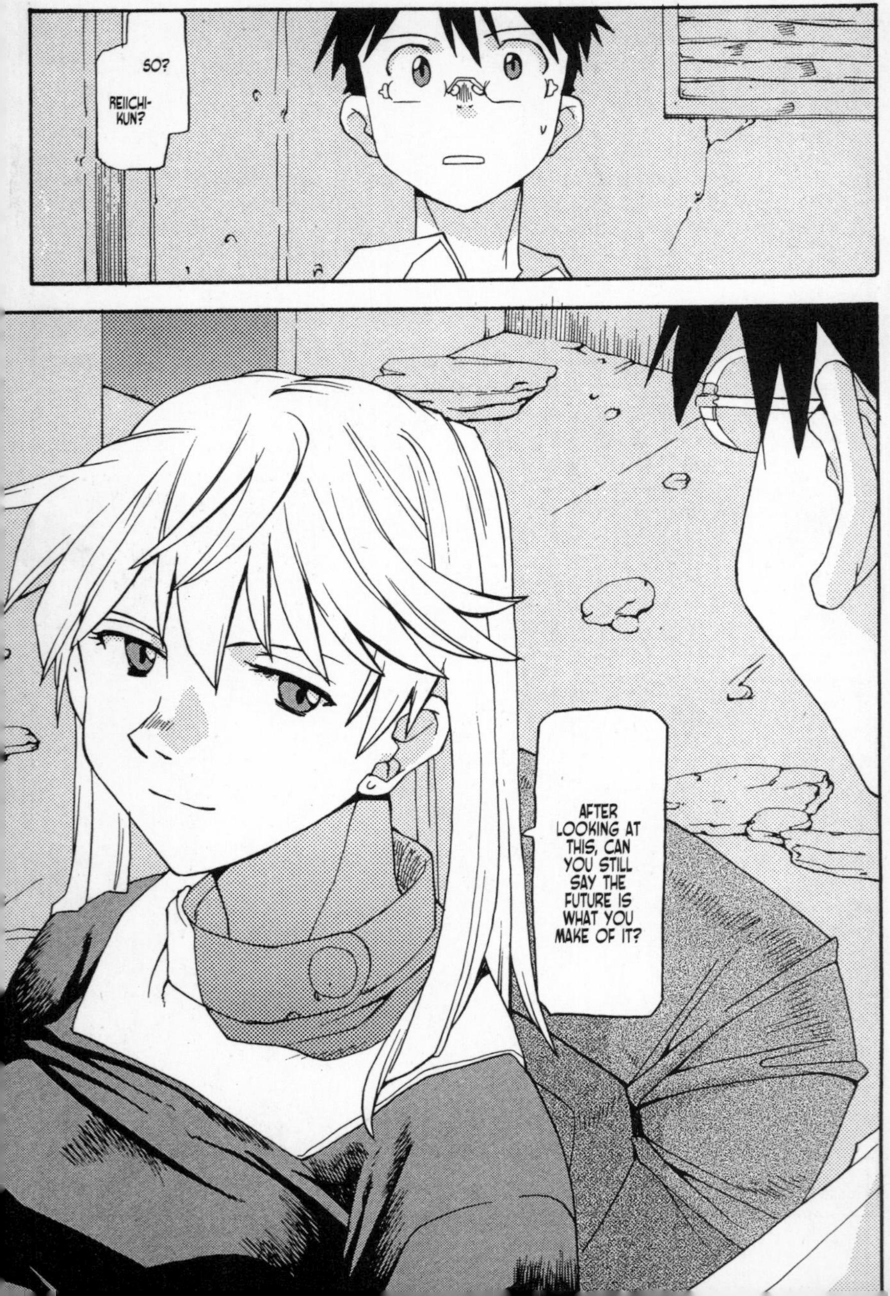
SO?
REIICHI-KUN?
AFTER LOOKING AT THIS, CAN YOU STILL SAY THE FUTURE IS WHAT YOU MAKE OF IT?

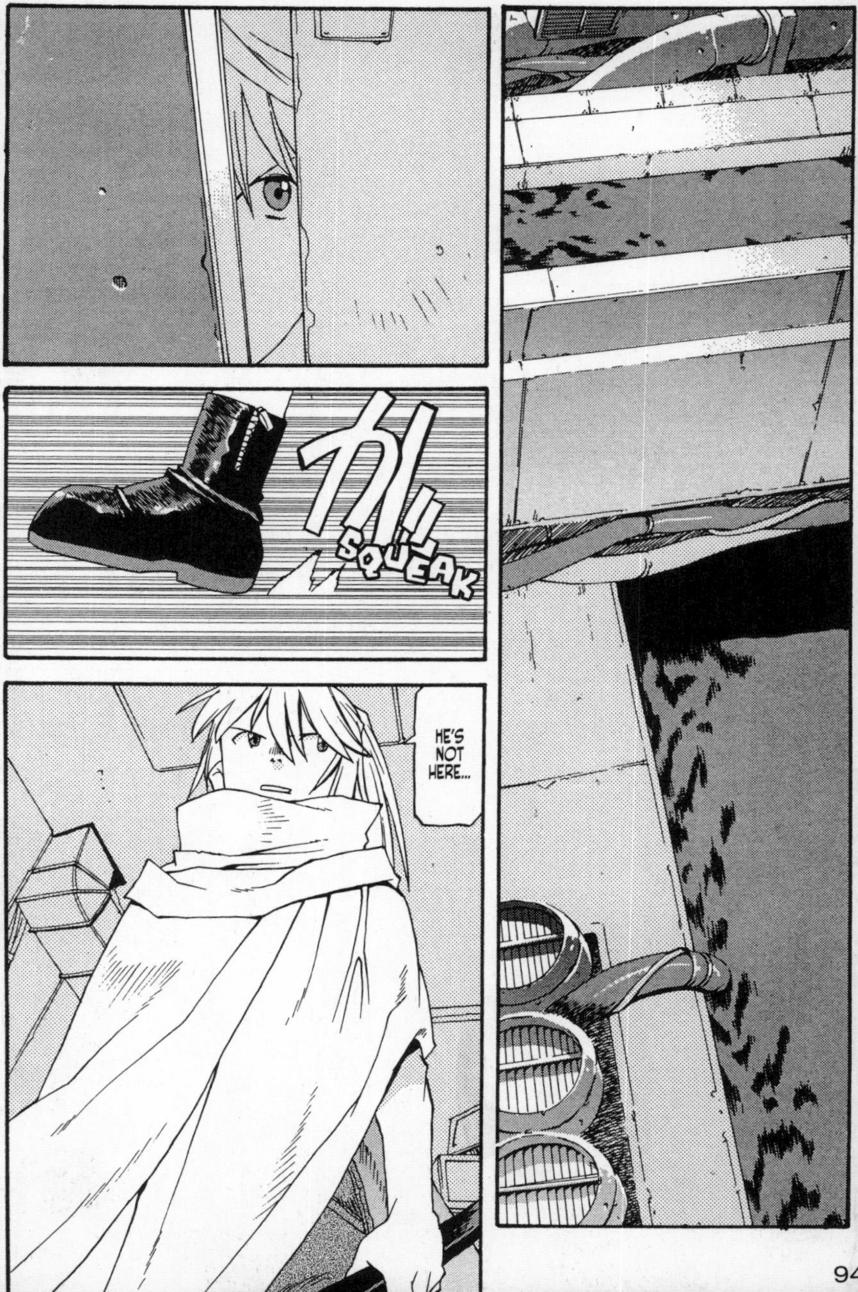
SQUEAK
HE'S NOT HERE...

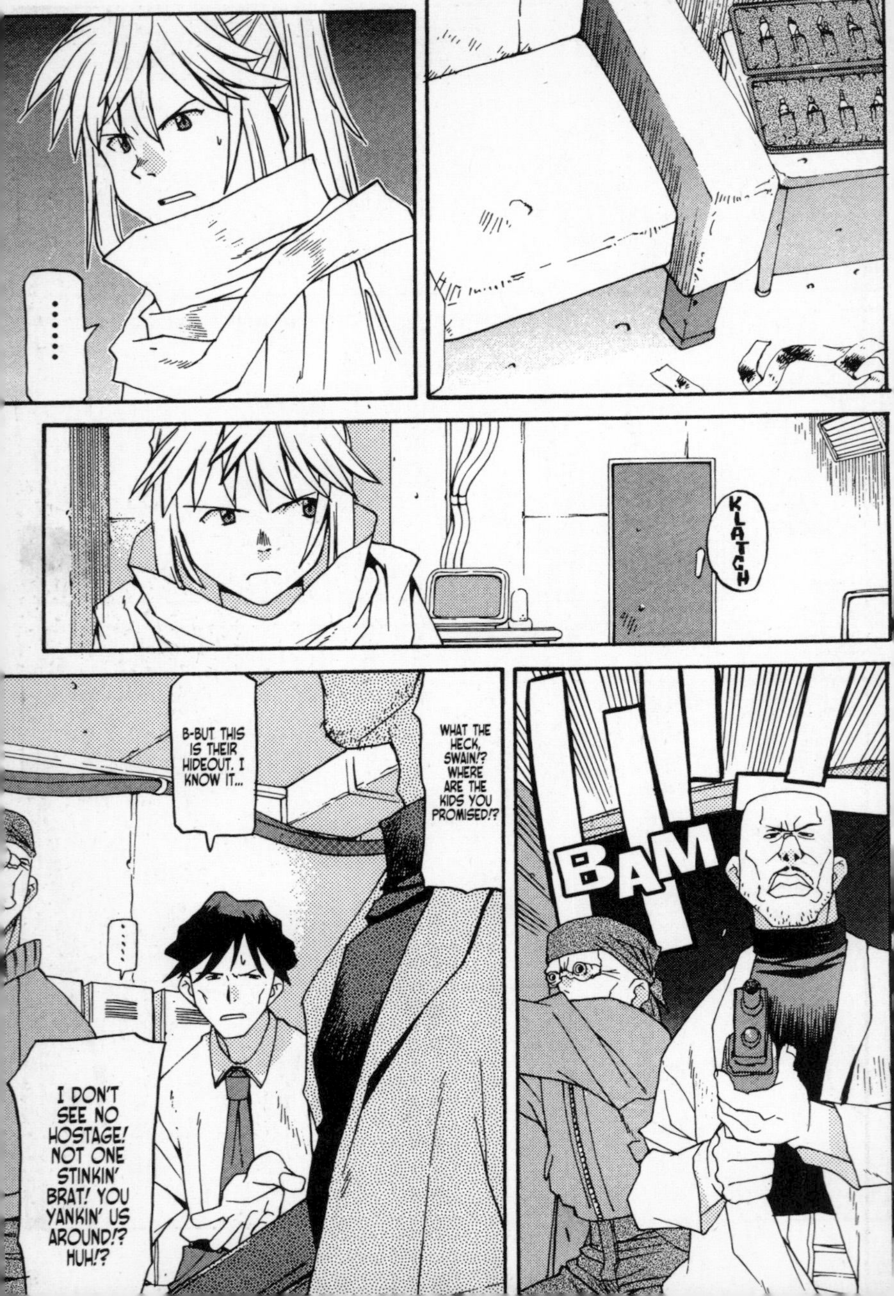
……
KLATCH
BAM
WHAT THE HECK, SWAIN!? WHERE ARE THE KIDS YOU PROMISED!?
B-BUT THIS IS THEIR HIDEOUT. I KNOW IT...
……
I DON'T SEE NO HOSTAGE! NOT ONE STINKIN' BRAT! YOU YANKIN' US AROUND!? HUH!?

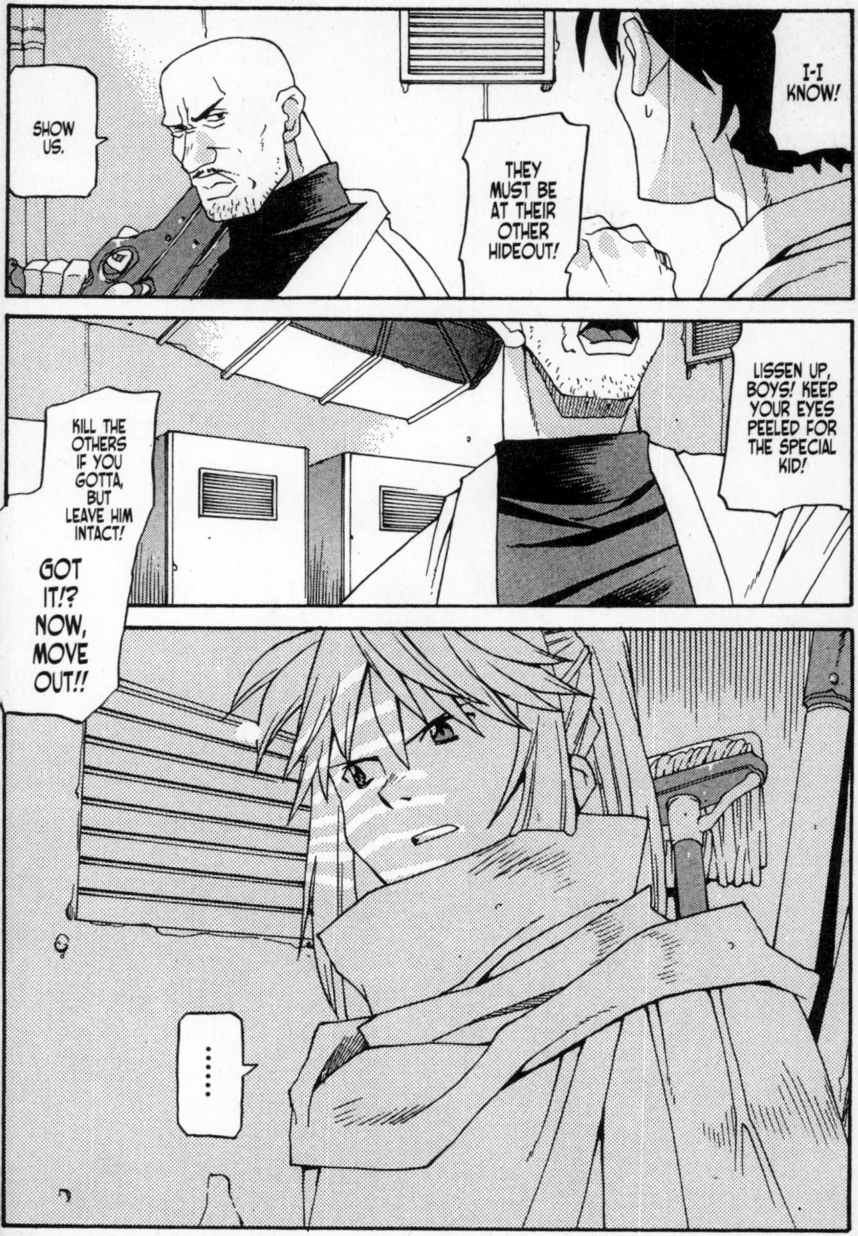
I-I KNOW!
THEY MUST BE AT THEIR OTHER HIDEOUT!
SHOW US.
LISSEN UP, BOYS! KEEP YOUR EYES PEELED FOR THE SPECIAL KID!
KILL THE OTHERS IF YOU GOTTA, BUT LEAVE HIM INTACT!
GOT IT!? NOW, MOVE OUT!!
......

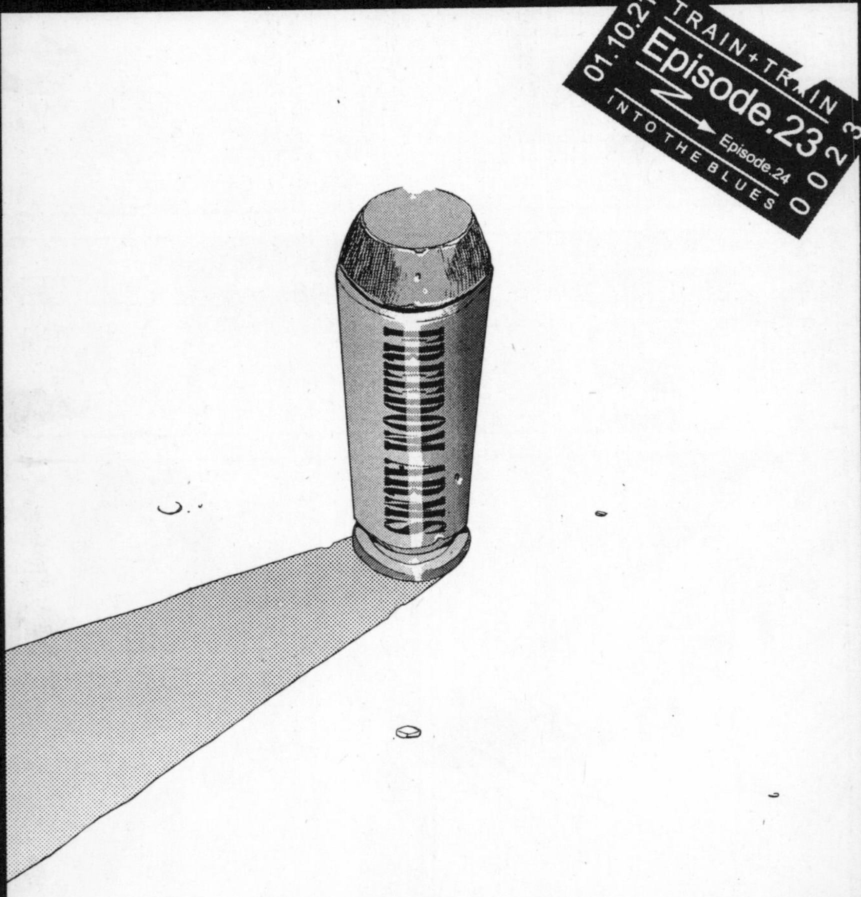

01.10.21
TRAIN+TRAIN
Episode.23
Episode.24
INTO THE BLUES
0023

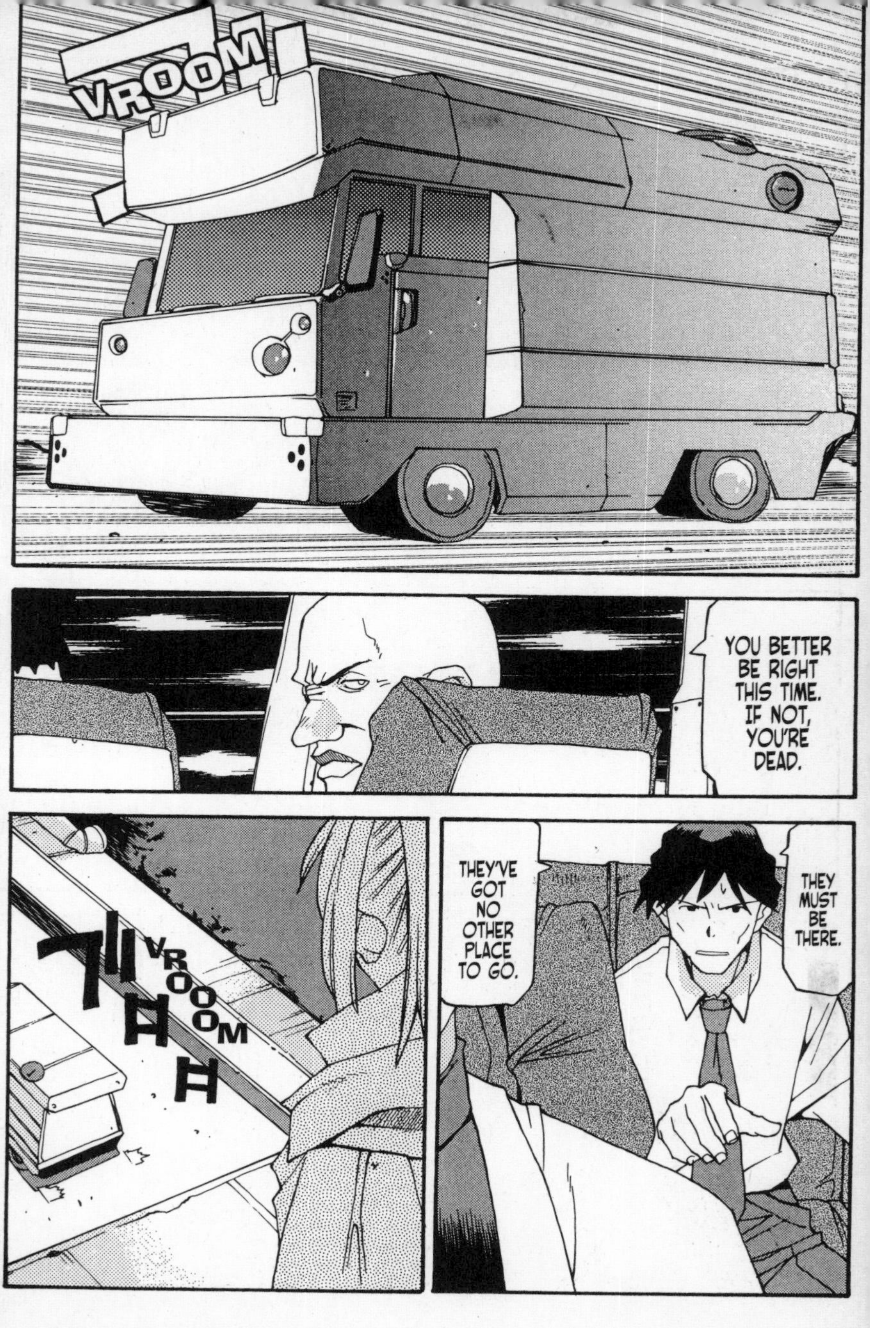
VROOM
YOU BETTER BE RIGHT THIS TIME. IF NOT, YOU'RE DEAD.
THEY MUST BE THERE.
THEY'VE GOT NO OTHER PLACE TO GO.
VROOOOM

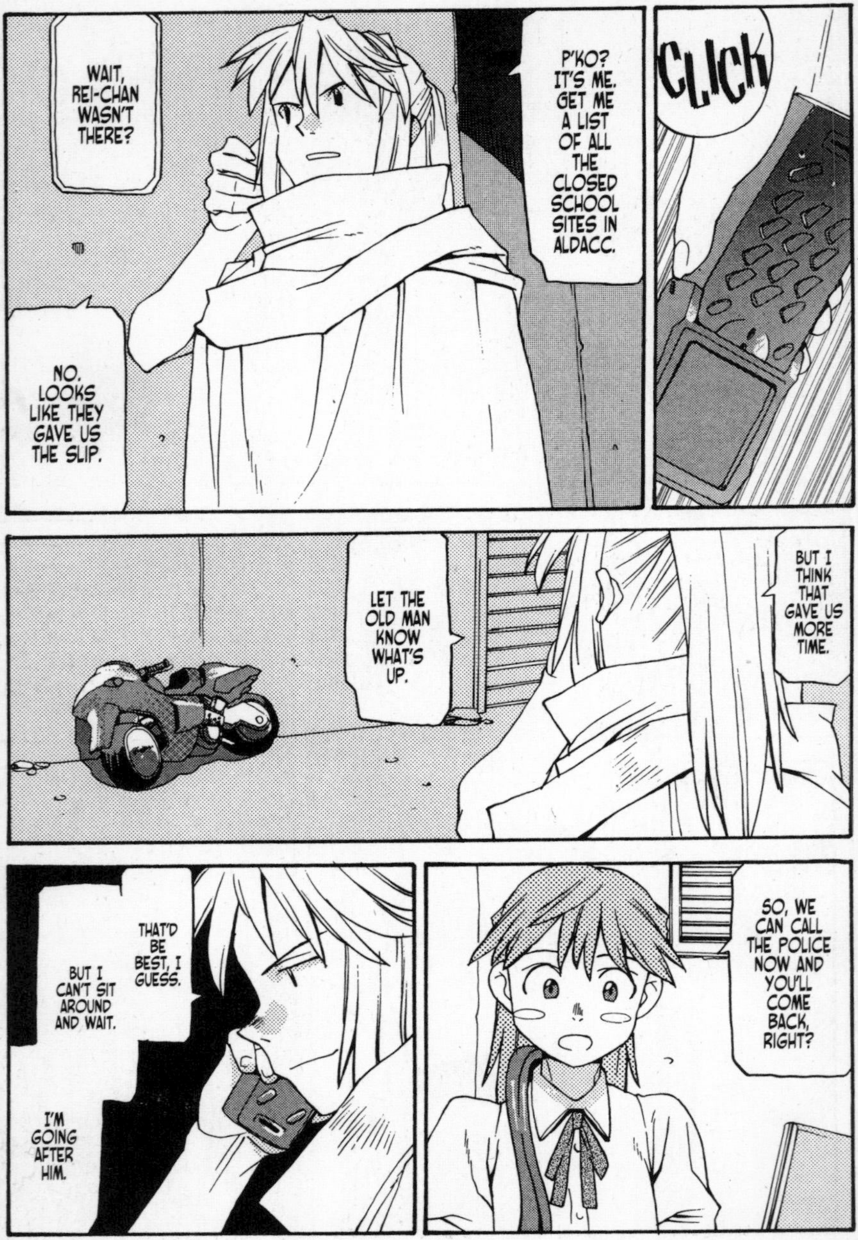
CLICK
P'KO? IT'S ME. GET ME A LIST OF ALL THE CLOSED SCHOOL SITES IN ALDACC.
WAIT, REI-CHAN WASN'T THERE?
NO. LOOKS LIKE THEY GAVE US THE SLIP.
BUT I THINK THAT GAVE US MORE TIME.
LET THE OLD MAN KNOW WHAT'S UP.
SO, WE CAN CALL THE POLICE NOW AND YOU'LL COME BACK, RIGHT?
THAT'D BE BEST, I GUESS.
BUT I CAN'T SIT AROUND AND WAIT.
I'M GOING AFTER HIM.

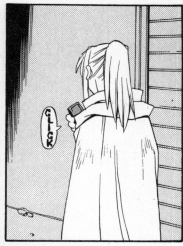

CLICK

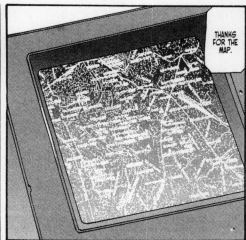

THANKS FOR THE MAP.

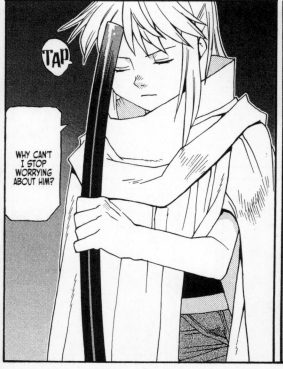

TAP

WHY CAN'T I STOP WORRYING ABOUT HIM?

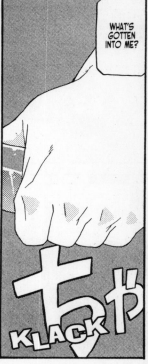

WHAT'S GOTTEN INTO ME?

KLACK

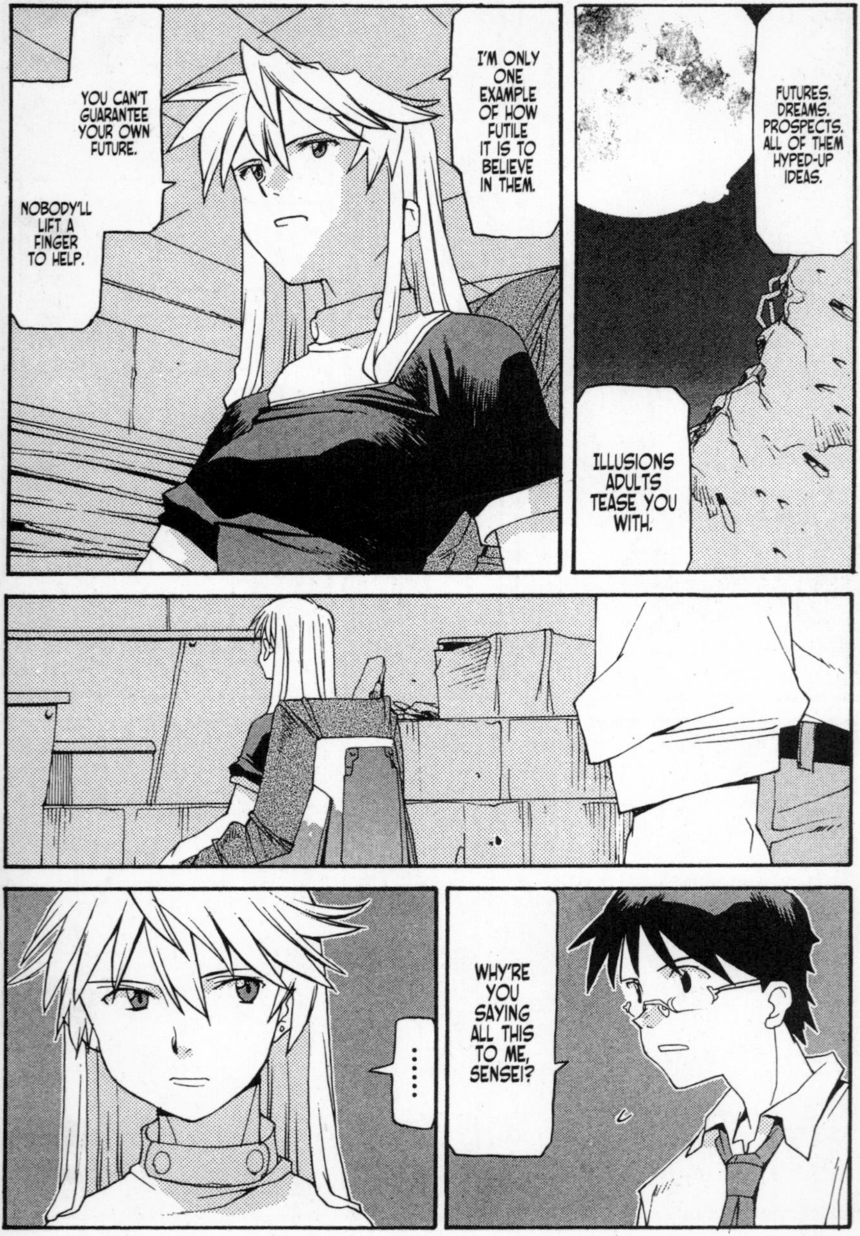
FUTURES. DREAMS. PROSPECTS. ALL OF THEM HYPED-UP IDEAS.
ILLUSIONS ADULTS TEASE YOU WITH.
I'M ONLY ONE EXAMPLE OF HOW FUTILE IT IS TO BELIEVE IN THEM.
YOU CAN'T GUARANTEE YOUR OWN FUTURE.
NOBODY'LL LIFT A FINGER TO HELP.
WHY'RE YOU SAYING ALL THIS TO ME, SENSEI?
......

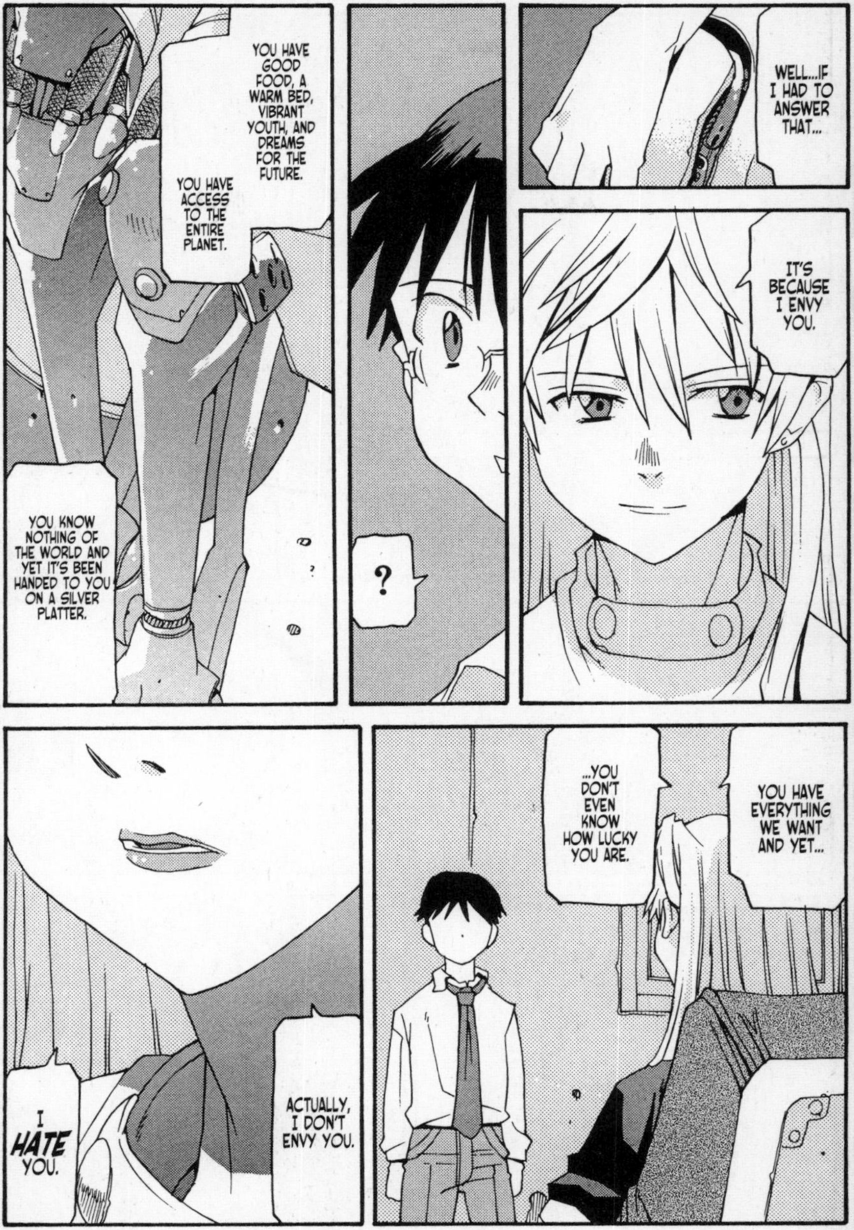
WELL...IF I HAD TO ANSWER THAT...
IT'S BECAUSE I ENVY YOU.
?
YOU HAVE GOOD FOOD, A WARM BED, VIBRANT YOUTH, AND DREAMS FOR THE FUTURE.
YOU HAVE ACCESS TO THE ENTIRE PLANET.
YOU KNOW NOTHING OF THE WORLD AND YET IT'S BEEN HANDED TO YOU ON A SILVER PLATTER.
YOU HAVE EVERYTHING WE WANT AND YET...
...YOU DON'T EVEN KNOW HOW LUCKY YOU ARE.
ACTUALLY, I DON'T ENVY YOU.
I **HATE** YOU.

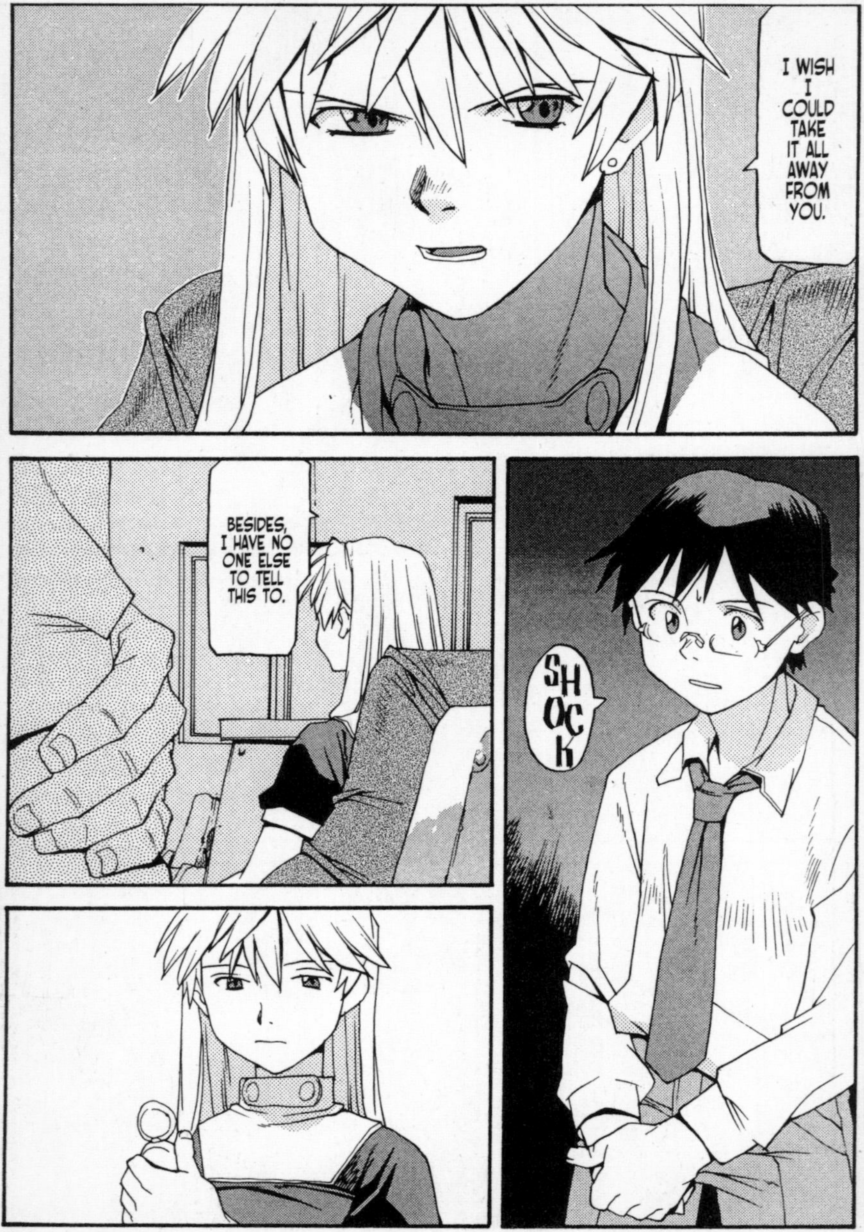
I WISH I COULD TAKE IT ALL AWAY FROM YOU.
SHOCK
BESIDES, I HAVE NO ONE ELSE TO TELL THIS TO.

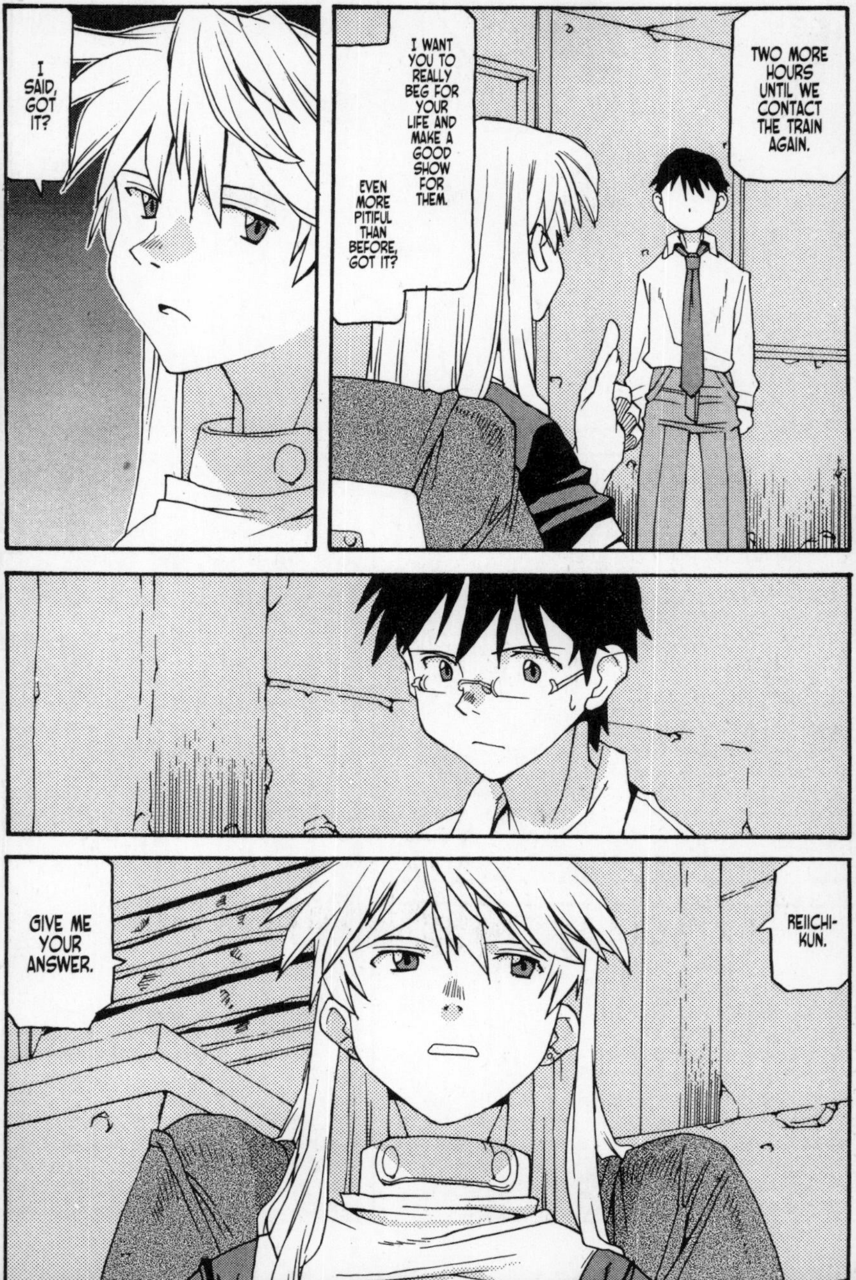
TWO MORE HOURS UNTIL WE CONTACT THE TRAIN AGAIN.
I WANT YOU TO REALLY BEG FOR YOUR LIFE AND MAKE A GOOD SHOW FOR THEM.
EVEN MORE PITIFUL THAN BEFORE, GOT IT?
I SAID, GOT IT?
REIICHI-KUN.
GIVE ME YOUR ANSWER.

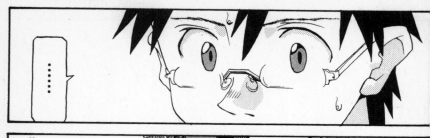

. . . . .

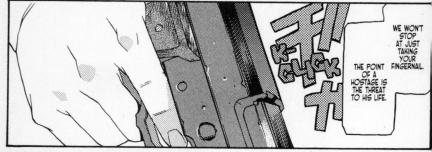

THE POINT OF A HOSTAGE IS THE THREAT TO HIS LIFE.

WE WON'T STOP AT JUST TAKING YOUR FINGERNAIL.

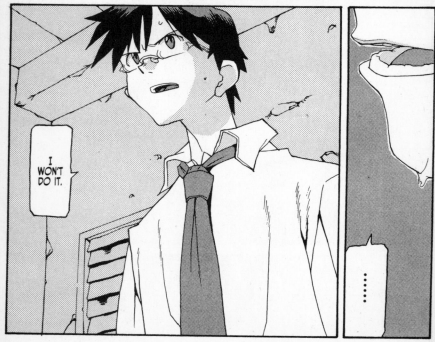

I WON'T DO IT.

. . . . .

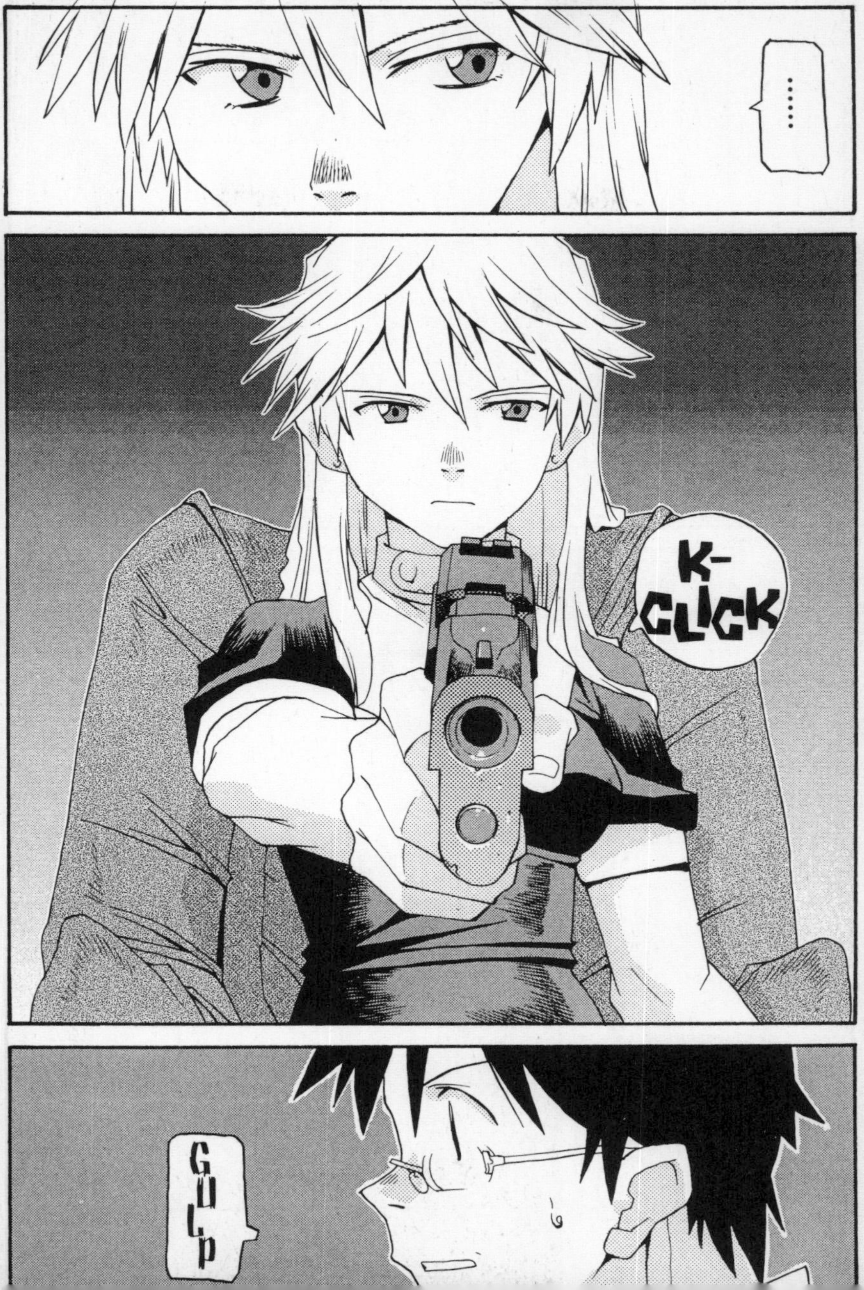
......
K-CLICK
GULP

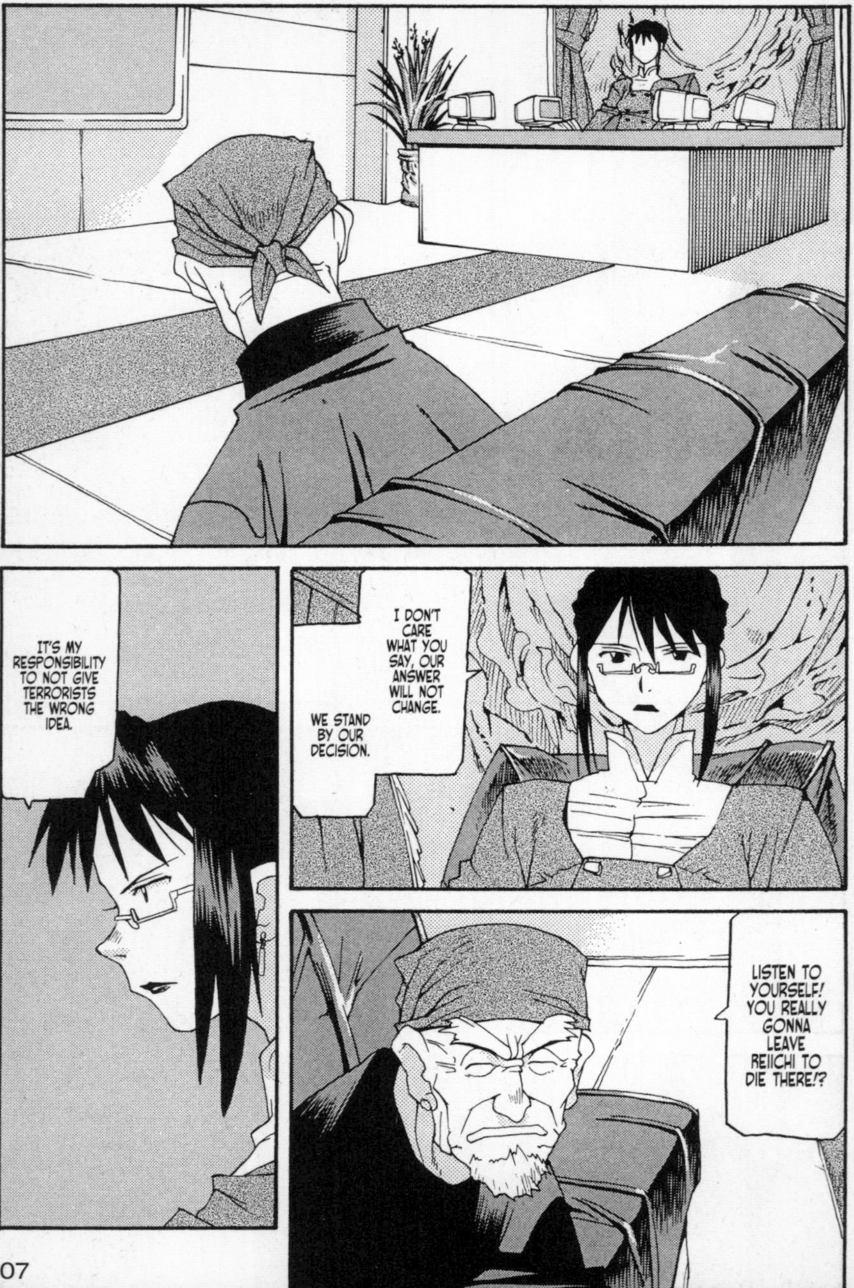
I DON'T CARE WHAT YOU SAY, OUR ANSWER WILL NOT CHANGE.
WE STAND BY OUR DECISION.
LISTEN TO YOURSELF! YOU REALLY GONNA LEAVE REIICHI TO DIE THERE!?
IT'S MY RESPONSIBILITY TO NOT GIVE TERRORISTS THE WRONG IDEA.

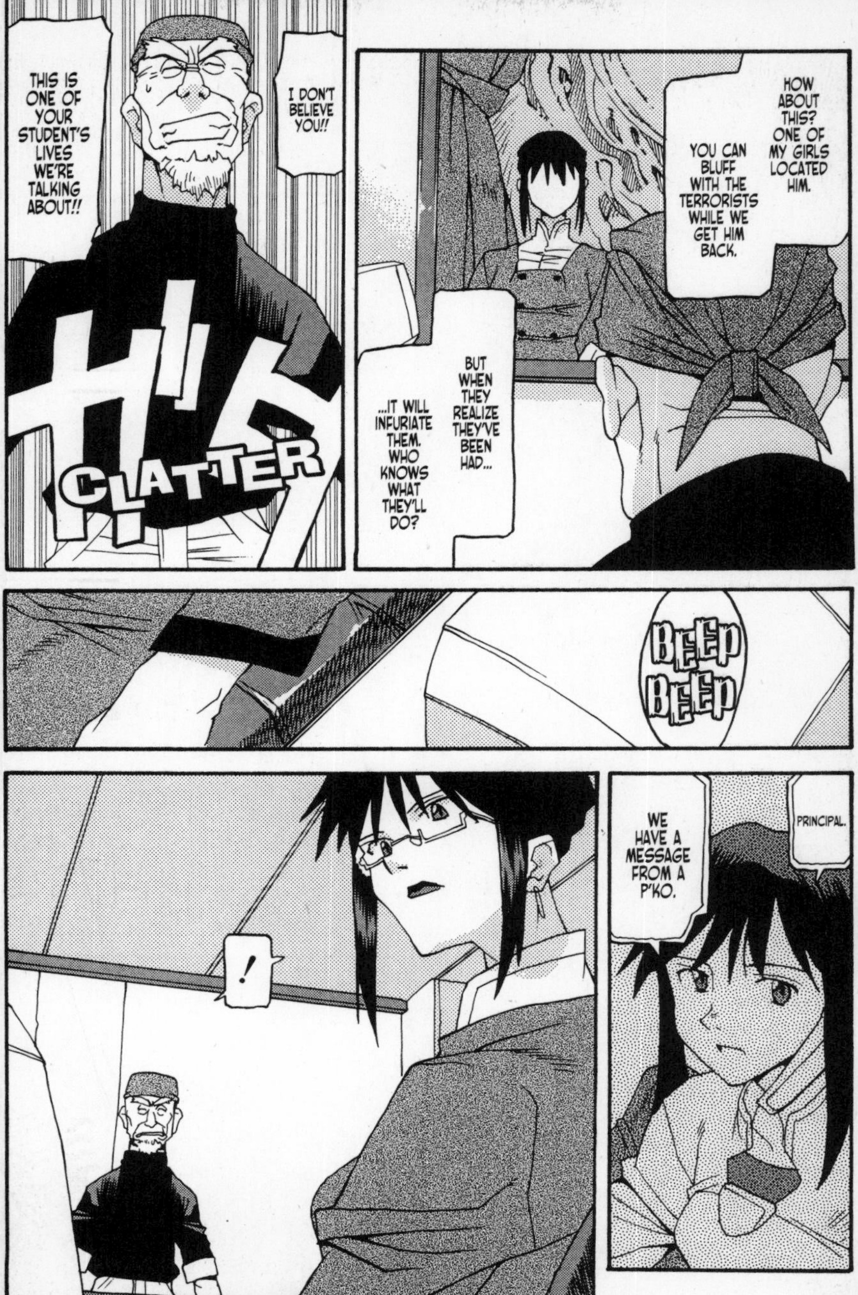
HOW ABOUT THIS? ONE OF MY GIRLS LOCATED HIM.
YOU CAN BLUFF WITH THE TERRORISTS WHILE WE GET HIM BACK.
BUT WHEN THEY REALIZE THEY'VE BEEN HAD...
...IT WILL INFURIATE THEM. WHO KNOWS WHAT THEY'LL DO?
I DON'T BELIEVE YOU!!
THIS IS ONE OF YOUR STUDENT'S LIVES WE'RE TALKING ABOUT!!
CLATTER
BEEP BEEP
PRINCIPAL.
WE HAVE A MESSAGE FROM A P'KO.
!

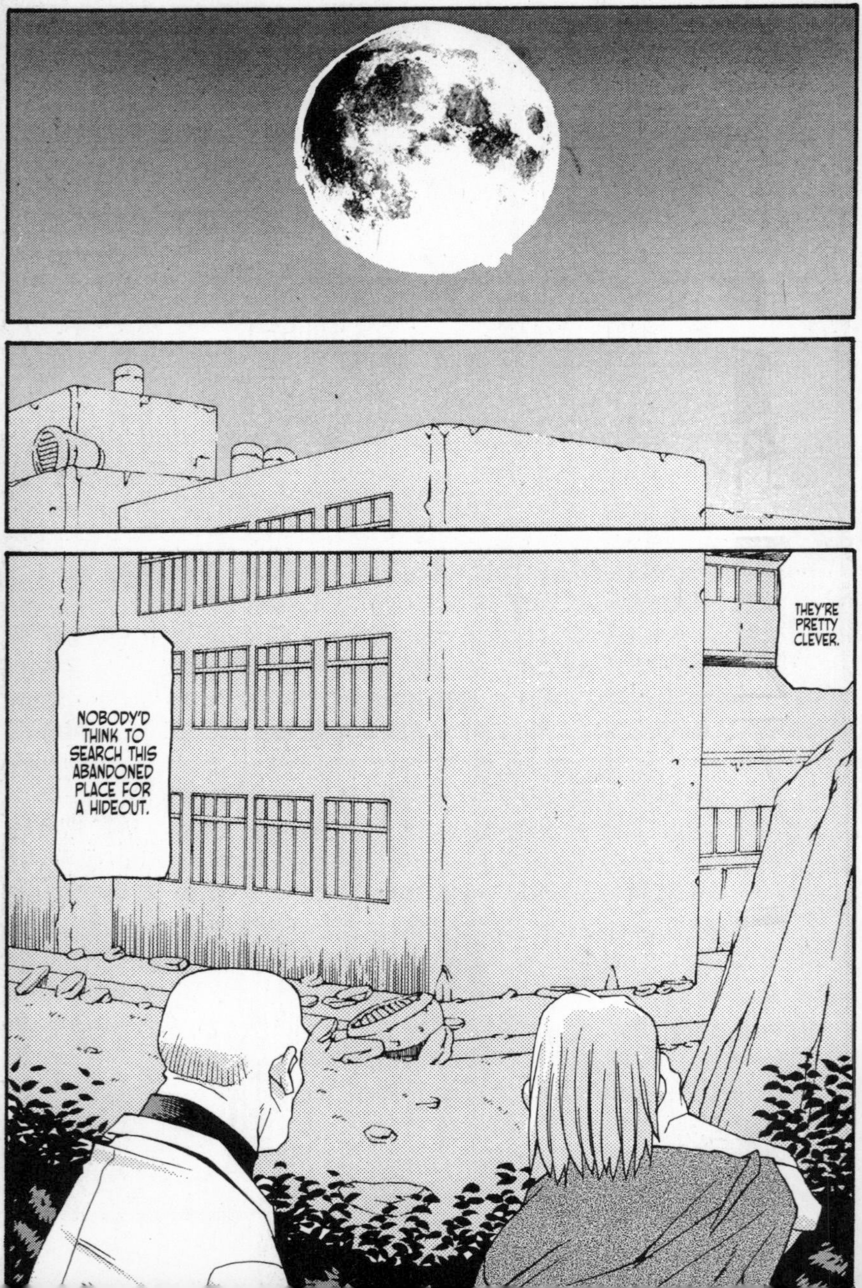
THEY'RE PRETTY CLEVER.
NOBODY'D THINK TO SEARCH THIS ABANDONED PLACE FOR A HIDEOUT.

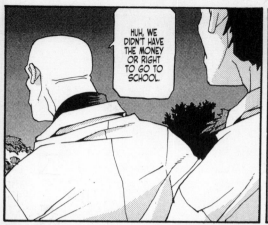

HUH, WE DIDN'T HAVE THE MONEY OR RIGHT TO GO TO SCHOOL.

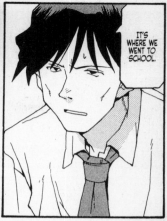

IT'S WHERE WE WENT TO SCHOOL.

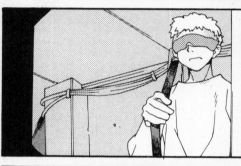

I SPOTTED A KID. MUST BE A LOOKOUT.

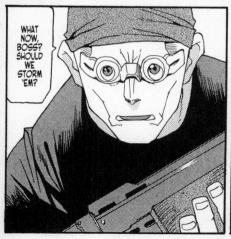

WHAT NOW, BOSS? SHOULD WE STORM 'EM?

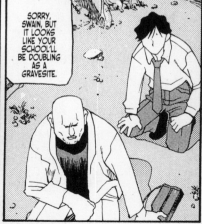

SORRY, SWAIN, BUT IT LOOKS LIKE YOUR SCHOOL'LL BE DOUBLING AS A GRAVESITE.

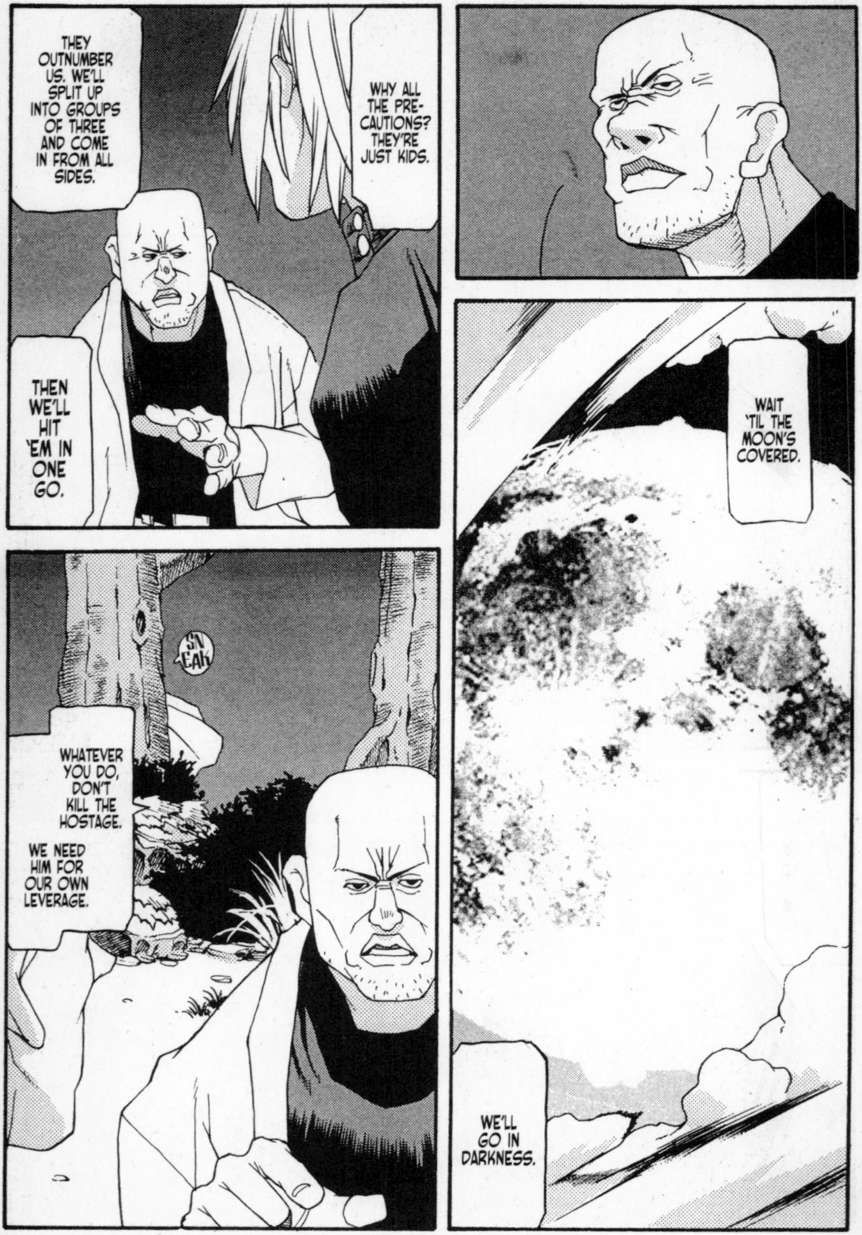
THEY OUTNUMBER US. WE'LL SPLIT UP INTO GROUPS OF THREE AND COME IN FROM ALL SIDES.
WHY ALL THE PRE-CAUTIONS? THEY'RE JUST KIDS.
THEN WE'LL HIT 'EM IN ONE GO.
SNEAK
WHATEVER YOU DO, DON'T KILL THE HOSTAGE.
WE NEED HIM FOR OUR OWN LEVERAGE.
WAIT 'TIL THE MOON'S COVERED.
WE'LL GO IN DARKNESS.

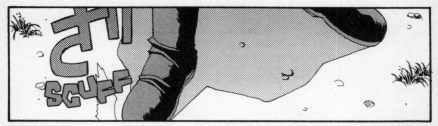

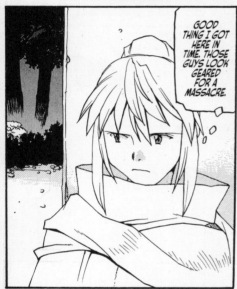

GOOD THING I GOT HERE IN TIME. THOSE GUYS LOOK GEARED FOR A MASSACRE.

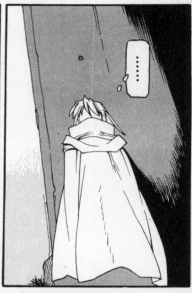

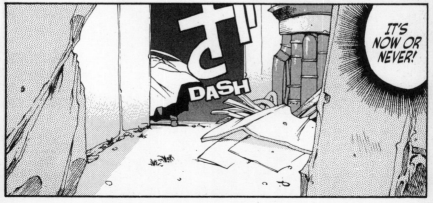

IT'S NOW OR NEVER!

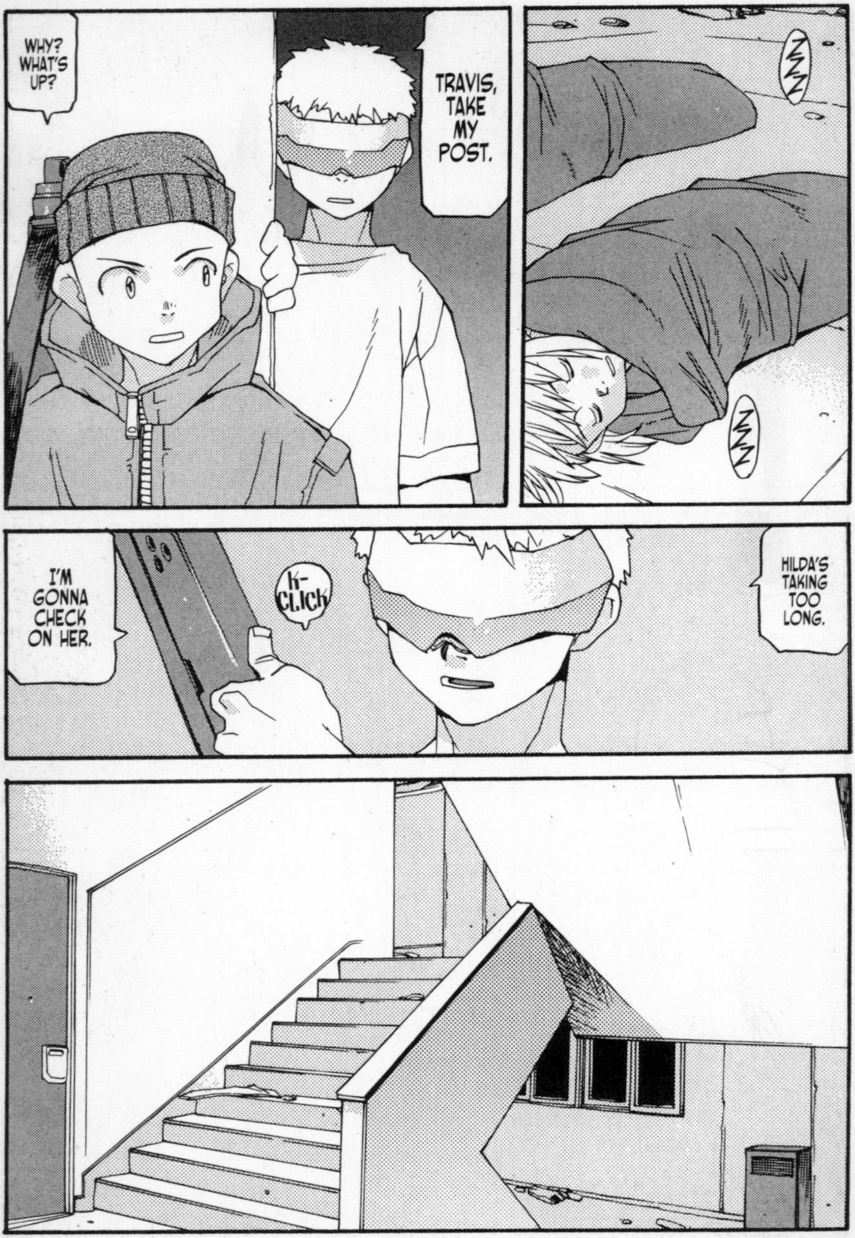
ZZZ
ZZZ
TRAVIS, TAKE MY POST.
WHY? WHAT'S UP?
HILDA'S TAKING TOO LONG.
K-CLICK
I'M GONNA CHECK ON HER.

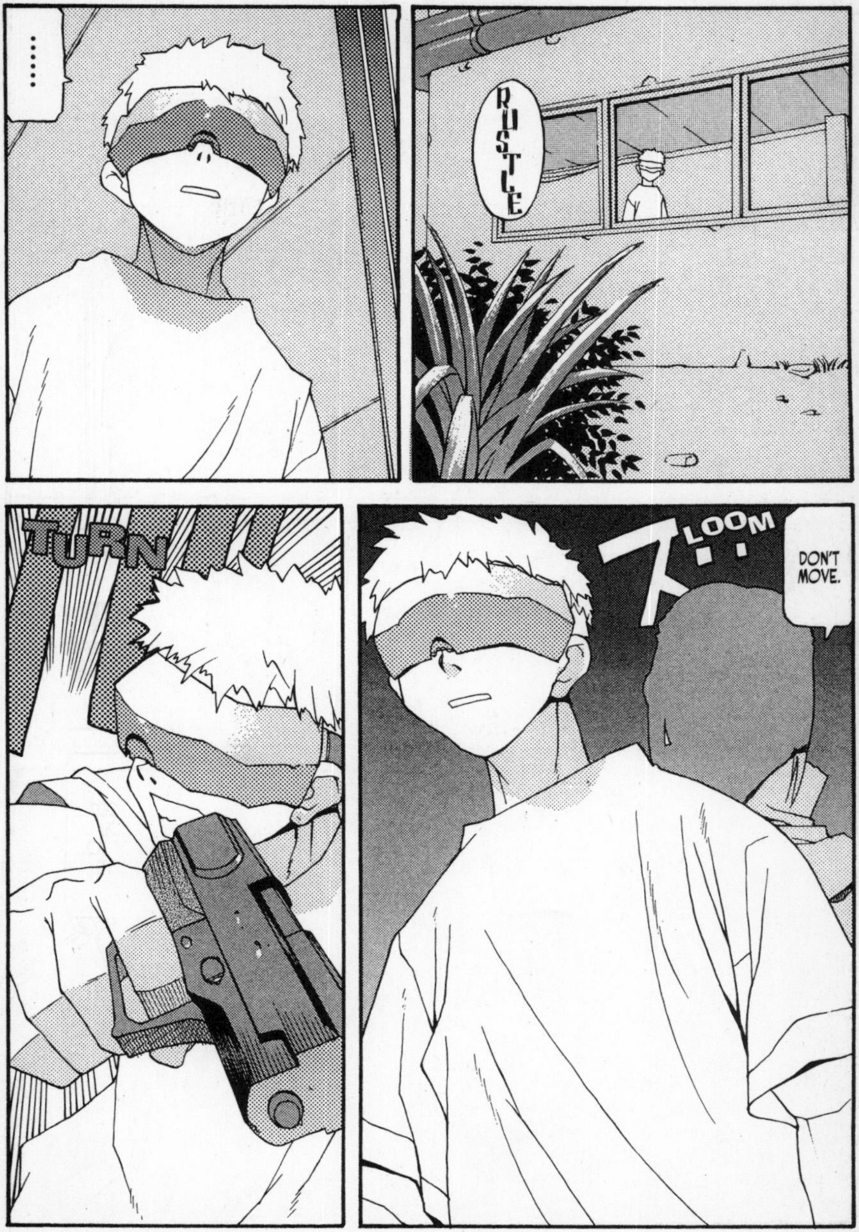
RUSTLE
......
ZLOOM
DON'T MOVE.
TURN

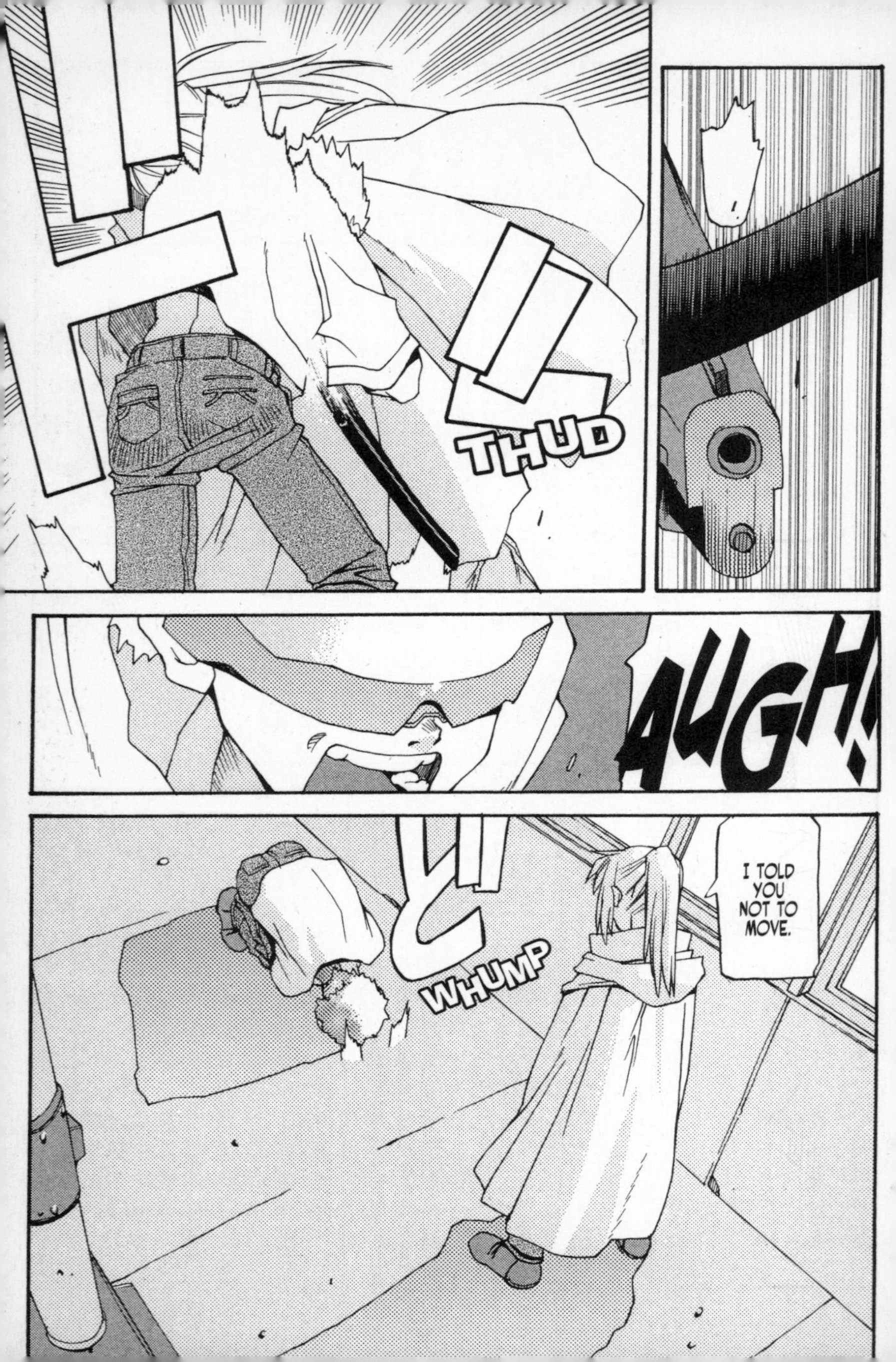
THUD
AUGH!!
I TOLD YOU NOT TO MOVE.
WHUMP

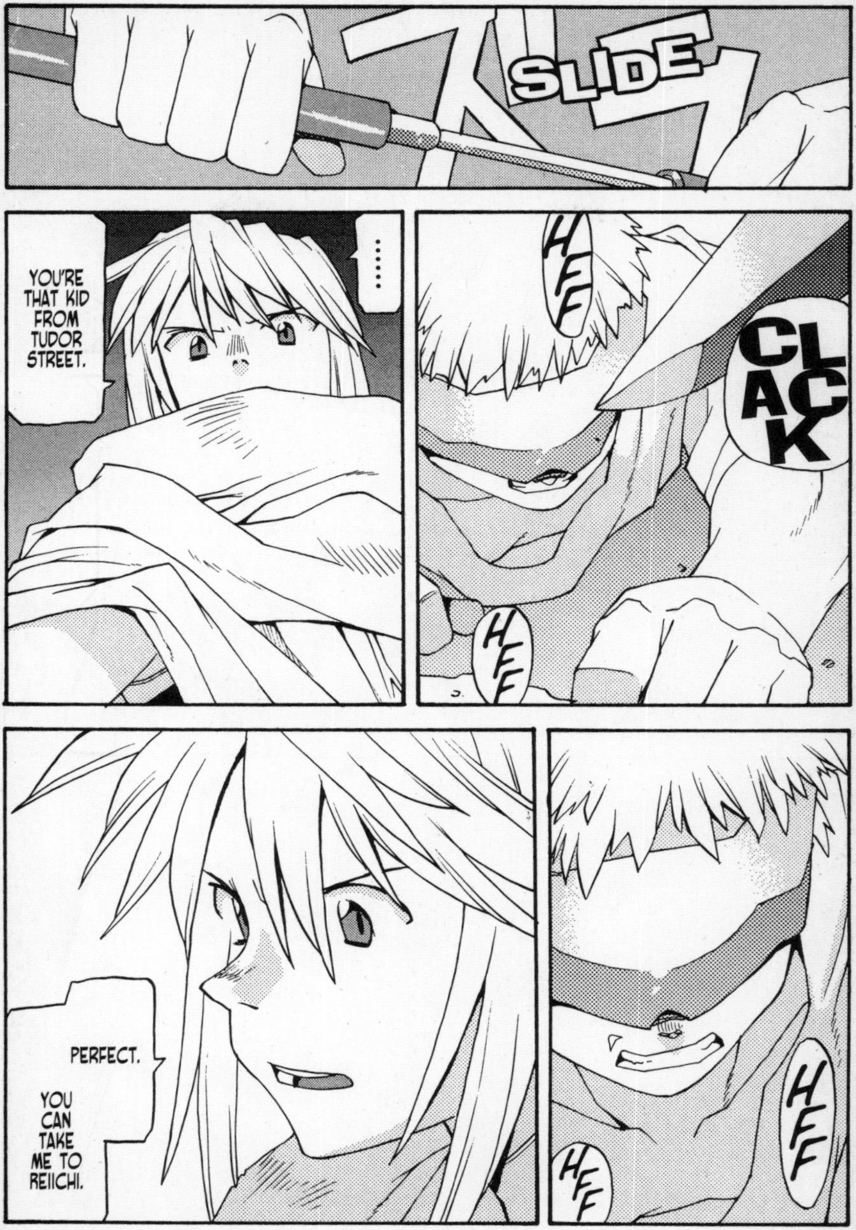
SLIDE
HFF
CLACK
HFF
......
YOU'RE THAT KID FROM TUDOR STREET.
HFF
HFF
PERFECT.
YOU CAN TAKE ME TO REIICHI.

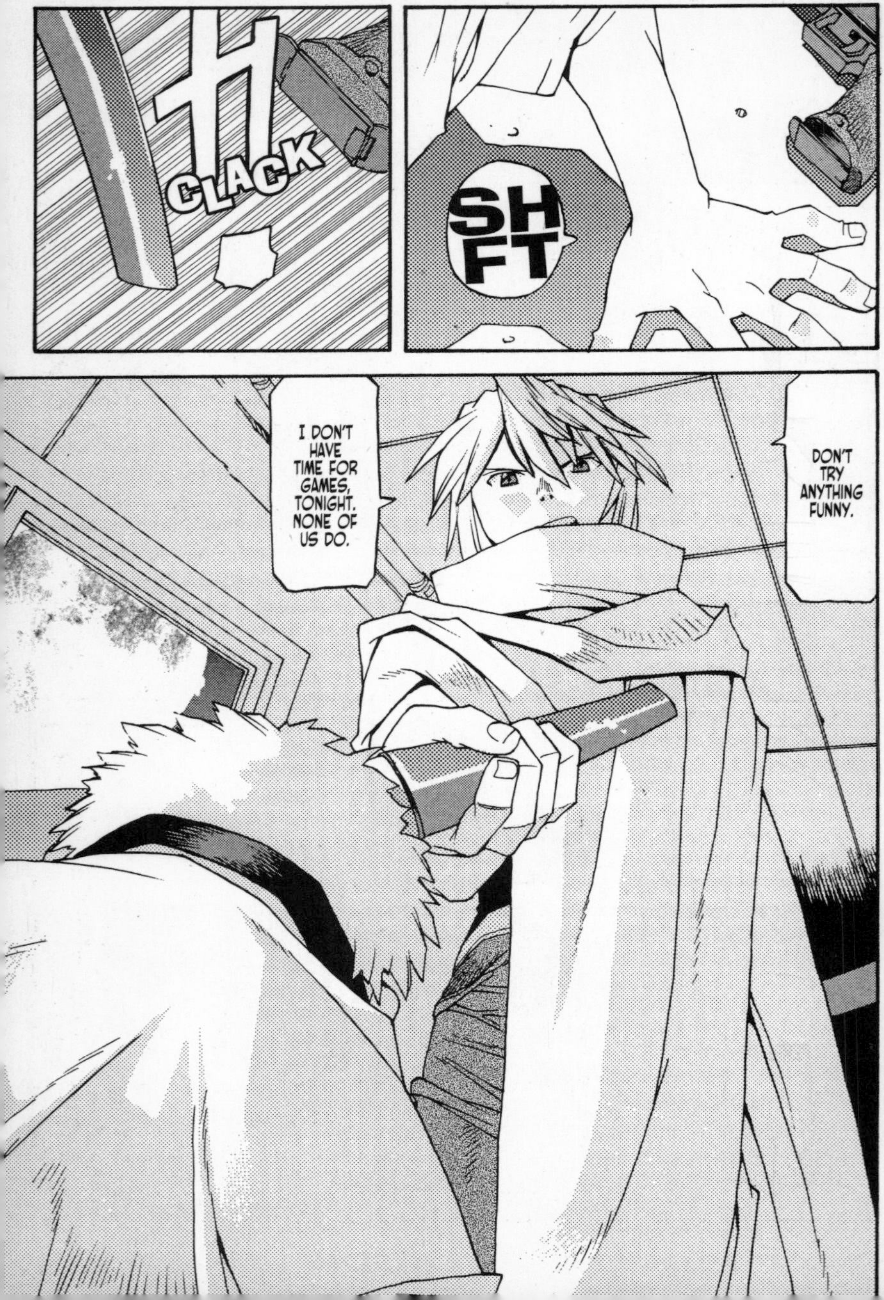

SHFT
CLACK
DON'T TRY ANYTHING FUNNY.
I DON'T HAVE TIME FOR GAMES, TONIGHT. NONE OF US DO.

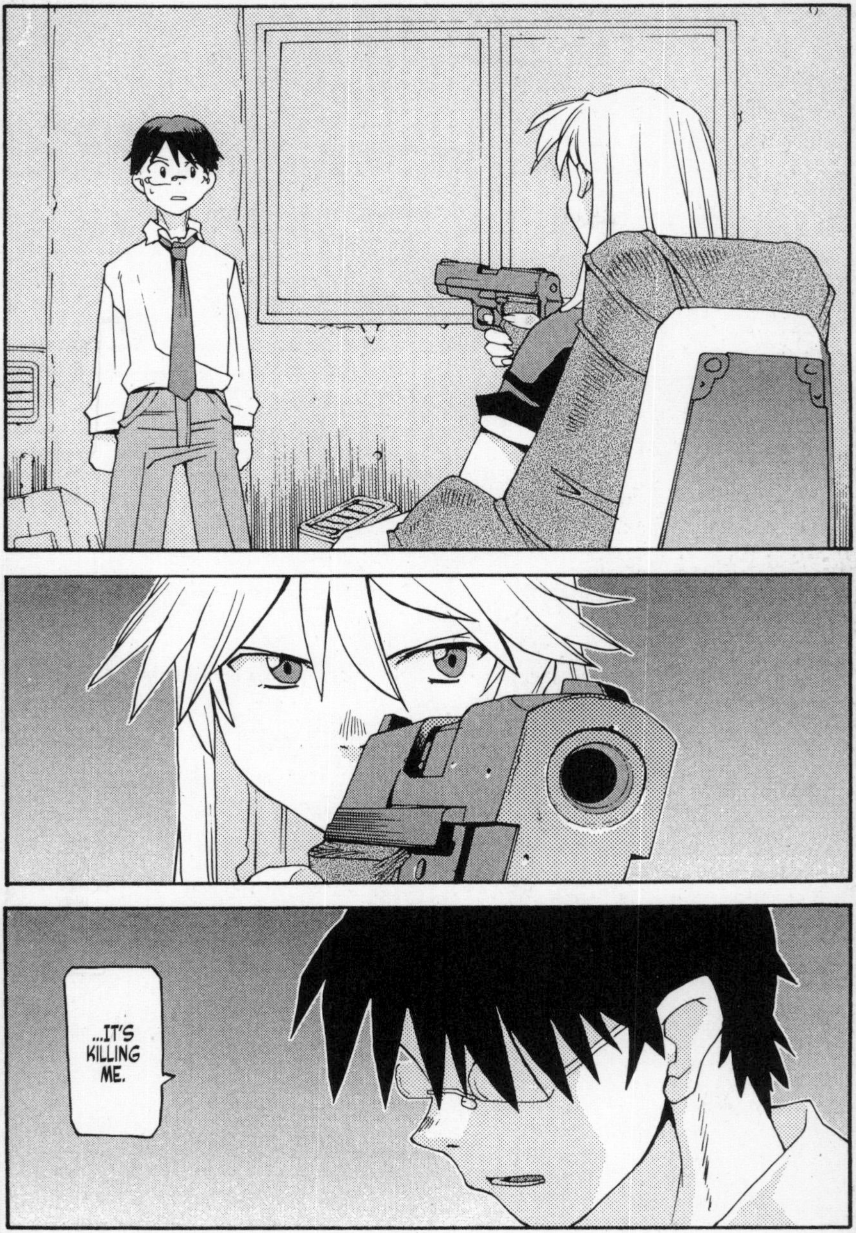
...IT'S KILLING ME.

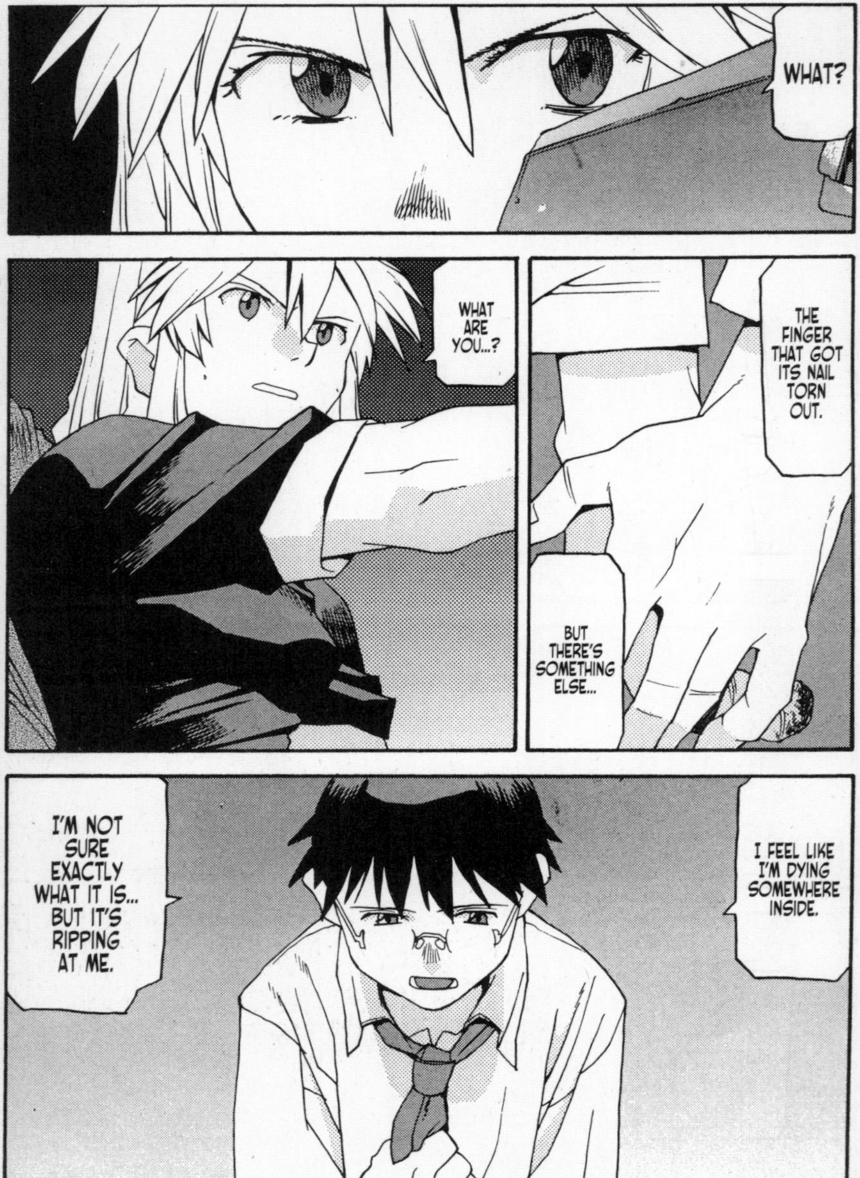
WHAT?
THE FINGER THAT GOT ITS NAIL TORN OUT.
BUT THERE'S SOMETHING ELSE...
WHAT ARE YOU...?
I FEEL LIKE I'M DYING SOMEWHERE INSIDE.
I'M NOT SURE EXACTLY WHAT IT IS... BUT IT'S RIPPING AT ME.

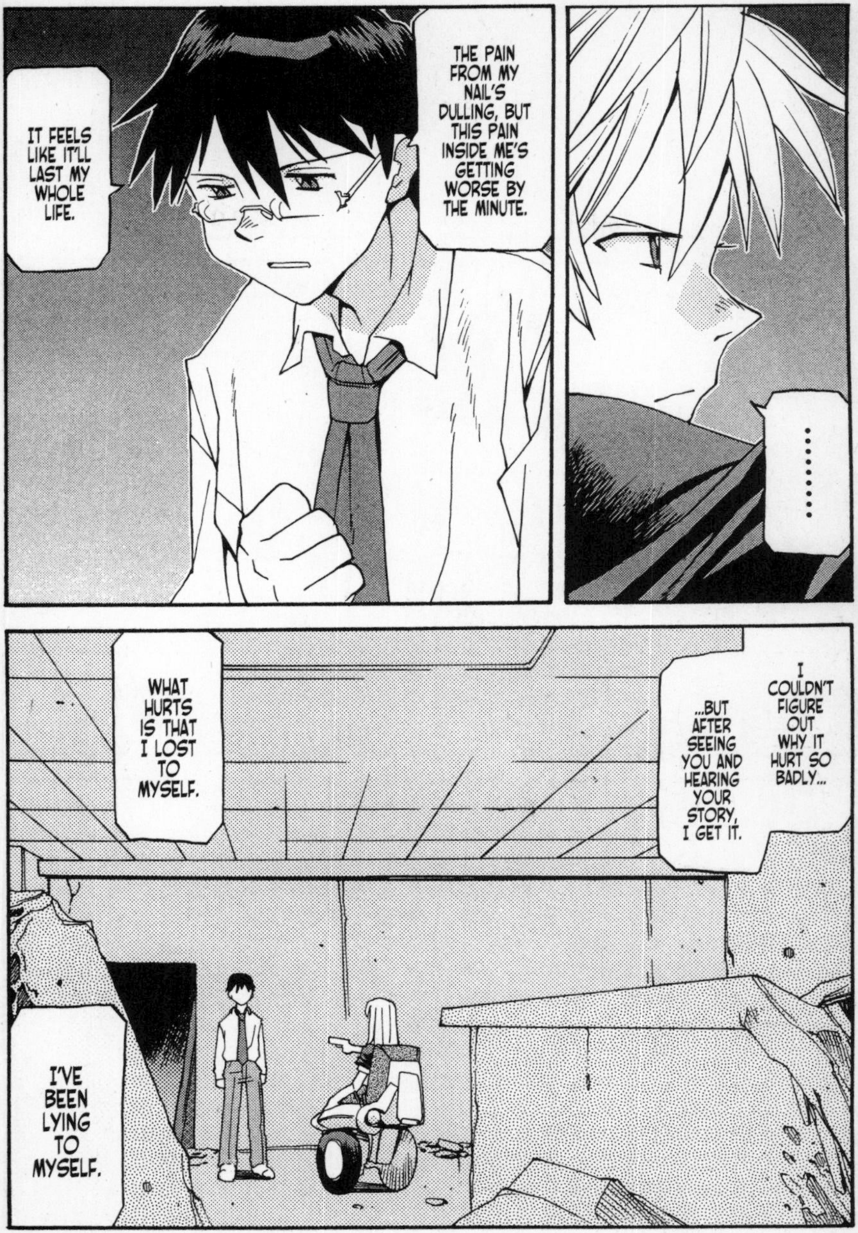
........
THE PAIN FROM MY NAIL'S DULLING, BUT THIS PAIN INSIDE ME'S GETTING WORSE BY THE MINUTE.
IT FEELS LIKE IT'LL LAST MY WHOLE LIFE.
I COULDN'T FIGURE OUT WHY IT HURT SO BADLY...
...BUT AFTER SEEING YOU AND HEARING YOUR STORY, I GET IT.
WHAT HURTS IS THAT I LOST TO MYSELF.
I'VE BEEN LYING TO MYSELF.

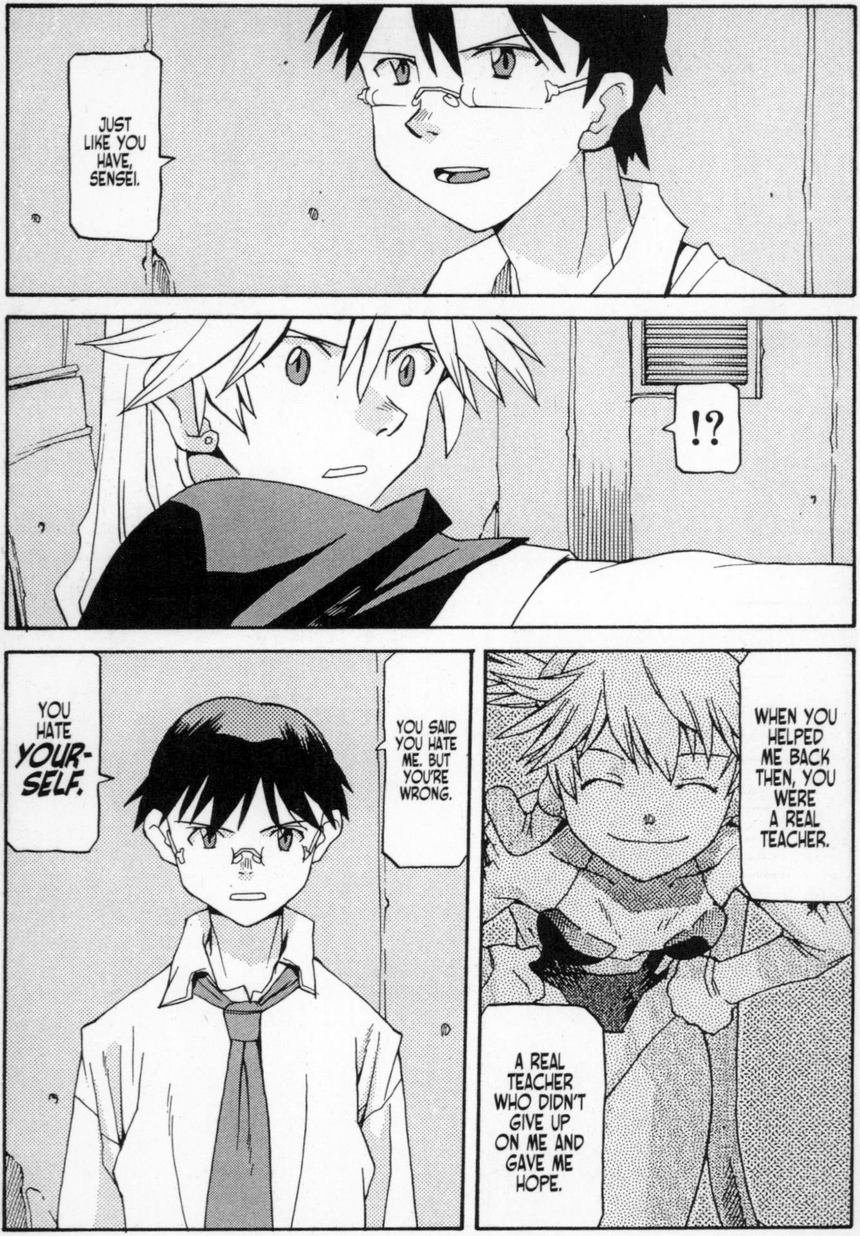
JUST LIKE YOU HAVE, SENSEI.
!?
WHEN YOU HELPED ME BACK THEN, YOU WERE A REAL TEACHER.
A REAL TEACHER WHO DIDN'T GIVE UP ON ME AND GAVE ME HOPE.
YOU SAID YOU HATE ME. BUT YOU'RE WRONG.
YOU HATE ***YOURSELF.***

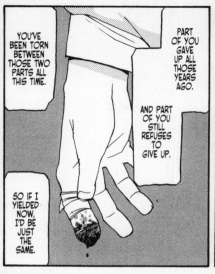

YOU'VE BEEN TORN BETWEEN THOSE TWO PARTS ALL THIS TIME.

PART OF YOU GAVE UP ALL THOSE YEARS AGO.

AND PART OF YOU STILL REFUSES TO GIVE UP.

SO IF I YIELDED NOW, I'D BE JUST THE SAME.

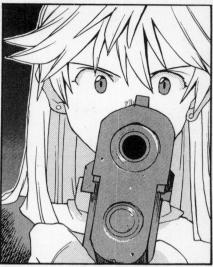

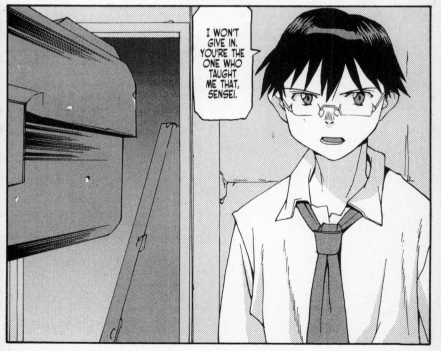

I WON'T GIVE IN. YOU'RE THE ONE WHO TAUGHT ME THAT, SENSEI.

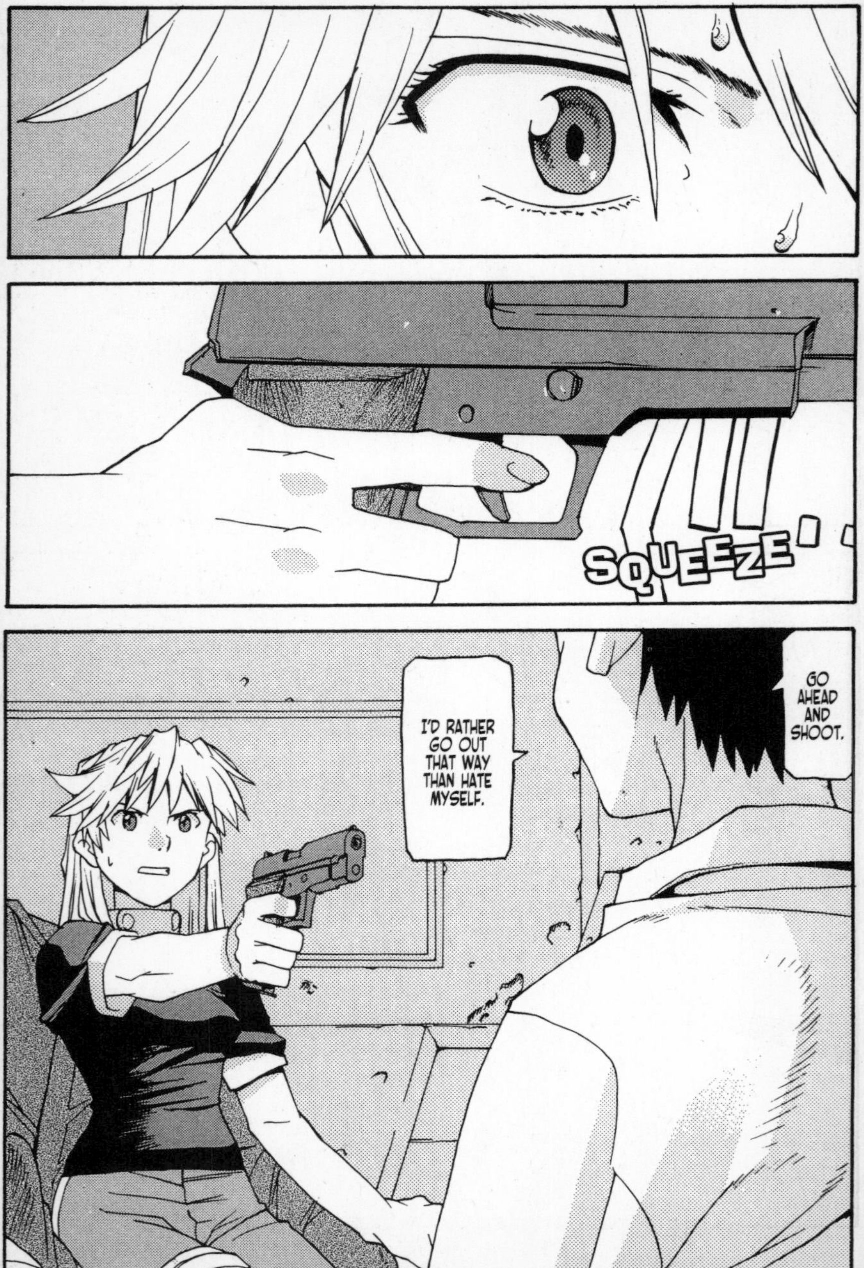
SQUEEZE...
GO AHEAD AND SHOOT.
I'D RATHER GO OUT THAT WAY THAN HATE MYSELF.

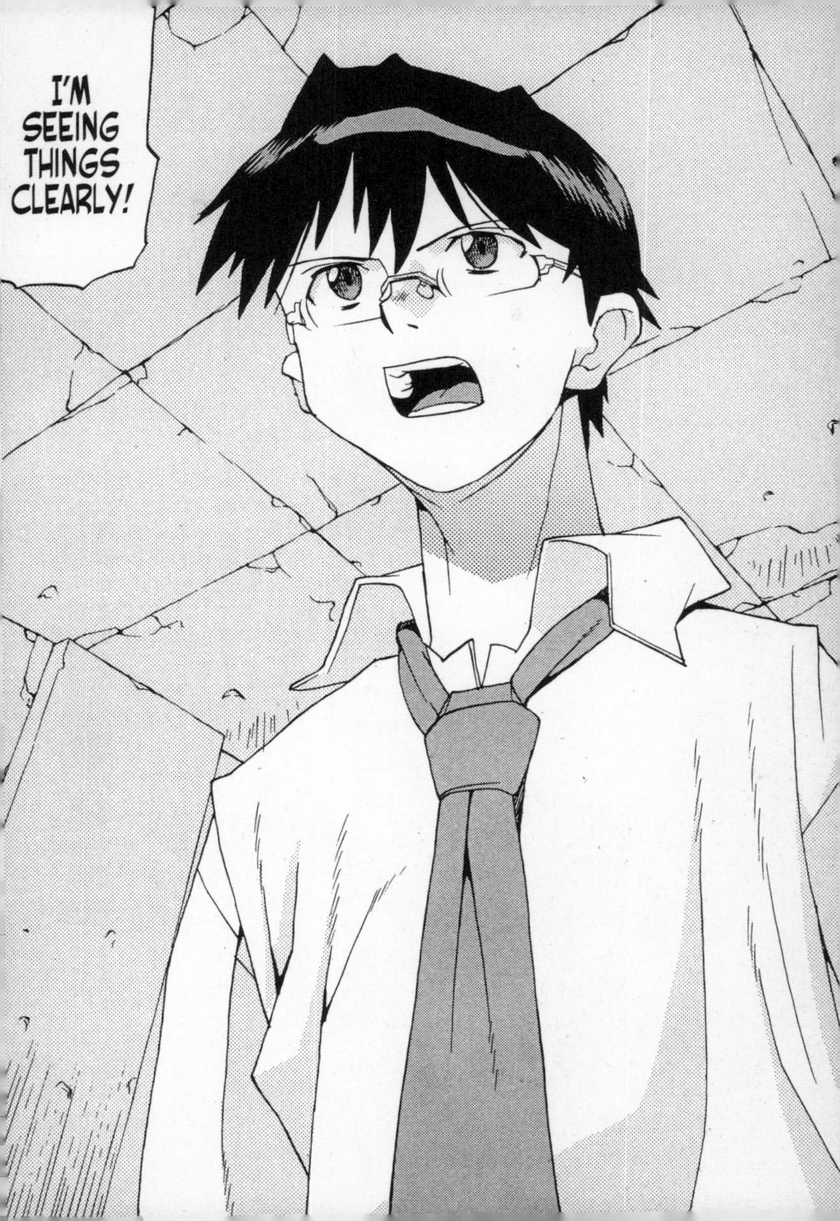
I'M SEEING THINGS CLEARLY!

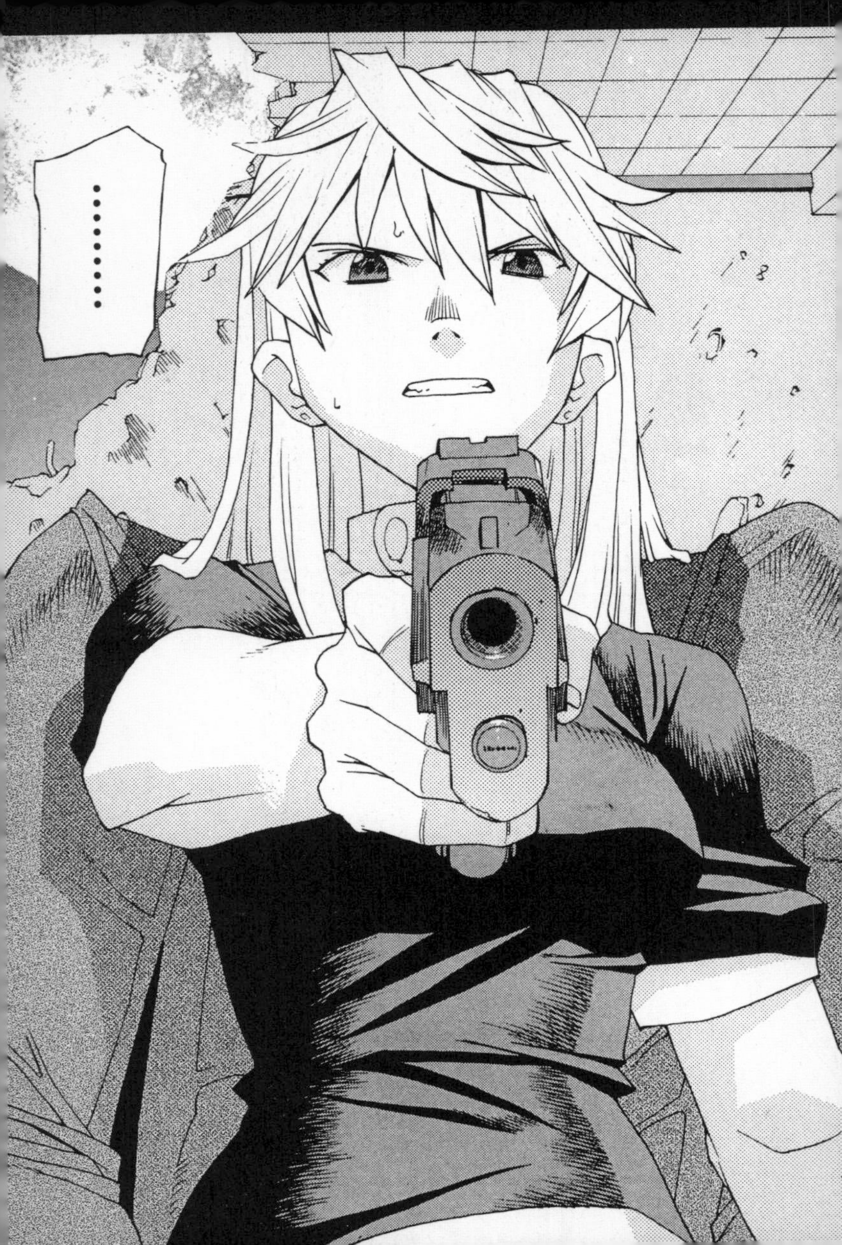
……

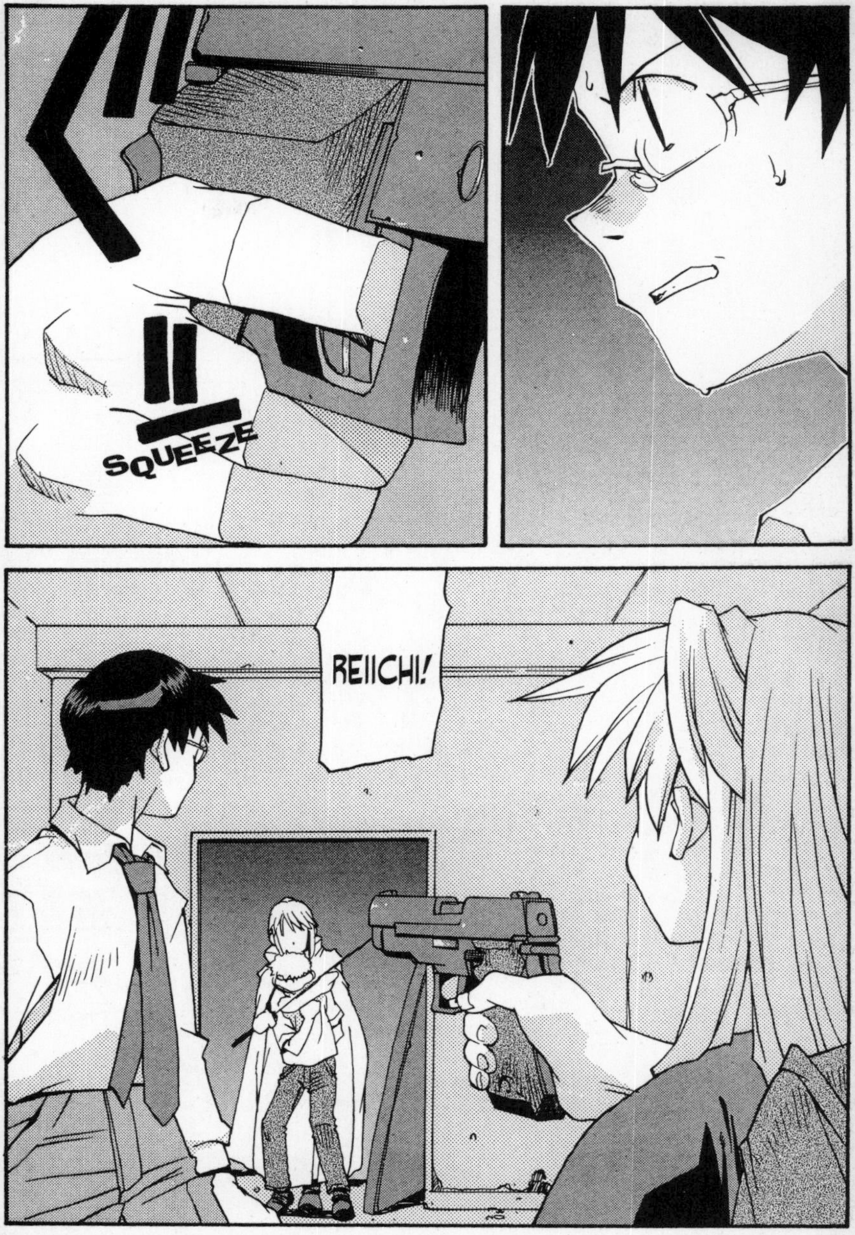
SQUEEZE
REIICHI!

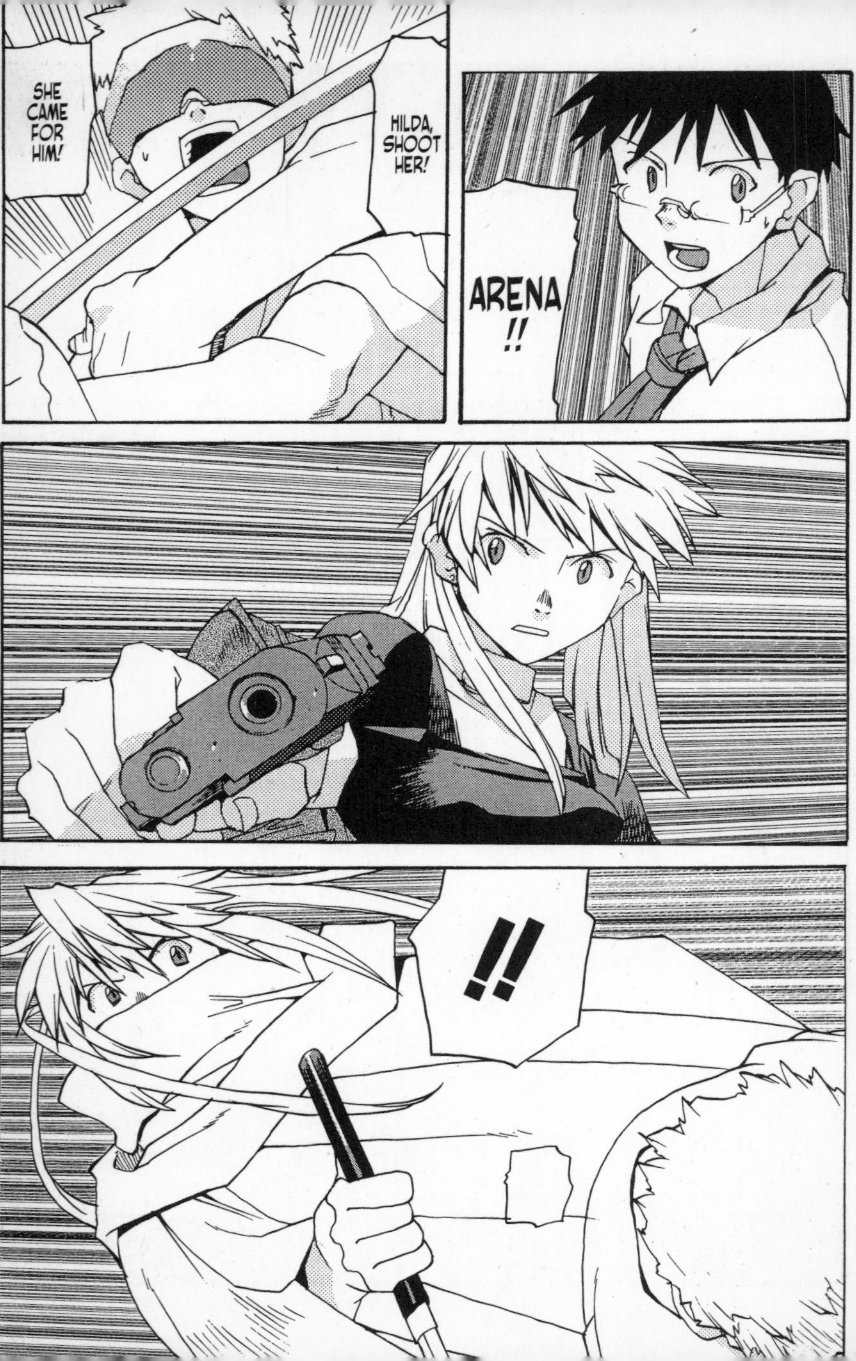
ARENA !!
HILDA, SHOOT HER!
SHE CAME FOR HIM!
!!

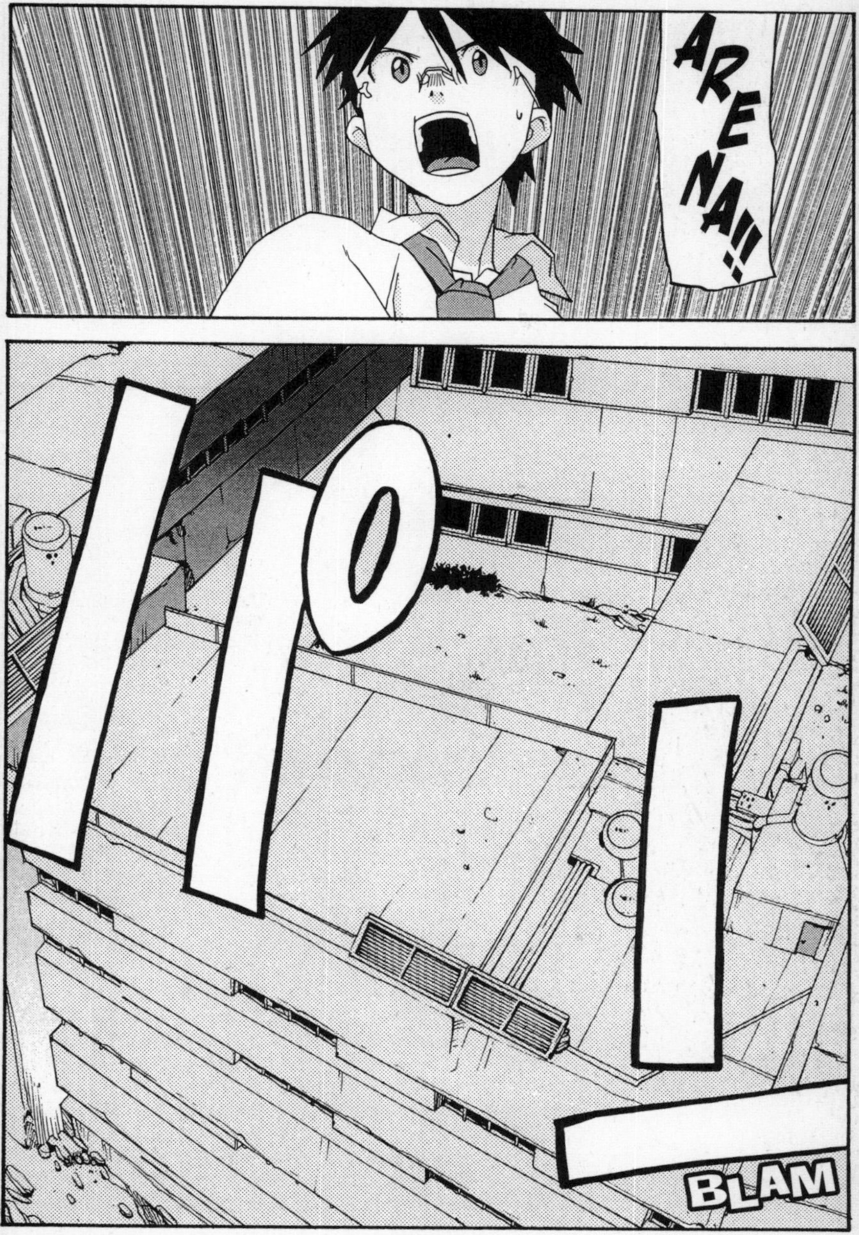
ARENA!!
BLAM

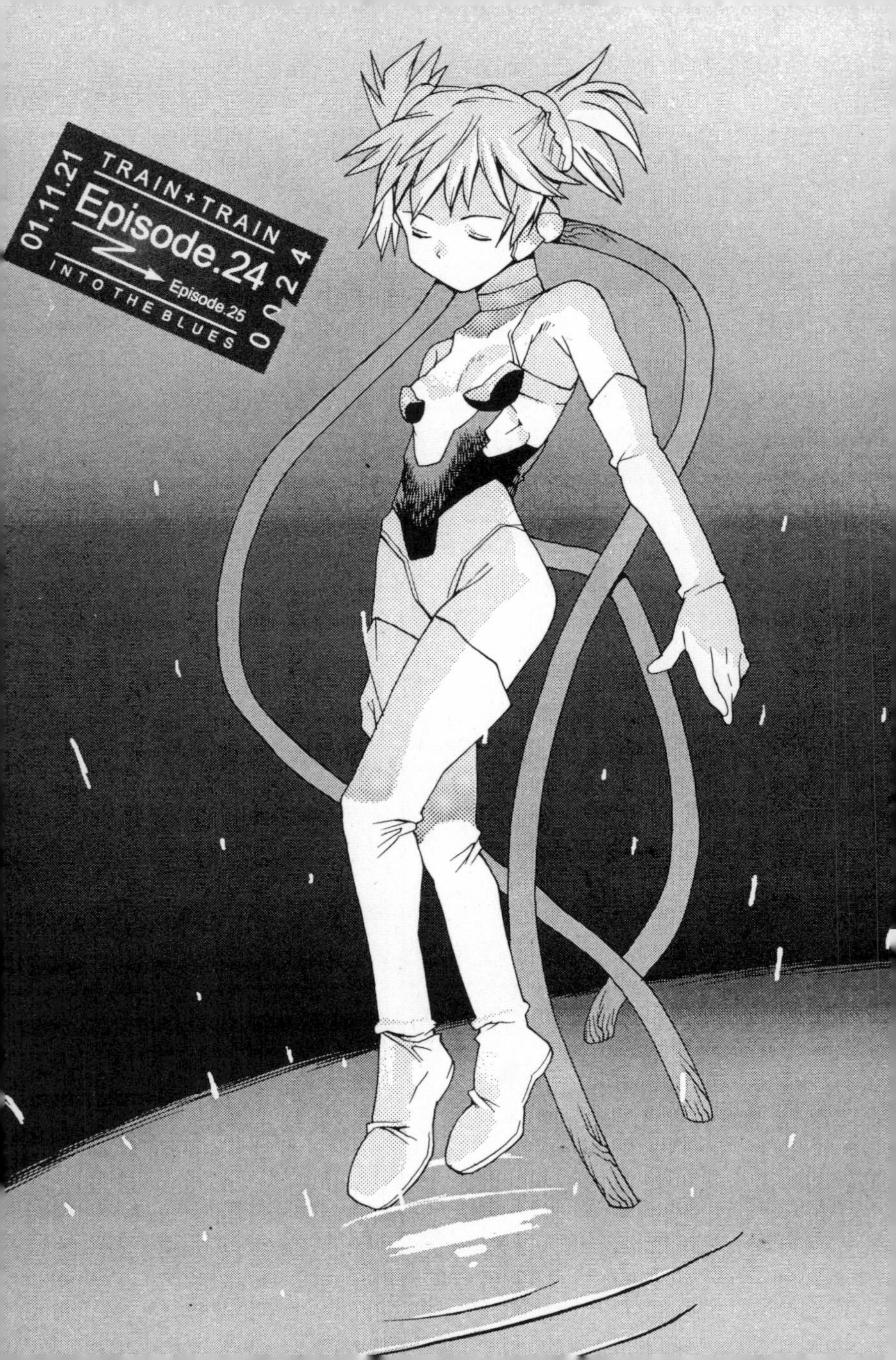
01.11.21
TRAIN+TRAIN
Episode.24
Episode.25
INTO THE BLUES
0024

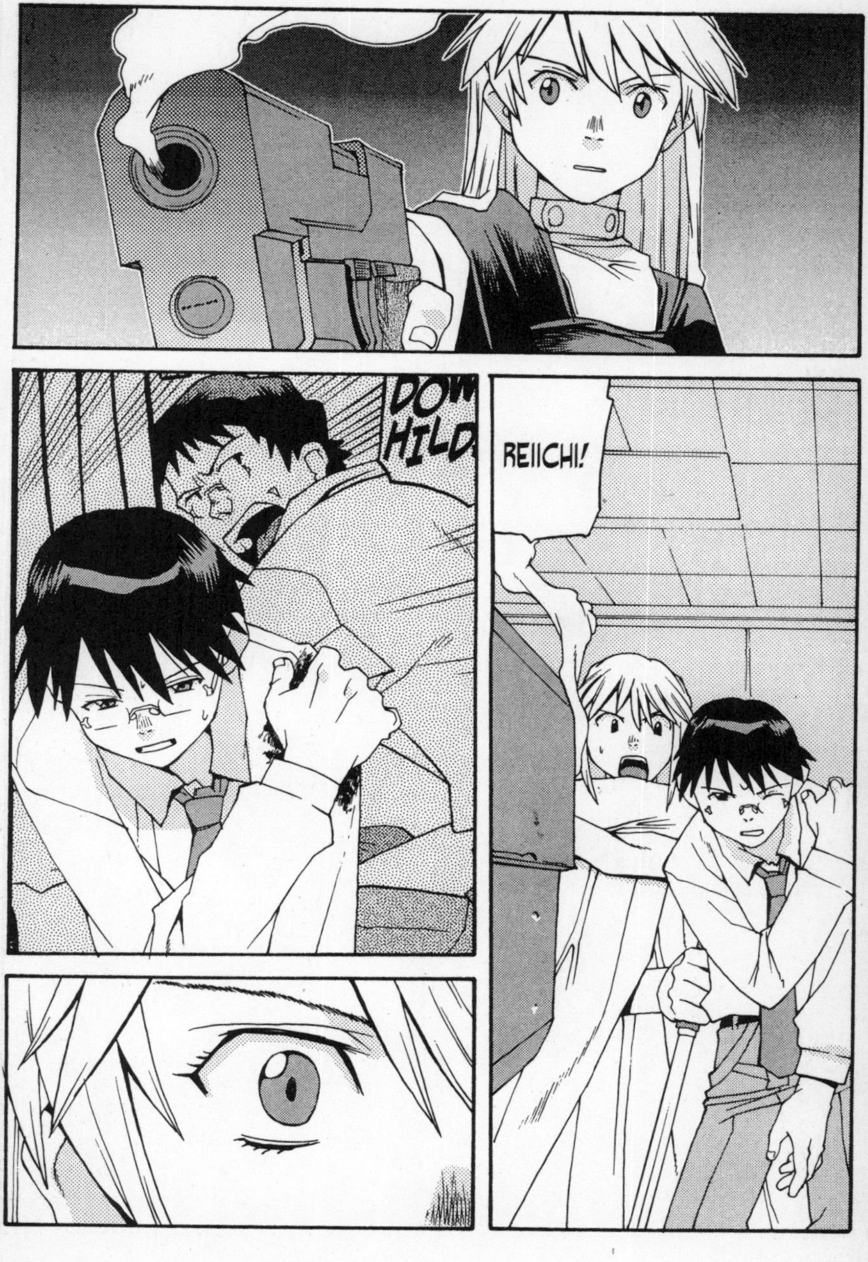
REIICHI!
DOW
HILD

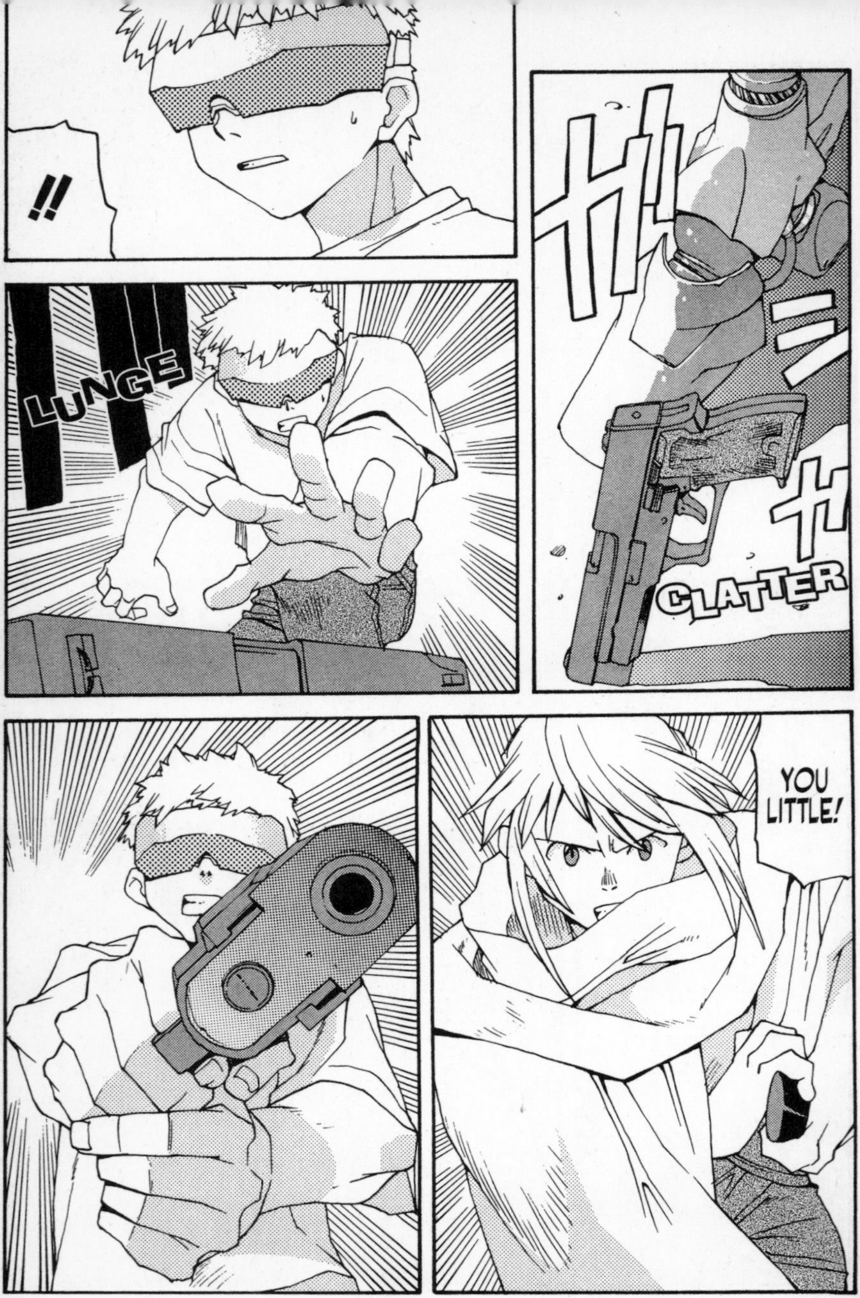
CLATTER
!!
LUNGE
YOU LITTLE!

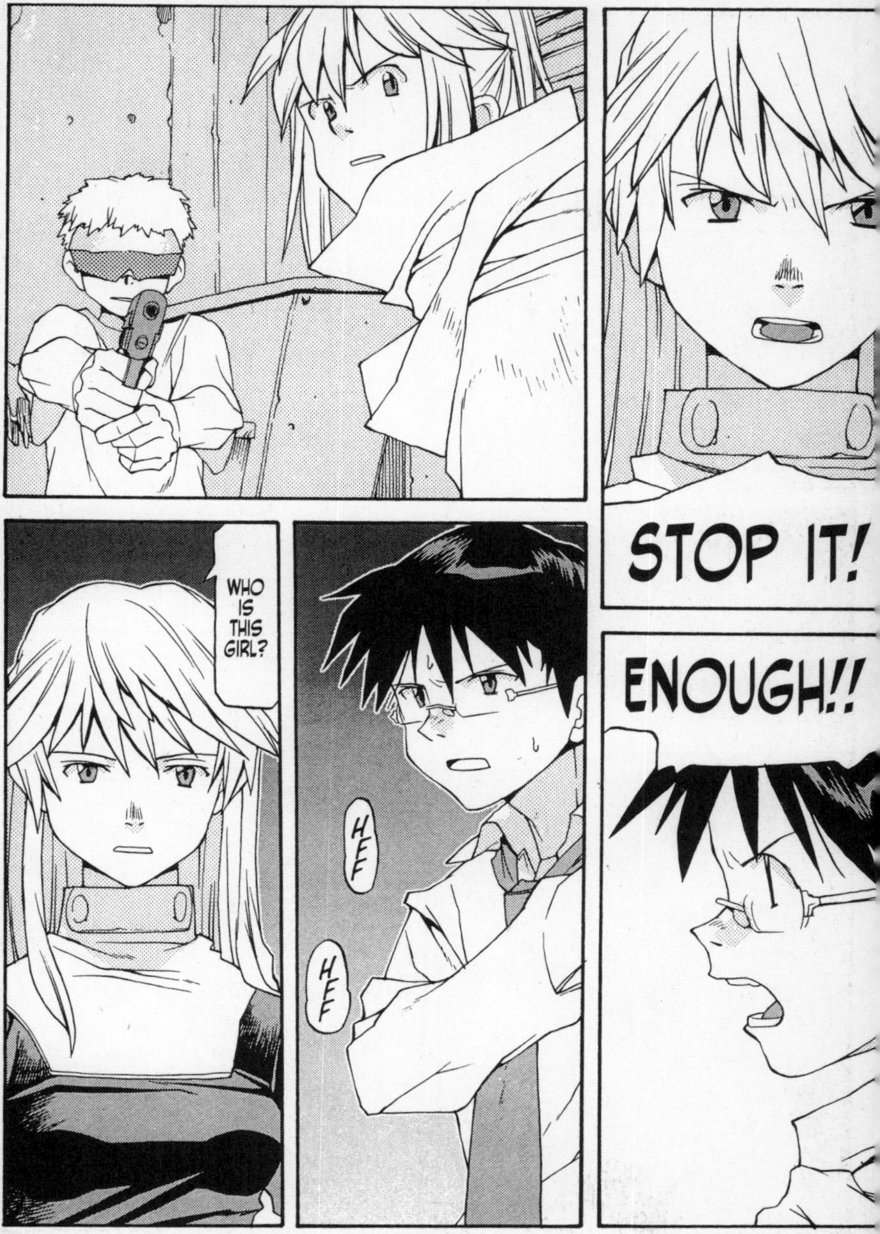
STOP IT!
ENOUGH!!
HEFF
HEFF
WHO IS THIS GIRL?

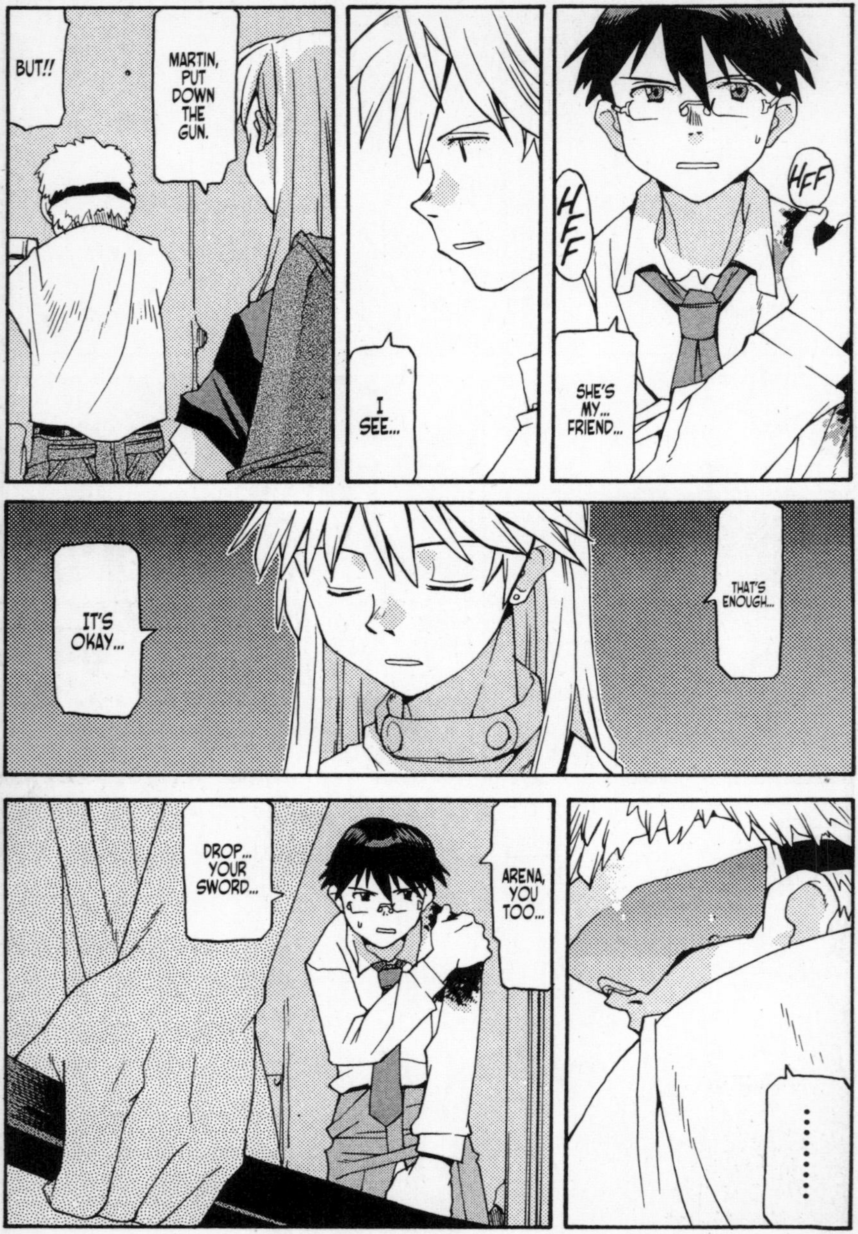
HFF
HFF
SHE'S MY... FRIEND...
I SEE...
MARTIN, PUT DOWN THE GUN.
BUT!!
THAT'S ENOUGH...
IT'S OKAY...
......
ARENA, YOU TOO...
DROP... YOUR SWORD...

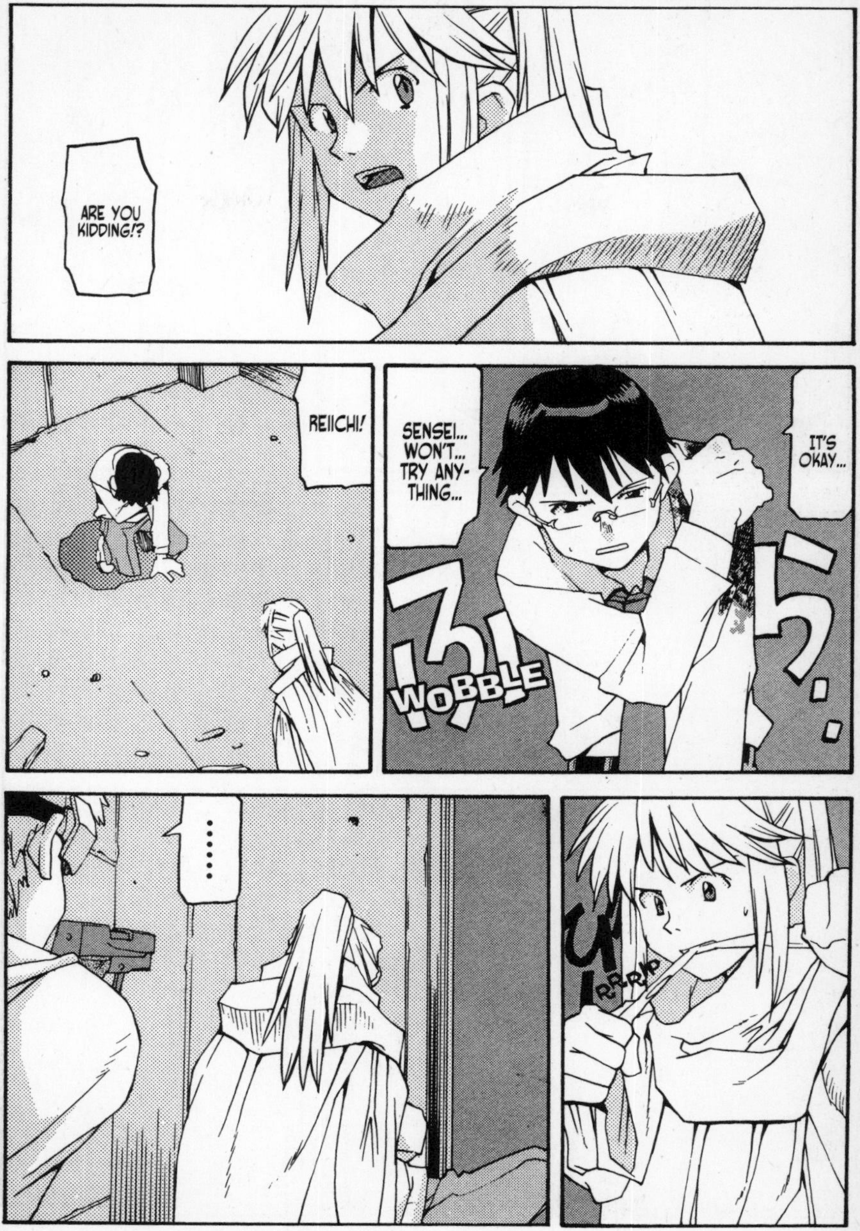
ARE YOU KIDDING!?
IT'S OKAY...
SENSEI... WON'T... TRY ANYTHING...
WOBBLE
REIICHI!
R-R-RRIP
......

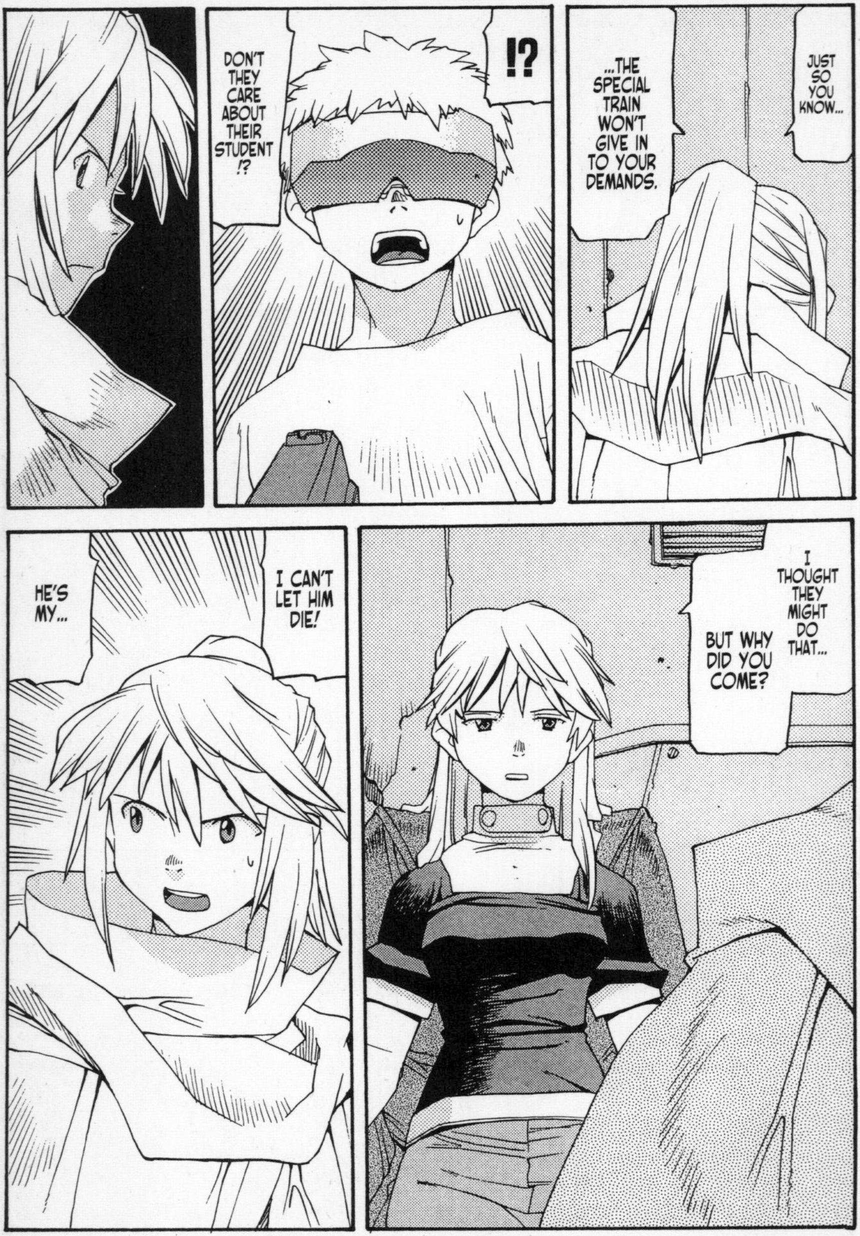
JUST SO YOU KNOW...
...THE SPECIAL TRAIN WON'T GIVE IN TO YOUR DEMANDS.
!?
DON'T THEY CARE ABOUT THEIR STUDENT !?
I THOUGHT THEY MIGHT DO THAT...
BUT WHY DID YOU COME?
I CAN'T LET HIM DIE!
HE'S MY...

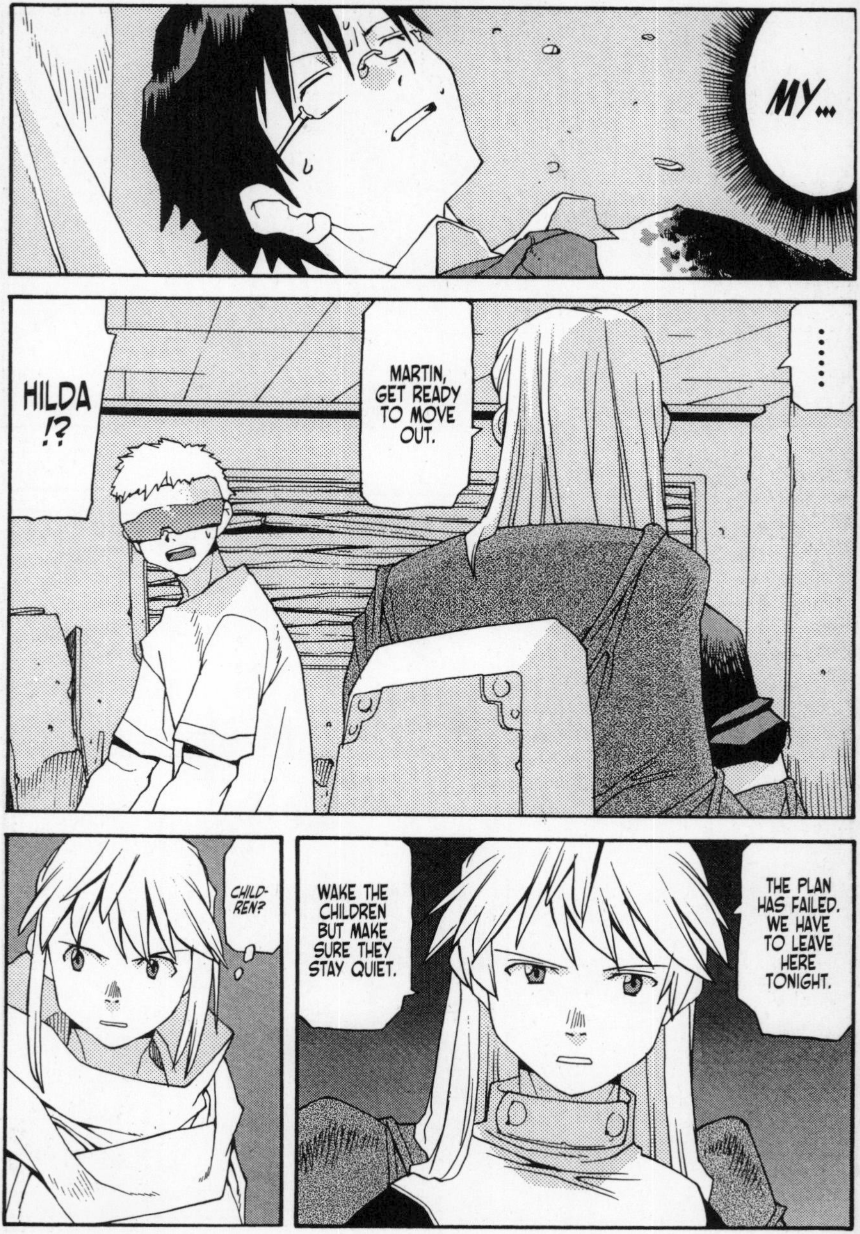

MY...
......
MARTIN, GET READY TO MOVE OUT.
HILDA !?
THE PLAN HAS FAILED. WE HAVE TO LEAVE HERE TONIGHT.
WAKE THE CHILDREN BUT MAKE SURE THEY STAY QUIET.
CHILD-REN?

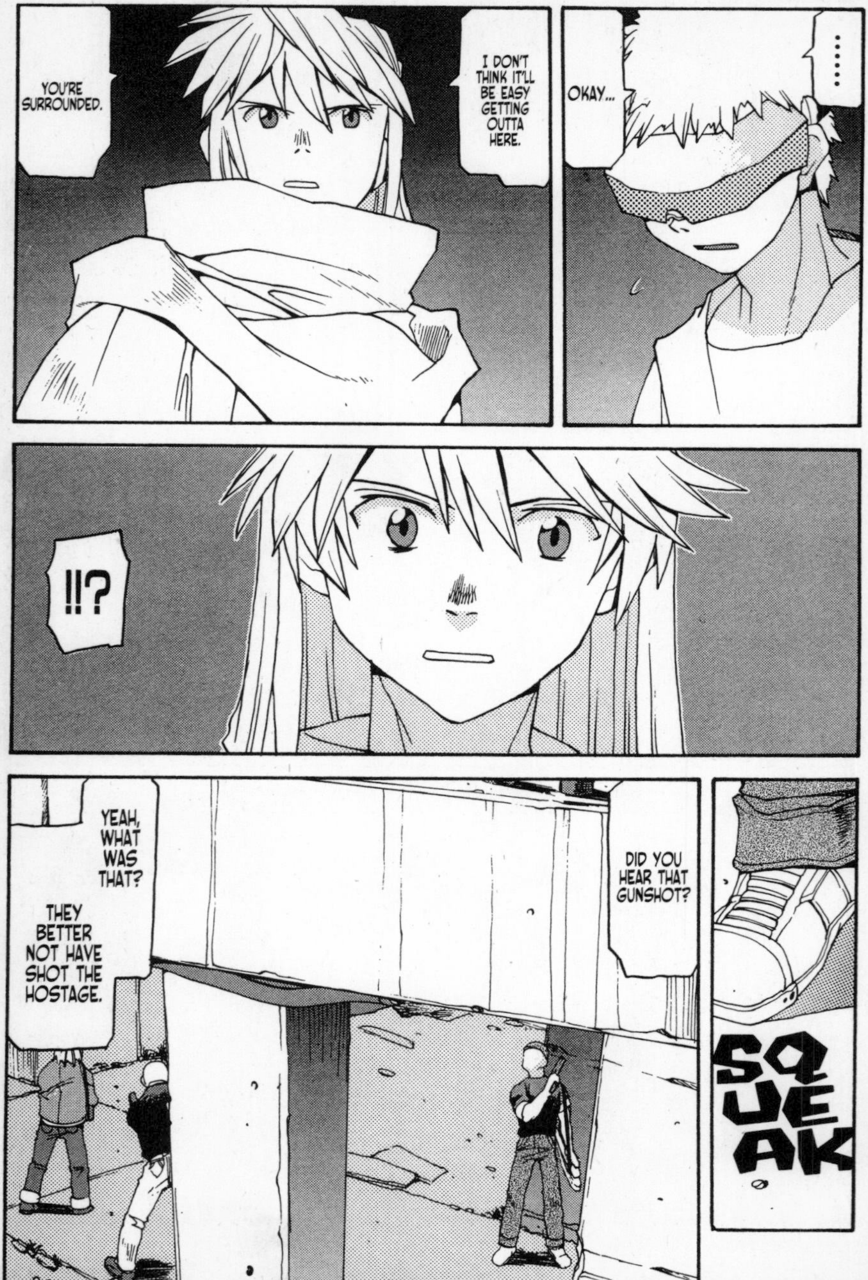
......
OKAY...
I DON'T THINK IT'LL BE EASY GETTING OUTTA HERE.
YOU'RE SURROUNDED.
!!?
SQUEAK
DID YOU HEAR THAT GUNSHOT?
YEAH, WHAT WAS THAT?
THEY BETTER NOT HAVE SHOT THE HOSTAGE.

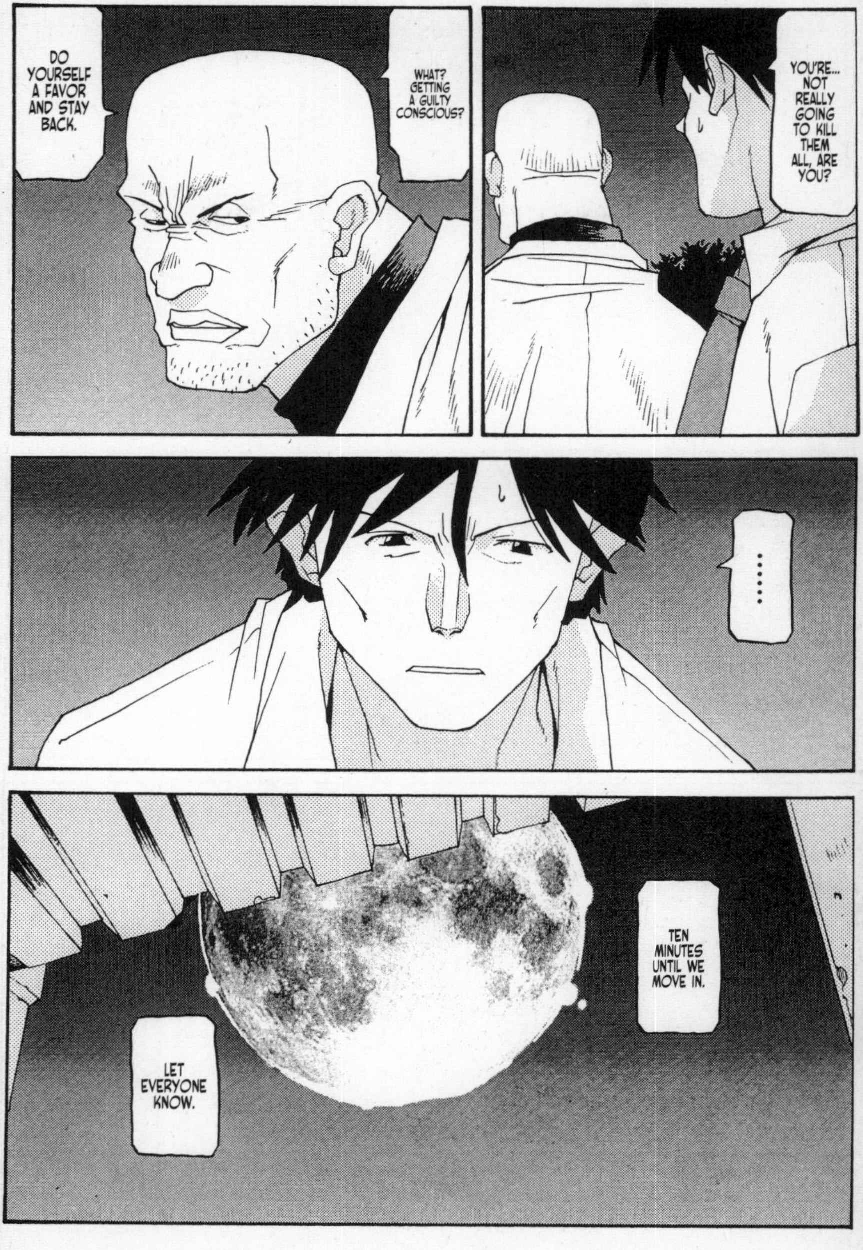
YOU'RE... NOT REALLY GOING TO KILL THEM ALL, ARE YOU?
WHAT? GETTING A GUILTY CONSCIOUS?
DO YOURSELF A FAVOR AND STAY BACK.
......
TEN MINUTES UNTIL WE MOVE IN.
LET EVERYONE KNOW.

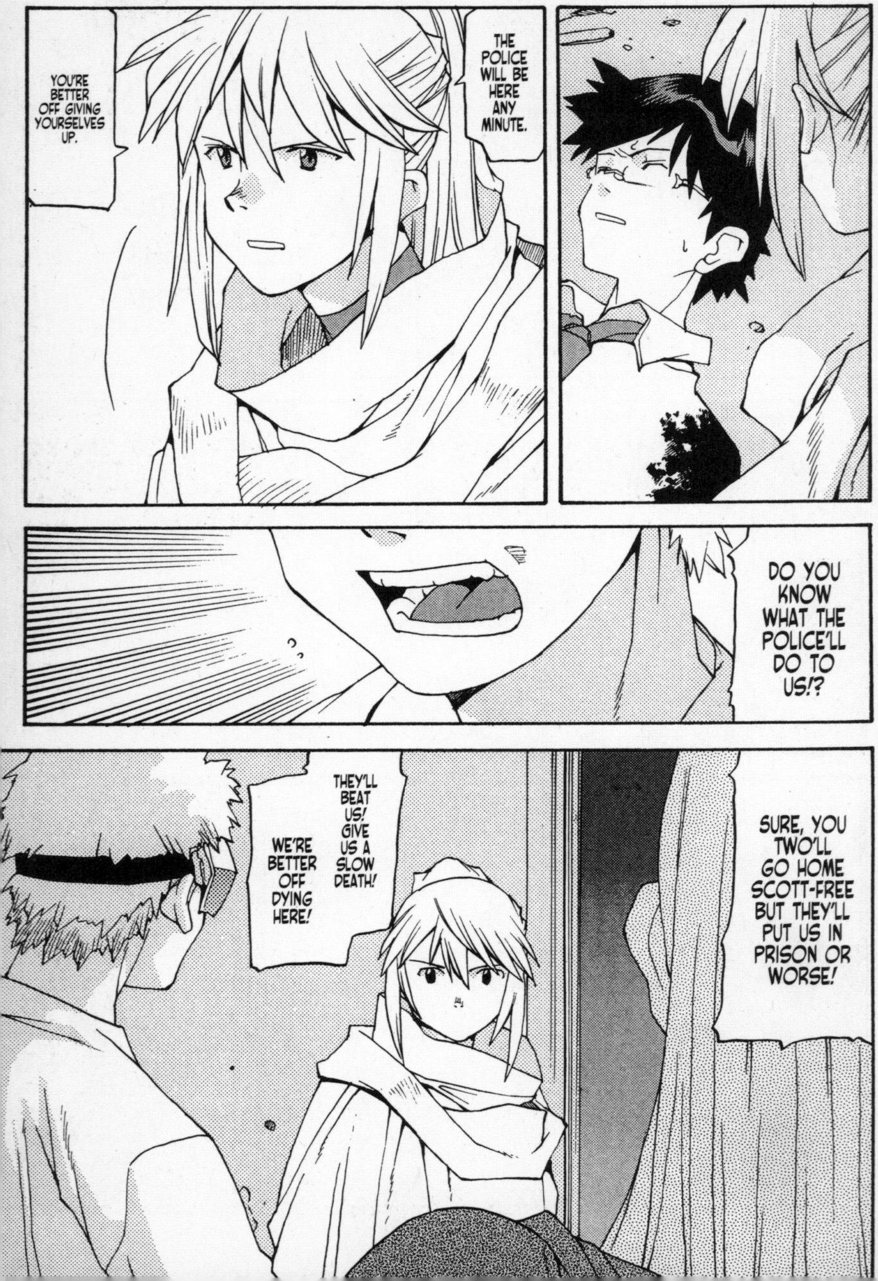
THE POLICE WILL BE HERE ANY MINUTE.
YOU'RE BETTER OFF GIVING YOURSELVES UP.
DO YOU KNOW WHAT THE POLICE'LL DO TO US!?
SURE, YOU TWO'LL GO HOME SCOTT-FREE BUT THEY'LL PUT US IN PRISON OR WORSE!
THEY'LL BEAT US! GIVE US A SLOW DEATH!
WE'RE BETTER OFF DYING HERE!

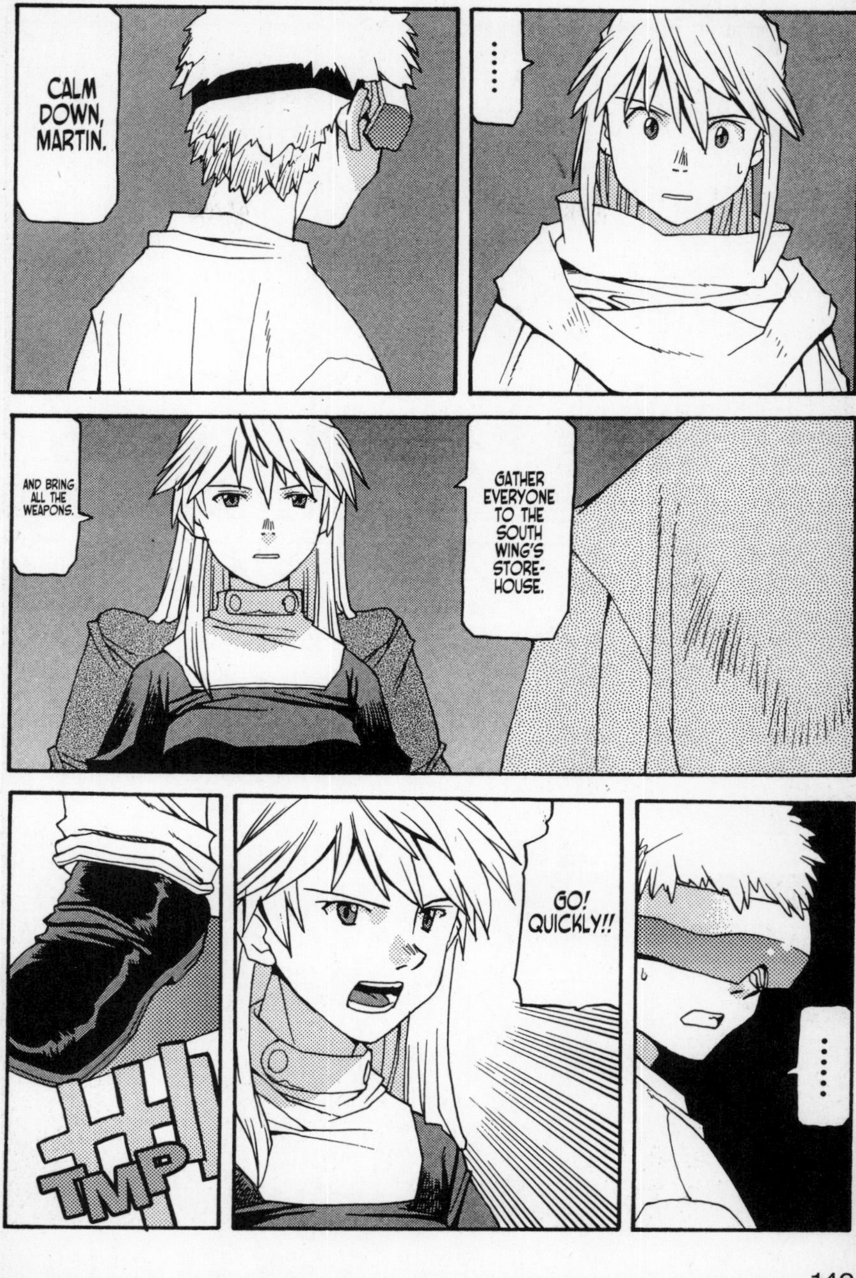
......
CALM DOWN, MARTIN.
GATHER EVERYONE TO THE SOUTH WING'S STORE-HOUSE.
AND BRING ALL THE WEAPONS.
......
GO! QUICKLY!!
TMP!!

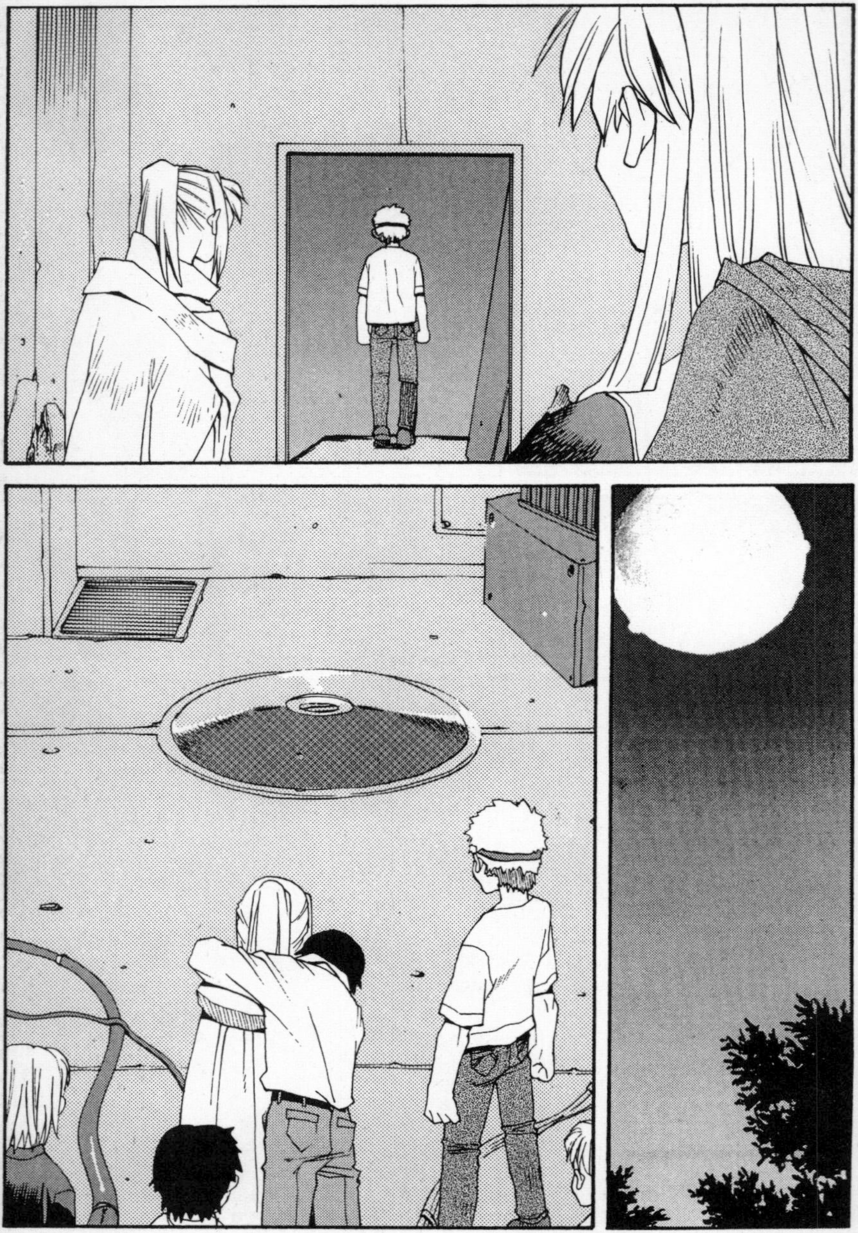

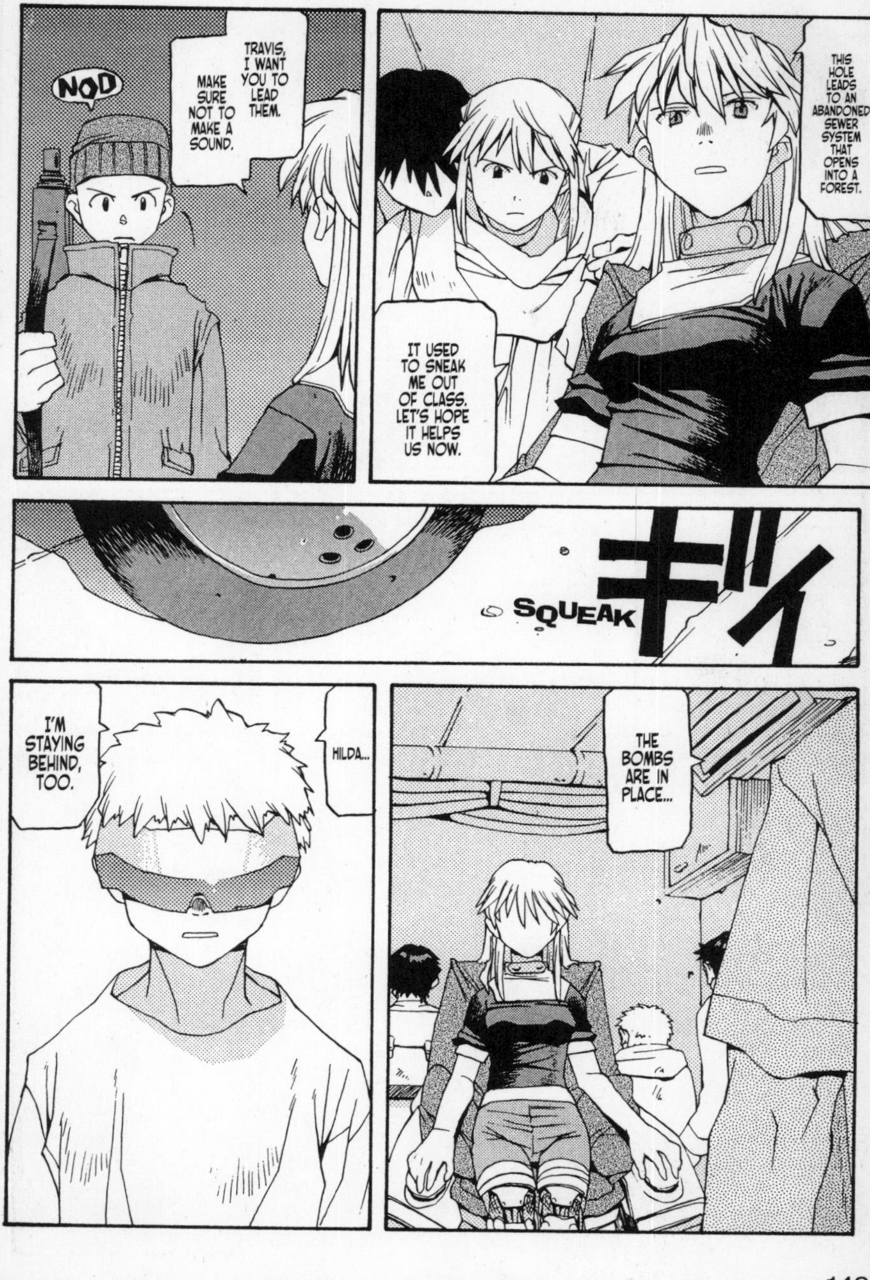
THIS HOLE LEADS TO AN ABANDONED SEWER SYSTEM THAT OPENS INTO A FOREST.
IT USED TO SNEAK ME OUT OF CLASS. LET'S HOPE IT HELPS US NOW.
TRAVIS, I WANT YOU TO LEAD THEM.
MAKE SURE NOT TO MAKE A SOUND.
NOD
SQUEAK
THE BOMBS ARE IN PLACE...
HILDA...
I'M STAYING BEHIND, TOO.

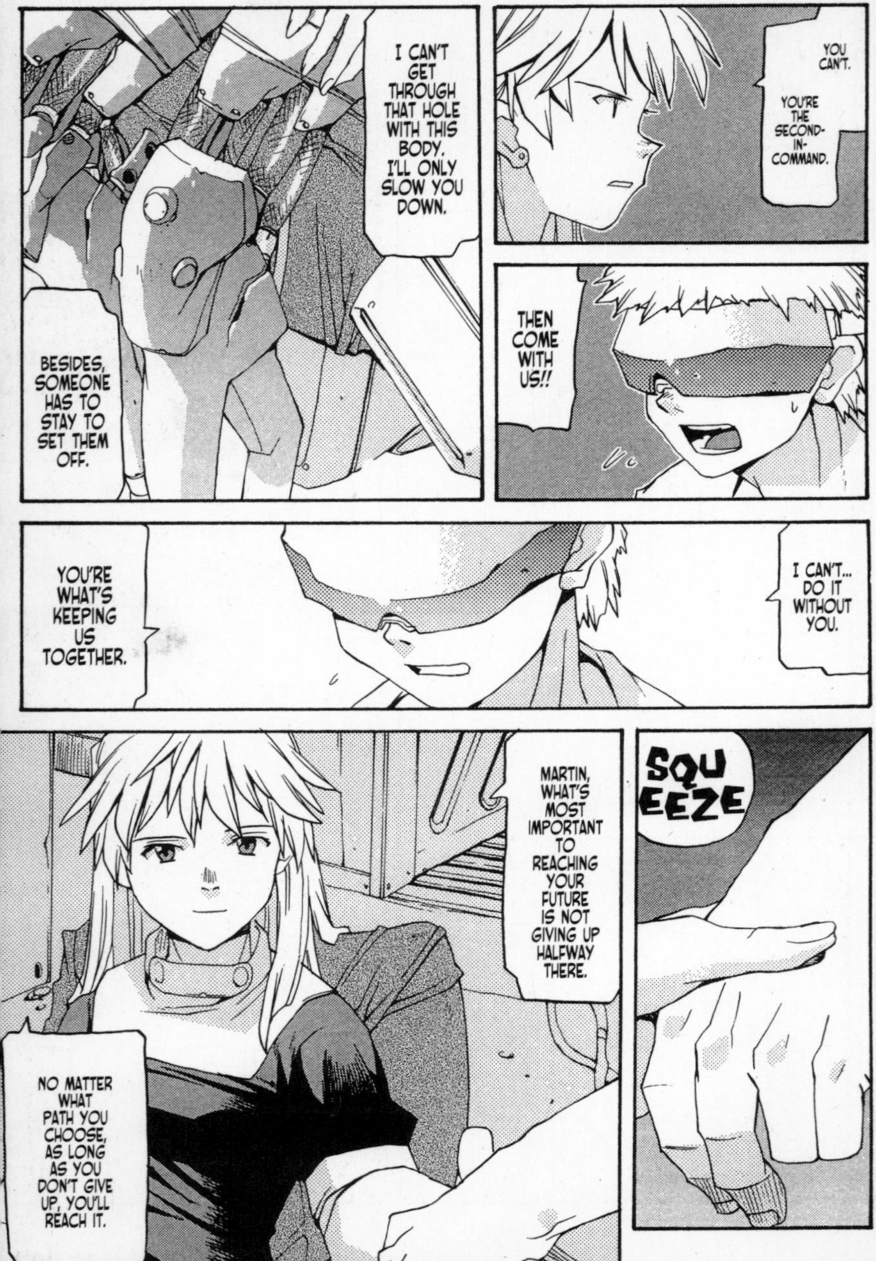
YOU CAN'T.
YOU'RE THE SECOND-IN-COMMAND.
THEN COME WITH US!!
I CAN'T GET THROUGH THAT HOLE WITH THIS BODY. I'LL ONLY SLOW YOU DOWN.
BESIDES, SOMEONE HAS TO STAY TO SET THEM OFF.
I CAN'T... DO IT WITHOUT YOU.
YOU'RE WHAT'S KEEPING US TOGETHER.
SQUEEZE
MARTIN, WHAT'S MOST IMPORTANT TO REACHING YOUR FUTURE IS NOT GIVING UP HALFWAY THERE.
NO MATTER WHAT PATH YOU CHOOSE, AS LONG AS YOU DON'T GIVE UP, YOU'LL REACH IT.

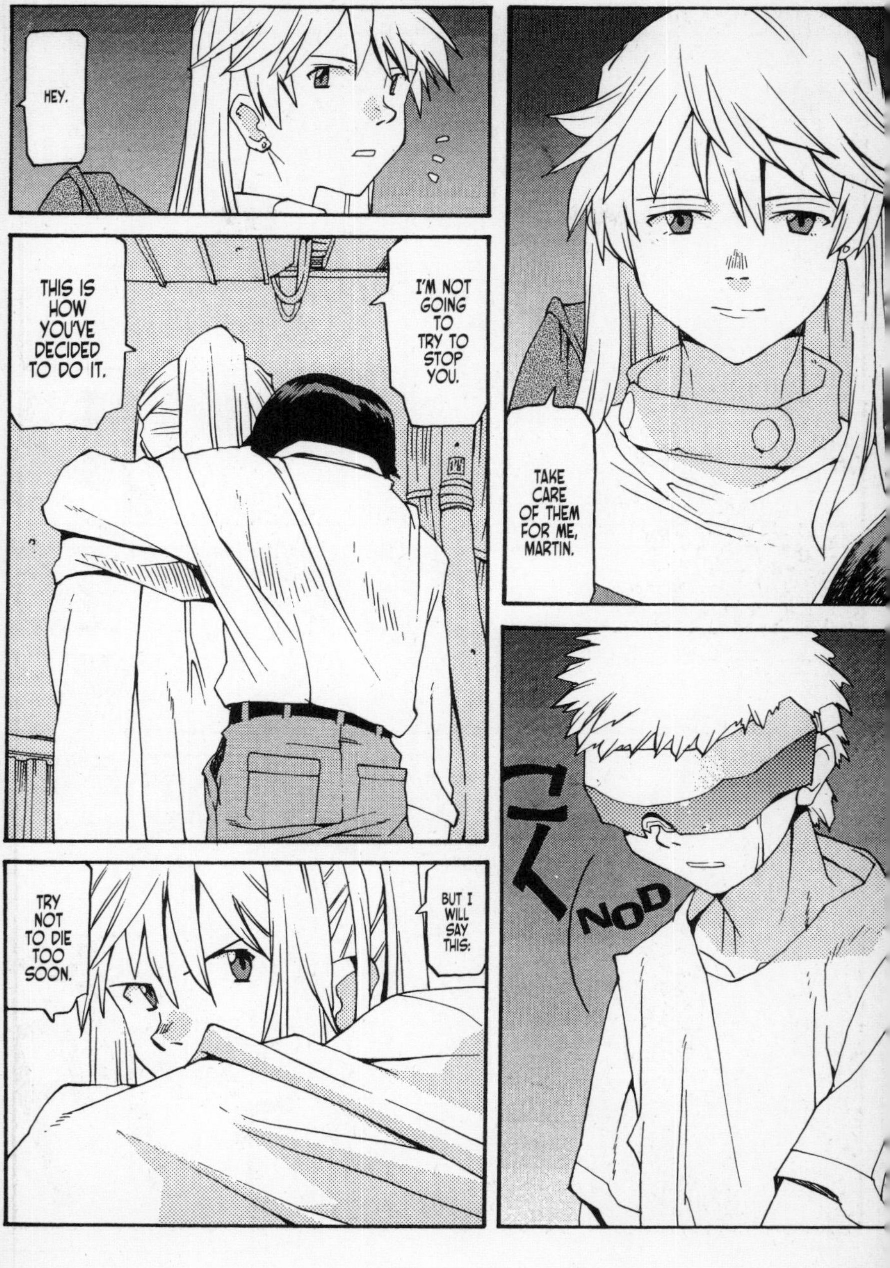
TAKE CARE OF THEM FOR ME, MARTIN.
HEY.
I'M NOT GOING TO TRY TO STOP YOU.
THIS IS HOW YOU'VE DECIDED TO DO IT.
NOD
BUT I WILL SAY THIS:
TRY NOT TO DIE TOO SOON.

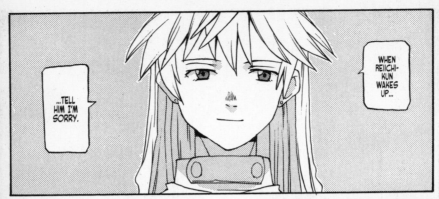

WHEN REIICHI-KUN WAKES UP...

...TELL HIM I'M SORRY.

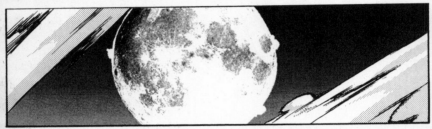

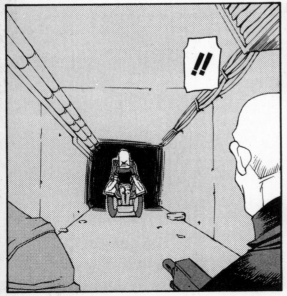

!!

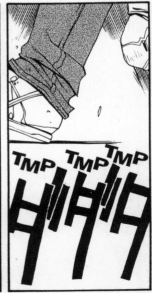

TMP TMP TMP

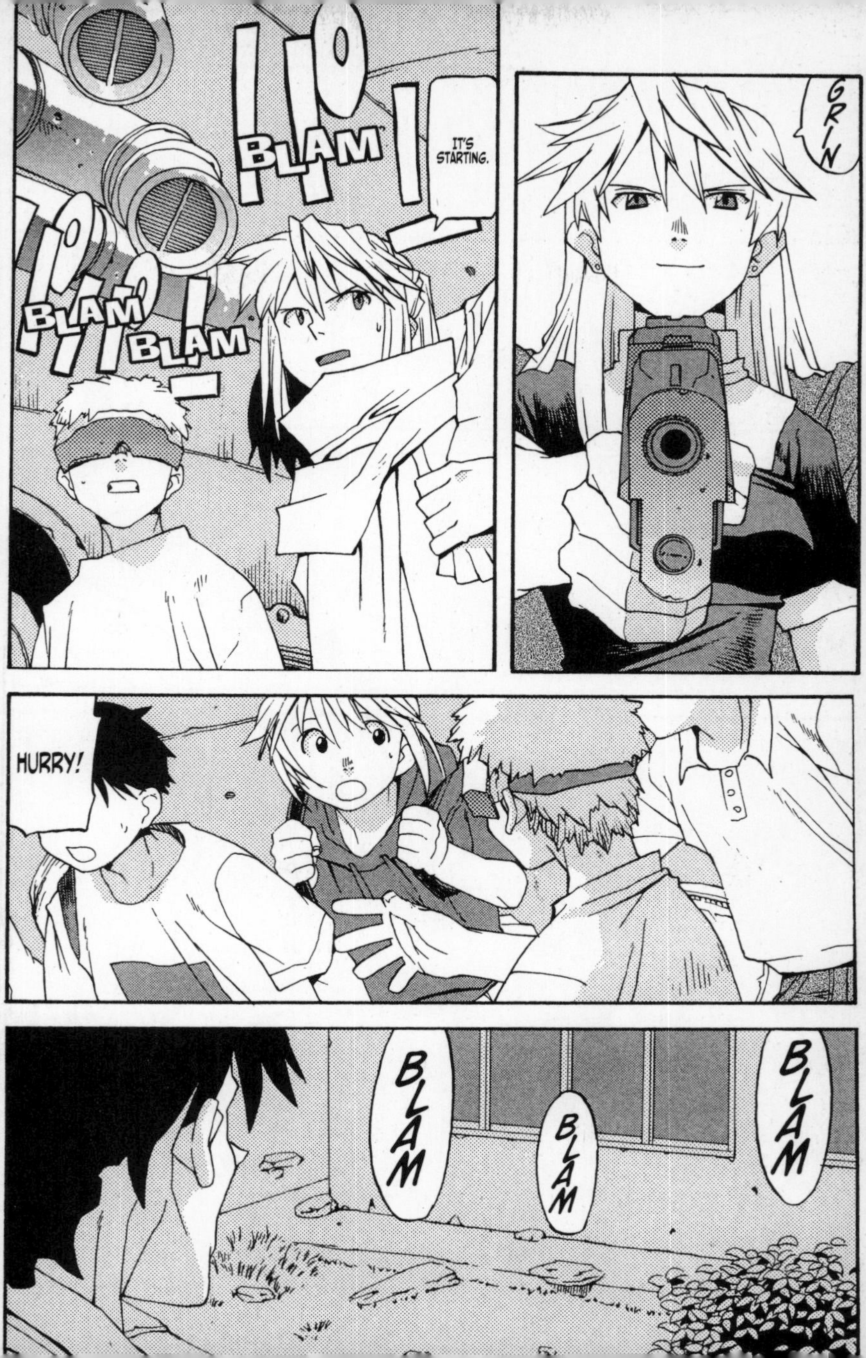
GRIN
IT'S STARTING.
BLAM
BLAM
BLAM
HURRY!
BLAM
BLAM
BLAM

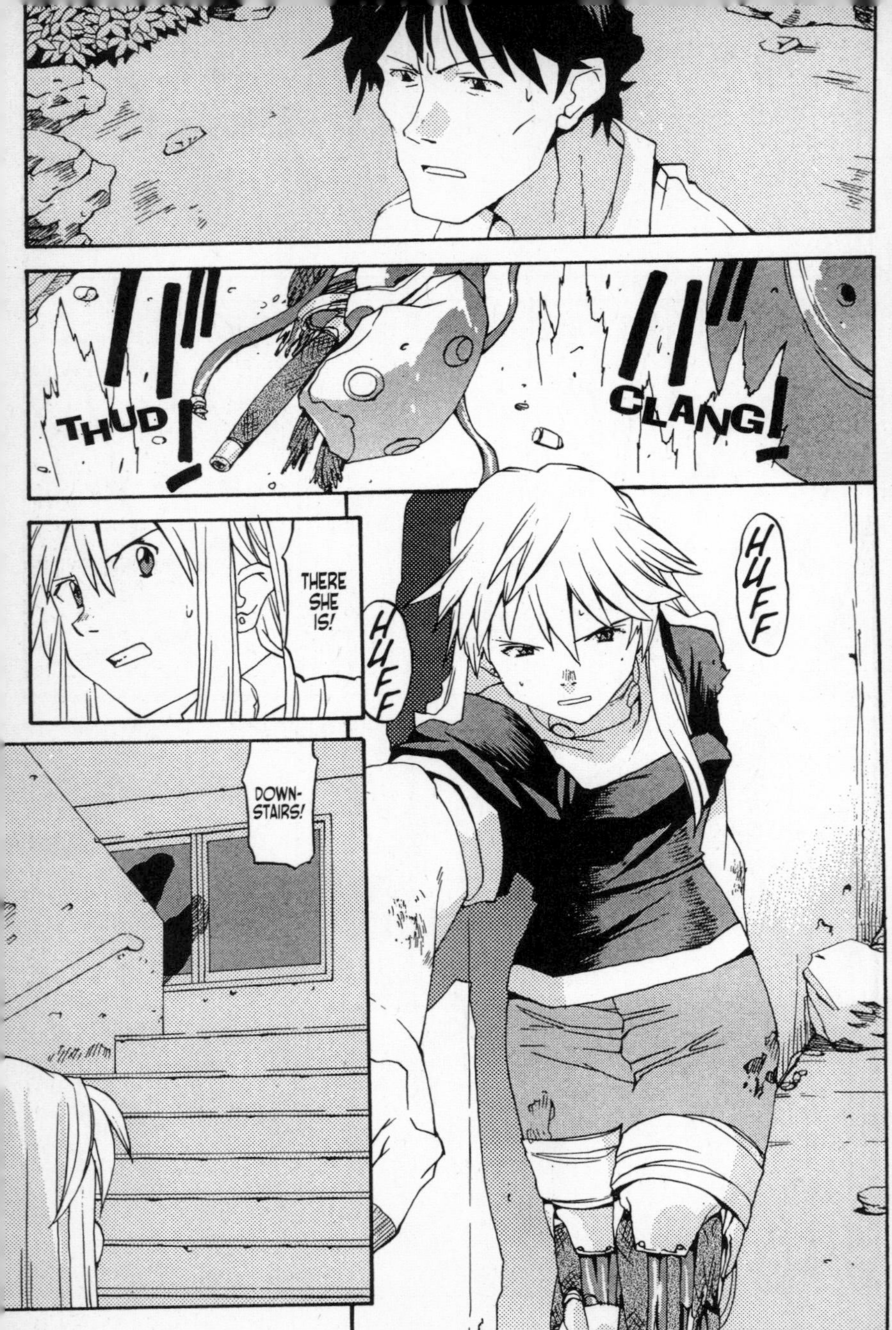
CLANG!
THUD!
HUFF
HUFF
THERE SHE IS!
DOWN-STAIRS!

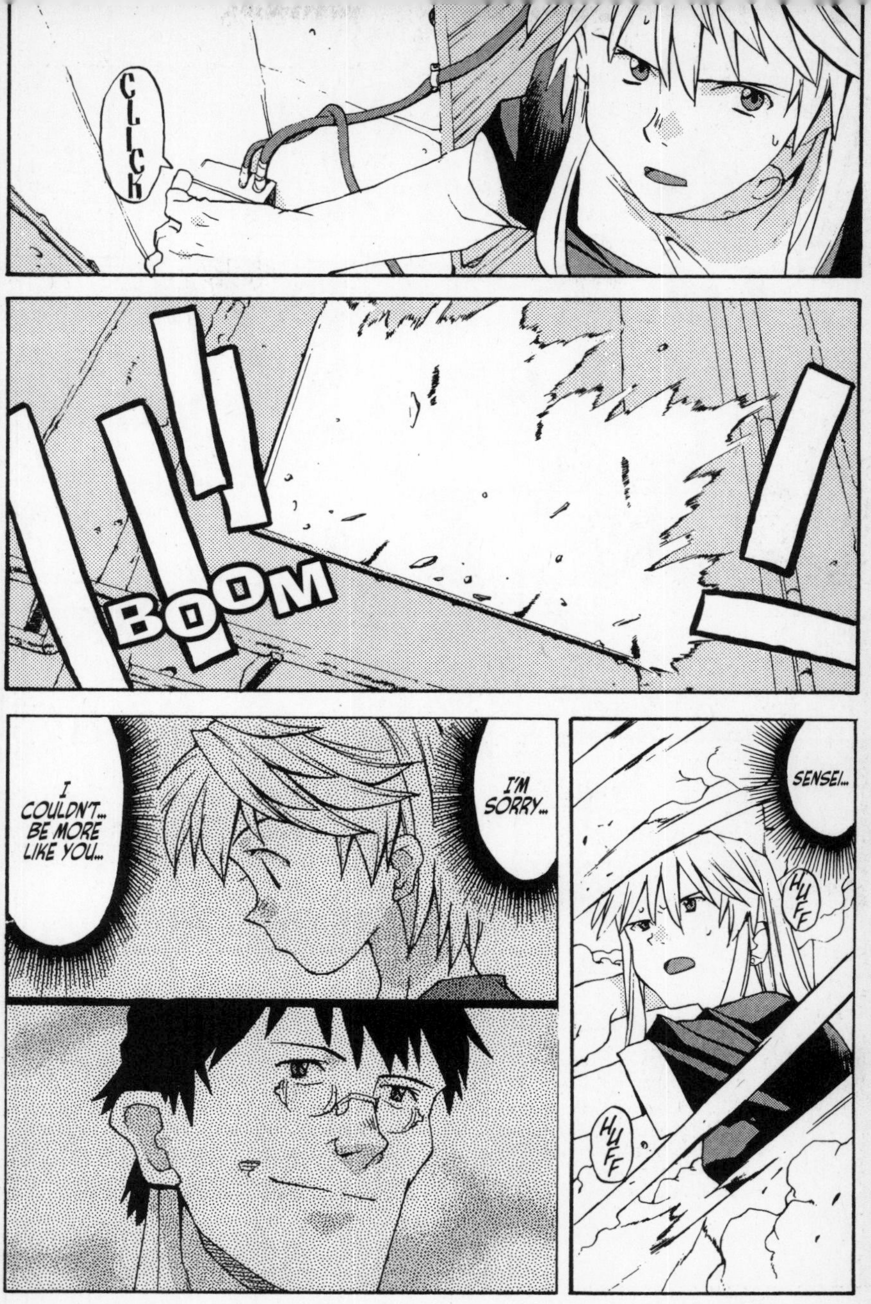
CLICK
BOOM
SENSEI...
HUFF
HUFF
I'M SORRY...
I COULDN'T... BE MORE LIKE YOU...

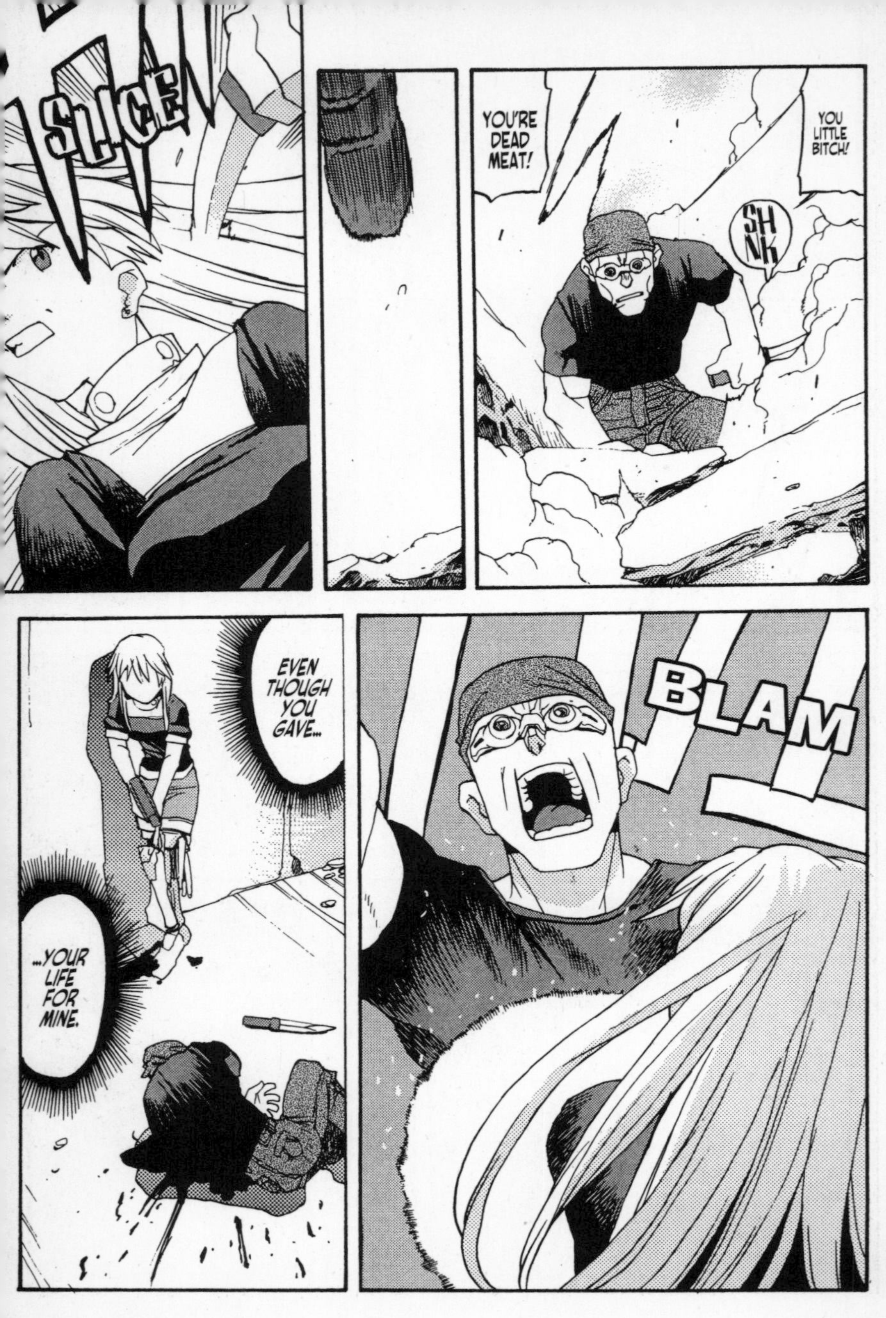
YOU LITTLE BITCH!
YOU'RE DEAD MEAT!
SHNK
SLICE
BLAM
EVEN THOUGH YOU GAVE...
...YOUR LIFE FOR MINE.

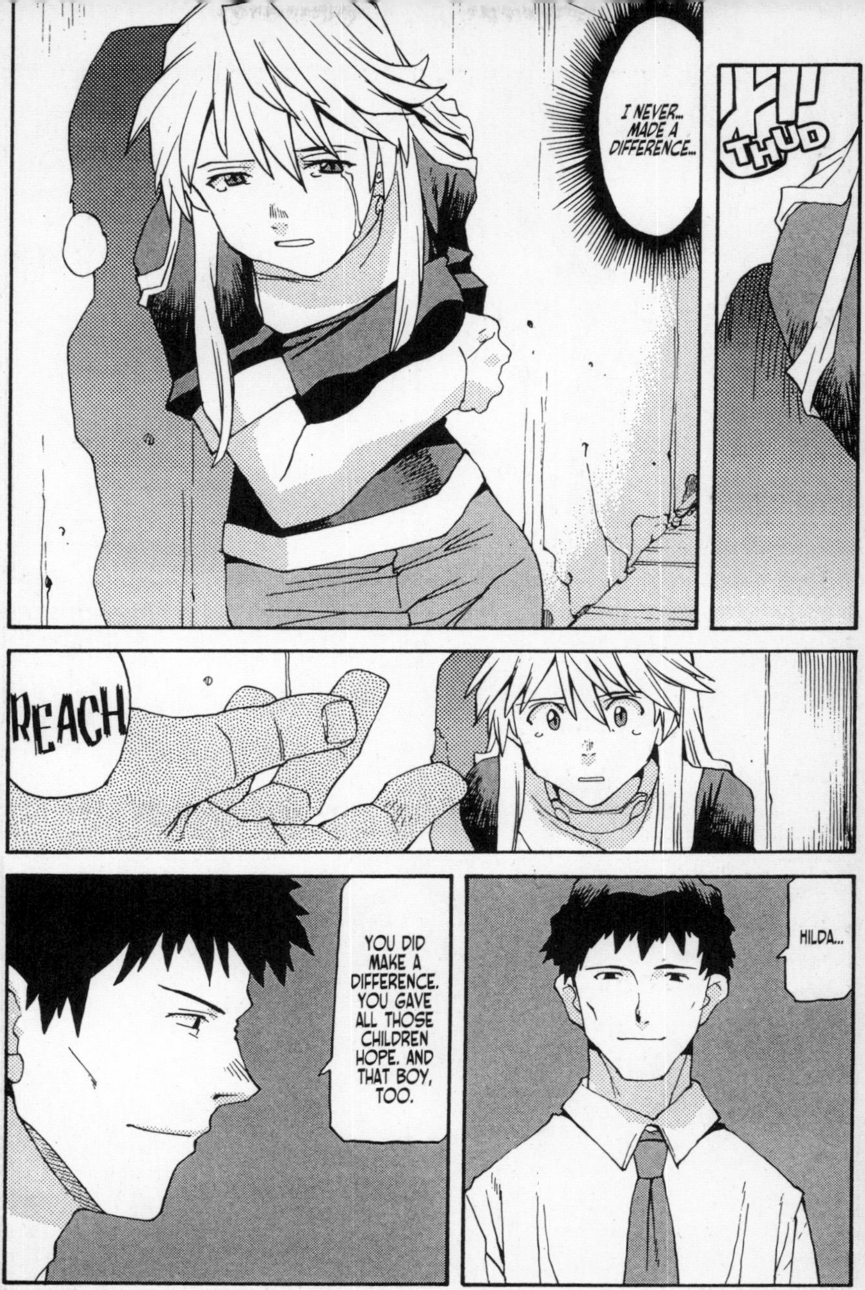
THUD
I NEVER... MADE A DIFFERENCE...
REACH
HILDA...
YOU DID MAKE A DIFFERENCE. YOU GAVE ALL THOSE CHILDREN HOPE. AND THAT BOY, TOO.

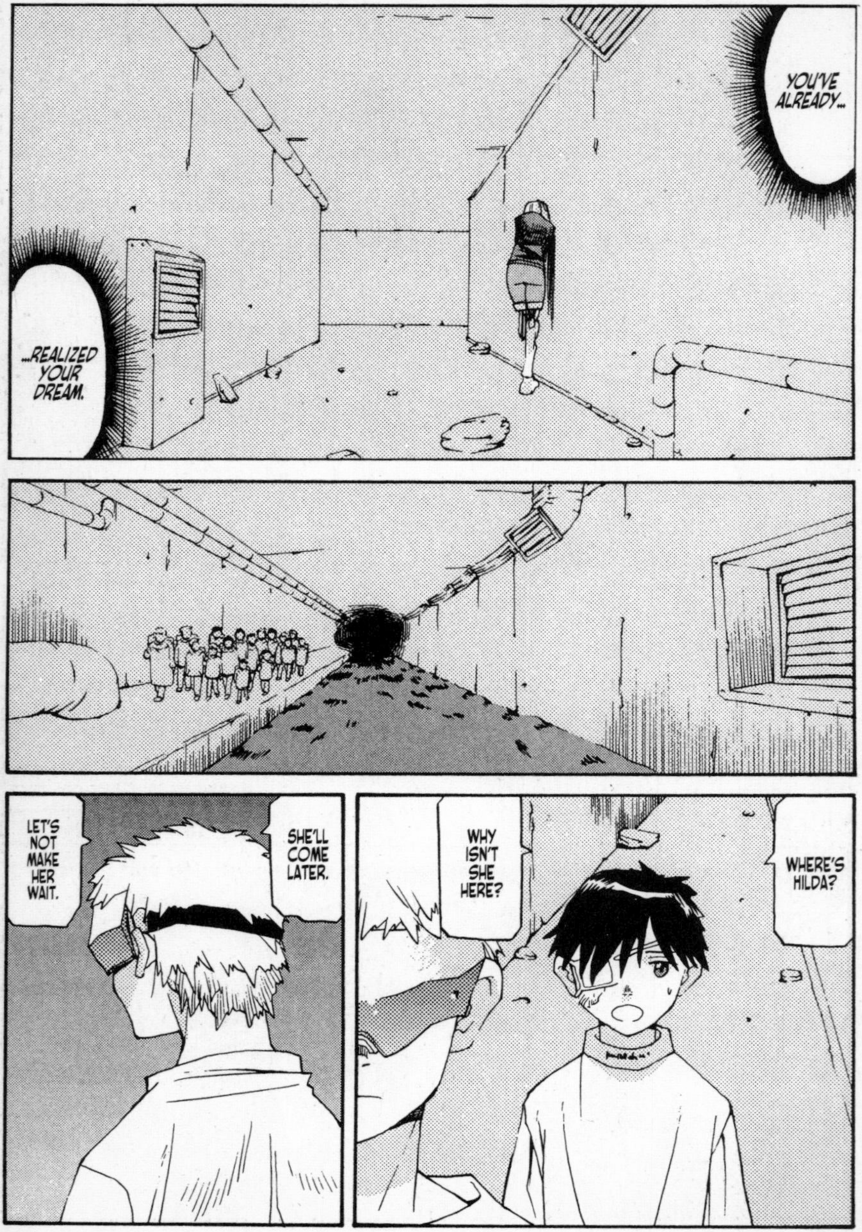
YOU'VE ALREADY...
...REALIZED YOUR DREAM.
WHERE'S HILDA?
WHY ISN'T SHE HERE?
SHE'LL COME LATER.
LET'S NOT MAKE HER WAIT.

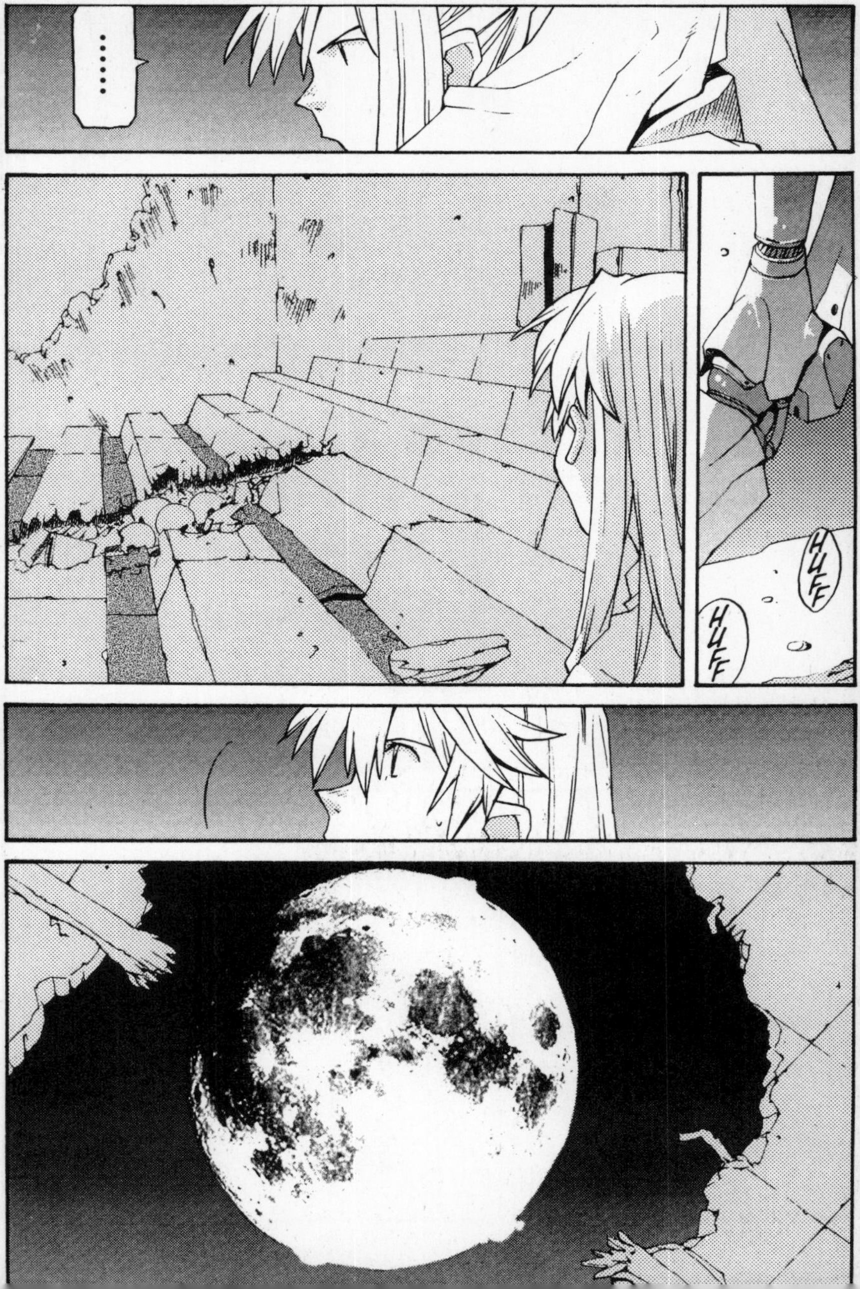
......
HUFF
HUFF

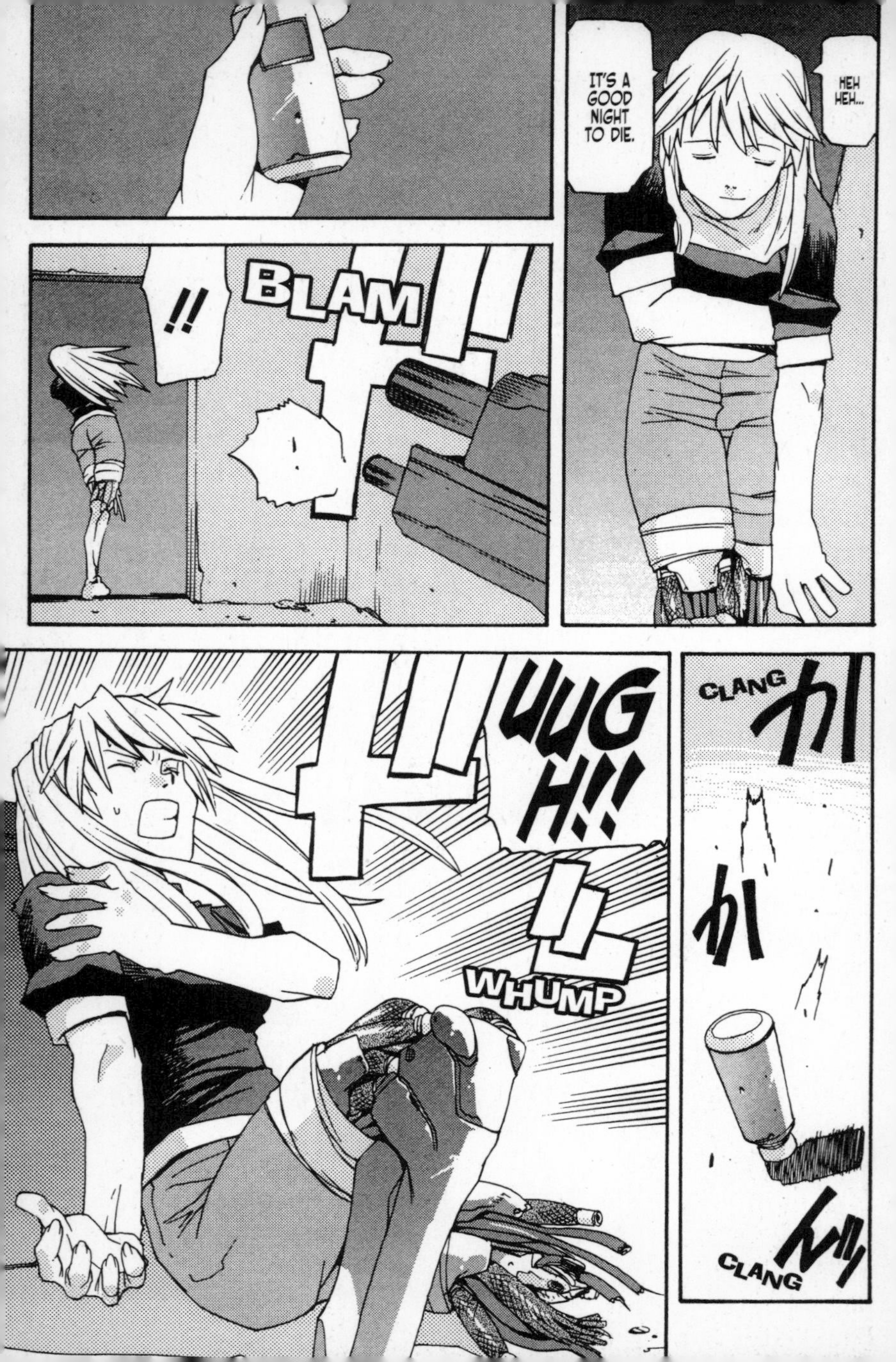
HEH HEH...
IT'S A GOOD NIGHT TO DIE.
BLAM
!!
CLANG
CLANG
UUGH!!
WHUMP

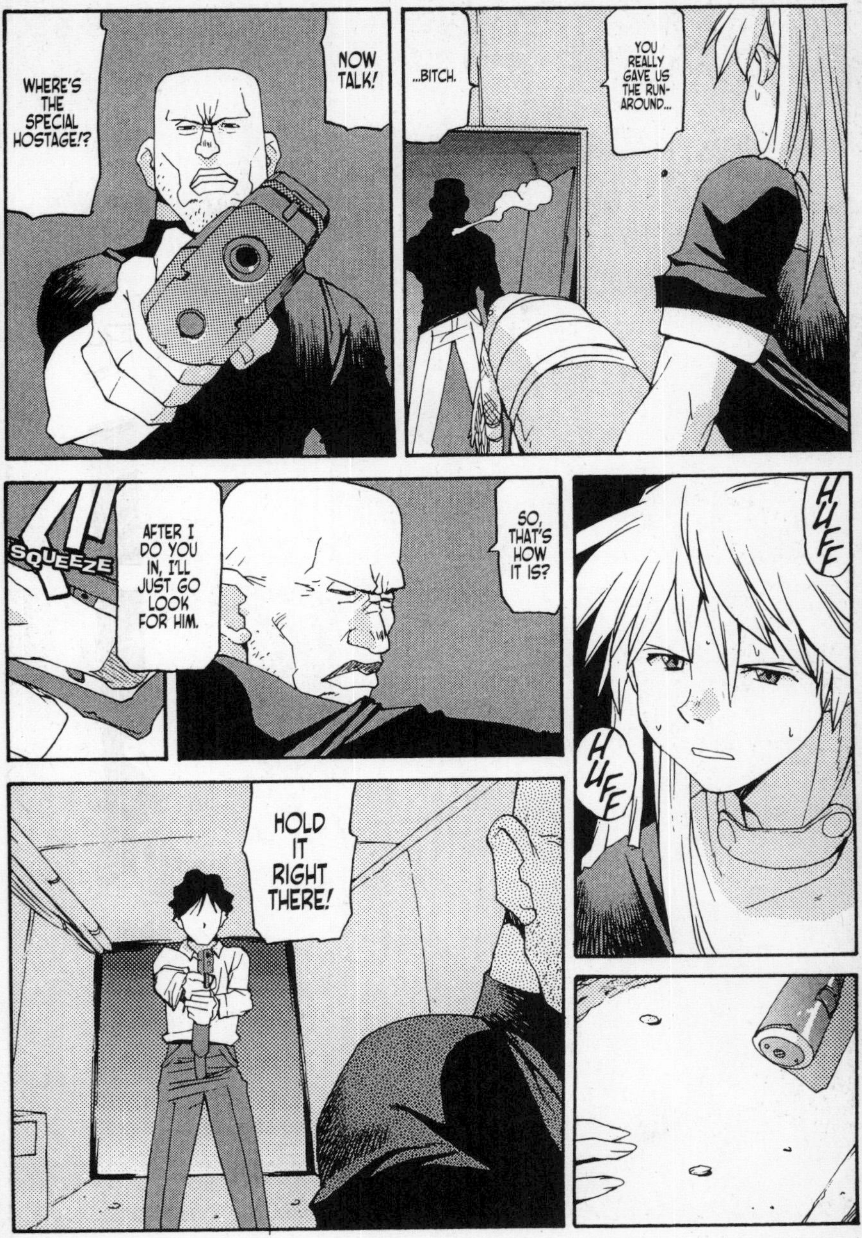
YOU REALLY GAVE US THE RUN-AROUND...
...BITCH.
NOW TALK!
WHERE'S THE SPECIAL HOSTAGE!?
HUFF
HUFF
SO, THAT'S HOW IT IS?
AFTER I DO YOU IN, I'LL JUST GO LOOK FOR HIM.
SQUEEZE
HOLD IT RIGHT THERE!

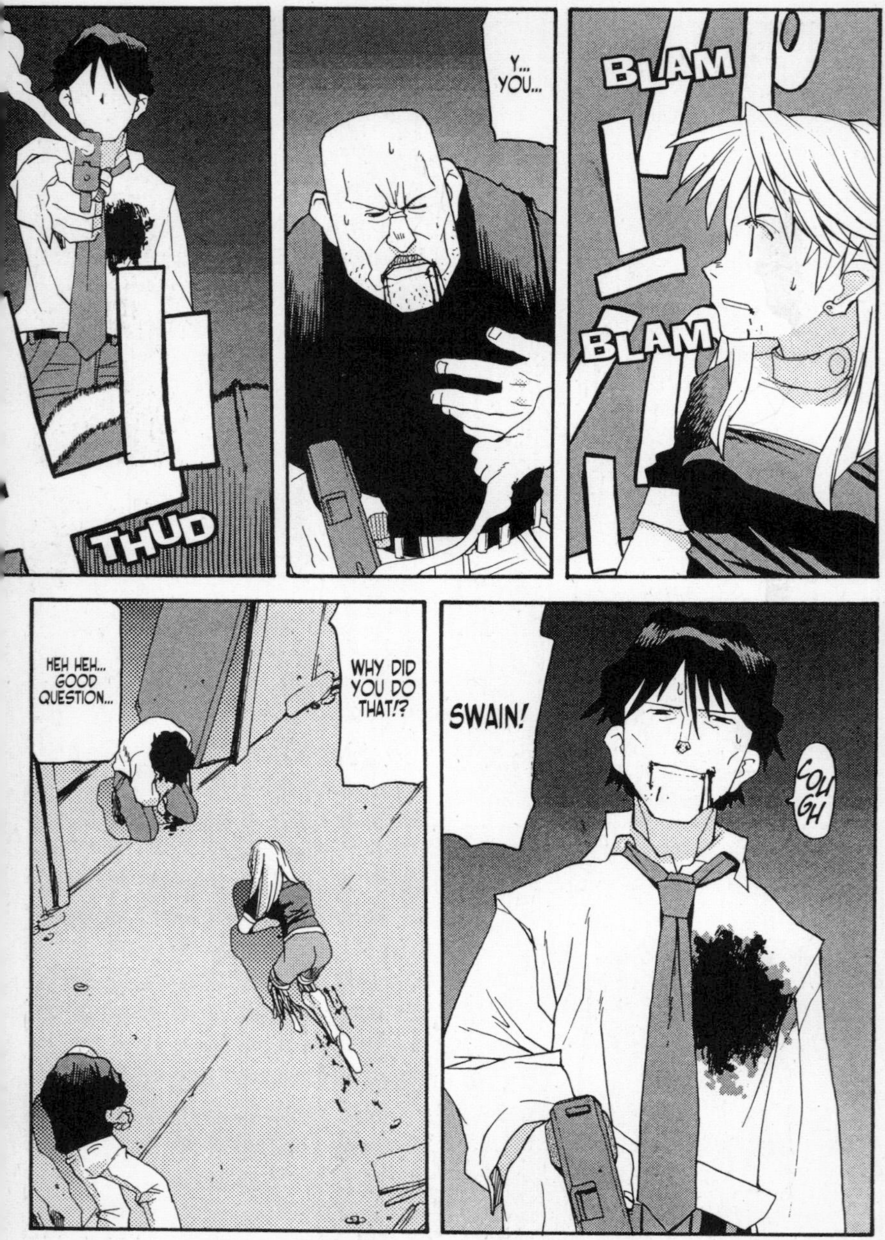
BLAM
BLAM
Y... YOU...
THUD
COUGH
SWAIN!
WHY DID YOU DO THAT!?
HEH HEH... GOOD QUESTION...

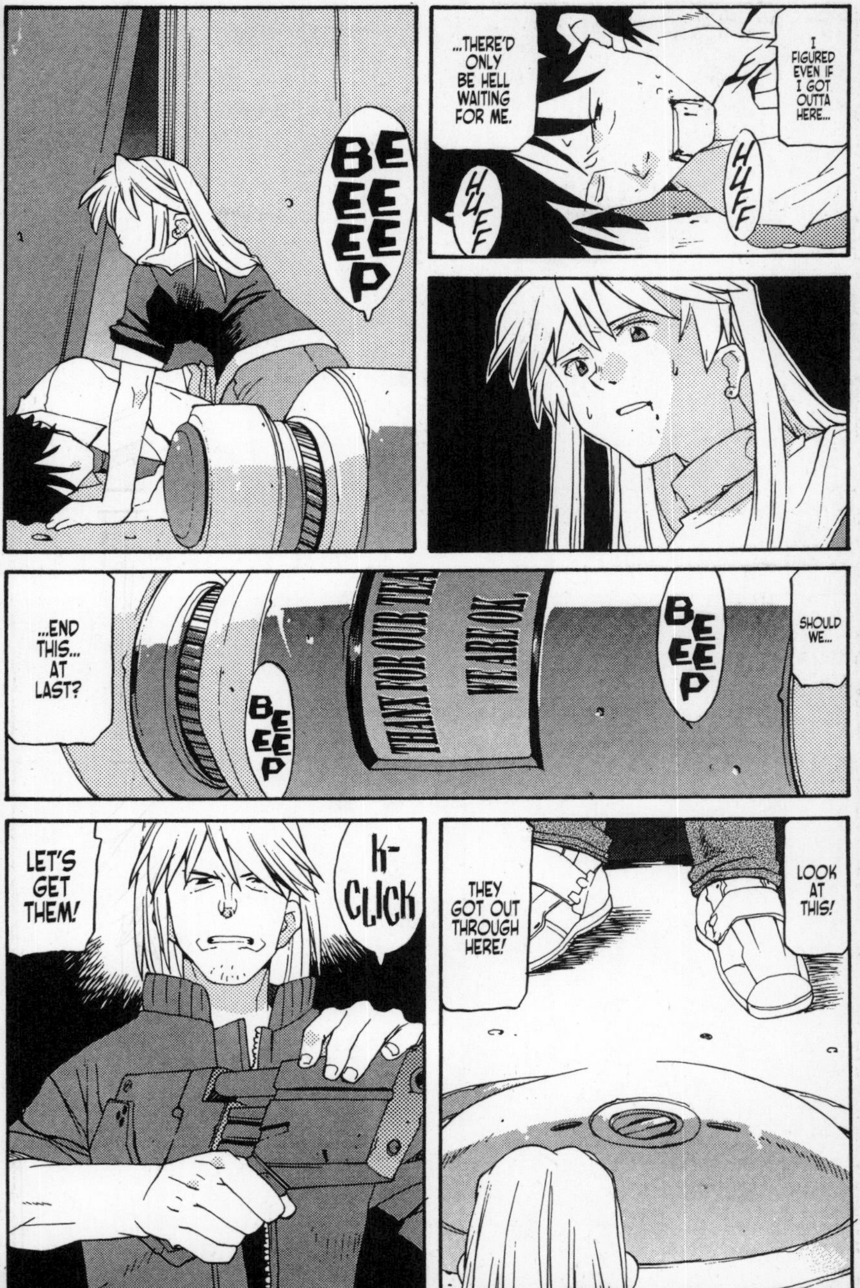
I FIGURED EVEN IF I GOT OUTTA HERE...
HUFF
...THERE'D ONLY BE HELL WAITING FOR ME.
HUFF
BEEEEEP
SHOULD WE...
BEEP
THANX FOR OUR TEA
WE ARE OK.
BEEEP
...END THIS... AT LAST?
LOOK AT THIS!
THEY GOT OUT THROUGH HERE!
K-CLICK
LET'S GET THEM!

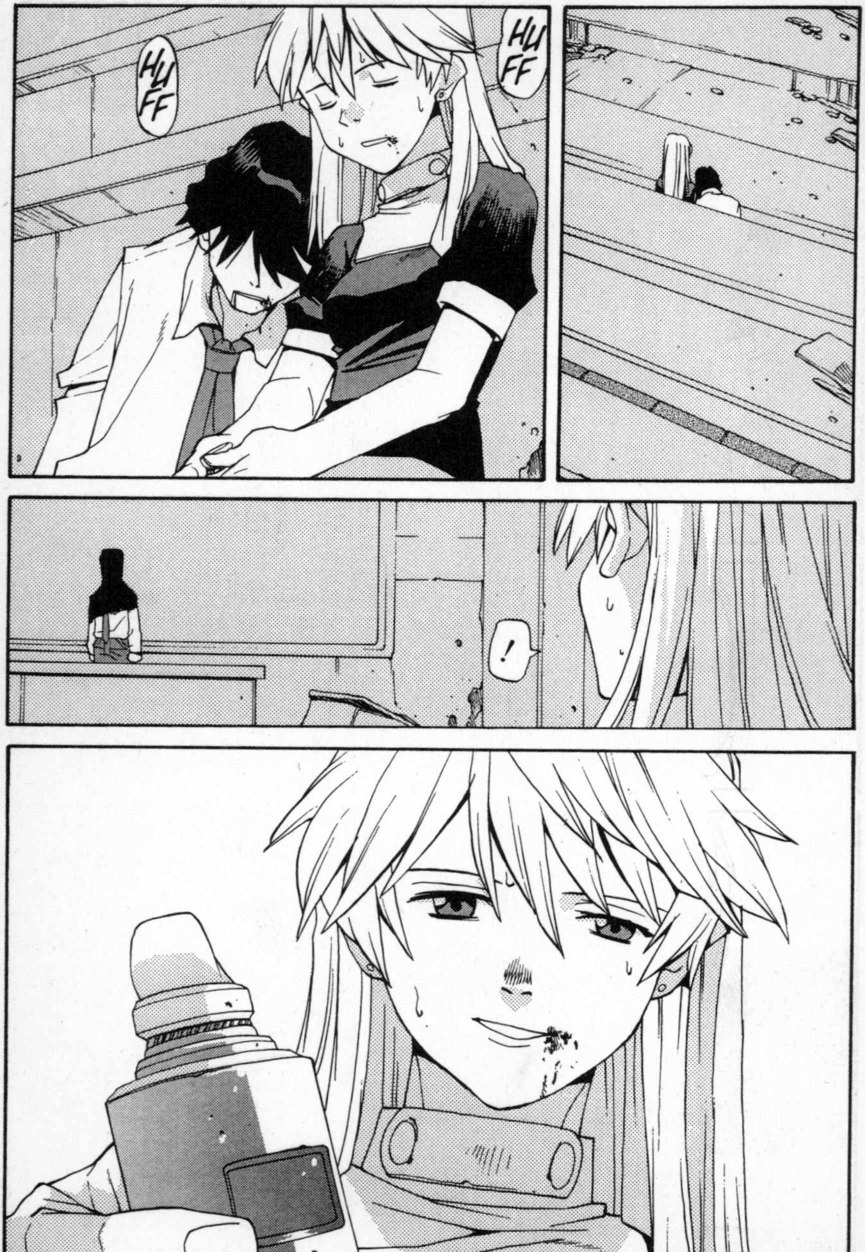
HUFF
HUFF
!

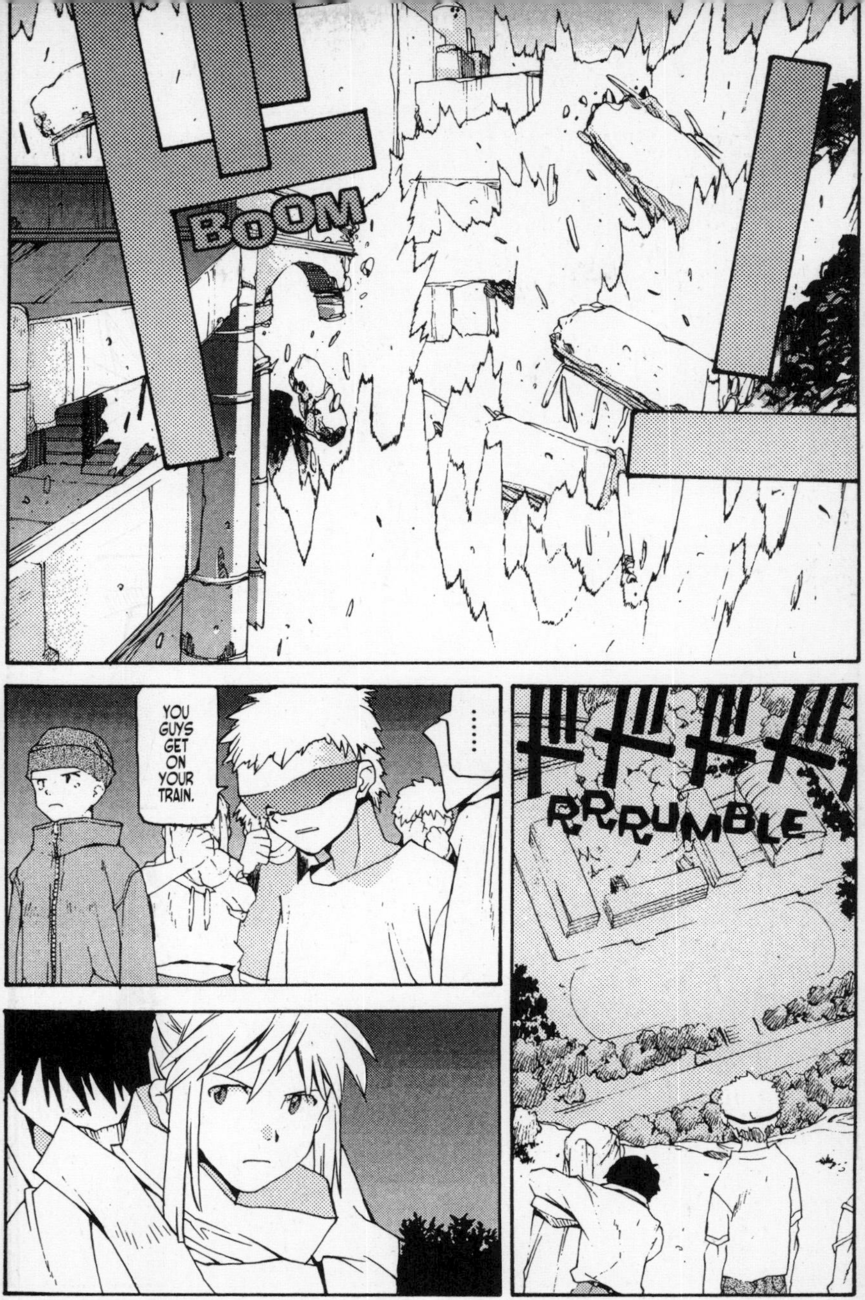
BOOM
RRRUMBLE
......
YOU GUYS GET ON YOUR TRAIN.

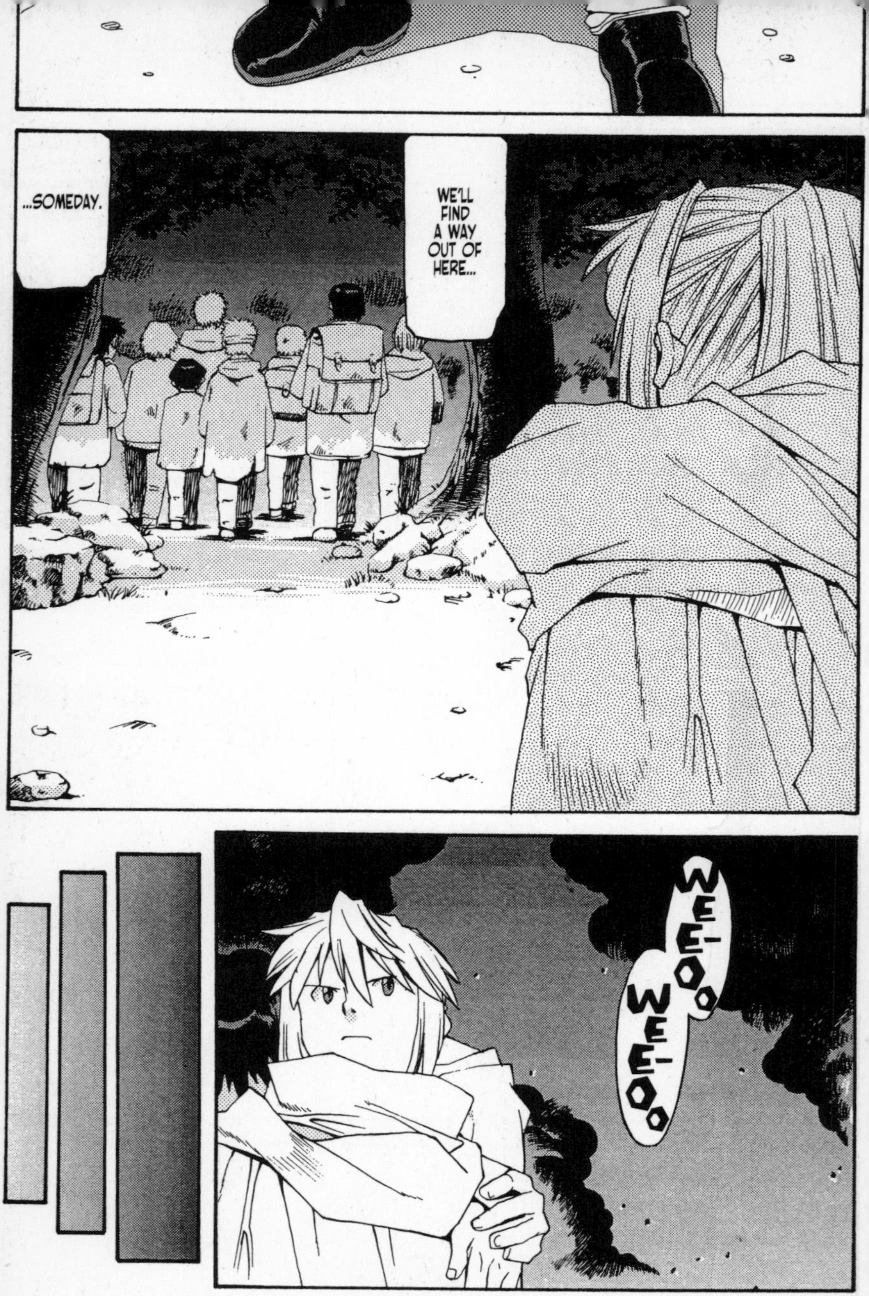
WE'LL FIND A WAY OUT OF HERE...
...SOMEDAY.
WEE-OO WEE-OO

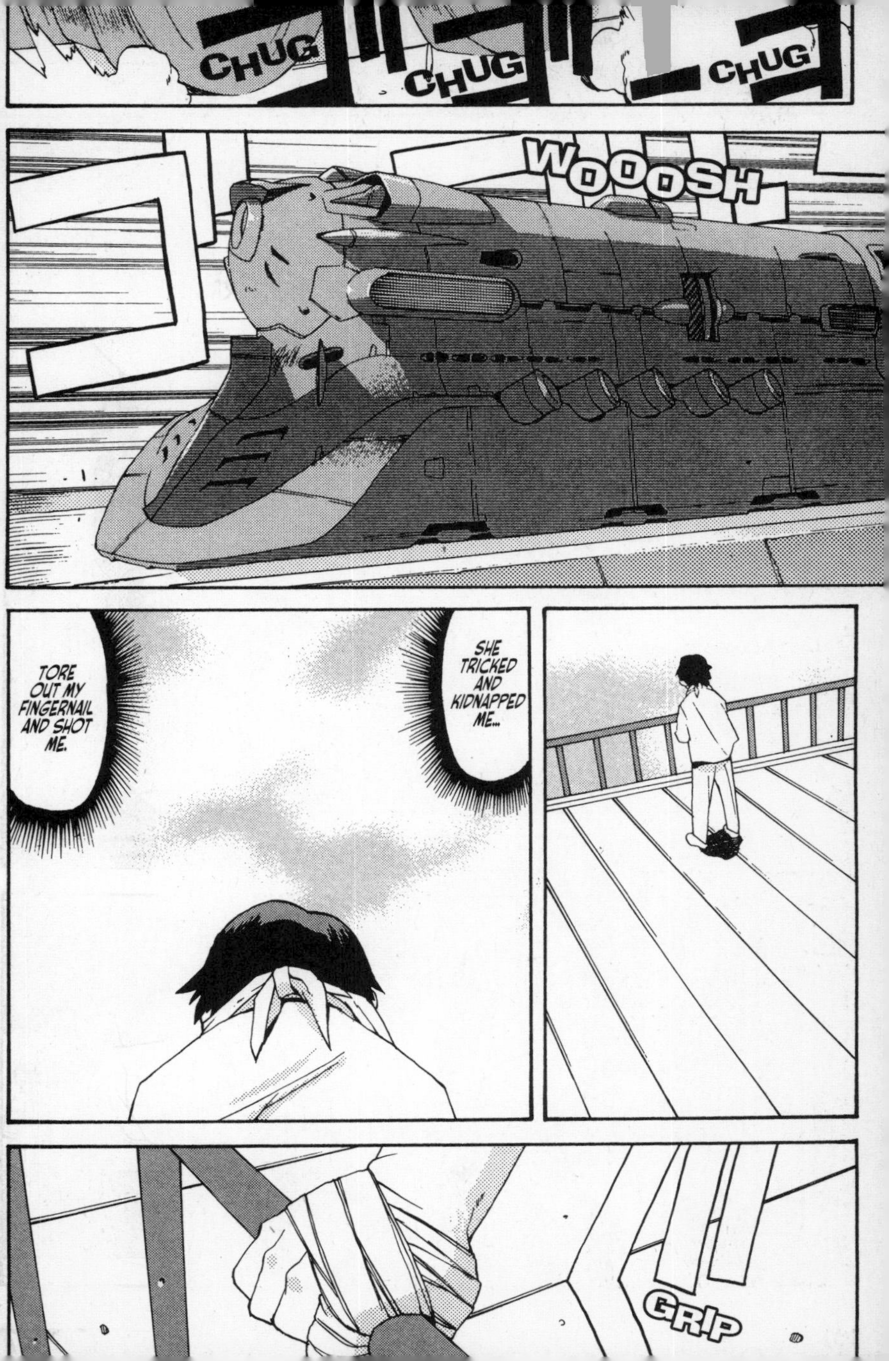
CHUG
CHUG
CHUG
WOOOSH
SHE TRICKED AND KIDNAPPED ME...
TORE OUT MY FINGERNAIL AND SHOT ME.
GRIP

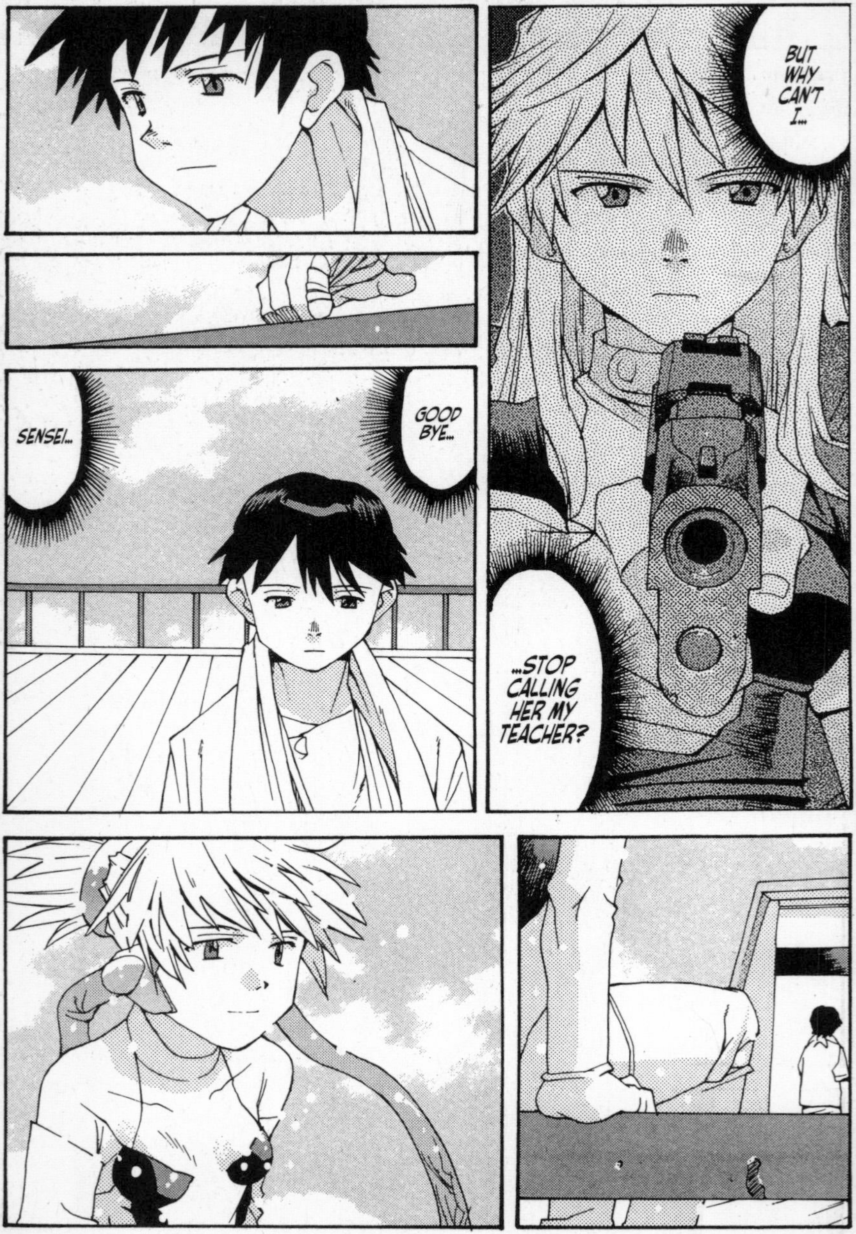
BUT WHY CAN'T I...
...STOP CALLING HER MY TEACHER?
GOOD BYE...
SENSEI...

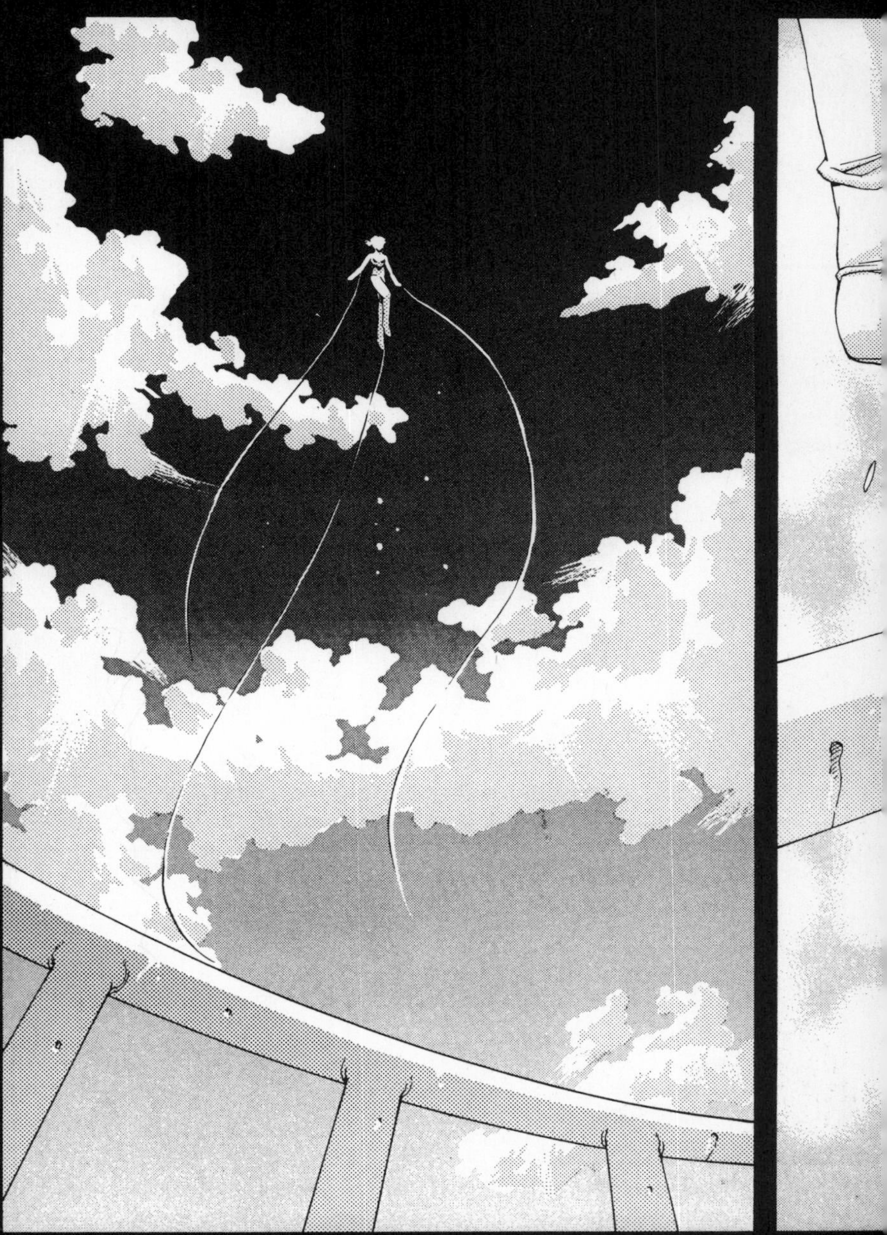

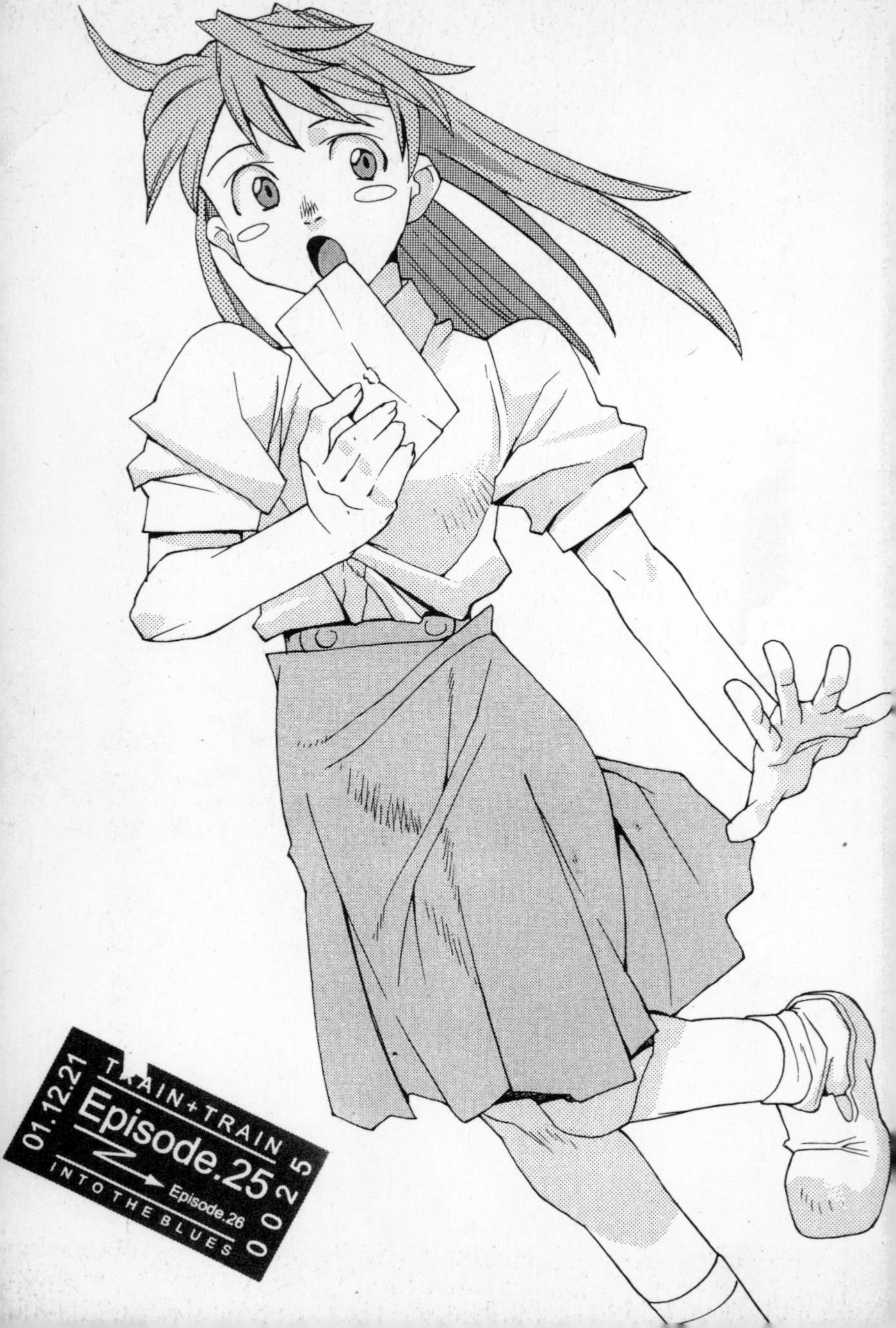
01.12.21
TRAIN+TRAIN
Episode.25
Episode.26
INTO THE BLUES
0025

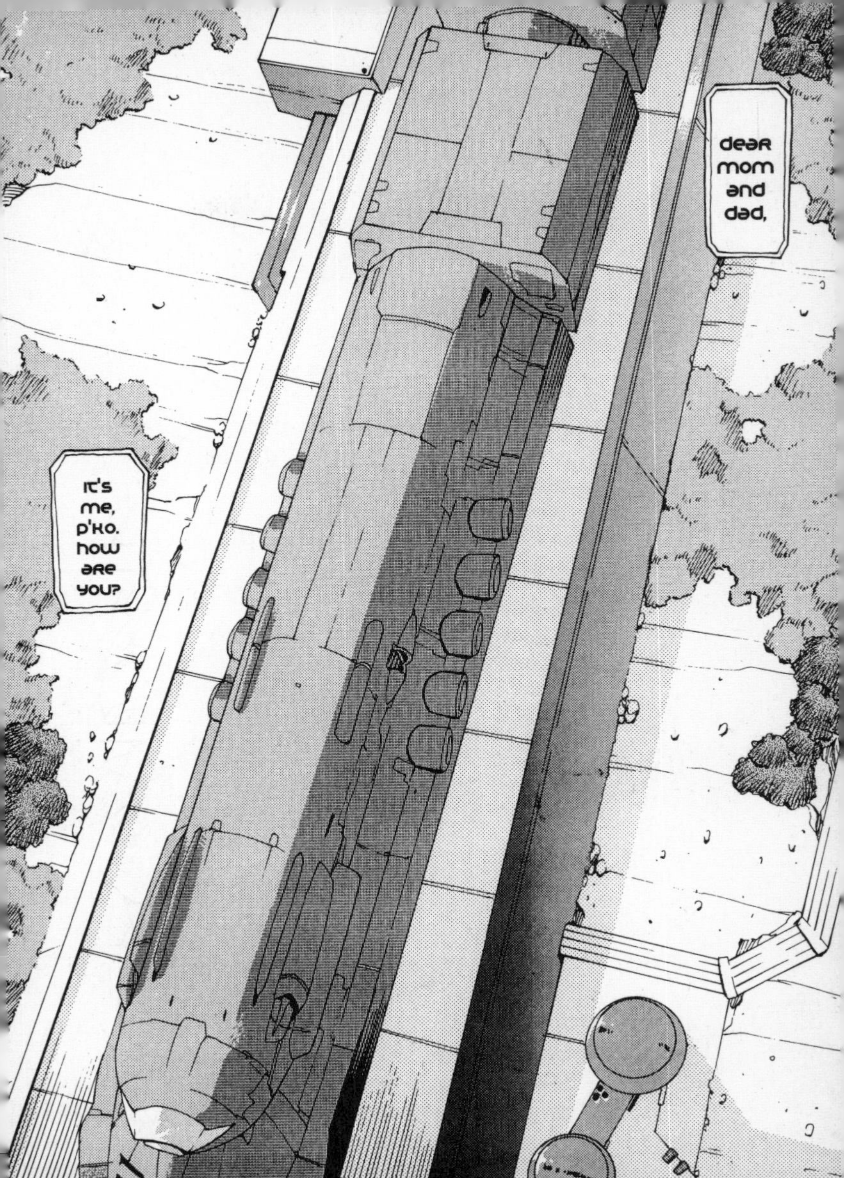
dear mom and dad,
it's me, p'ko. how are you?

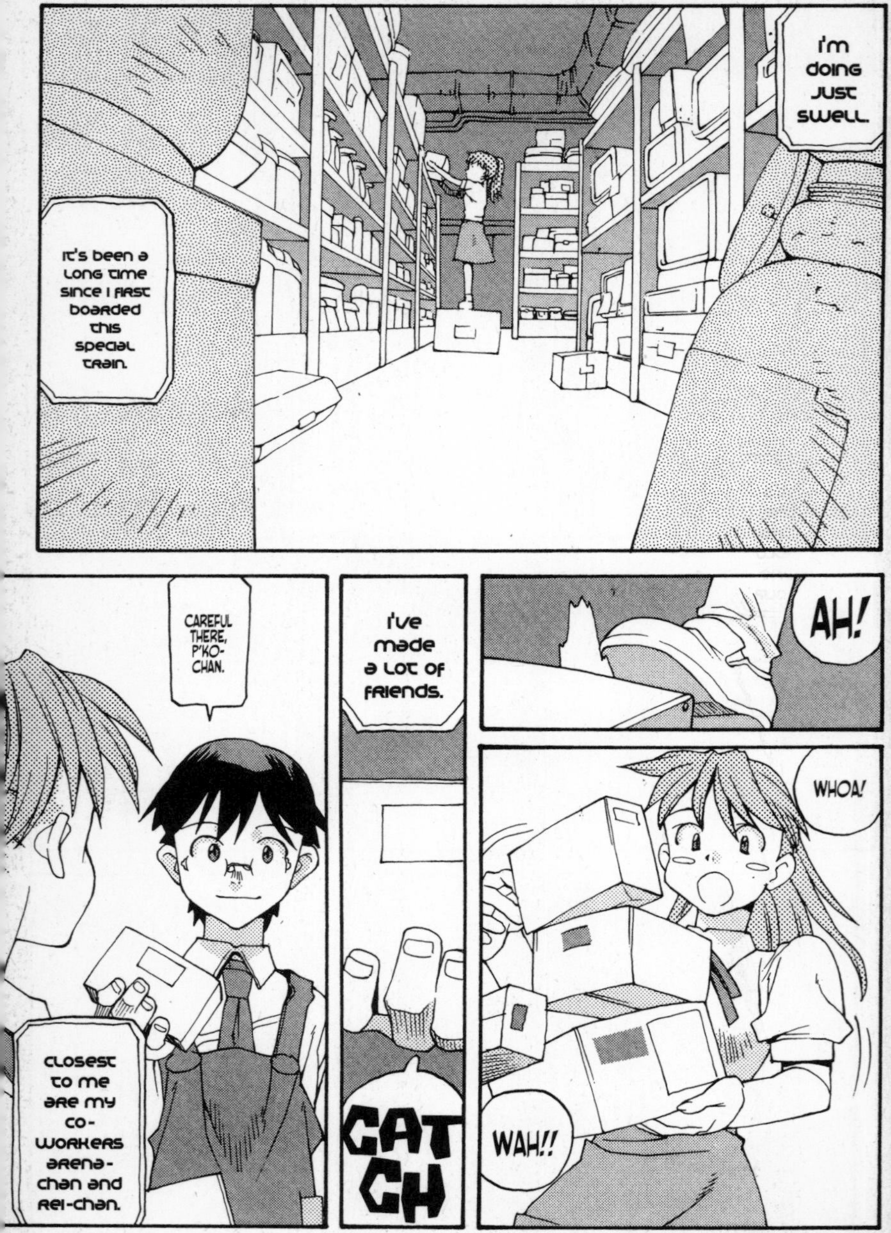
I'm doing just swell.
It's been a long time since I first boarded this special train.
AH!
WHOA!
WAH!!
I've made a lot of friends.
CATCH
CAREFUL THERE, P'KO-CHAN.
Closest to me are my co-workers Arena-chan and Rei-chan.

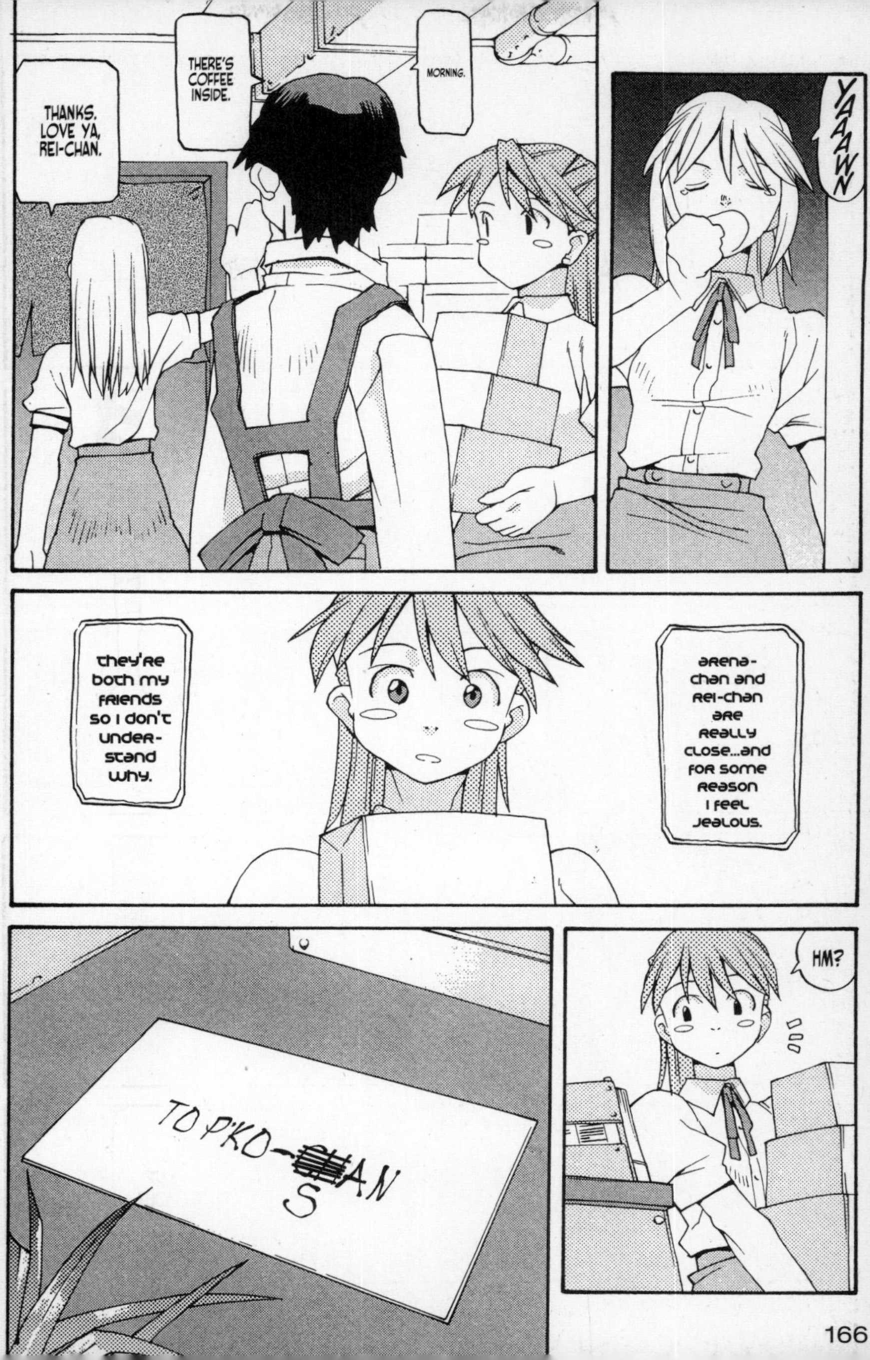
YAAAWN
MORNING.
THERE'S COFFEE INSIDE.
THANKS. LOVE YA, REI-CHAN.
arena-chan and rei-chan are really close...and for some reason I feel jealous.
they're both my friends so I don't understand why.
HM?
TO P'KO- AN
S

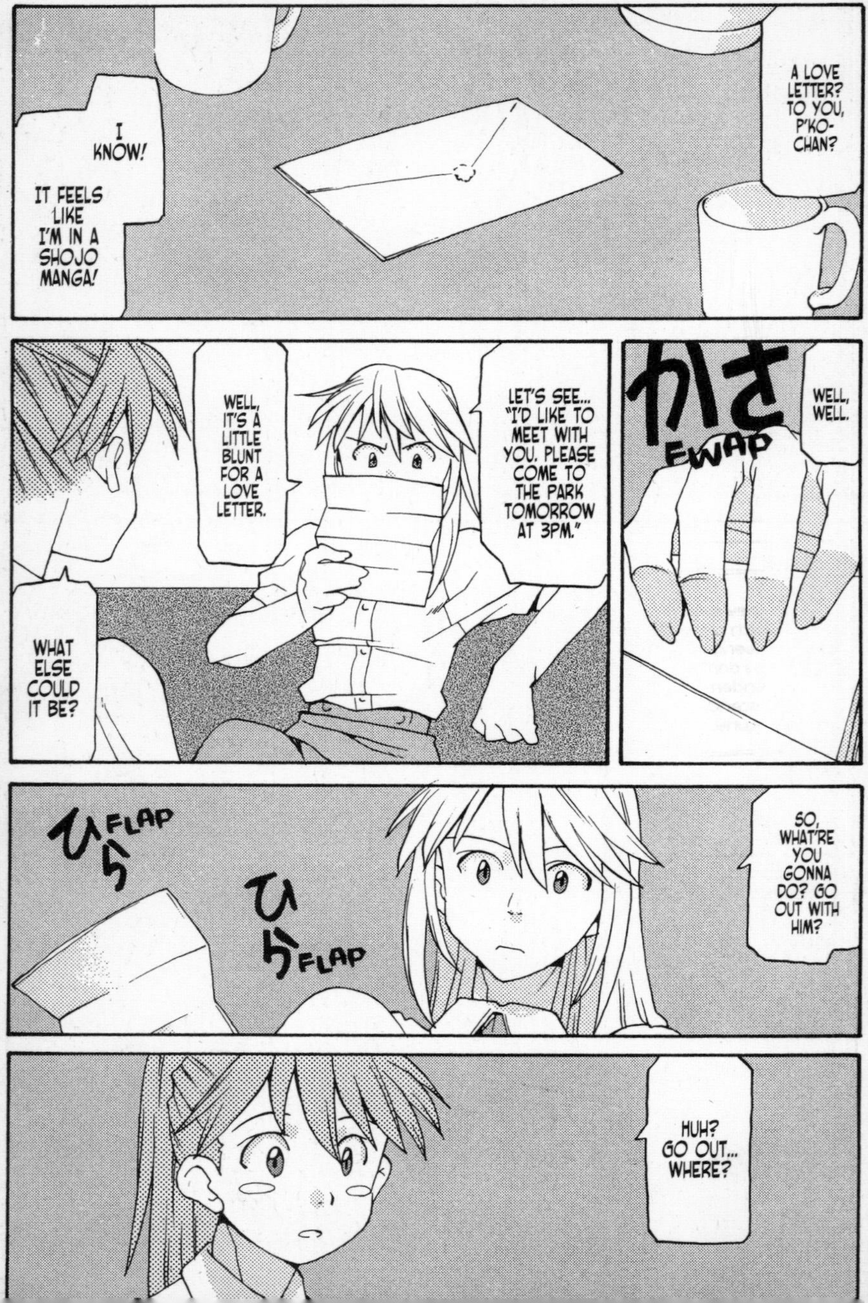
A LOVE LETTER? TO YOU, P'KO-CHAN?
I KNOW!
IT FEELS LIKE I'M IN A SHOJO MANGA!
WELL, WELL.
かさ FWAP
LET'S SEE... "I'D LIKE TO MEET WITH YOU. PLEASE COME TO THE PARK TOMORROW AT 3PM."
WELL, IT'S A LITTLE BLUNT FOR A LOVE LETTER.
WHAT ELSE COULD IT BE?
SO, WHAT'RE YOU GONNA DO? GO OUT WITH HIM?
ひら FLAP
ひら FLAP
HUH? GO OUT... WHERE?

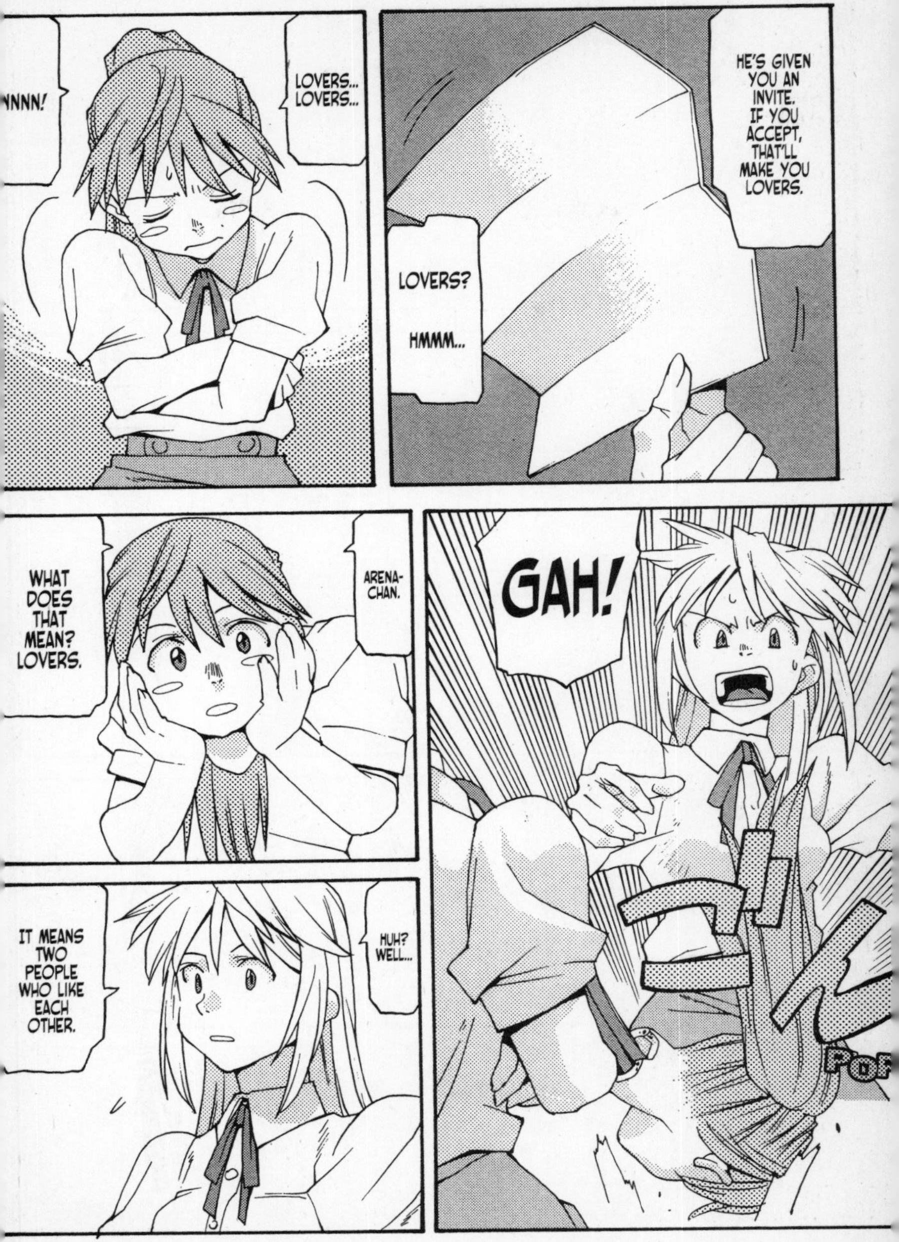
HE'S GIVEN YOU AN INVITE. IF YOU ACCEPT, THAT'LL MAKE YOU LOVERS.
LOVERS?
HMMM...
LOVERS... LOVERS...
NNNN!
GAH!
POF
ARENA-CHAN.
WHAT DOES THAT MEAN? LOVERS.
HUH? WELL...
IT MEANS TWO PEOPLE WHO LIKE EACH OTHER.

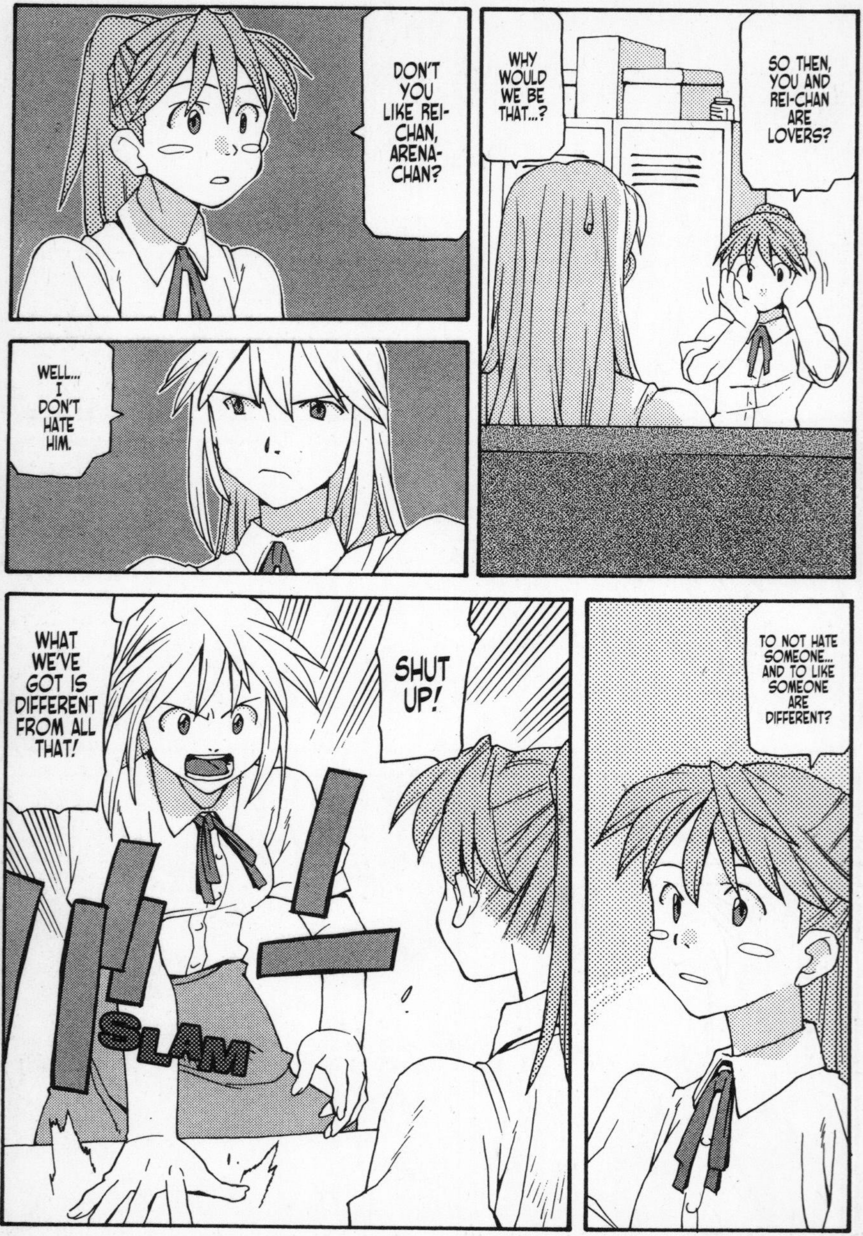
SO THEN, YOU AND REI-CHAN ARE LOVERS?
WHY WOULD WE BE THAT...?
DON'T YOU LIKE REI-CHAN, ARENA-CHAN?
WELL... I DON'T HATE HIM.
TO NOT HATE SOMEONE... AND TO LIKE SOMEONE ARE DIFFERENT?
SHUT UP!
WHAT WE'VE GOT IS DIFFERENT FROM ALL THAT!
SLAM

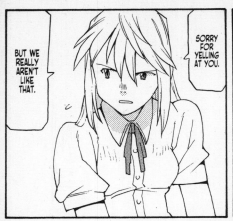

BUT WE REALLY AREN'T LIKE THAT.

SORRY FOR YELLING AT YOU.

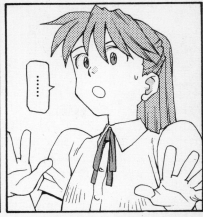

. . . .

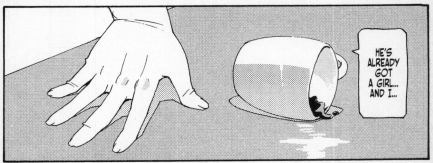

HE'S ALREADY GOT A GIRL... AND I...

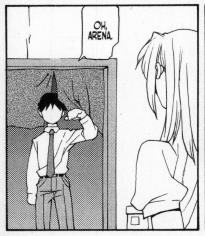

OH, ARENA.

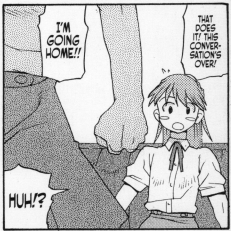

I'M GOING HOME!!

THAT DOES IT! THIS CONVERSATION'S OVER!

HUH!?

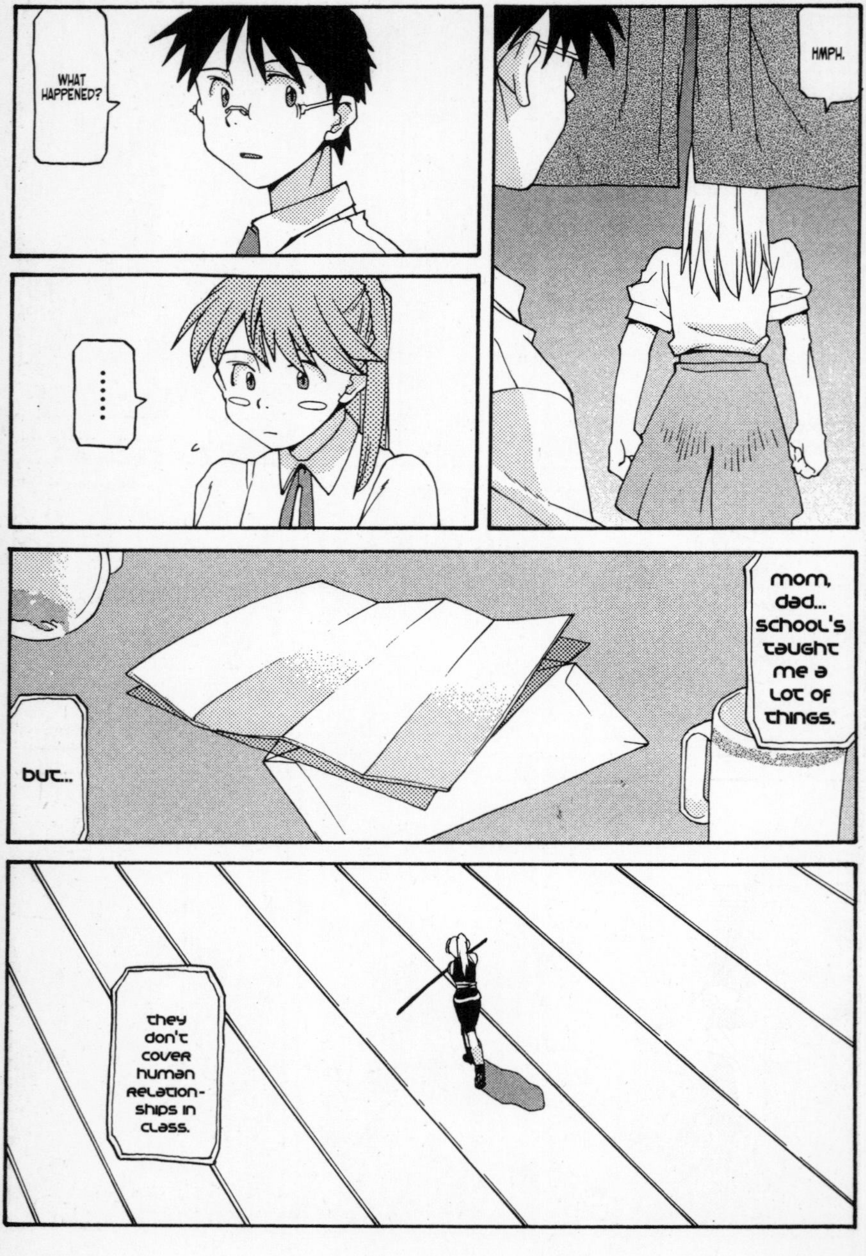
HMPH.
WHAT HAPPENED?
......
mom, dad... school's taught me a lot of things.
but...
they don't cover human relation-ships in class.

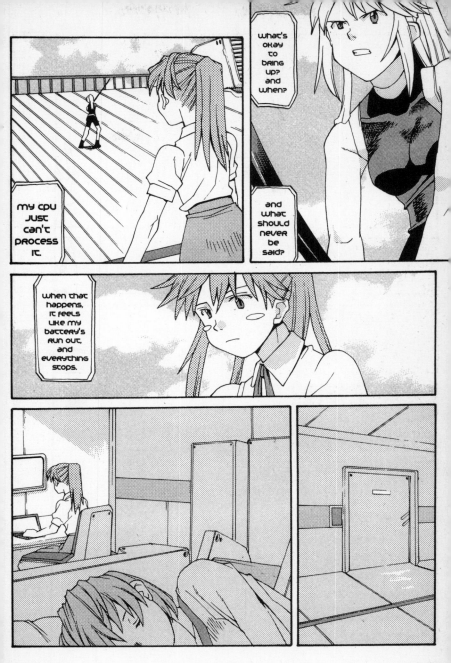

WHAT'S OKAY TO BRING UP? AND WHEN?

MY CPU JUST CAN'T PROCESS IT.

AND WHAT SHOULD NEVER BE SAID?

WHEN THAT HAPPENS, IT FEELS LIKE MY BATTERY'S RUN OUT, AND EVERYTHING STOPS.

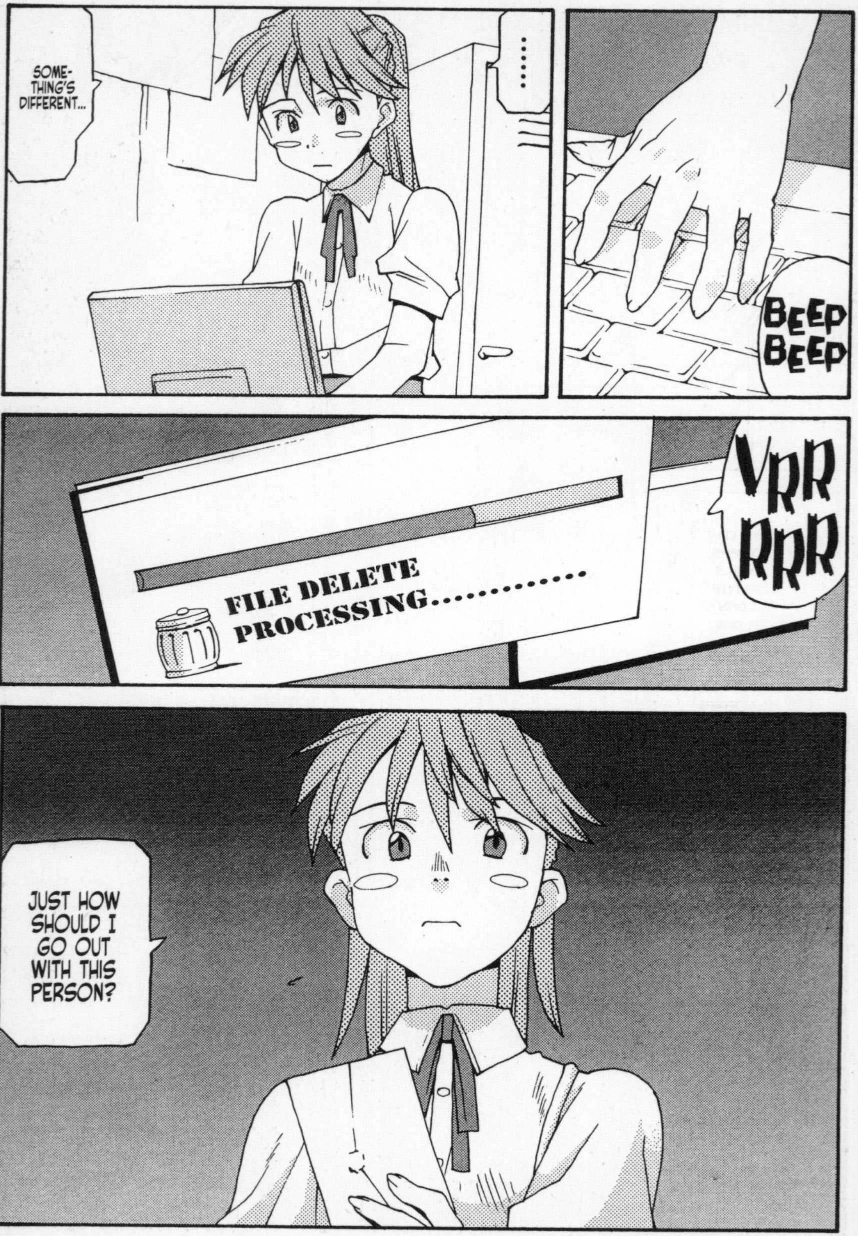
BEEP BEEP
......
SOME-THING'S DIFFERENT...
VRR RRR
FILE DELETE PROCESSING............
JUST HOW SHOULD I GO OUT WITH THIS PERSON?

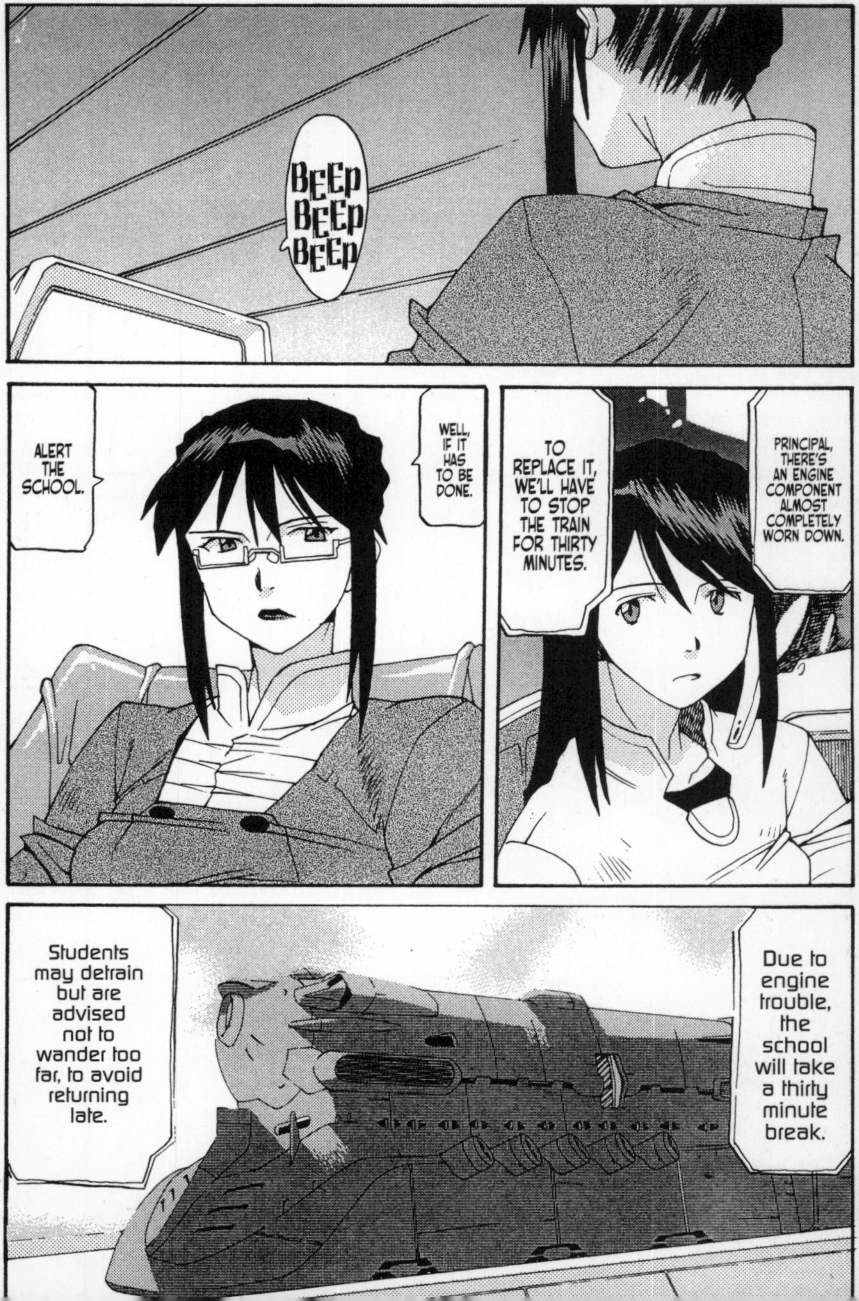
BEEP BEEP BEEP
PRINCIPAL, THERE'S AN ENGINE COMPONENT ALMOST COMPLETELY WORN DOWN.
TO REPLACE IT, WE'LL HAVE TO STOP THE TRAIN FOR THIRTY MINUTES.
WELL, IF IT HAS TO BE DONE.
ALERT THE SCHOOL.
Due to engine trouble, the school will take a thirty minute break.
Students may detrain but are advised not to wander too far, to avoid returning late.

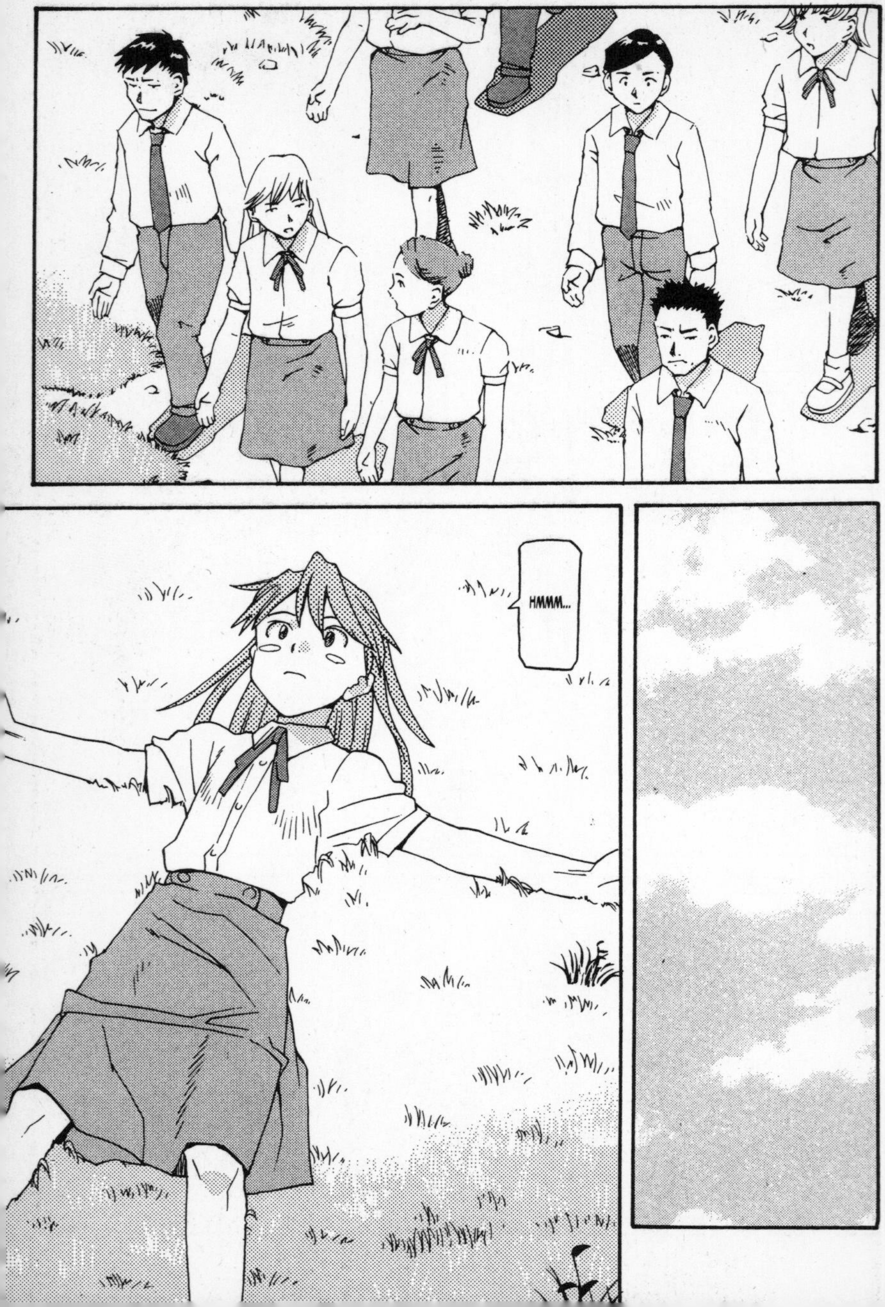
HMMM...

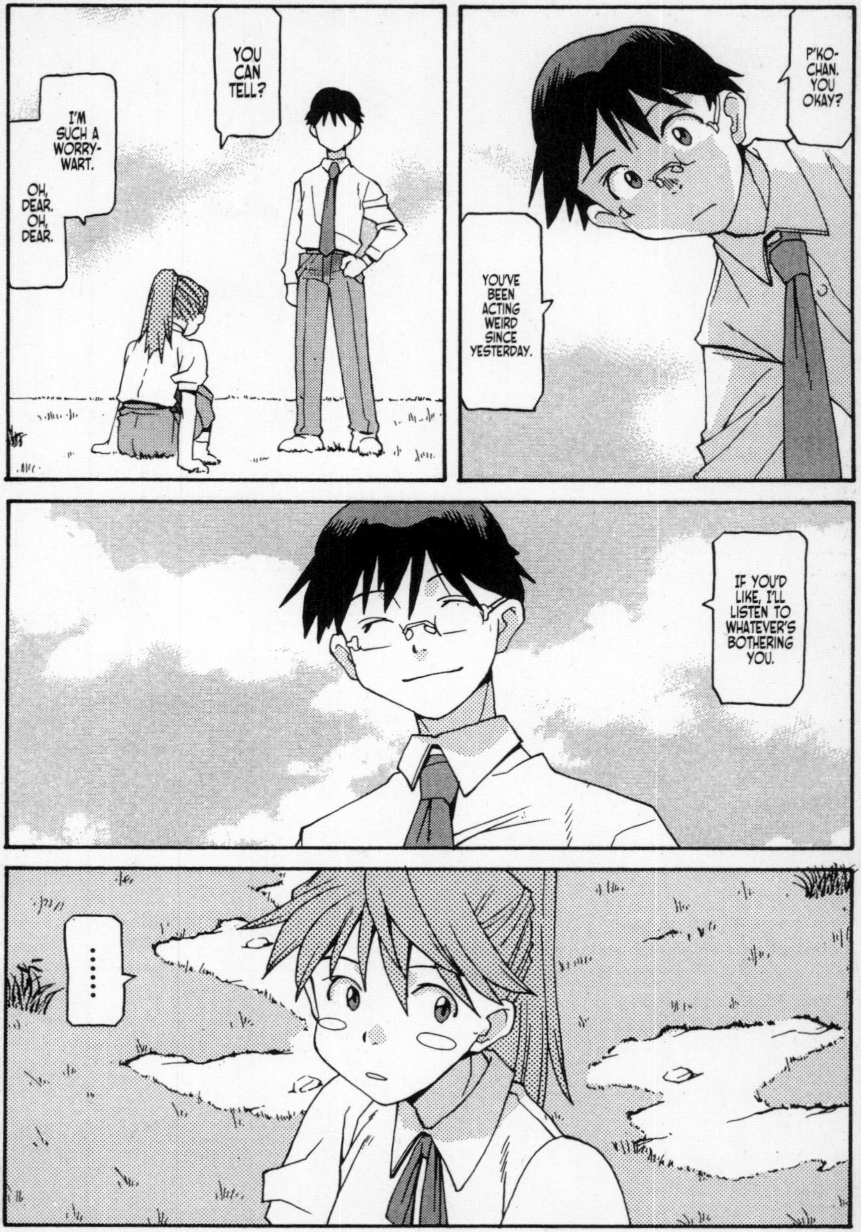
P'KO-CHAN. YOU OKAY?
YOU'VE BEEN ACTING WEIRD SINCE YESTERDAY.
YOU CAN TELL?
I'M SUCH A WORRY-WART.
OH, DEAR. OH, DEAR.
IF YOU'D LIKE, I'LL LISTEN TO WHATEVER'S BOTHERING YOU.
......

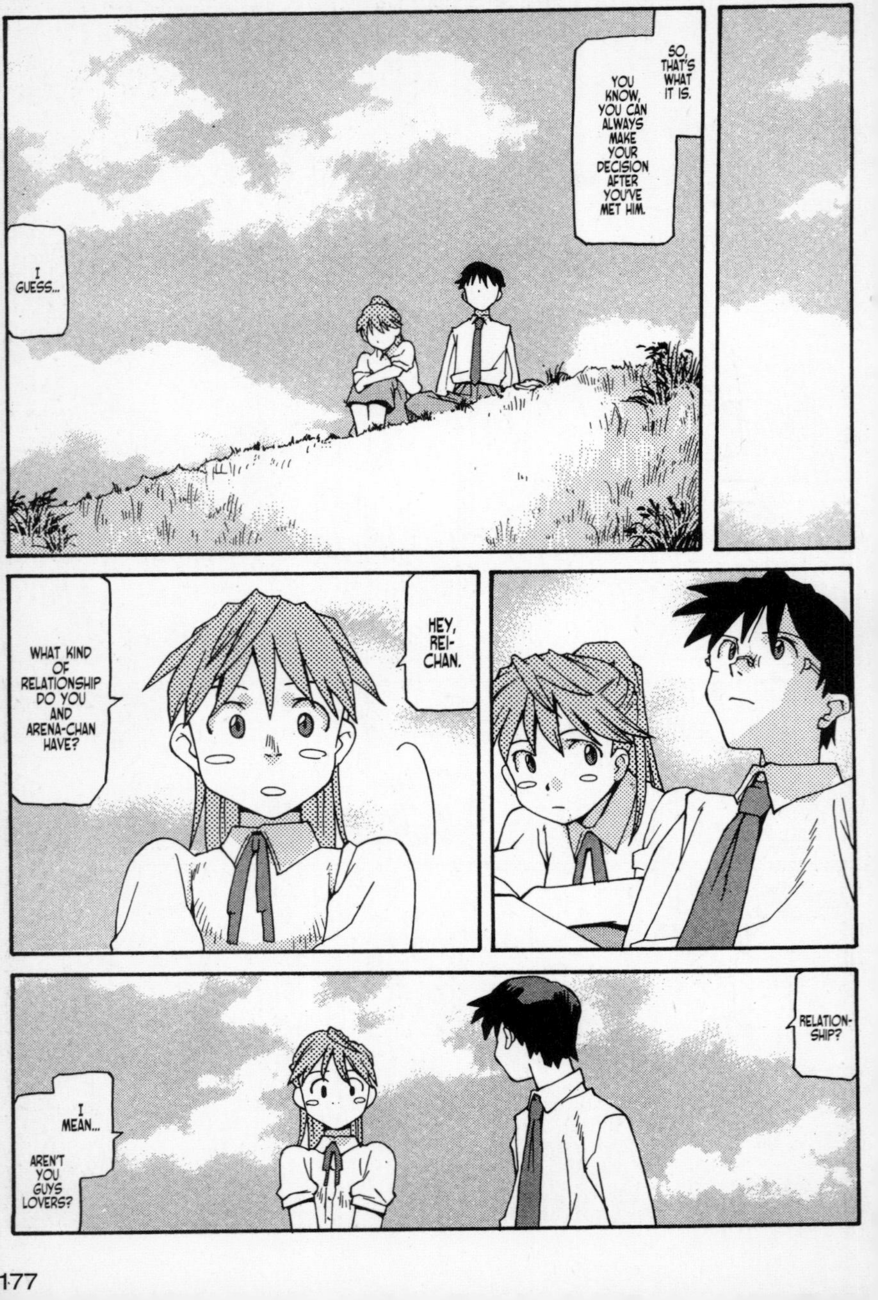
SO, THAT'S WHAT IT IS.
YOU KNOW, YOU CAN ALWAYS MAKE YOUR DECISION AFTER YOU'VE MET HIM.
I GUESS...
HEY, REI-CHAN.
WHAT KIND OF RELATIONSHIP DO YOU AND ARENA-CHAN HAVE?
RELATION-SHIP?
I MEAN...
AREN'T YOU GUYS LOVERS?

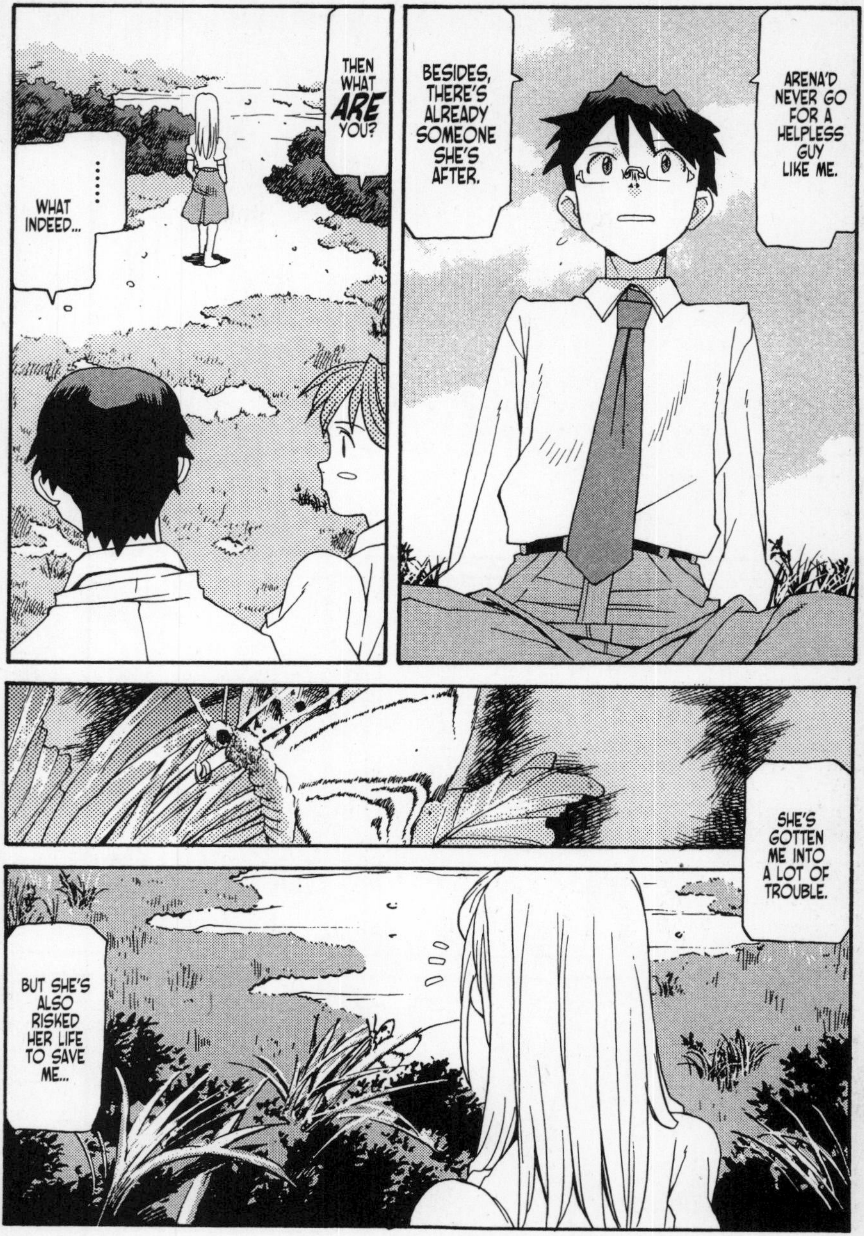
ARENA'D NEVER GO FOR A HELPLESS GUY LIKE ME.
BESIDES, THERE'S ALREADY SOMEONE SHE'S AFTER.
THEN WHAT ARE YOU?
......
WHAT INDEED...
SHE'S GOTTEN ME INTO A LOT OF TROUBLE.
BUT SHE'S ALSO RISKED HER LIFE TO SAVE ME...

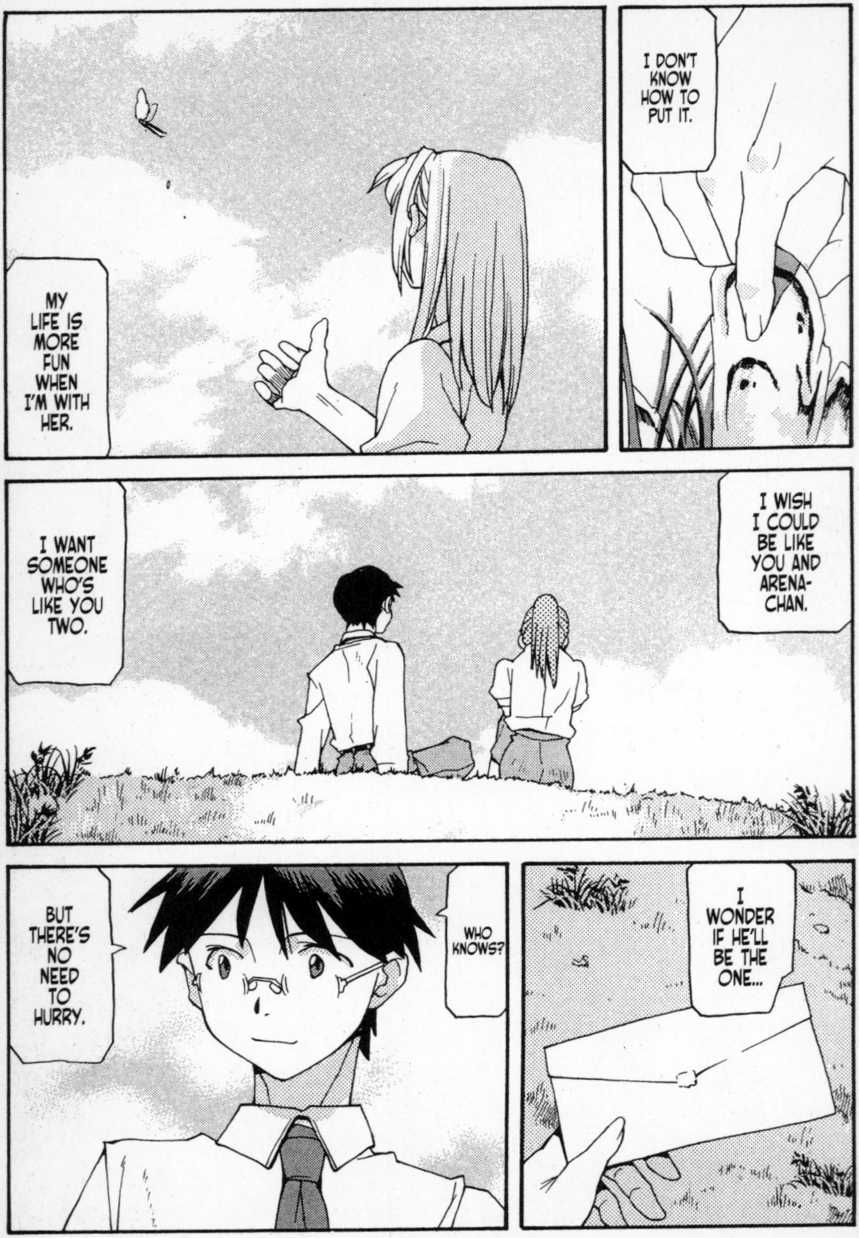
I DON'T KNOW HOW TO PUT IT.
MY LIFE IS MORE FUN WHEN I'M WITH HER.
I WISH I COULD BE LIKE YOU AND ARENA-CHAN.
I WANT SOMEONE WHO'S LIKE YOU TWO.
I WONDER IF HE'LL BE THE ONE...
WHO KNOWS?
BUT THERE'S NO NEED TO HURRY.

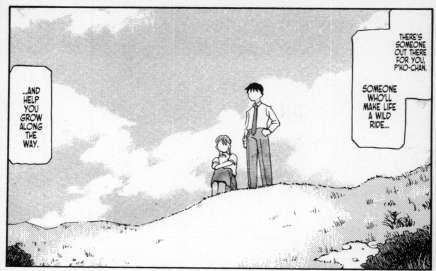

THERE'S SOMEONE OUT THERE FOR YOU, P'KO-CHAN.

SOMEONE WHO'LL MAKE LIFE A WILD RIDE...

...AND HELP YOU GROW ALONG THE WAY.

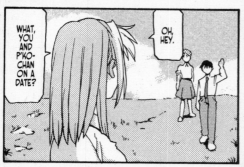

WHAT, YOU AND P'KO-CHAN ON A DATE?

OH, HEY.

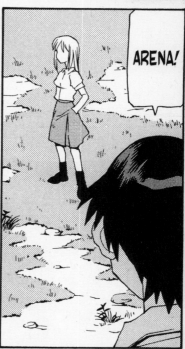

ARENA!

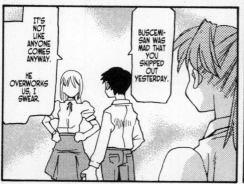

IT'S NOT LIKE ANYONE COMES ANYWAY.

HE OVERWORKS US, I SWEAR.

BUSCEMI-SAN WAS MAD THAT YOU SKIPPED OUT YESTERDAY.

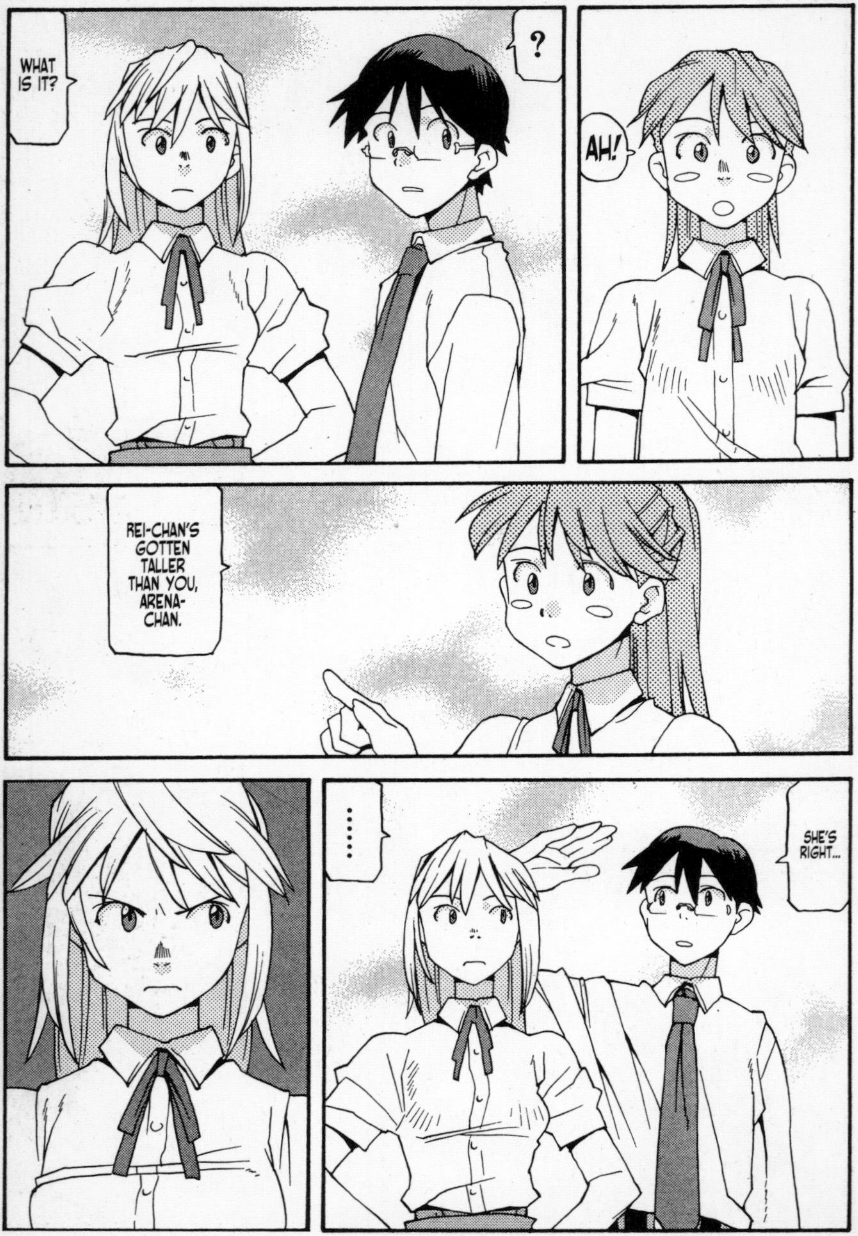
AH!
?
WHAT IS IT?
REI-CHAN'S GOTTEN TALLER THAN YOU, ARENA-CHAN.
SHE'S RIGHT...
......

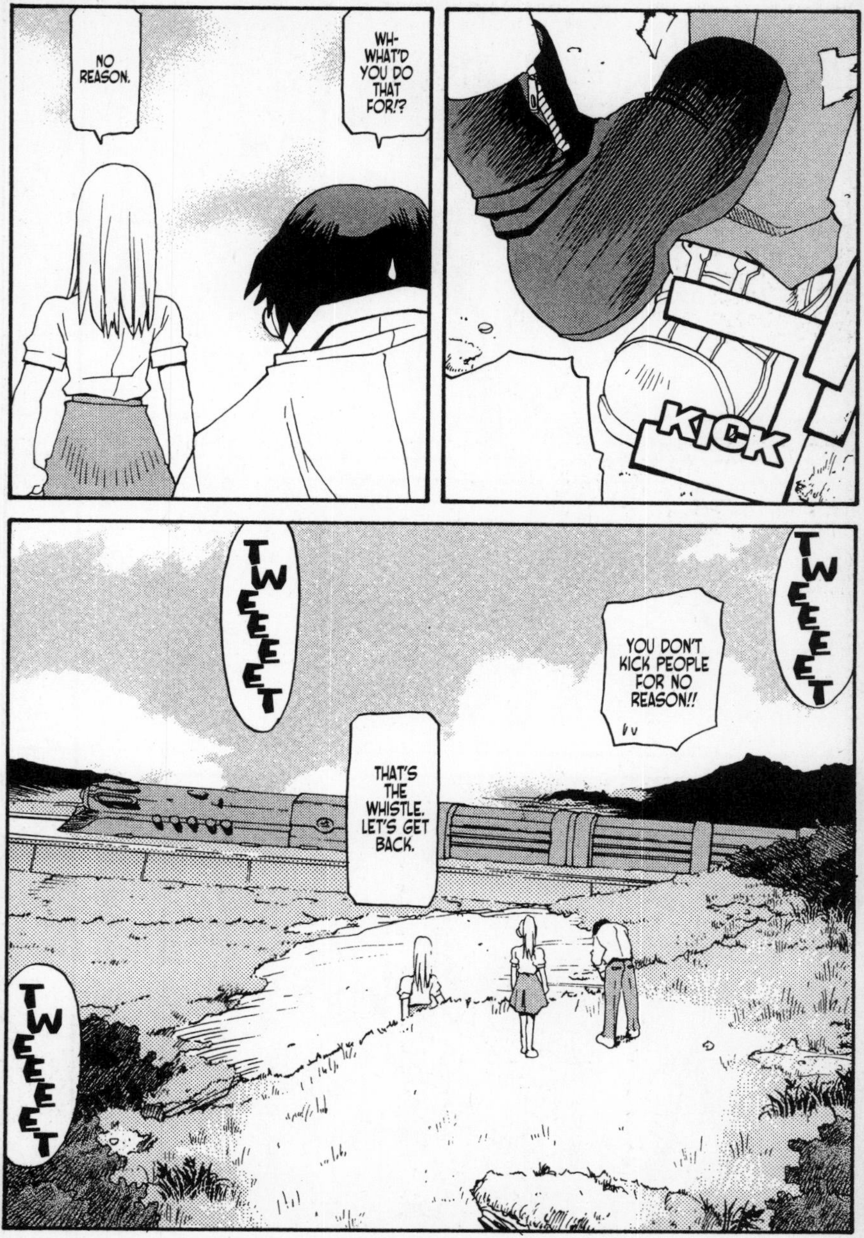
KICK
WH- WHAT'D YOU DO THAT FOR!?
NO REASON.
TWEEEET
YOU DON'T KICK PEOPLE FOR NO REASON!!
TWEEEET
THAT'S THE WHISTLE. LET'S GET BACK.
TWEEEET

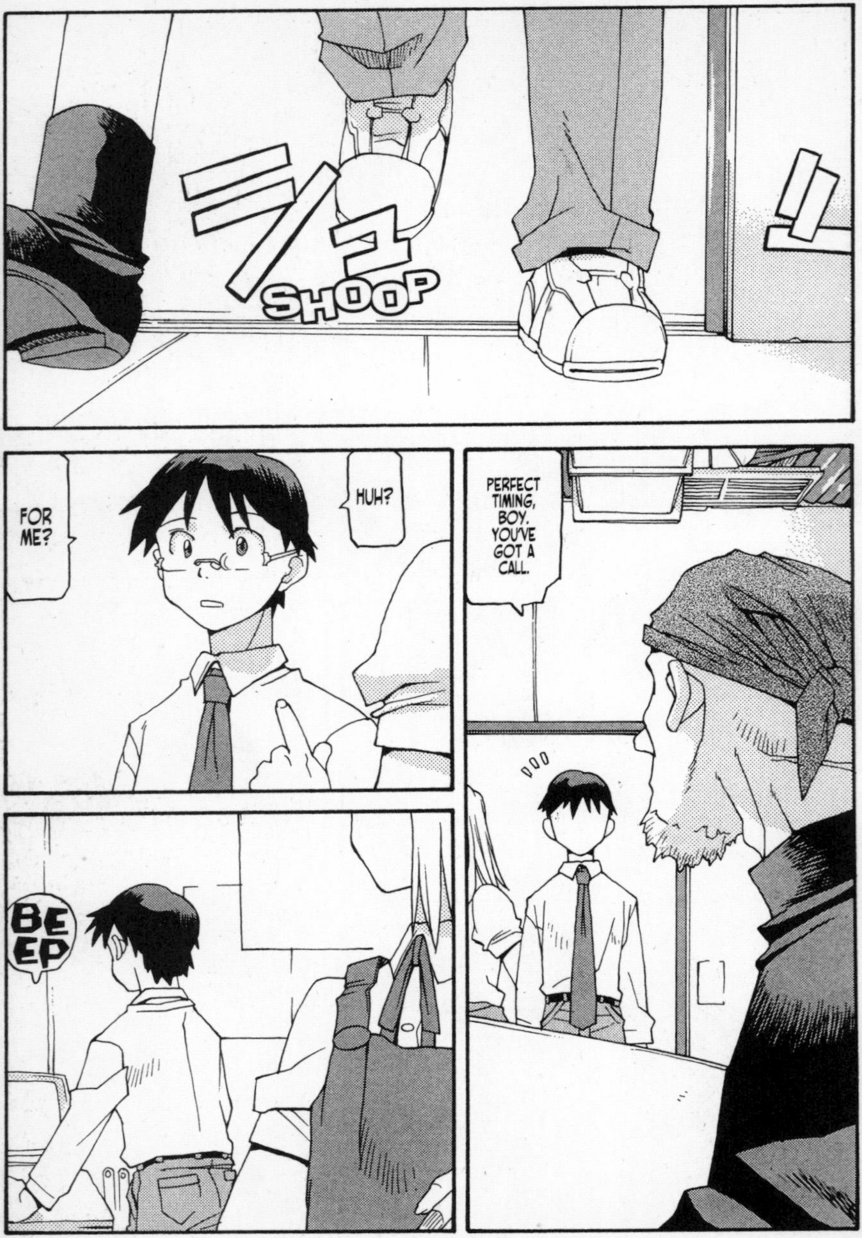
SHOOP
PERFECT TIMING, BOY. YOU'VE GOT A CALL.
HUH?
FOR ME?
BEEP

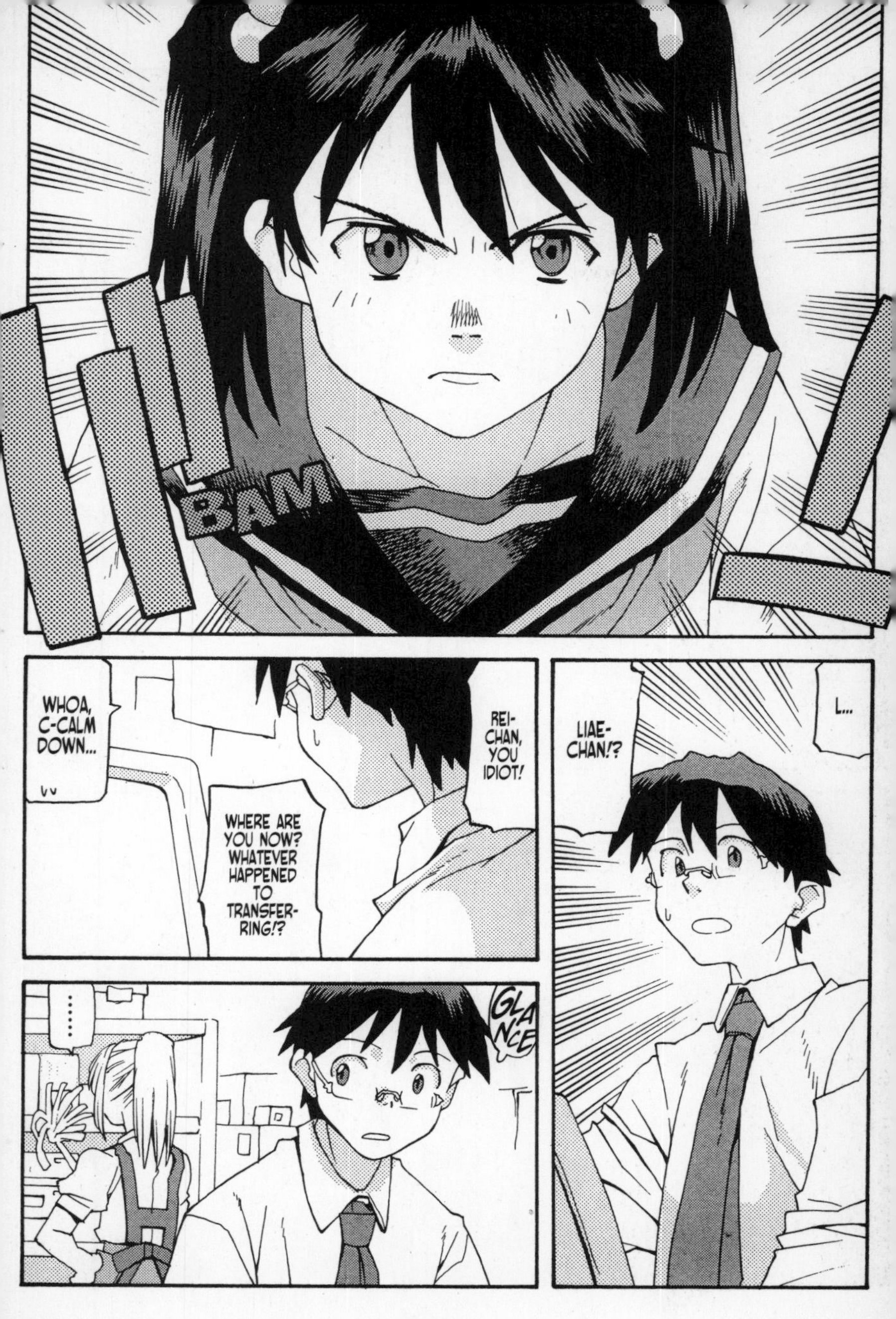
BAM
L...
LIAE-CHAN!?
REI-CHAN, YOU IDIOT!
WHERE ARE YOU NOW? WHATEVER HAPPENED TO TRANSFER-RING!?
WHOA, C-CALM DOWN...
GLANCE
......

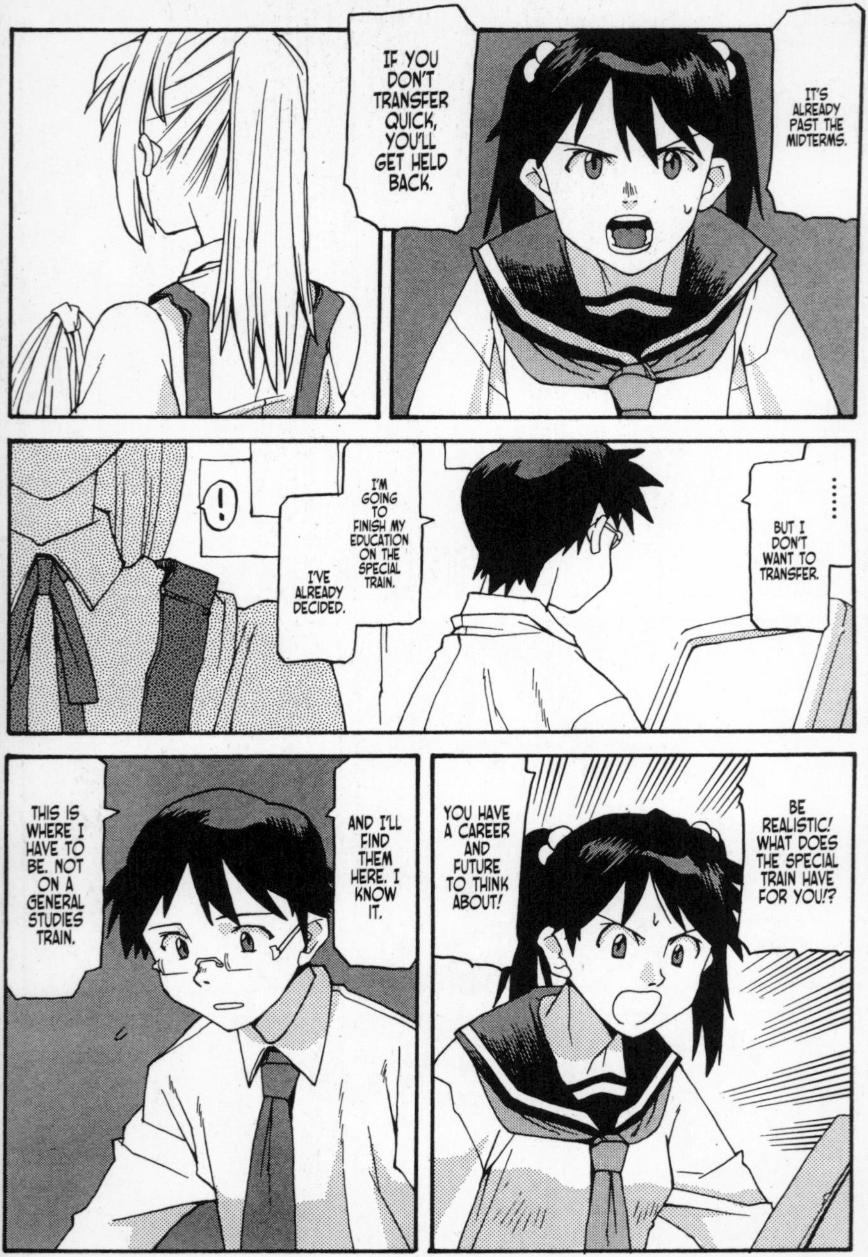
IT'S ALREADY PAST THE MIDTERMS.
IF YOU DON'T TRANSFER QUICK, YOU'LL GET HELD BACK.
......
BUT I DON'T WANT TO TRANSFER.
I'M GOING TO FINISH MY EDUCATION ON THE SPECIAL TRAIN.
I'VE ALREADY DECIDED.
!
BE REALISTIC! WHAT DOES THE SPECIAL TRAIN HAVE FOR YOU!?
YOU HAVE A CAREER AND FUTURE TO THINK ABOUT!
AND I'LL FIND THEM HERE. I KNOW IT.
THIS IS WHERE I HAVE TO BE. NOT ON A GENERAL STUDIES TRAIN.

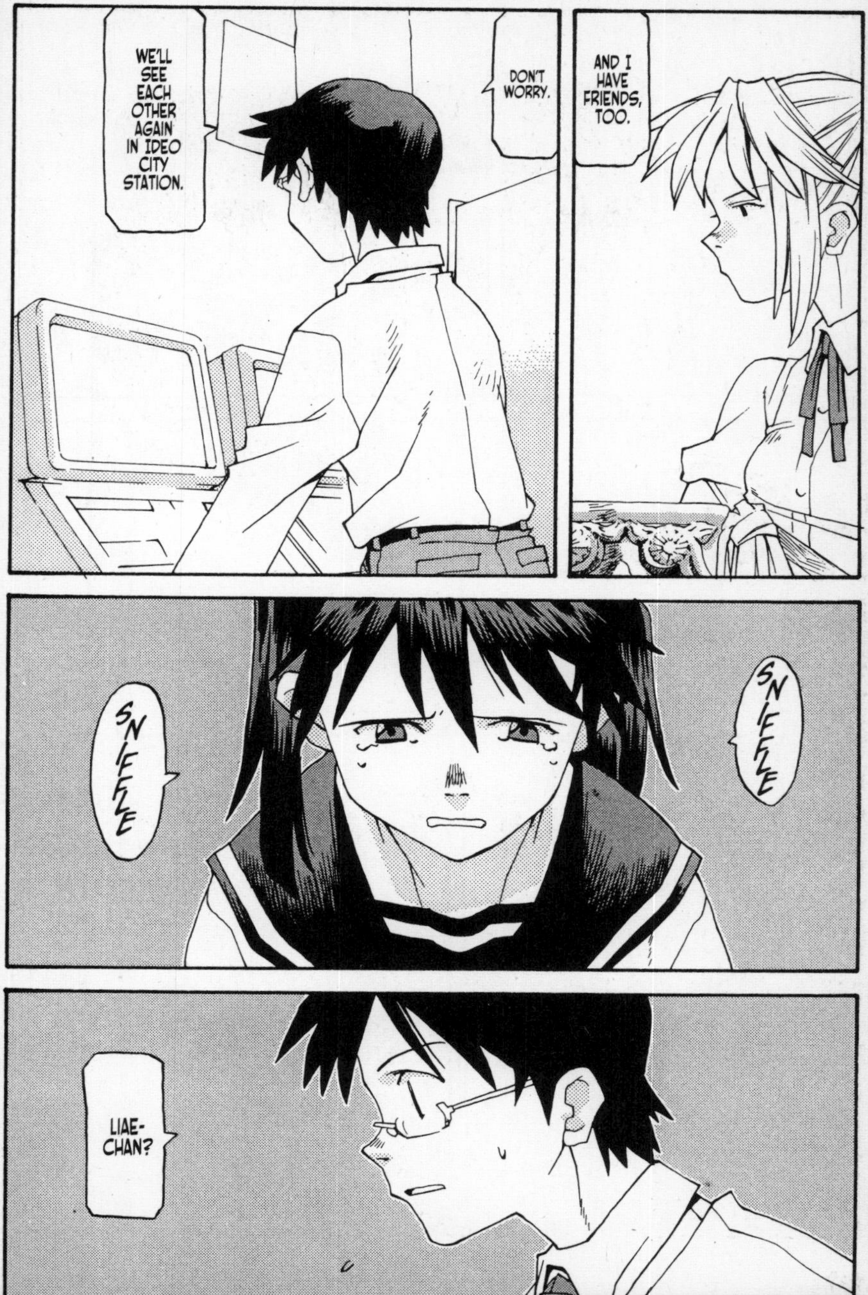
AND I HAVE FRIENDS, TOO.
DON'T WORRY.
WE'LL SEE EACH OTHER AGAIN IN IDEO CITY STATION.
SNIFFLE
SNIFFLE
LIAE-CHAN?

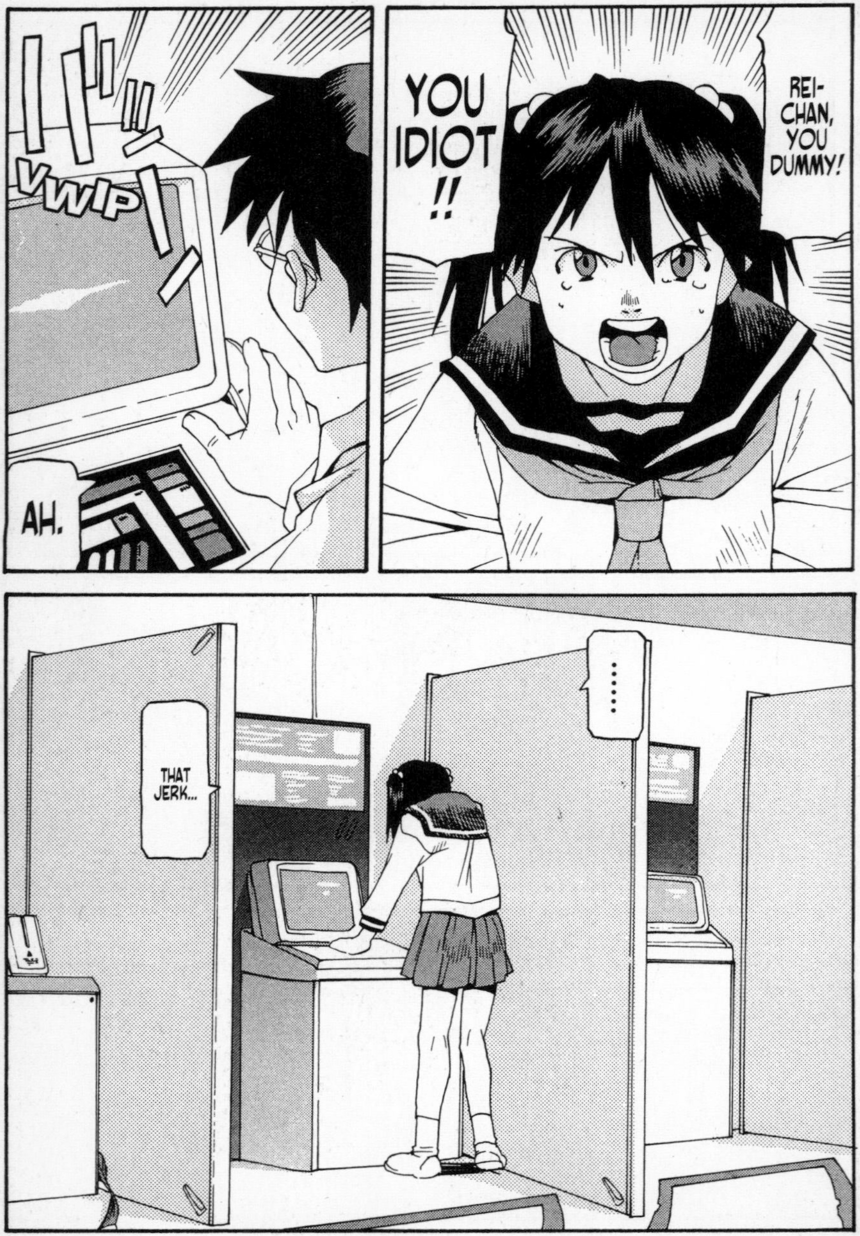
REI-CHAN, YOU DUMMY!
YOU IDIOT!!
VWIP
AH.
......
THAT JERK...

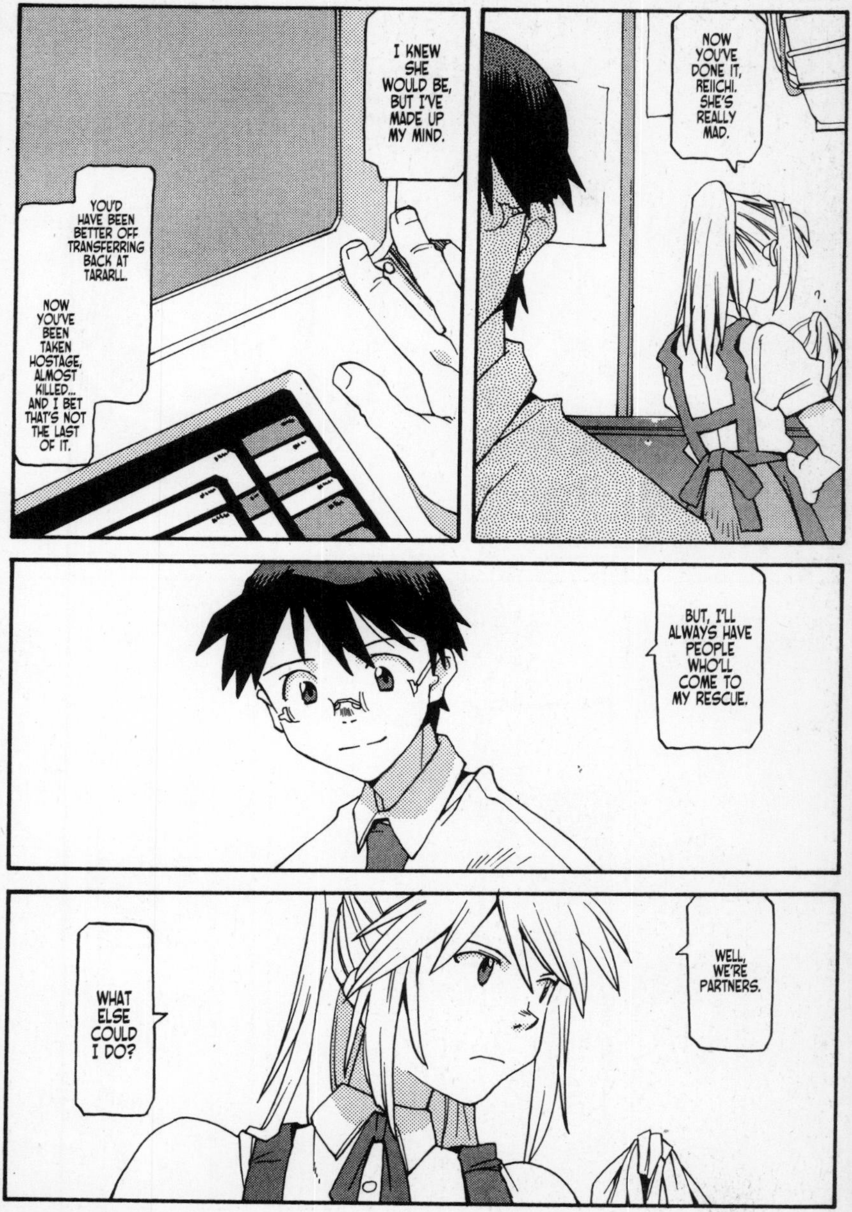
NOW YOU'VE DONE IT, REIICHI. SHE'S REALLY MAD.
I KNEW SHE WOULD BE, BUT I'VE MADE UP MY MIND.
YOU'D HAVE BEEN BETTER OFF TRANSFERRING BACK AT TARARLL.
NOW YOU'VE BEEN TAKEN HOSTAGE, ALMOST KILLED... AND I BET THAT'S NOT THE LAST OF IT.
BUT, I'LL ALWAYS HAVE PEOPLE WHO'LL COME TO MY RESCUE.
WELL, WE'RE PARTNERS.
WHAT ELSE COULD I DO?

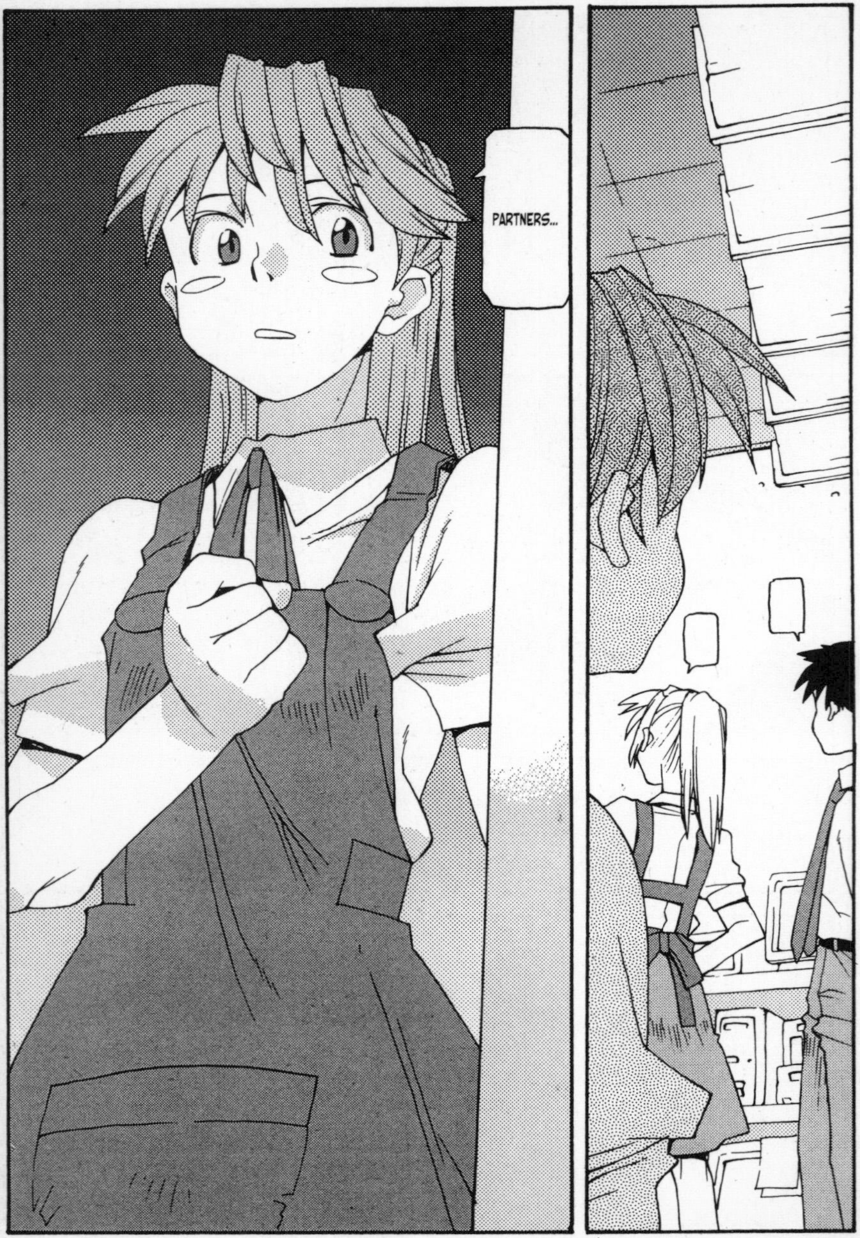
PARTNERS...

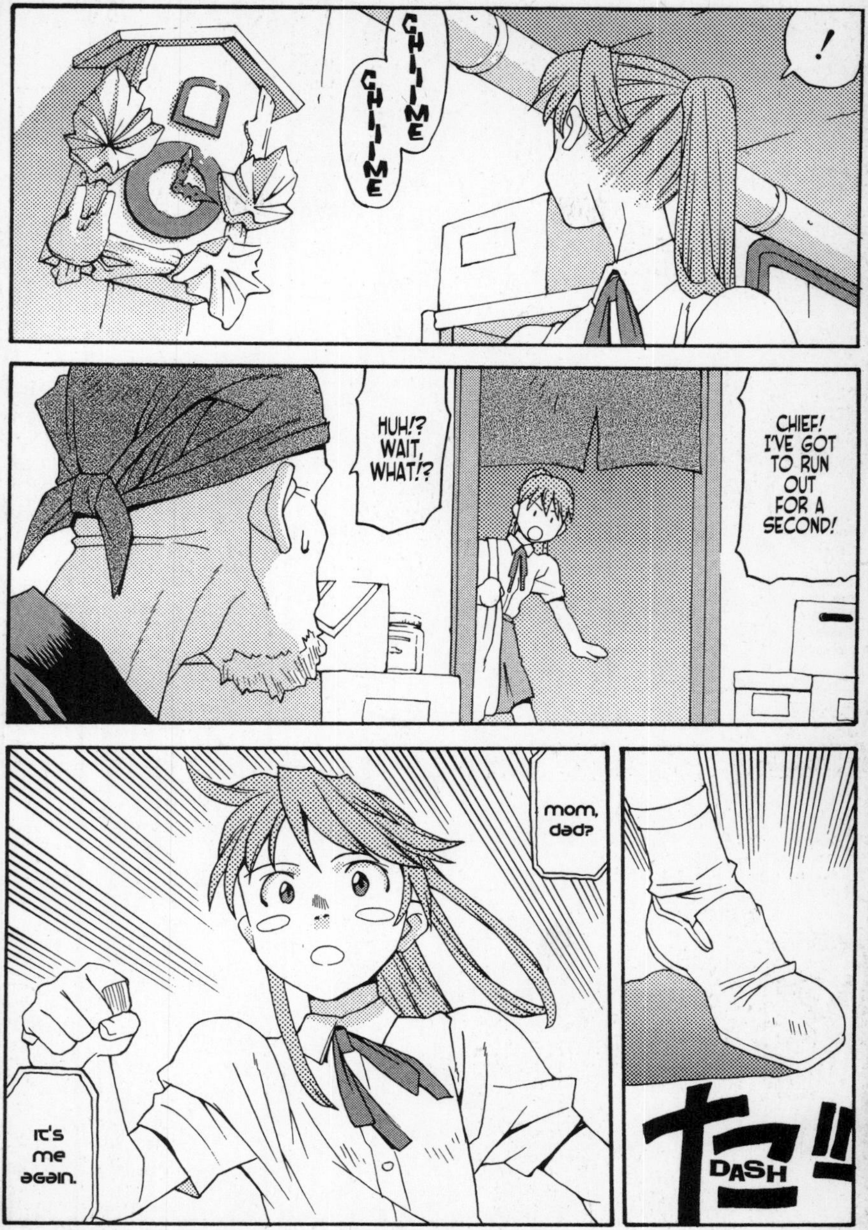
!
CHIIIME
CHIIIME
CHIEF! I'VE GOT TO RUN OUT FOR A SECOND!
HUH!? WAIT, WHAT!?
DASH
mom, dad?
It's me again.

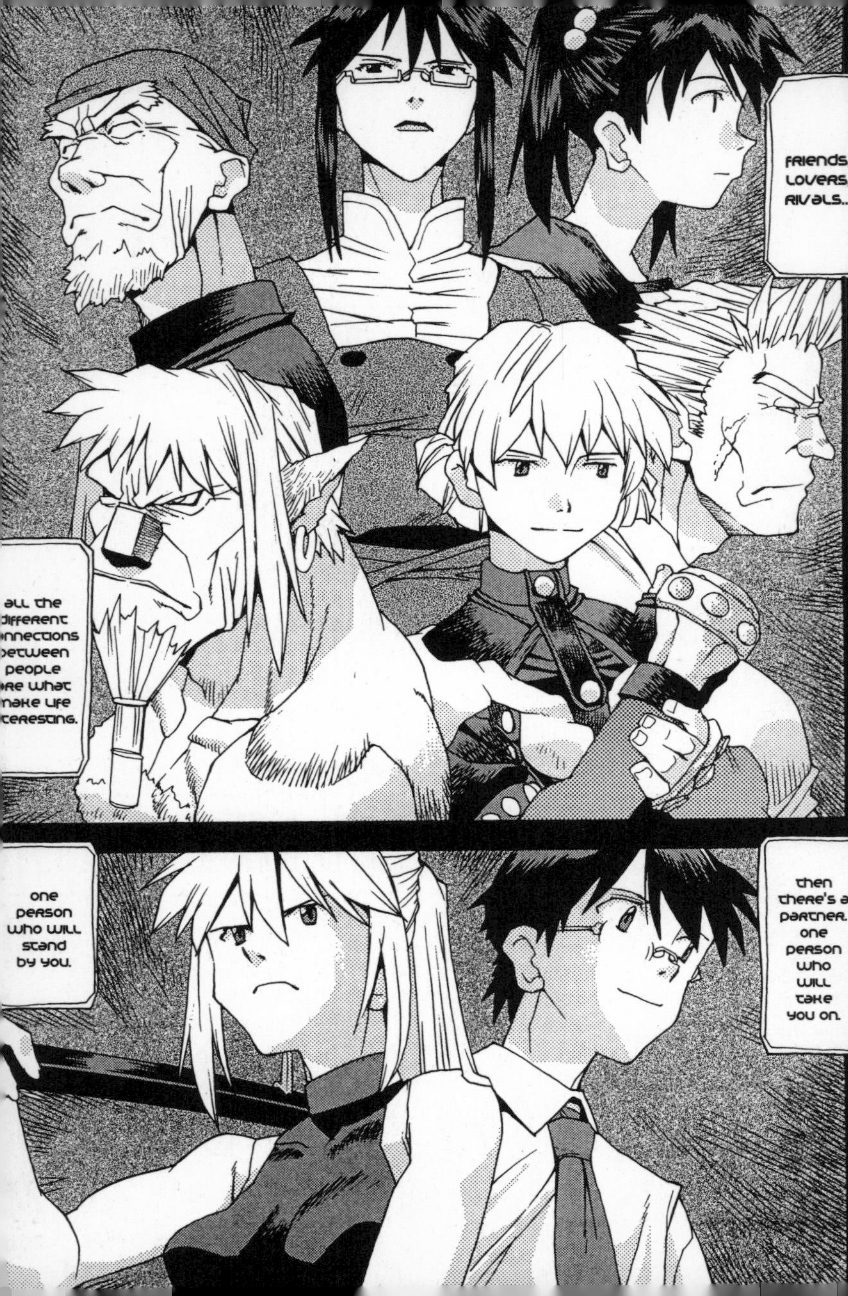
Friends, lovers, rivals...
all the different nnections etween people re what nake life teresting.
Then there's a partner. One person who will take you on.
One person who will stand by you.

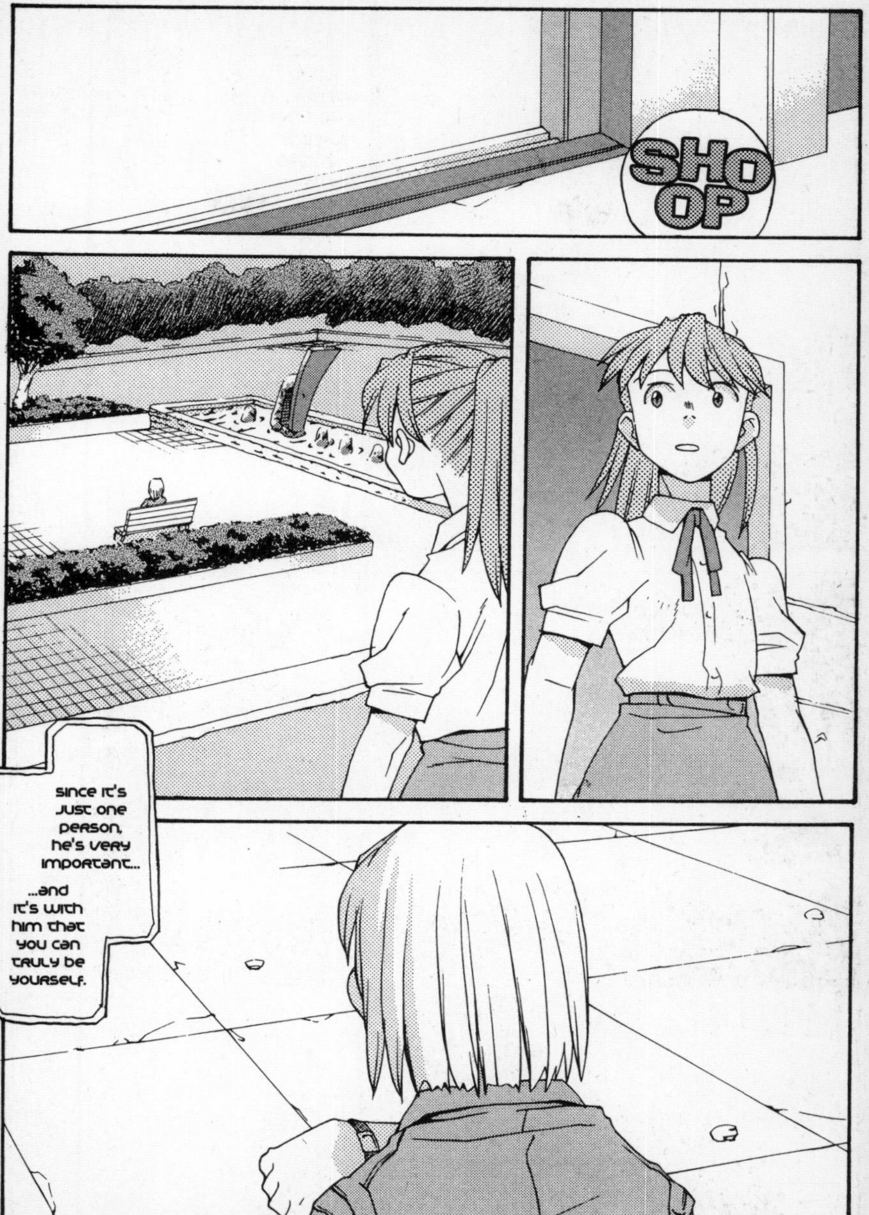
SHOOP
Since it's just one person, he's very important...
...and it's with him that you can truly be yourself.

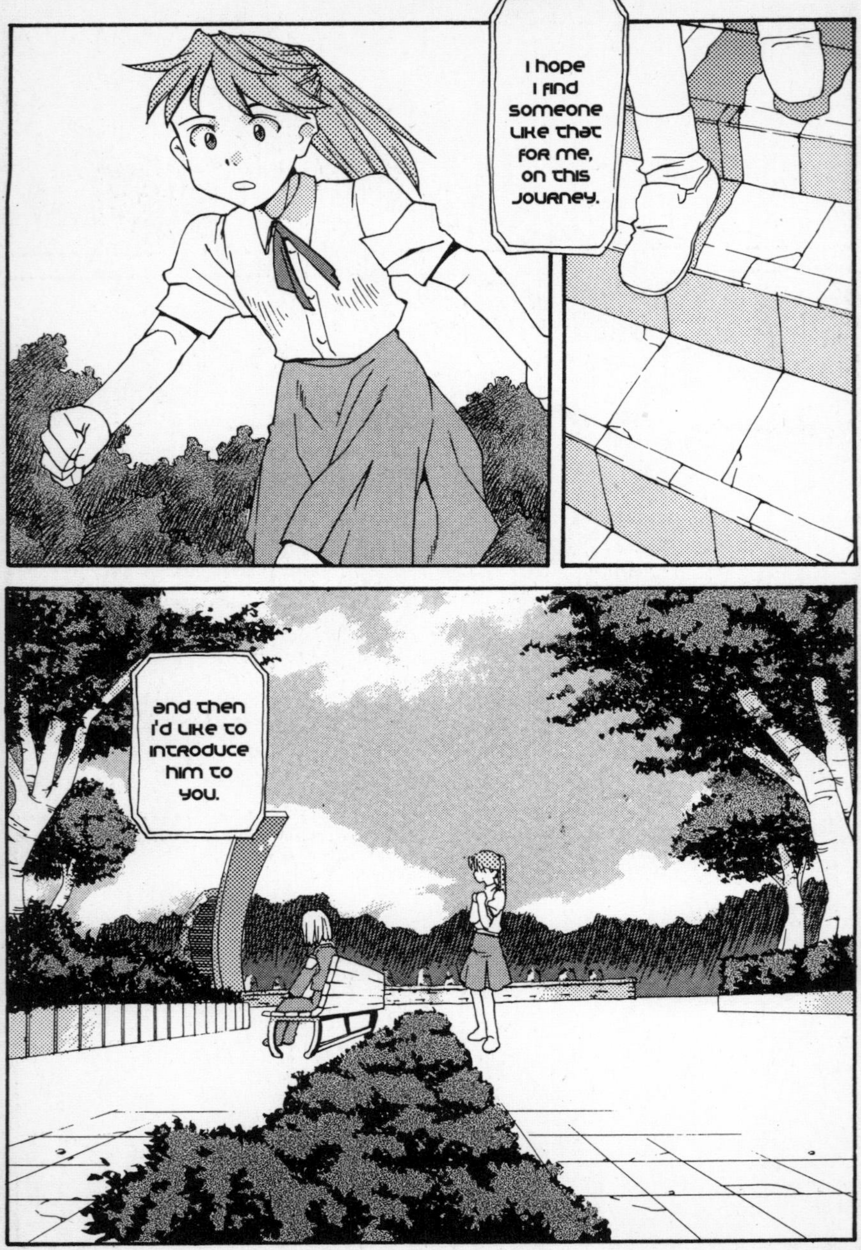
I hope I find someone like that for me, on this journey.
and then I'd like to introduce him to you.

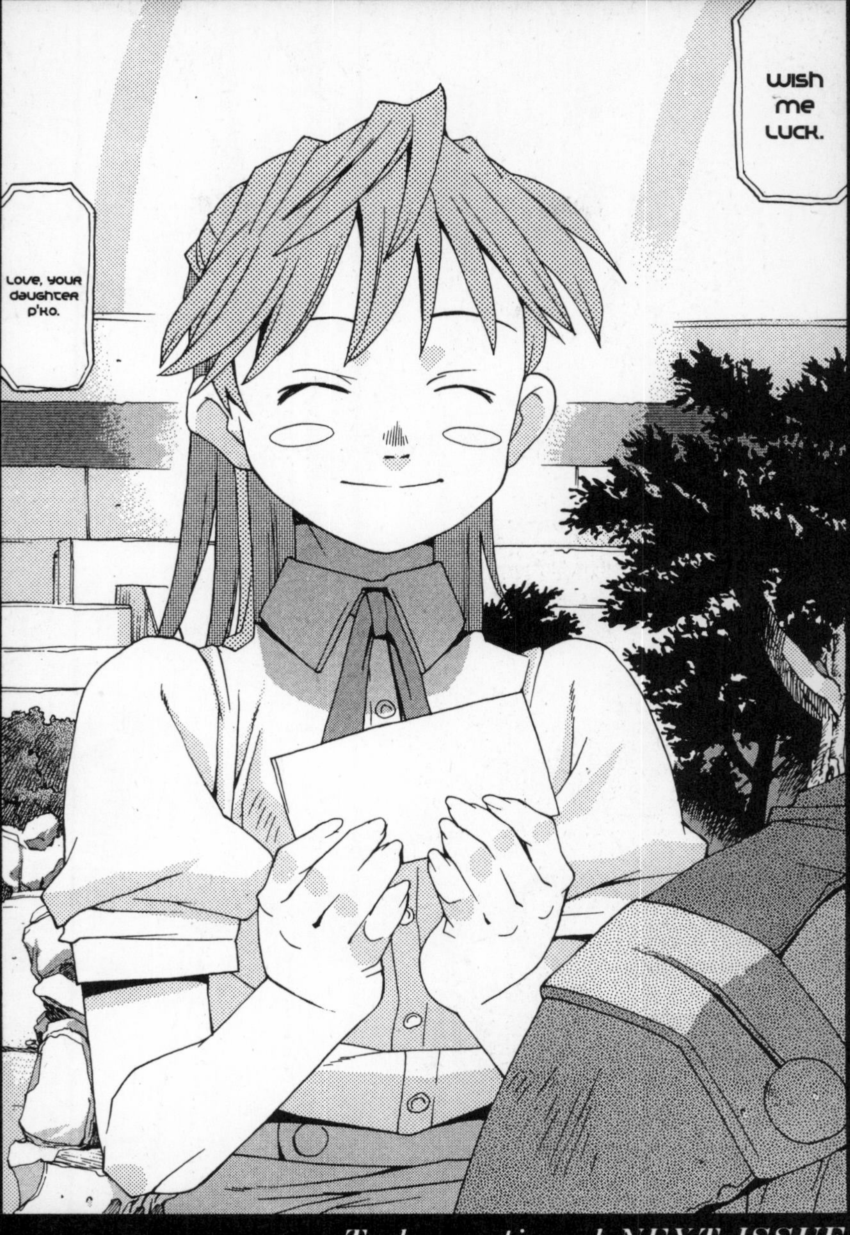
WISH ME LUCK.
LOVE, YOUR DAUGHTER P'KO.

*To be continued NEXT ISSUE*

**Illustration by TOMOMASA TAKUMA**
**Text by HIDEYUKI KURATA**

TRAIN+TRAIN PLOT WRITER'S NOTE
FILE NO. 006

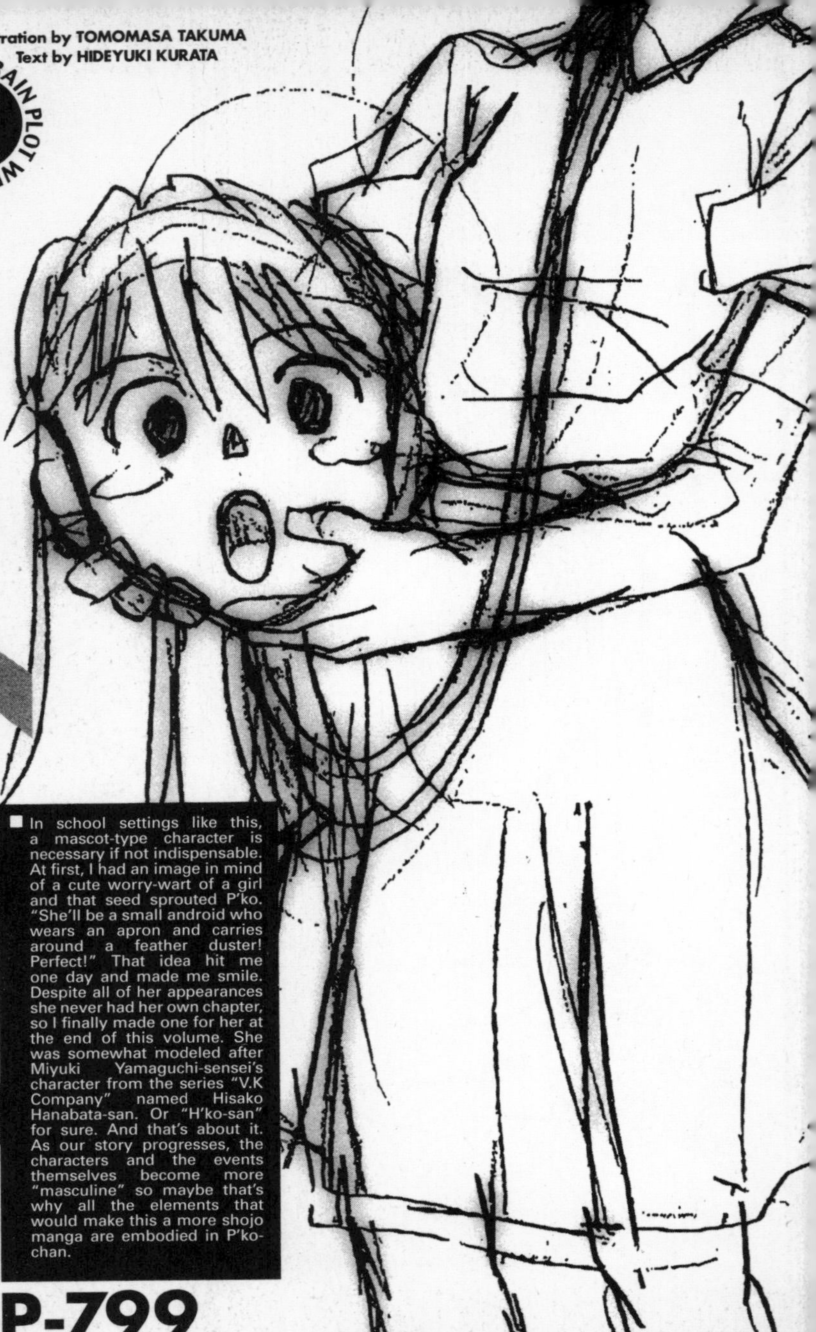

■ In school settings like this, a mascot-type character is necessary if not indispensable. At first, I had an image in mind of a cute worry-wart of a girl and that seed sprouted P'ko. "She'll be a small android who wears an apron and carries around a feather duster! Perfect!" That idea hit me one day and made me smile. Despite all of her appearances she never had her own chapter, so I finally made one for her at the end of this volume. She was somewhat modeled after Miyuki Yamaguchi-sensei's character from the series "V.K Company" named Hisako Hanabata-san. Or "H'ko-san" for sure. And that's about it. As our story progresses, the characters and the events themselves become more "masculine" so maybe that's why all the elements that would make this a more shojo manga are embodied in P'ko-chan.

# P-799

# HILDA

Hilda's a character that I was still coming to understand while writing her. At first, she was just going to be a tutor for when Reiichi had to take his make-up class and that would be it. However, when I decided to use her for a smooth transition into the Aldacc arc, just as expected, she completely stole the spotlight. I recall that during the drafting phase, I realized she didn't need my help at all. Letting her do her thing to work herself so well into the story was one of the happiest moments of the process. Even now, I feel I don't quite know her fully so I'll have to wrap up my little talk about her here. She wasn't really modeled after anybody. As a side-note, while this chapter was being serialized was when the terrorist attack on NY happened. Real life terrorism is far more terrifying, irrational, and impacting.

TRAIN+TRAIN PLOT WRITER'S NOTE

FILE NO. 007

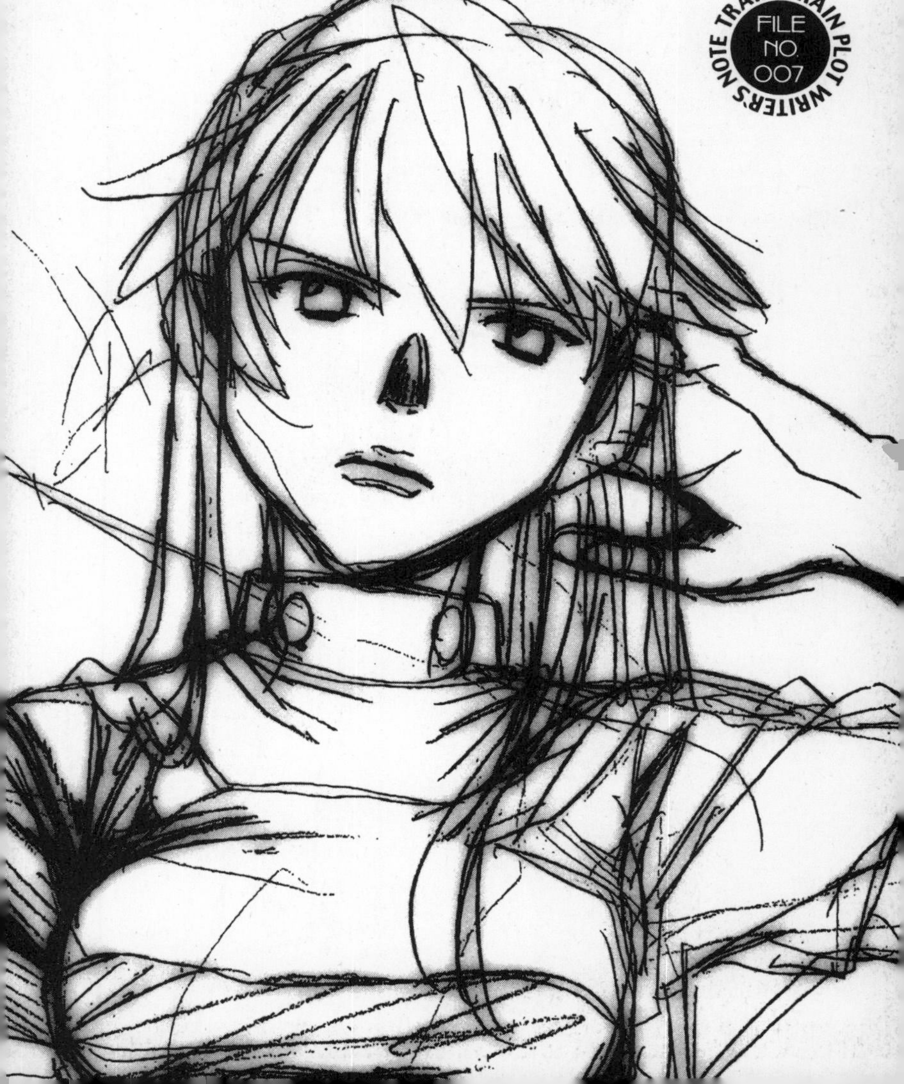

TRAIN

Tomomasa Takuma
作画たくま朋正

Hi, this is Tomomasa Takuma.
TRAIN+TRAIN is finally up to volume 4 where things really start to change.
Due to my hospitalization halfway through the serialization, I had to take a break for a couple of months but I finally got back on track and ready for more.
At the back of volume 1, I wrote about how I wondered how Arena and Reiichi would influence each other. Now at volume 4, the two have experienced so much that though they still collide on some things, they've helped each other grow a lot more.
I'm sure there are still plenty of things awaiting them at the stations to come.
How will Arena and Reiichi overcome future hardships now? And what will the "final stop" be for the two?
I'm looking very much forward to it myself.

December 27, 2001
Tomomasa Takuma

Hideyuki Kurata
原作倉田英之

It's volume 3 of the manga version of "TRAIN+TRAIN" where original developments from the novel version start taking place. I tried to write for the manga keeping in mind those who'd already read the novel version, but the atmosphere and content is overall so different, I'm rather surprised myself.
The story and characters have strayed quite far from what I'd imagined in my head as they find their own individual paths. It's like I'm onboard a train that I can't see the next station. I know that there always is a last station so I suppose the only problem is how I'll get the rest of the characters to arrive there.
In this volume, Reiichi succeeded in establishing his persona, so from now on Arena will take the center stage of the story. Putting her in the main position over Reiichi is going to be trying, but hey, it's their story. I just hope that you stick around to the very end.

December 27, 2001
Hideyuki Kurata

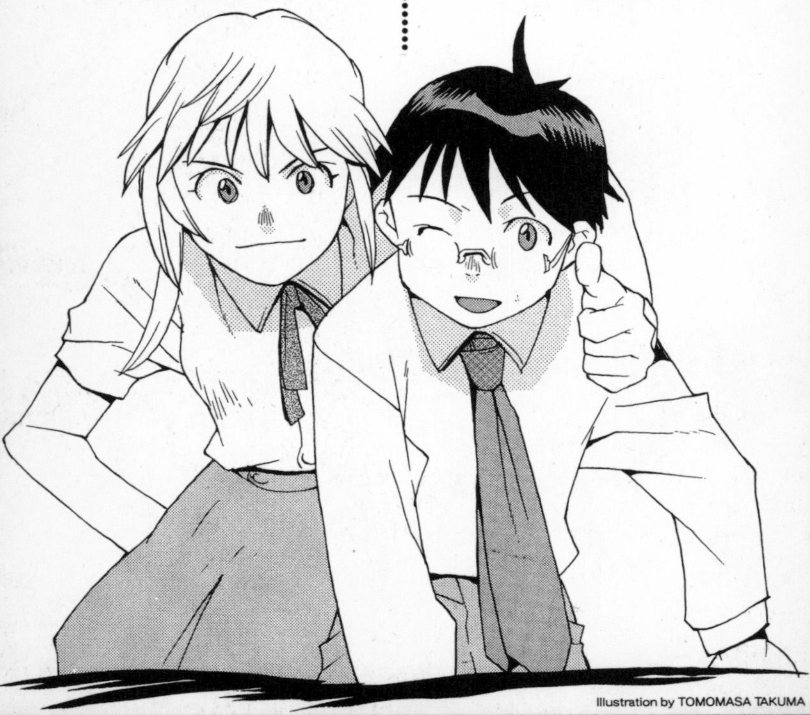

Illustration by TOMOMASA TAKUMA

TRAIN

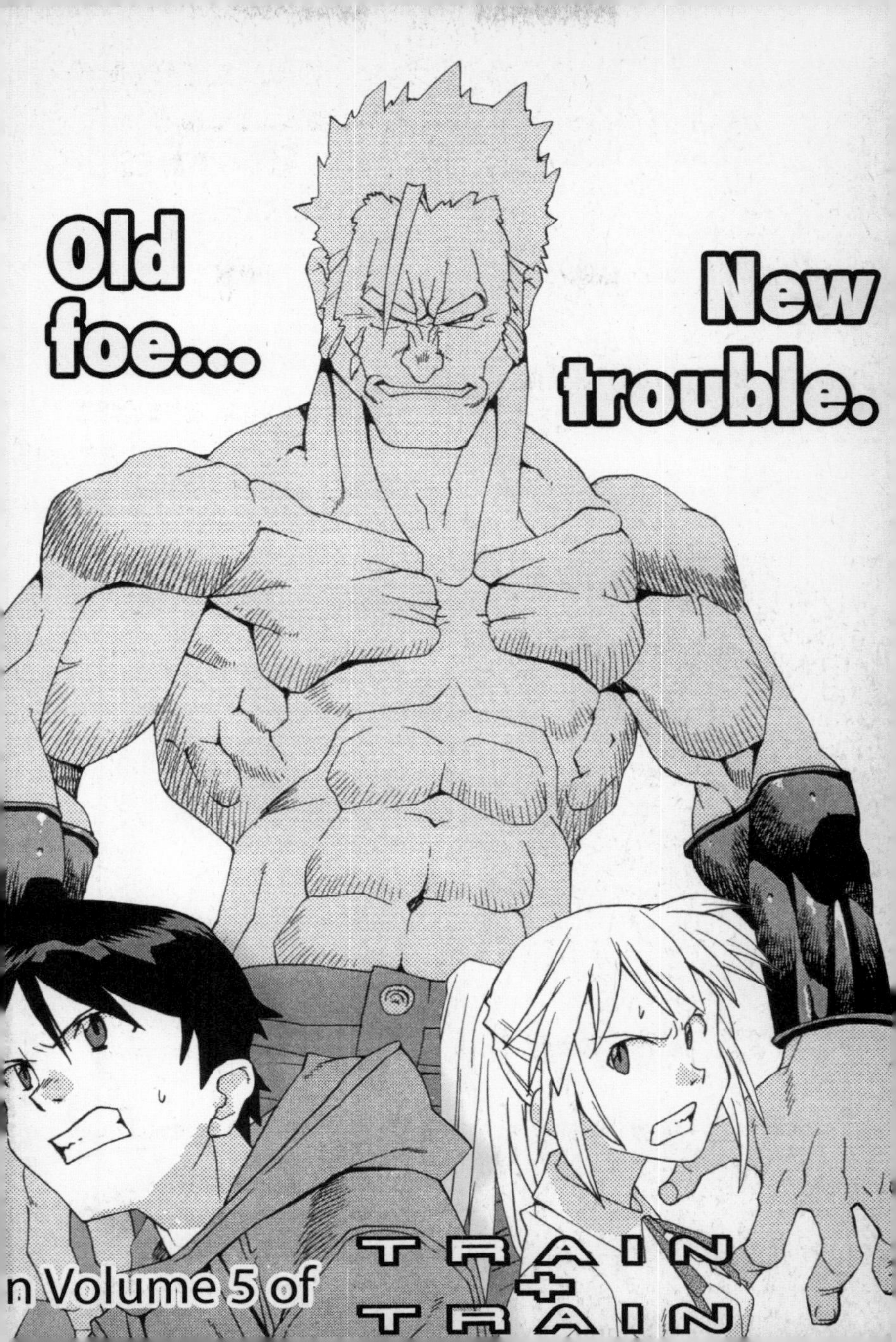
Old foe...
New trouble.
n Volume 5 of
TRAIN + TRAIN

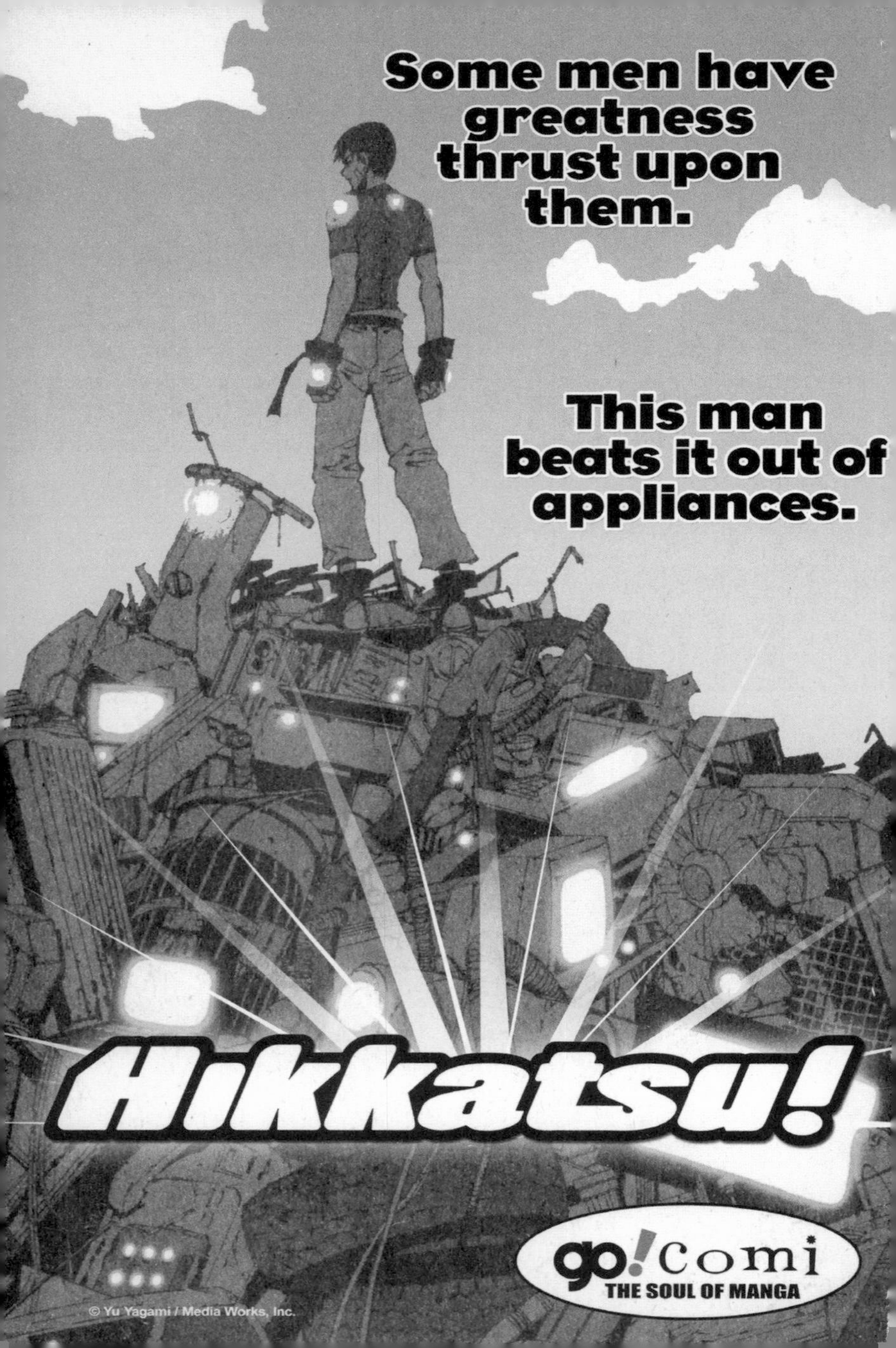
Some men have greatness thrust upon them.
This man beats it out of appliances.
Hikkatsu!
go!comi
THE SOUL OF MANGA
© Yu Yagami / Media Works, Inc.

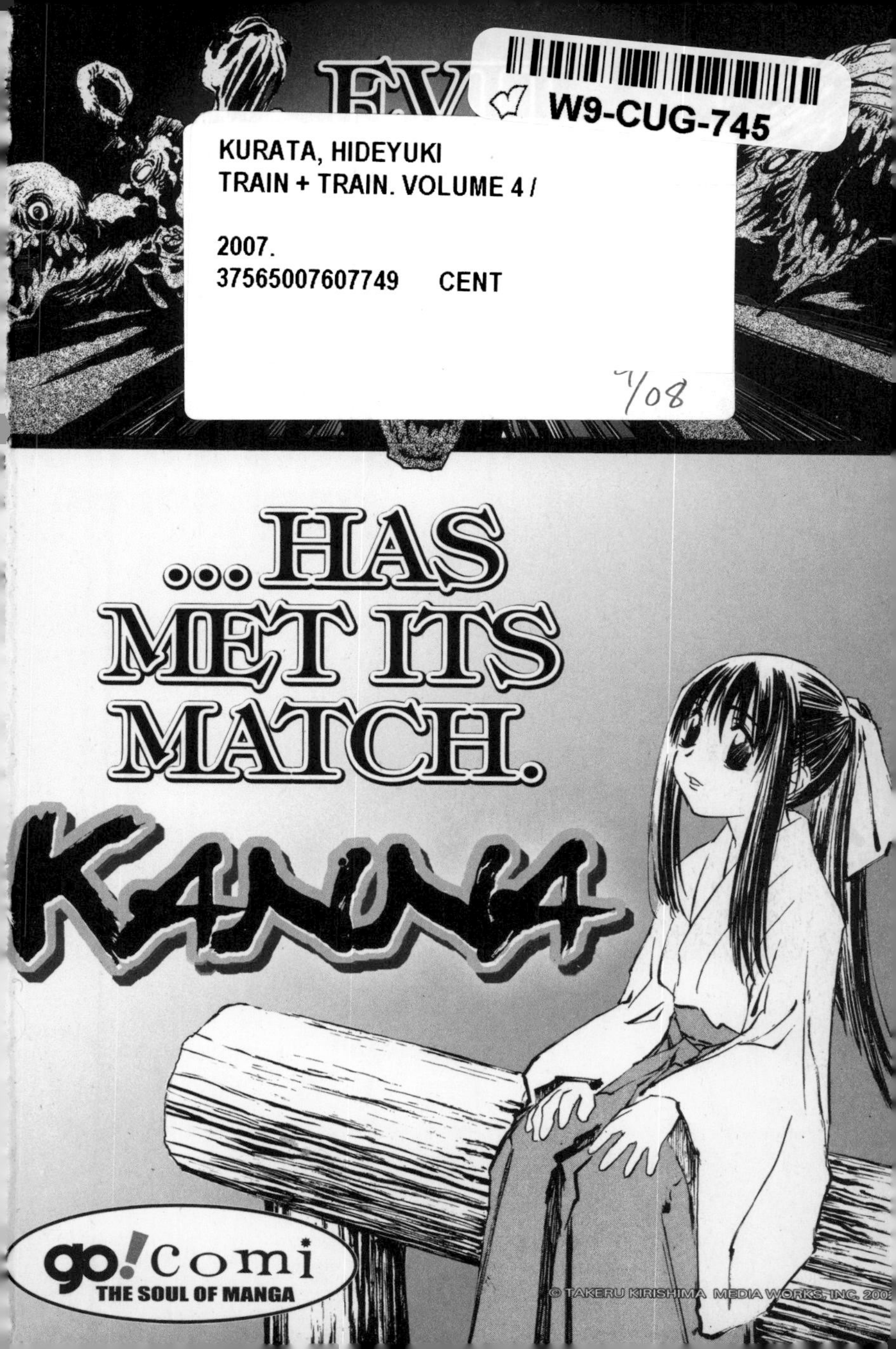
...HAS
MET ITS
MATCH.
KANNA
go!comi
THE SOUL OF MANGA
© TAKERU KIRISHIMA MEDIA WORKS, INC. 200